THE HISTORY OF WITCHCRAFT AND DEMONOLOGY

MONTAGUE
SUMMERS

BRISTOL PARK BOOKS / NEW YORK

To

PATRICK,

in memory of Loreto and Our Lady's Holy House, as also of Our Lady's miraculous Picture at Campocavallo, Our Lady of Pompeii, La Consolata of Turin, Consolatrix Afflictorum in S. Caterina ai Funari at Rome, la Santissima Vergine del Parto of S. Agostino, the Madonna della Strada at the Gesù, La Nicopeja of San Marco at Venice, Notre-Dame-de-Bonne-Nouvelle of Rennes, Notre-Dame de Grande Puissance of Lamballe, and all the Italian and French Madonnas at whose shrines we have worshipped.

Bristol Park Books
252 W. 38th Street
New York, NY 10018

ISBN: 978-0-88486-474-5

Printed in the United States of America

CONTENTS

INTRODUCTION

The history of Witchcraft, a subject as old as the world and as wide as the world,—since I understand for the present purpose by Witchcraft, Sorcery, Black Magic, Necromancy, secret Divination, Satanism, and every kind of malign occult art,—at once confronts the writer with a most difficult problem. He is called upon to exercise a choice, and his dilemma is by no means made the easier owing to the fact he is acutely conscious that whichever way he may decide he is laying himself open to damaging and not impertinent criticism. Since it is essential that his work should be comprised within a reasonable compass he may elect to attempt a bird's-eye view of the whole range from China to Peru, from the half-articulate, rhythmic incantations of primitive man at the dawn of life to the last spiritistic fad and manifestation at yesterday's séance or circle, in which case his pages will most certainly be thin and often superficial: or again he may rather concentrate upon one or two features in the history of Witchcraft, deal with these at some length, stress some few forgotten facts whose importance is now neglected and unrealized, utilize new material the result of laborious research, but all this at the expense of inevitable omissions, of hiatus, of self-denial, the avoidance of fascinating by-ways and valuable inquiry, of silence when he would fain be entering upon discussion and exposition. With a full sense of its drawbacks and danger I have selected the second method, since in dealing with a topic such as Witchcraft where there is no human hope of recording more than a tithe of the facts I believe it is better to give a documented account of certain aspects rather than to essay a somewhat huddled and confused conspectus of the whole, for such, indeed, even at best is itself bound to have no inconsiderable gaps and lacunæ, however carefully we endeavour to make it complete. I am conscious, then, that there is scarcely a paragraph in the present work which might not easily be expanded into a page, scarcely a page which might not to its great advantage become a chapter, and certainly not a chapter that would not be vastly improved were it elaborated to a volume.

Many omissions are, as I have said, a necessary consequence of the plan I have adopted ; or, indeed, I venture to suppose, of any other plan which contemplates the treatment of so universal a subject as Witchcraft. I can but offer my apologies to these students who come to this History to find details of Finnish magic and the sorceries of Lapland, who wish to inform themselves concerning Tohungaism among the Maoris, Hindu devilry and enchantments, the Bersekir of Iceland, Siberian Shamanism, the blind Pan Sus and Mutangs of Korea, the Chinese Wu-po, Serbian lycanthropy, negro Voodoism, the dark lore of old Scandinavia and Islam. I trust my readers will believe that I regret as much as any the absence of these from my work, but after all in any human endeavour there are practical limitations of space.

In a complementary and companion volume I am intending to treat the epidemic of Witchcraft in particular localities, the British Isles, France, Germany, Italy, New England, and other countries. Many famous cases, the Lancashire witch-trials, the activities of Matthew Hopkins, Gilles de Rais, Gaufridi, Urbain Grandier, Cotton Mather and the Salem sorceries, will then be dealt with and discussed in some detail.

It is a surprising fact that amongst English writers Witchcraft in Europe has not of recent years received anything like adequate attention from serious students of history, who strangely fail to recognize the importance of this tragic belief both as a political and a social factor. Magic, the genesis of magical cults and ceremonies, the ritual of primitive peoples, traditional superstitions, and their ancillary lore, have been made the subject of vast and erudite studies, mostly from an anthropological and folk-loristic point of view, but the darker side of the subject, the history of Satanism seems hardly to have been attempted.

Possibly one reason for this neglect and ignorance lies in the fact that the heavy and crass materialism, which was so prominent a feature during the greater part of the eighteenth and nineteenth centuries in England, intellectually disavowed the supernatural, and attempted not without some success to substitute for religion a stolid system of respectable morality. Since Witchcraft was entirely exploded it would, at best, possess merely an antiquarian interest, and even so, the exhumation of a disgusting and contemptible superstition was not to be encouraged. It were more seemly to forget the uglier side of the past. This was the attitude which prevailed for more than a hundred and fifty years, and when Witchcraft came under discussion by such narrowly prejudiced and inefficient writers as Lecky or Charles Mackay they are not even concerned to discuss the possibility of the accounts given by the earlier authorities, who, as they premise, were all mistaken, extravagant, purblind, and misled. The cycle of time has had its revenge, and this rationalistic superstition is dying fast. The extraordinary vogue of and immense adherence to Spiritism would alone prove that, whilst the widespread interest that is taken in mysticism is a yet healthier sign that the world will no longer be content to be fed on dry husks and the chaff of straw. And these are only just two indications, and by no means the most significant, out of many.

It is quite impossible to appreciate and understand the true lives of men and women in Elizabethan and Stuart England, in the France of Louis XIII and his son, in the Italy of the Renaissance and the Catholic Reaction—to name but three countries and a few definite periods—unless we have some realization of the part that Witchcraft played in those ages amid the affairs of these kingdoms. All classes were concerned from Pope to peasant, from Queen to cottage gill.

Accordingly as actors are "the abstracts and brief chronicles of the time" I have given a concluding chapter which deals with Witchcraft as seen upon the stage, mainly concentrating upon the English theatre. This review has not before been attempted, and since Witchcraft was so formidable a social evil and so intermixed with all stations of life it is obvious that we can find few better contemporary illustrations of it than in the drama, for the playwright ever had his finger upon the public pulse. Until the development of the novel it was the theatre alone that mirrored manners and history.

There are many general French studies of Witchcraft of

the greatest value, amongst which we may name such standard works as Antoine-Louis Daugis, *Traité sur la magie, le sortilège, les possessions, obsessions et maléfices*, 1732; Jules Garinet, *Histoire de la Magie en France depuis le commencement de la monarchie jusqu'à nos jours*, 1818; Michelet's famous *La Sorcière;* Alfred Maury, *La Magie et l'Astrologie*, 3rd edition, 1868; L'Abbé Lecanu, *Histoire de Satan;* Jules Baissac, *Les grands Jours de la Sorcellerie*, 1890; Theodore de Cauzons, *La Magie et la Sorcellerie en France*, 4 vols., 1910, etc.

In German we have Eberhard Hauber's *Bibliotheca Magica;* Roskoff's *Geschichte des Teufels*, 1869; Soldan's *Geschichte der Hexenprozesse* (neu bearbeitet von Dr. Heinrich Heppe), 1880; Friedrich Leitschuch's *Beitræge zur Geschichte des Hexenwesens in Franken*, 1883; Johan Dieffenbach's *Der Hexenwahn vor und nach der Glaubensspaltung in Deutschland*, 1886; Schreiber's *Die Hexenprozesse im Breisgau;* Ludwig Rapp's *Die Hexenprozesse und ihre Gegner aus Tirol;* Joseph Hansen's *Quellen und Untersuchungen zur Geschichte des Hexenwahns*, 1901; and very many more admirably documented studies.

In England the best of the older books must be recommended with necessary reservations. Thomas Wright's *Narratives of Sorcery and Magic*, 2 vols., 1851, is to be commended as the work of a learned antiquarian who often referred to original sources, but it is withal sketchy and can hardly satisfy the careful scholar. Some exceptionally good writing and sound, clear, thinking are to be met with in Dr. F. G. Lee's *The Other World*, 2 vols., 1875; *More Glimpses of the World Unseen*, 1878; *Glimpses in the Twilight*, 1885; and *Sight and Shadows*, 1894, all of which deserve to be far more widely known, since they well repay an unhurried and repeated perusal.

Quite recent work is represented by Professor Wallace Notestein's *History of Witchcraft in England from* 1558 *to* 1718, published in 1911. This intimate study of a century and a half concentrates, as its title tells, upon England alone. It is supplied with ample and useful appendixes. In respect of the orderly marshalling of his facts, garnered from the trials and other sources—no small labour—Professor Notestein deserves a generous meed of praise; his interpretation of the facts and his deductions may not unfairly be criticized. Although his incredulity must surely now and again be shaken by the cumulative force of reiterated and corroborative evidence, nevertheless he refuses to admit even the possibility that persons who at any rate affected supernatural powers held clandestine meetings after nightfall in obscure and lonely places for purposes and plots of their own. If human testimony is worth anything at all, unless we are to be more Pyrrhonian than the famous Dr. Marphurius himself who would never say, "Je suis venu; mais; Il me semble que je suis venu," when in 1612 Roger Nowell had swooped down on the Lancashire coven and carried off Elizabeth Demdike with three other beldames to durance vile in Lancaster Castle, Elizabeth Device summoned the whole Pendle gang to her home at Malking Tower, in order that they might discuss the situation and contrive the delivery of the prisoners. As soon as they had forgathered, they all sat down to dinner, and had a good north country spread of beef, bacon, and roast mutton. Surely there is nothing very remarkable in this; and the evidence as given in Thomas Potts' famous narrative, *The Wonderfull Discoverie of Witches in the countie of Lancaster* (London, 1613), bears the very hall-mark and impress of truth: "The persons aforesaid had to their dinners Beefe, Bacon, and roasted Mutton; which Mutton (as this Examinates said brother said) was of a Wether of Christopher Swyers of Barley: which Wether was brought in the night before into this Examinates mothers house by the said Iames Deuice, the Examinates said brother: and in this Examinates sight killed and eaten." But Professor Notestein will none of it. He writes: "The concurring evidence in the Malking Tower story is of no more compelling character than that to be found in a multitude of Continental stories of witch gatherings which have been shown to be the outcome of physical or mental pressure and of leading questions. It seems unnecessary to accept even a substratum of fact" (p. 124). In the face of such sweeping and dogmatic assertion mere evidence is no use at all. For we know that the Continental stories of witch gatherings are with very few exceptions the chronicle of actual fact. It must be confessed that such feeble scepticism, which repeatedly mars his summary of the witch-trials, is a serious blemish in Professor Notestein's work, and in view of his industry much to be regretted.

Miss M. A. Murray does not for a moment countenance any such summary dismissal and uncritical rejection of evidence. Her careful reading of the writers upon Witchcraft has justly convinced her that their statements must be accepted. Keen intelligences and shrewd investigators such as Gregory XV, Bodin, Guazzo, De Lancre, D'Espagnet, La Reynie, Boyle, Sir Matthew Hale, Glanvill, were neither deceivers nor deceived. The evidence must stand, but as Miss Murray finds herself unable to admit the logical consequence of this, she hurriedly starts away with an arbitrary, "the statements do not bear the construction put upon them," and in *The Witch-Cult in Western Europe* (1921) proceeds to develop a most ingenious, but, as I show, a wholly untenable hypothesis. Accordingly we are not surprised to find that many of the details Miss Murray has collected in her painstaking pages are (no doubt unconsciously) made to square with her preconceived theory. However much I may differ from Miss Murray in my outlook, and our disagreement is, I consider, neither slight nor superficial, I am none the less bound to commend her frank and courageous treatment of many essential particulars which are all too often suppressed, and in consequence a false and counterfeit picture has not unseldom been drawn.

So vast a literature surrounds modern Witchcraft, for frankly such is Spiritism in effect, that it were no easy task to mention even a quota of those works which seem to throw some real light upon a complex and difficult subject. Among many which I have found useful are Surbled, *Spiritualisme et spiritisme* and *Spirites et médiums ;* Gutberlet, *Der Kampf um die Seele ;* Dr. Marcel Viollet, *Le spiritisme dans ses rapports avec la folie ;* J. Godfrey Raupert, *Modern Spiritism* and *Dangers of Spiritualism ;* the Very Rev. Alexis Lépicier, O.S.M., *The Unseen World ;* the Rev. A. V. Miller, *Sermons on Modern Spiritualism ;* Lapponi, *Hypnotism and Spiritism ;* the late Monsignor Hugh Benson's *Spiritualism* (*The History of Religions*); Elliot O'Donnell's *The Menace of Spiritualism ;* and Father Simon Blackmore's *Spiritism : Facts and Frauds*, 1925. My own opinion of this movement has been formed not only from reading studies and monographs which treat of every phase of the question from all points of view, but also by correspondence and discussion with ardent devotees of the cult, and, not least, owing to the admissions and warnings of those who have abandoned these dangerous practices, revelations made in such circumstances, however, as altogether to preclude even a hint as to their definite import and scope.

The History of Witchcraft is full of interest to the theologian, the psychologist, the historian, and cannot be ignored. But it presents a very dark and terrible aspect, the details of which in the few English studies that claim serious attention have almost universally been unrecorded, and, indeed, deliberately burked and shunned. Such treatment is unworthy and unscholarly to a degree, reprehensible and dishonest.

The work of Professor Notestein, for example, is gravely vitiated, owing to the fact that he has completely ignored the immodesty of the witch-cult and thus extenuated its evil. He is, indeed, so uncritical, I would even venture to say so unscholarly, as naïvely to remark (p. 300): "No one who has not read for himself can have any notion of the vile character of the charges and confessions embodied in the witch pamphlets. It is an aspect of the question which has not been discussed in these pages." Such a confession is amazing. One cannot write in dainty phrase of Satanists and the Sabbat. However loathly the disease the doctor must not hesitate to diagnose and to probe. This ostrich-like policy is moral cowardice. None of the Fathers and great writers of the Church were thus culpably prudish. When S. Epiphanius has to discuss the Gnostics, he describes in detail their abominations, and pertinently remarks: "Why should I shrink from speaking of the things you do not fear to do? By speaking thus, I hope to fill you with horror of the turpitudes you commit." And S. Clement of Alexandria says: "I am not ashamed to name the parts of the body wherein the fœtus is formed and nourished; and why, indeed, should I be, since God was not ashamed to create them?"

A few authors have painted the mediæval witch in pretty colours on satin. She has become a somewhat eccentric but kindly old lady, shrewd and perspicacious, with a knowledge of healing herbs and simples, ready to advise and aid her neighbours who are duller-witted than she; not disdaining in return a rustic present of a flitch, meal, a poult or eggs from the farm-yard. And so for no very definite reason she fell an easy prey to fanatic judges and ravening inquisitors, notoriously the most ignorant and stupid of mortals, who caught her, swum her in a river, tried her, tortured her, and finally burned her at the stake. Many modern writers, more sceptical still, frankly relegate the witch to the land of nursery tales and Christmas pantomime; she never had any real existence other than as Cinderella's fairy godmother or the Countess D'Aulnoy's Madame Merluche.

I have even heard it publicly asserted from the lecture platform by a professed student of the Elizabethan period that the Elizabethans did not, of course, as a matter of fact believe in Witchcraft. It were impossible to imagine that men of the intellectual standard of Shakespeare, Ford, Jonson, Fletcher, could have held so idle a chimæra, born of sick fancies and hysteria. And his audience acquiesced with no little complacency, pleased to think that the great names of the past had been cleared from the stigma of so degrading and gross a superstition. A few uneducated peasants here and there may have been morbid and ignorant enough to dream of witches, and the poets used these crones and hags with effect in ballad and play. But as for giving any actual credence to such fantasies, most assuredly our great Elizabethans were more enlightened than that! And, indeed, Witchcraft is a phase of and a factor in the manners of the seventeenth century, which in some quarters there seems a tacit agreement almost to ignore.

All this is very unhistorical and very unscientific. In the following pages I have endeavoured to show the witch as she really was—an evil liver; a social pest and parasite; the devotee of a loathly and obscene creed; an adept at poisoning, blackmail, and other creeping crimes; a member of a powerful secret organization inimical to Church and State; a blasphemer in word and deed; swaying the villagers by terror and superstition; a charlatan and a quack sometimes; a bawd; an abortionist; the dark counsellor of lewd court ladies and adulterous gallants; a minister to vice and inconceivable corruption; battening upon the filth and foulest passions of the age.

My present work is the result of more than thirty years' close attention to the subject of Witchcraft, and during this period I have made a systematic and intensive study of the older demonologists, as I am convinced that their first-hand evidence is of prime importance and value, whilst since their writings are very voluminous and of the last rarity they have universally been neglected, and are allowed to accumulate thick dust undisturbed. They are, moreover, often difficult to read owing to technicalities of phrase and vocabulary. Among the most authoritative I may cite a few names: Sprenger (*Malleus Maleficarum*); Guazzo; Bartolomeo Spina, O.P.; John Nider, O.P.; Grilland; Jerome Mengo; Binsfeld; Gerson; Ulrich Molitor; Basin; Murner; Crespet; Anania; Henri Boguet; Bodin; Martin Delrio, S.J.; Pierre le Loyer; Ludwig Elich; Godelmann; Nicolas Remy; Salerini; Leonard Vair; De Lancre; Alfonso de Castro; Sebastian Michaelis, O.P.; Sinistrari; Perreaud; Dom Calmet; Sylvester Mazzolini, O.P. (Prierias). When we supplement these by the judicial records and the legal codes we have an immense body of material. In all that I have written I have gone to original sources, and it has been my endeavour fairly to weigh and balance the evidence, to judge without heat or prejudice, to give the facts and the comment upon them with candour, sincerity, and truth. At the same time I am very well aware that several great scholars for whom I have the sincerest personal regard and whose attainments I view with a very profound respect will differ from me in many particulars.

I am conscious that the rough list of books which I have drawn up does not deserve to be dignified with the title, Bibliography. It is sadly incomplete, yet should it, however inadequate, prove helpful in the smallest way it will have justified its inclusion. I may add that my Biblical quotations, save where expressly otherwise noted, are from the Vulgate or its translation into English commonly called the Douai Version.

In Festo S. Teresiæ, *V.*
1925.

THE HISTORY OF WITCHCRAFT

CHAPTER I

THE WITCH: HERETIC AND ANARCHIST

"SORCIER est celuy qui par moyens Diaboliques sciemment s'efforce de paruenir à quel que chose." ("A sorcerer is one who by commerce with the Devil has a full intention of attaining his own ends.") With these words the profoundly erudite jurisconsult Jean Bodin, one of the acutest and most strictly impartial minds of his age, opens his famous *De la Demonomanie des Sorciers*,[1] and it would be, I imagine, hardly possible to discover a more concise, exact, comprehensive, and intelligent definition of a Witch. The whole tremendous subject of Witchcraft, especially as revealed in its multifold and remarkable manifestations throughout every district of Southern and Western Europe from the middle of the thirteenth until the dawn of the eighteenth century,[2] has it would seem in recent times seldom, if ever, been candidly and fairly examined. The only sound sources of information are the contemporary records; the meticulously detailed legal reports of the actual trials; the vast mass of pamphlets which give eye-witnessed accounts of individual witches and reproduce evidence *uerbatim* as told in court; and, above all, the voluminous and highly technical works of the Inquisitors and demonologists, holy and reverend divines, doctors *utriusque iuris*, hard-headed, slow, and sober lawyers,—learned men, scholars of philosophic mind, the most honourable names in the universities of Europe, in the forefront of literature, science, politics, and culture; monks who kept the conscience of kings, pontiffs; whose word would set Europe aflame and bring an emperor to his knees at their gate.

It is true that Witchcraft has formed the subject of a not inconsiderable literature, but it will be found that inquirers have for the most part approached this eternal and terrible chapter in the history of humanity from biassed, although wholly divergent, points of view, and in consequence it is often necessary to sift more or less thoroughly their partial presentation of their theme, to discount their unwarranted commentaries and illogical conclusions, and to get down in time to the hard bed-rock of fact.

In the first place we have those writings and that interest which may be termed merely antiquarian. Witchcraft is treated as a curious by-lane of history, a superstition long since dead, having no existence among, nor bearing upon, the affairs of the present day. It is a field for folk-lore, where one may gather strange flowers and noxious weeds. Again, we often recognize the romantic treatment of Witchcraft. 'Tis the Eve of S. George, a dark wild night, the pale moon can but struggle thinly through the thick massing clouds. The witches are abroad, and hurtle swiftly aloft, a hideous covey, borne headlong on the skirling blast. In delirious tones they are yelling foul mysterious words as they go: "Har! Har! Har! Altri! Altri!" To some peak of the Brocken or lonely Cevennes they haste, to the orgies of the Sabbat, the infernal Sacraments, the dance of Acheron, the sweet and fearful fantasy of evil, "Vers les stupres impurs et les baisers immondes."[3] Hell seems to vomit its foulest dregs upon the shrinking earth; a loathsome shape of obscene horror squats huge and monstrous upon the ebon throne; the stifling air reeks with filth and blasphemy; faster and faster whirls the witches' lewd lavolta; shriller and shriller the cornemuse screams; and then a wan grey light flickers in the Eastern sky; a moment more and there sounds the loud clarion of some village chanticleer; swift as thought the vile phantasmagoria vanishes and is sped, all is quiet and still in the peaceful dawn.

But both the antiquarian and the romanticist reviews of Witchcraft may be deemed negligible and impertinent so far as the present research is concerned, however entertaining and picturesque such treatment proves to many readers, affording not a few pleasant hours, whence they are able to draw highly dramatic and brilliantly coloured pictures of old time sorceries, not to be taken too seriously, for these things never were and never could have been.[4]

The rationalist historian and the sceptic, when inevitably confronted with the subject of Witchcraft, chose a charmingly easy way to deal with these intensely complex and intricate problems, a flat denial of all statements which did not fit, or could not by some means be squared with, their own narrow prejudice. What matter the most irrefragable evidence, which in the instance of any other accusation would unhesitatingly have been regarded as final. What matter the logical and reasoned belief of centuries, of the most cultured peoples, the highest intelligences of Europe? Any appeal to authority is, of course, useless, as the sceptic repudiates all authority—save his own. Such things could not be. We must argue from that axiom, and therefore anything which it is impossible to explain away by hallucination, or hysteria, or auto-suggestion, or any other vague catch-word which may chance to be fashionable at the moment, must be uncompromisingly rejected, and a note of superior pity, to candy the so suave yet crushingly decisive judgement, has proved of great service upon more occasions than one. Why examine the evidence? It is really useless and a waste of time, because we know that the allegations are all idle and ridiculous; the "facts" sworn to by innumerable witnesses, which are repeated in changeless detail century fter century in every country, in every town, simply did not take place. How so absolute and entire falsity of these facts can be demonstrated the sceptic omits to inform us, but we must unquestioningly accept his infallible authority in the face of reason, evidence, and truth.

Yet supposing that with clear and candid minds we proceed carefully to investigate this accumulated evidence, to inquire into the circumstances of a number of typical cases, to compare the trials of the fifteenth century in France with the trials of the seventeenth century in England, shall we not find that amid obvious accretions of fantastic and superfluous detail a certain very solid substratum of a permanent and invaried character is unmistakably to be traced throughout the whole? This cannot in reason be denied, and here we have the core and the enduring reality of Witchcraft and the witch-cult throughout the ages.

There were some gross superstitions; there were some unbridled imaginations; there was deception, there was legerdemain; there was phantasy; there was fraud; Henri Boguet seems, perhaps, a trifle credulous, a little eager to explain obscure practices by an instant appeal to the supernormal; Brother Jetzer, the Jacobin of Berne, can only have been either the tool of his superiors or a cunning impostor; Matthew Hopkins was an unmitigated scoundrel who preyed upon the fears of the Essex franklins whilst he emptied their pockets; Lord Torphichen's son was an idle mischievous boy whose pranks not merely deluded both his father and the Rev. Mr. John Wilkins, but caused considerable mystification and amaze throughout the whole of Calder; Anne Robinson, Mrs. Golding's maid, and the two servant lasses of Baldarroch were prestidigitators of no common sleight and skill; and all these examples of ignorance, gullibility, malice, trickery, and imposture might easily be multiplied twenty times over and twenty times again, yet when every allowance has been made, every possible explanation exhausted, there persists a congeries of solid proven fact which cannot be ignored, save indeed by the purblind prejudice of the rationalist, and cannot be accounted for, save that we recognize there were and are individuals and organizations deliberately, nay, even enthusiastically, devoted to the service of evil, greedy of such emotions and experiences, rewards the thraldom of wickedness may bring.

The sceptic notoriously refuses to believe in Witchcraft, but a sanely critical examination of the evidence at the witch-trials will show that a vast amount of the modern vulgar incredulity is founded upon a complete misconception of the facts, and it may be well worth while quite briefly to review and correct some of the more common objections that are so loosely and so repeatedly maintained. There are many points which are urged as proving the fatuous absurdity and demonstrable impossibility of the whole system, and yet there is not one of these phenomena which is not capable of a satisfactory, and often a simple, elucidation. Perhaps the first thought of a witch that will occur to the man in the street is that of a hag on a broomstick flying up the chimney through the air. This has often been pictorially impressed on his imagination, not merely by woodcuts and illustrations traditionally presented in books, but by the brush of great painters such as Queverdo's *Le Départ au Sabbat*, *Le Départ pour le Sabbat* of David Teniers, and Goya's midnight fantasies. The famous Australian artist, Norman Lindsay, has a picture *To The Sabbat*[5] where witches are depicted wildly rushing through the air on the backs of grotesque pigs and hideous goats. Shakespeare, too, elaborated the idea, and "Hover through the fog and filthy air" has impressed itself upon the English imagination. But to descend from the airy realms of painting and poetry to the hard ground of actuality. Throughout the whole of the records there are very few instances when a witness definitely asserted that he had seen a witch carried through the air mounted upon a broom or stick of any kind, and on every occasion there is patent and obvious exaggeration to secure an effect. Sometimes the witches themselves boasted of this means of transport to impress their hearers. Boguet records that Claudine Boban, a young girl whose head was turned with pathological vanity, obviously a monomaniac who must at all costs occupy the centre of the stage and be the cynosure of public attention, confessed that she had been to the Sabbat, and this was undoubtedly the case; but to walk or ride on horseback to the Sabbat were far too ordinary methods of locomotion, melodrama and the marvellous must find their place in her account and so she alleged: "that both she and her mother used to mount on a broom, and so making their exit by the chimney in this fashion they flew through the air to the Sabbat."[6] Julian Cox (1664) said that one evening when she was in the fields about a mile away from the house "there came riding towards her three persons upon three Broom-staves, born up about a yard and a half from the ground."[7] There is obvious exaggeration here; she saw two men and one woman bestriding brooms and leaping high in the air. They were, in fact, performing a magic rite, a figure of a dance. So it is recorded of the Arab crones that "In the time of the Munkidh the witches rode about naked on a stick between the graves of the cemetery of Shaizar."[8] Nobody can refuse to believe that the witches bestrode sticks and poles and in their ritual capered to and fro in this manner, a sufficiently grotesque, but by no means an impossible, action. And this bizarre ceremony, evidence of which—with no reference to flying through the air—is frequent, has been exaggerated and transformed into the popular superstition that sorcerers are carried aloft and so transported from place to place, a wonder they were all ready to exploit in proof of their magic powers. And yet it is not impossible that there should have been actual instances of levitation. For, outside the lives of the Saints, spiritistic séances afford us examples of this supernormal phenomenon, which, if human evidence is worth anything at all, are beyond all question proven.

As for the unguents wherewith the sorcerers anointed themselves we have the actual formulæ for this composition, and Professor A. J. Clark, who has examined these,[9] considers that it is possible a strong application of such liniments might produce unwonted excitement and even delirium. But long ago the great demonologists recognized and laid down that of themselves the unguents possessed no such properties as the witches supposed. "The ointment and lotion are just of no use at all to witches to aid their journey to the Sabbat," is the well-considered opinion of Boguet who,[10] speaking with confident precision and finality, on this point is in entire agreement with the most sceptical of later rationalists.

The transformation of witches into animals and the extraordinary appearance at their orgies of "the Devil" under many a hideously unnatural shape, two points which have been repeatedly held up to scorn as self-evident impossibilities and proof conclusive of the untrustworthiness of the evidence and the incredibility of the whole system, can both be easily and fairly interpreted in a way which offers a complete and convincing explanation of these prodigies. The first metamorphosis, indeed, is mentioned and fully explained in the *Liber Pœnitentialis*[11] of S. Theodore, seventh Archbishop of Canterbury (668–690), capitulum xxvii, which code includes under the rubric *De Idolatria et Sacrilegio* "qui in Kalendas Ianuarii in ceruulo et in uitula uadit," and prescribes: "If anyone at the Kalends of January goes about as a stag or a bull; that is, making himself into a wild animal and dressing in the skin of a herd animal, and putting on the heads of beasts; those who in such wise transform themselves into the appearance of a wild animal, penance for three years because this is devilish." These ritual masks, furs, and hides, were, of course, exactly those the witches at certain ceremonies were wont to don for their Sabbats. There is ample proof that "the Devil" of the Sabbat was very frequently a human being, the Grand Master of the district, and since his officers and immediate attendants were also termed "Devils" by the witches some confusion has on occasion ensued. In a few cases where sufficient details are given it is possible actually to identify "the Devil" by name. Thus, among a list of suspected persons in the reign of Elizabeth we have "Ould Birtles, the great devil, Roger Birtles and his wife, and Anne Birtles."[12] The evil William, Lord Soulis, of Hermitage Castle, often known as "Red Cap," was "the Devil" of a coven of sorcerers. Very seldom "the Devil" was a woman. In May, 1569, the Regent of Scotland was present at S. Andrews "quhair a notabill sorceres callit Nicniven was condemnit to the death and burnt." Now Nicniven is the Queen of Elphin, the Mistress of the Sabbat, and this office had evidently been filled by this witch whose real name is not recorded. On 8 November, 1576, Elizabeth or Bessy Dunlop, of Lyne, in the Barony of Dalry, Ayrshire, was tried for sorcery, and she confessed that a certain mysterious Thom Reid had met her and demanded that she should renounce Christianity and her baptism, and apparently worship him. There can be little doubt that he was "the Devil" of a coven, for the original details, which are very full, all point to this. He seems to have played his part with some forethought and skill, since when the accused stated that she often saw him in the churchyard of Dalry, as also in the streets of Edinburgh, where he walked to and fro among other people and handled goods that were exposed on bulks for sale without attracting any special notice, and was thereupon asked why she did not address him, she replied that he had forbidden her to recognize him on any such occasion unless he made a sign or first actually accosted her. She was "convict and burnt."[13] In the case of Alison Peirson, tried 28 May, 1588, "the Devil" was actually her kinsman, William Sympson, and she "wes conuict of the vsing of Sorcerie and Witchcraft, with the Inuocatioun of the spreitis of the Deuill; speciallie in the visioune and forme of ane Mr. William Sympsoune, hir cousing and moder-brotheris-sone, quha sche affermit wes ane grit scoller and doctor of medicin."[14] *Conuicta et combusta* is the terse record of the margin of the court-book.

One of the most interesting identifications of "the Devil" occurs in the course of the notorious trials of Dr. Fian and his associates in 1590–1. As is well known, the whole crew was in league with Francis Stewart, Earl of Bothwell, and even at the time well-founded gossip, and something more than gossip, freely connected his name with the spells, Sabbats, and orgies of the witches. He was vehemently suspected of the black art; he was an undoubted client of warlocks and poisoners; his restless ambition almost overtly aimed at the throne, and the witch covens were one and all frantically attempting the life of King James. There can be no sort of doubt that Bothwell was the moving force who energized and directed the very elaborate and numerous organization of demonolaters, which was almost accidentally brought to light, to be fiercely crushed by the draconian vengeance of a monarch justly frightened for his crown and his life.

In the nineteenth century both Albert Pike of Charleston and his successor Adriano Lemmi have been identified upon abundant authority as being Grand Masters of societies practising Satanism, and as performing the hierarchical functions of "the Devil" at the modern Sabbat.

God, so far as His ordinary presence and action in Nature are concerned, is hidden behind the veil of secondary causes, and when God's ape, the Demon, can work so successfully and obtain not merely devoted adherents but fervent worshippers by human agency, there is plainly no need for him to manifest himself in person either to particular individuals or at the Sabbats, but none the less, that he can do so and has done so is certain, since such is the sense of the Church, and there are many striking cases in the records and trials which are to be explained in no other way.

That, as Burns Begg pointed out, the witches not unseldom "seem to have been undoubtedly the victims of unscrupulous and designing knaves, who personated Satan"[15] is no palliation of their crimes, and therefore they are not one whit the less guilty of sorcery and devil-worship, for this was their hearts' intention and desire. Nor do I think that the man who personated Satan at their assemblies was so much an unscrupulous and designing knave as himself a demonist, believing intensely in the reality of his own dark powers, wholly and horribly dedicated and doomed to the service of evil.

We have seen that the witches were upon occasion wont to array themselves in skins and ritual masks and there is complete evidence that the hierophant at the Sabbat, when a human being played that rôle, generally wore a corresponsive, if somewhat more elaborate, disguise. Nay more, as regards the British Isles at least—and it seems clear that in other countries the habit was very similar—we possess a pictorial representation of "the Devil" as he appeared to the witches. During the famous Fian trials Agnes Sampson confessed: "The deuell wes cled in ane blak goun with ane blak hat vpon his head. . . . His faice was terrible, his noise lyk the bek of ane egle, greet bournyng eyn; his handis and leggis wer herry, with clawes vpon his handis, and feit lyk the griffon."[16] In the pamphlet *Newes from Scotland, Declaring the Damnable life and death of Doctor Fian*[17] we have a rough woodcut, repeated twice, which shows "the Devil" preaching from the North Berwick pulpit to the whole coven of witches, and allowing for the crudity of the draughtsman and a few unimportant differences of detail—the black gown and hat are not portrayed—the demon in the picture is exactly like the description Agnes Sampson gave. It must be remembered, too, that at the Sabbat she was obviously in a state of morbid excitation, in part due to deep cups of heady wine, the time was midnight, the place a haunted old church, the only light a few flickering candles that burned with a ghastly blue flame.

Now "the Devil" as he is shown in the *Newes from Scotland* illustration is precisely the Devil who appears upon the title-page of Middleton and Rowley's Masque, *The World tost at Tennis*, 4to, 1620. This woodcut presents an episode towards the end of the masque, and here the Devil in traditional disguise, a grim black hairy shape with huge beaked nose, monstrous claws, and the cloven hoofs of a griffin, in every particular fits the details so closely observed by Agnes

Sampson. I have no doubt that the drawing for the masque was actually made in the theatre, for although this kind of costly and decorative entertainment was almost always designed for court or some great nobleman's house we know that *The World tost at Tennis* was produced with considerable success on the public stage " By the Prince his Seruants." The dress, then, of "the Devil" at the Sabbats seems frequently to have been an elaborate theatrical costume, such as might have been found in the stock wardrobe of a rich playhouse at London, but which would have had no such associations for provincial folk and even simpler rustics.

From time to time the sceptics have pointed to the many cases upon record of a victim's sickness or death following the witch's curse, and have incredulously inquired if it be possible that a malediction should have such consequences. Whilst candidly remarking that personally I believe there is power for evil and even for destruction in such a bane, that a deadly anathema launched with concentrated hate and all the energy of volition may bring unhappiness and fatality in its train, I would—since they will not allow this—answer their objections upon other lines. When some person who had in any way annoyed the witch was to be harmed or killed, it was obviously convenient, when practicable, to follow up the symbolism of the solemn imprecation, or it might be of the melted wax image riddled with pins, by a dose of subtly administered poison, which would bring about the desired result, whether sickness or death; and from the evidence concerning the witches' victims, who so frequently pined owing to a wasting disease, it seems more than probable that lethal drugs were continually employed, for as Professor A. J. Clark records " the society of witches had a very creditable knowledge of the art of poisoning,"[18] and they are known to have freely used aconite, deadly nightshade (belladonna), and hemlock.

So far then from the confessions of the witches being mere hysteria and hallucination they are proved, even upon the most material interpretation, to be in the main hideous and horrible fact.

In choosing examples to demonstrate this I have as yet referred almost entirely to the witchcraft which raged from the middle of the thirteenth to the beginning of the eighteenth century, inasmuch as that was the period when the diabolic cult reached its height, when it spread as a blight and a scourge throughout Europe and flaunted its most terrific proportions. But it must not for a moment be supposed, as has often been superficially believed, that Witchcraft was a product of the Middle Ages, and that only then did authority adopt measures of repression and legislate against the warlock and the sorceress. If attention has been concentrated upon that period it is because during those and the succeeding centuries Witchcraft blazed forth with unexampled virulence and ferocity, that it threatened the peace, nay in some degree, the salvation of mankind. But even pagan emperors had issued edicts absolutely forbidding goetic theurgy, confiscating grimoires (*fatidici libri*), and visiting necromancers with death. In A.U.C. 721 during the triumvirate of Octavius, Antony, and Lepidus, all astrologers and charmers were banished.[19] Maecenas called upon Augustus to punish sorcerers, and plainly stated that those who devote themselves to magic are despisers of the gods.[20] More than two thousand popular books of spells, both in Greek and Latin, were discovered in Rome and publicly burned.[21] In the reign of Tiberius a decree of the Senate exiled all traffickers in occult arts; Lucius Pituanius, a notorious wizard, they threw from the Tarpeian rock, and another, Publius Martius, was executed *more prisco* outside the Esquiline gate.[22]

Under Claudius the Senate reiterated the sentence of banishment: "De mathematicis Italia pellendis factum Senatus consultum, atrox et irritum," says Tacitus.[23] During the few months he was emperor Vitellius proceeded with implacable severity against all soothsayers and diviners; many of whom, when accused, he ordered for instant execution, not even affording them the tritest formality of a trial.[24] Vespasian, again, his successor, refused to permit scryers and enchanters to set foot in Italy, strictly enforcing the existent statutes.[25] It is clear from all these stringent laws, and the list of examples might be greatly extended, that although under the Cæsars omens were respected, oracles were consulted, the augurs honoured, and haruspices revered, the dark influences and foul criminality of the reverse of that dangerous science were recognized and its professors punished with the full force of repeated legislation.

M. de Cauzons has expressed himself somewhat vigorously when speaking of writers who trace the origins of Witchcraft to the Middle Ages: "C'est une mauvaise plaisanterie," he remarks,[26] "ou une contrevérité flagrante, d'affirmer que la sorcellerie naquit au Moyen-Age, et d'attribuer son existence à l'influence ou aux croyances de l'Eglise." (It is either a silly jest or inept irony to pretend that Witchcraft arose in the Middle Ages, to attribute its existence to the influence or the beliefs of the Catholic Church.)

An even more erroneous assertion is the charge which has been not infrequently but over-emphatically brought forward by partial ill-documented historians to the effect that the European crusade against witches, the stern and searching prosecutions with the ultimate penalty of death at the stake, are entirely due to the Bull *Summis desiderantes affectibus*, 5 December, 1484, of Pope Innocent VIII; or that at any rate this famous document, if it did not actually initiate the campaign, blew to blasts of flame and fury the smouldering and half-cold embers. This is most preposterously affirmed by Mackay, who does not hesitate to write[27]: "There happened at that time to be a pontiff at the head of the Church who had given much of his attention to the subject of Witchcraft, and who, with the intention of rooting out the supposed crime, did more to increase it than any other man that ever lived. John Baptist Cibo, elected to the papacy in 1485,[28] under the designation of Innocent VIII, was sincerely alarmed at the number of witches, and launched forth his terrible manifesto against them. In his celebrated bull of 1488, he called the nations of Europe to the rescue of the Church of Christ upon earth, 'imperilled by the arts of Satan'" which last sentence seems to be a very fair statement of fact. Lecky notes the Bull of Innocent which, he extravagantly declares, "gave a fearful impetus to the persecution."[29] Dr. Davidson, in a brief but slanderous account of this great pontiff, gives angry prominence to his severity "against sorcerers, magicians, and witches."[30] It is useless to cite more of these superficial and crooked judgements; but since even authorities of weight and value have been deluded and fallen into the snare it is worth while labouring the point a little and stressing the fact that the Bull of Innocent VIII was only one of a long series of Papal ordinances dealing with the suppression of a monstrous and almost universal evil.[31]

The first Papal Bull directly launched against the black art and its professors was that of Alexander IV, 13 December, 1258, addressed to the Franciscan inquisitors. And it is worth while here to examine precisely what was the earlier connotation of the terms "inquisitor" and "inquisition," so often misunderstood, as our research, though brief, will throw a flood of light upon the subject of Witchcraft, and, moreover, incidentally will serve to explain how that those writers who assign the beginnings of Witchcraft to the Middle Ages, although most certainly and even demonstrably in error, have at any rate been very subtilely and easily led wrong, since sorcery in the Middle Ages was violently unmasked and the whole horrid craft then first authoritatively exposed in its darkest colours and most abominable manifestations, as had indeed existed from the first, but had been carefully hidden and scrupulously concealed.

By the term Inquisition (*inquirere* = to look into) is now generally understood a special ecclesiastical institution for combating or suppressing heresy, and the Inquisitors are the officials attached to the said institution, more particularly judges who are appointed to investigate the charges of heresy and to try the persons brought before them on those charges. During the first twelve centuries the Church was loath to deal with heretics save by argument and persuasion; obstinate and avowed heretics were, of course, excluded from her communion, a defection which in the ages of faith, naturally involved them in many and great difficulties. S. Augustine,[32] S. John Chrysostom,[33] S. Isidore of Seville[34] in the seventh century, and a number of other Doctors and Fathers held that for no cause whatsoever should the Church shed blood; but, on the other hand, the imperial successors of Constantine justly considered that they were obliged to have a care for the material welfare of the Church here on earth, and that heresy is always inevitably and inextricably entangled with attempts on the social order, always anarchical, always political. Even the pagan persecutor Diocletian recognized this fact, which heretics, until they obtain the upper hand, have throughout the ages consistently denied and endeavoured to disguise. For in 287, less than two years after his accession, he sent to the stake the leaders of the Manichees; the majority of their followers were beheaded, and a few less culpable sent to perpetual forced labour in the government mines. Again in 296 he orders their extermination (*stirpitus amputari*) as a sordid, vile, and impure sect. So the Christian Cæsars, persuaded that the protection of orthodoxy was their sacred duty, began to issue edicts for the suppression of heretics as being traitors and anti-social revolutionaries.[35] But the Church protested, and when Priscillian, Bishop of Avila, being found guilty of heresy and sorcery,[36] was condemned to death by Maximus at Trier in 384, S. Martin of Tours addressed the Emperor in such plain terms that it was solemnly promised the sentence should not be carried into effect. However, the pledge was broken, and S. Martin's indignation was such that for a long while he refused to hold communion with those who had been in any way responsible for the execution, which S. Ambrose roundly stigmatized as a heinous crime.[37] Even more crushing were the words of Pope S. Siricius, before whom Maximus was fain to humble himself in lowliest penitence, and the supreme pontiff actually excommunicated Bishop Felix of Trier for his part in the deed.

From time to time heretics were put to death under the civil law to which they were amenable, as in 556 when a band of Manichees were executed at Ravenna. Pope Pelagius I, who was consecrated that very year, when Paulinus of Fossombrone, rejecting his authority, openly stirred up schism and revolt, merely relegated the recalcitrant bishop to a monastery. Saint Cæsarius of Arles, who died in 547, speaking[38] of the punishment to be meted out to those who obstinately persevere in overt paganism, recommends that they should first be remonstrated with and reprimanded, that they should if possible be thus persuaded of their errors; but if they persist certain corporal chastisement is to be given; and in extreme cases a course of domestic discipline, the cutting of the hair close as a mark of indignity and confinement within doors under restraint, may be adopted. There is no hint of anything more than private measures, no calling in of any ecclesiastical authority, far less an appeal to any punitive tribunal.

In the days of Charlemagne the aged Elipandus, Archbishop of Toledo, taught an offshoot of the Nestorian heresy, Adoptionism, a crafty but deadly error, to which he won the slippery dialectician Felix of Urgel. Felix, as a Frankish prelate, was summoned to Aix-la-Chapelle. A synod condemned his doctrine and he recanted, only to retract his words and to reiterate his blasphemies. He was again condemned, and again he recanted. But he proved shifty and tricksome to the last. For after his death Agobar of Lyons found amongst his papers a scroll asserting that of this heresy he was fully persuaded, in spite of any contradictions to which he might hypocritically subscribe. Yet Felix only suffered a short detention at Rome, whilst no measures seem to have been taken against Elipandus, who died in his errors. It was presumably considered that orthodoxy could be sufficiently served and vindicated by the zeal of such great names as Beatus, Abbot of Libana; Etherius, Bishop of Osma; S. Benedict of Aniane; and the glorious Alcuin.[39]

Some forty years later, about the middle of the ninth century, Gothescalch, a monk of Fulda, caused great scandal by obstinately and impudently maintaining that Christ had not died for all mankind, a foretaste of the Calvinistic heresy. He was condemned at the Synods of Mainz in 848, and of Kiersey-sur-Oise in 849, being sentenced to flogging and imprisonment, punishments then common in monasteries for various infractions of the rule. In this case, as particularly flagrant, it was Hincmar, Archbishop of Rheims, a prelate notorious for his severity, who sentenced the culprit to incarceration. But Gothescalch had by his pernicious doctrines been the cause of serious disturbances; and his inflammatory harangues had excited tumults, sedition, and unrest, bringing odium upon the sacred habit. The sentence of the Kiersey Synod ran: "Frater Goteschalc . . . quia et ecclesiastica et ciuilia negotia contra propositum et nomen monachi conturbare iura ecclesiastica præsumpsisti, durissimis uerberibus te cagistari et secundum ecclesiasticas regulas ergastulo retrudi, auctoritate episcopali decernimus." (Brother Gothescalch, . . . because thou hast dared—contrary to thy monastic calling and vows—to concern thyself in worldly as well as spiritual businesses and hast violated all ecclesiastical law and order, by our episcopal authority we condemn thee to be severely scourged and according to the provision of the Church to be closely imprisoned.)

From these instances it will be seen that the Church throughout all those centuries of violence, rapine, invasion, and war, when often primitive savagery reigned supreme and the most hideous cruelty was the general order of the day, dealt very gently with the rebel and the heretic, whom she might have executed wholesale with the greatest ease; no voice would have been raised in protest save that of her own pontiffs, doctors, and Saints; nay, rather, such repression would have been universally applauded as eminently proper and just. But it was the civil power who arraigned the anarch and the misbeliever, who sentenced him to death.

About the year 1000, however, the venom of Manichæism obtained a new footing in the West, where it had died out early in the sixth century. Between 1030–40 an important Manichæan community was discovered at the Castle of Monteforte, near Asti, in Piedmont. Some of the members were arrested by the Bishop of Asti and a number of noblemen in the neighbourhood, and upon their refusal to retract the civil arm burned them. Others, by order of the Archbishop of Milan, Ariberto, were brought to that city since he hoped to convert them. They answered his efforts by attempts to make proselytes; whereupon Lanzano, a prominent noble and leader of the popular party, caused the magistrates to intervene and when they had been taken into the custody of the State they were executed without further respite. For the next two hundred years Manichæism spread its infernal teaching in secret until, towards the year 1200, the plague had infected all Italy and Southern Europe, had reached northwards to Germany, where it was completely organized, and was not unknown in England, since as early as 1159 thirty foreign Manichees had privily settled here. They were discovered in 1166, and handed over to the secular authorities by the Bishops of the Council of Oxford. In high wrath Henry II ordered them to be scourged, branded in the forehead, and cast adrift in the cold of winter, straightly forbidding any to succour such vile criminals, so all perished from cold and exposure. Manichæism furthermore split up into an almost infinite number of sects and systems, prominent amongst which were the Cathari, the Aldonistæ and Speronistæ, the Concorrezenses of Lombardy, the Bagnolenses, the Albigenses, Pauliciani, Patarini, Bogomiles, the Waldenses, Tartarins, Beghards, Pauvres de Lyon.

It must be clearly borne in mind that these heretical bodies with their endless ramifications were not merely exponents of erroneous religious and intellectual beliefs by which they morally corrupted all who came under their influence, but they were the avowed enemies of law and order, red-hot anarchists who would stop at nothing to gain their ends. Terrorism and secret murder were their most frequent weapons. In 1199 the Patarini followers of Ermanno of Parma and Gottardo of Marsi, two firebrands of revolt, foully assassinated S. Peter Parenzo, the governor of Orvieto. On 6 April, 1252, whilst returning from Como to Milan, as he passed through a lonely wood S. Peter of Verona was struck down by the axe of a certain Carino, a Manichæan bravo, who had been hired to the deed.[40] By such acts they sought to intimidate whole districts, and to compel men's allegiance with blood and violence. The Manichæan system was in truth a simultaneous attack upon the Church and the State, a desperate but well-planned organization to destroy the whole fabric of society, to reduce civilization to chaos. In the first instance, as the Popes began to perceive the momentousness of the struggle they engaged the bishops to stem the tide. At the Council of Tours, 1163, Alexander III called upon the bishops of Gascony to take active measures for the suppression of these revolutionaries, but at the Lateran Council of 1179 it was found these disturbers of public order had sown such sedition in Languedoc that an appeal was made to the secular power to check the evil. In 1184 Lucius III issued from Verona his Bull *Ad Abolendam* which expressly mentions many of the heretics by name, Cathari, Patarini, Humiliati, Pauvres de Lyon, Pasagians, Josephins, Aldonistæ. The situation had fast developed and become serious. Heretics were to be sought out and suitably punished, by which, however, capital punishment is not intended. Innocent III, although adding nothing essential to these regulations yet gave them fuller scope and clearer definition. In his Decretals he precisely speaks of accusation, denunciation, and inquisition, and it is obvious that these measures were necessary in the face of a great secret society aiming at nothing less than the destruction of the established order, for all the sectaries were engaged upon the most zealous propaganda, and their adherents had spread like a network over the greater part of Europe. The members bore the title of "brother" and "sister," and had words and signs by which the initiate could recognize one another without betraying themselves to others.[41] Ivan de Narbonne, who was converted from this heresy, in a letter to Giraldus, Archbishop of Bordeaux, as quoted by Matthew of Paris, says that in every city where he travelled he was always able to make himself known by signs.[42]

It was necessary that the diocesan bishops should be assisted in their heavy task of tracking down heretics, and accordingly the Holy See had resource to legates who were furnished with extraordinary powers to cope with so perplexing a situation. In 1177 as legate of Alexander III, Peter, Cardinal of San Crisogono, at the particular request of Count Raymond V, visited the Toulouse district to check the rising tide of Catharist doctrine.[43] In 1181, Henry, Abbot of Clairvaux, who had been in his suite, now Cardinal of Albano, as legate of the same Pope, received the submission of various heretical leaders, and, so extensive were his powers, solemnly deposed the Archbishops of Lyons and Narbonne. In 1203 Peter of Castelnau and Raoul were acting at Toulouse on behalf of Innocent III, seemingly with plenipotentiary authority. The next year Arnauld Amaury, Abbot of Citeaux, was joined to them to form a triple tribunal with absolute power to judge heretics in the provinces of Aix, Arles, Narbonne, and the adjoining dioceses. At the death of Innocent III (1216) there existed an organization to search out heretics; episcopal tribunals at which often sat an assessor (the future inquisitor) to watch the conduct of the case; and above all the legate to whom he might make a report. The legate, from his position, was naturally a prelate occupied with a vast number of urgent affairs—Arnauld Amaury, for example, was absent for a considerable time to take part in the General Chapter at Cluny—and gradually more and more authority was delegated to the assessor, who insensibly developed into the Inquisitor, a special but permanent judge acting in the name of the Pope, by whom he was invested with the right and the duty to deal legally with offences against the Faith. And as just at this time there came into being two new Orders, the Dominicans and Franciscans, whose members by their theological training and the very nature of their vows seemed eminently fitted to perform the inquisitorial task with complete success, absolutely uninfluenced by any worldly motive, it is natural that the new officials should have been selected from these Orders, and, owing to the importance attached by the Dominicans to the study of divinity, especially from their learned ranks.

It is very obvious why the Holy See so sagaciously preferred to assign the prosecution of heretics, a matter of the first importance, to an extraordinary tribunal rather than leave the trials in the hands of the bishops. Without taking into consideration the fact that these new duties would have seriously encroached upon, if not wholly absorbed, the time and activities of a bishop, the prelates who ruled most dioceses were the subject of some monarch with whom they might have come in conflict on many a delicate point which could easily be conceived to arise, and the result of such disagreement would have been fraught with endless political difficulties and internal embarrassments. A court of religious, responsible to the Pope alone, would act more fairly, more freely, without fear or favour. The profligate Philip I of France, for example, during his long, worthless, and dishonoured reign (1060–1108), by his evil courses drew upon himself the censure of the Church, whereupon he banished the Bishop of Beauvais and revoked the decisions of the episcopal courts.[44] In a letter[45] to William, Count of Poitiers, Pope S. Gregory VII energetically declares that if the King does not cease from molesting the bishops and interfering with their judicature a sentence of excommunication will be launched. In another letter the same pontiff complains of the disrespect shown to the ecclesiastical tribunals, and addressing the French bishops he cries: "Your king, who sooth to say should be termed not a king but a cruel tyrant, inspired by Satan, is the head and cause of these evils. For he has notoriously passed all his days in foulest crimes, in seeking to do wickedness and to ensue it."[46] The conflict of the bishops of a realm with an unworthy and evil monarch is a commonplace of history. These troubles could scarcely arise in the case of courts forane.

The words "inquisition" and "inquisitors" began definitely to acquire their accepted signification in the earlier half of the thirteenth century. Thus in 1235 Gregory IX writes to the Archbishop of Sens: "Know then that we have charged the Provincial of the Order of Preachers in this same realm to nominate certain of his brethren, who are best fitted for so weighty a business, as Inquisitors that they may proceed against all notorious evildoers in the aforesaid realm . . . and we also charge thee, dear Brother, that thou shouldest be instant and zealous in this matter of establishing an Inquisition by the appointment of those who seem to be best fitted for such a work, and let thy loins be girded, Brother, to fight boldly the battles of the Lord."[47] In 1246 Innocent IV wrote to the Superiors of the Franciscans giving them leave to recall at will: "those brethren who have been sent abroad to preach the Mystery of the Cross of Christ, or to seek out and take measure against the plague sore of heresy."[48]

All the heresies, and the Secret Societies of heretics, which infested Europe during the Middle Ages were Gnostic, and even more narrowly, Manichæan in character. The Gnostics arose almost with the advent of Christianity as a School or Schools who explained the teachings of Christ by blending them with the doctrines of pagan fantasts, and thus they claimed to have a Higher and a Wider Knowledge, the Γνῶσις, the first exponent of which was unquestionably Simon Magus. "Two problems borrowed from heathen philosophy," says Mansel,[49] "were intruded by Gnosticism on the Christian revelation, the problem of absolute existence, and the problem of the Origin of Evil." The Gnostics denied the existence of Free-will, and therefore Evil was not the result of Man's voluntary transgression, but must in some way have emanated from the Creator Himself. Arguing on these lines the majority asserted that the Creator must have been a malignant power, Lord of the Kingdom of Darkness, opposed to the Supreme and Ineffable God. This doctrine was taught by the Gnostic sects of Persia, which became deeply imbued with the religion of Zoroaster, who assumed the existence of two original and independent Powers of Good and of Evil. Each of these Powers is of equal strength, and supreme in his own dominions, whilst constant war is waged between the two. This doctrine was particularly held by the Syrian Gnostics, the Ophites, the Naasseni, the Peratæ, the Sethians, amongst whom the serpent was the principal symbol. As the Creator of the world was evil, the Tempter, the Serpent, was the benefactor of man. In fact, in some creeds he was identified with the Logos. The Cainites carried out the Ophite doctrines to their fullest logical conclusion. Since the Creator, the God of the Old Testament, is evil all that is commended by the Scripture must be evil, and conversely all that is condemned therein is good. Cain, Korah, the rebels, are to be imitated and admired. The one true Apostle was Judas Iscariot. This cult is very plainly marked in the Middle Ages among the Luciferians; and Cainite ceremonies have their place in the witches' Sabbat.[50]

All this Gnostic teaching was summed up in the gospel of the Persian Mani, who, when but a young man of twenty-six, seems first to have proclaimed in the streets and bazaars of Seleucia-Ctesiphon his supposed message on Sunday, 20 March, 242, the coronation festival of Shapur I. He did not meet with immediate success in his own country, but here and there his ideas took deep root. In 276–277, however, he was seized and crucified by the grandson of Shapur, Bahram I, his disciples being relentlessly pursued. Whenever Manichees were discovered they were brought to swift justice, executed, held up to universal hatred and contempt. They were considered by Moslems as not merely Unbelievers, the followers of a false impostor, but unnatural and unsocial, a menace to the State. It was for no light cause that the Manichee was loathed and abhorred both by faithful Christian and by those who proclaimed Mohammed as the true prophet of Allah. But later Manichæism spread in every direction to an extraordinary degree, which may perhaps be accounted for by the fact that it is in some sense a synthesis of the Gnostic philosophies, the theory of two eternal principles, good and evil, being especially emphasized.

Moreover, the historical Jesus, "the Jewish Messias, whom the Jews crucified," was "a devil, who was justly punished for interfering in the work of the Æon Jesus," who was neither born nor suffered death. As time went on, the elaborate cosmogony of Mani disappeared, but the idea that the Christ must be repudiated remained. And logically, then, worship is due to the enemy of Christ, and a sub-sect, the Messalians or Euchites, taught that divine honours must be paid to Satan, who is further to be propitiated by means of every possible outrage done to Christ. This, of course, is plain and simple Satanism openly avowed. Carpocrates even went so far as to aggravate the teaching of the Cainites, for he made the performance of every species of sin forbidden in the Old Testament a solemn duty, since this was the completest mode of showing defiance to the Evil Creator and Ruler of the World. This doctrine was wholly that of mediæval witches, and is flaunted by modern Satanists. Although the Manichees affected the greatest purity, it is quite certain that not unchastity but the act of generation alone was opposed to their views, secretly they practised the most hideous obscenities.[51] The Messalians in particular, vaunted a treatise *Asceticus*, which was condemned by the Third General Council of Ephesus (431) as "that filthy book of this heresy," and in Armenia, in the fifth century, special edicts were passed to restrain their immoralities, so that their very name became the equivalent for "lewdness." The Messalians survived unto the Middle Ages as Bogomiles.

Attention has already been drawn to the striking fact that even Diocletian legislated with no small vigour against the Manichees, and when we find Valentinian I and his son Gratian, although tolerant of other bodies, passing laws of equal severity in this regard (372), we feel that such interdiction is especially significant. Theodosius I, by a statute of 381, declared Manichees to be without civil rights, and incapable of inheriting; in the following year he condemned them to death, and in 389 he sternly directed the rigorous enforcement to the letter of these penalties.

Valentinian II confiscated their goods, annulled their wills, and sent them into exile. Honorius in 399 renewed the draconian measures of his predecessors; in 405 he heavily fined all governors of provinces or civil magistrates who were slack in carrying out his orders; in 407 he pronounced the sect outlaws and public criminals having no legal status whatsoever, and in 408 he reiterated the former enactments in meticulous detail to afford no loophole of escape. Theodosius II (423), again, repeated this legislation, whilst Valentinian III passed fresh laws in 425 and 445. Anastasius once more decreed the penalty of death, which was even extended by Justin and Justinian to converts from Manichæism who did not at once denounce their former co-religionists to the authorities. This catena of laws which aims at nothing less than extermination is of singular moment.

About 660 arose the Paulicians, a Manichæan sect, who rejected the Old Testament, the Sacraments, and the Priesthood. In 835 it was realized that the government of this body was political and aimed at revolution and red anarchy. In 970 John Zimisces fixed their headquarters in Thrace. In 1115 Alexis Comnenus established himself during the winter at Philippopolis, and avowed his intention of converting them, the only result being that the heretics were driven westward and spread rapidly in France and Italy.

The Bogomiles were also Manichees. They openly worshipped Satan, repudiating Holy Mass and the Passion, rejecting Holy Baptism for some foul ceremony of their own, and possessing a peculiar version of the Gospel of S. John. As Cathari these wretches had their centre for France at Toulouse; for Germany at Cologne; whilst in Italy, Milan, Florence, Orvieto, and Viterbo were their rallying-points. Their meetings were often held in the open air, on mountains, or in the depths of some lone valley; the ritual was very secret, but we know that at night they celebrated their Eucharist or Consolamentum, when all stood in a circle round a table covered with a white cloth and numerous torches were kindled, the service being closed by the reading of the first seventeen verses of their transfigured gospel. Bread was broken, but there is a tradition that the words of consecration were not pronounced according to the Christian formula; in some instances they were altogether omitted.

During the eleventh century, then, there began to spread throughout Europe a number of mysterious organizations whose adherents, in a secrecy that was all but absolute, practised obscure rites embodying their beliefs, the central feature of which was the adoration of the evil principle, the demon. But what is this save Satanism, or in other words Witchcraft? It is true that when these heresies came into sharp conflict with the Catholic Church they developed on lines which lost various non-essential accretions and Eastern subtleties of extravagant thought, but the motive of the Manichæan doctrines and of Witchcraft is one and the same, and the punishment of Manichees and of witches was the same death at the stake. The fact that these heretics were recognized as sorcerers will explain, as nothing else can, the severity of the statutes against them, evidence of no ordinary depravity, and early in the eleventh century Manichee and warlock are recognized as synonymous.

The sorcery of the Middle Ages, says Carl Haas, a learned and impartial authority, was born from the heresies of earlier epochs, and just as Christian authority had dealt with heresy, so did it deal with the spawn witchcraft. Both alike are the result of doubts, of faithlessness, a disordered imagination, pride and presumption, intellectual arrogance; sick phantasy both, they grow and flourish apace in shadow and sin, until right reasoning, and sometimes salutary force, are definitely opposed to them. The authors of the *Malleus Maleficarum* clearly identify heresy and Witchcraft. When the Prince Bishop of Bamberg, John George II Fuchs von Dornheim, (1623–33), built a strong prison especially for sorcerers, the *Drudenhaus*, he set over the great door a figure of Justice, and inscribed above Vergil's words: *Discite iustitiam moniti et non temnere Diuos* (*Æneid*, VI, 620),

(Behold, and learn to practise right,
Nor do the blessed Gods despite).

To the right and the left were engraved upon two panels, the one Latin, the other German, two verses from the Bible, 3 Kings ix. 8, 9; which are Englished as follows: "This house shall be made an example of: every one that shall pass by it shall be astonished, and shall hiss, and say: Why hath the Lord done thus to this land, and to this house? And they shall answer: Because they forsook the Lord their God, who brought their fathers out of the land of Egypt, and followed strange gods, and adored them, and worshipped them: therefore hath the Lord brought upon them all this evil." This is a concise summary of the basic reason for the prosecution of witches, the standpoint of Christian authority, whose professors justly and logically regarded sorcery as being in essence heresy, to be suppressed by the same measures, to be punished with the same penalties.

In connexion with the close correlation between Witchcraft and heresy there is a very remarkable fact, the significance of which has—so far as I am aware—never been noted. The full fury of prosecution burst over England during the first half of the seventeenth century, that is to say, shortly after the era of a great religious upheaval, when the work of rehabilitation and recovery so nobly initiated by Queen Mary I had been wrecked owing to the pride, lust, and baseness of her sister. In Scotland, envenomed to the core with the poison of Calvin and Knox, fire and cord were seldom at rest. It is clear that heresy had brought Witchcraft swiftly in its train. Ireland has ever been singularly free from Witchcraft prosecutions, and with the rarest exceptions —chiefly, if not solely, the famous Dame Alice Kyteler case of 1324—the few trials recorded are of the seventeenth century and engineered by the Protestant party. The reason for this exemption is plain. Until the stranger forced his way into Ireland, heresy had no foothold there. That the Irish firmly believed in witches, we know, but the Devil's claws were finely clipped.

In 1022 a number of Manichees were burned alive by order of Robert I. They had been condemned by a Synod at Orleans and refused to recant their errors.[52] A contemporary document clearly identifies them with witches, worshippers of the Demon, who appeared to them under the form of an animal. Other abominable rites are fully set forth, comparable to the pages of Sprenger, Bodin, Boguet, De Lancre, Guazzo, and the rest. The account runs as follows : " Before we proceed to other details I will at some length inform those who are as yet ignorant of these matters, how that food which they call Food from Heaven is made and provided. On certain nights of the year they all meet together in an appointed house, each one of them carrying a lantern in his hand. They then begin to sing the names of various demons, as though they were chanting a litany, until suddenly they perceive that the Devil has appeared in the midst of them in the shape of some animal or other. As he would seem to be visible to them all in some mysterious way they immediately extinguish the lights, and each one of them as quickly as he can seizes upon the woman, who chances to be nearest at hand. . . . When a child happens to be born . . . on the eighth day they all meet together and light a large fire in their midst, and then the child is passed through the fire, ceremonially, according to the sacrifices of the old heathen, and finally is burnt in the flames. The ashes are collected and reserved, with the same veneration as Christians are wont to reserve the Blessed Sacrament, and they give those who are on the point of death a portion of these ashes as if it were the Viaticum. There appears to be such power infused by the Devil into the said ashes that a man who belongs to these heretics and happens to have tasted even the smallest quantity of these ashes can scarcely ever be persuaded to abandon his heresies and to turn his thoughts towards the true path. It must suffice to give only these details, as a warning to all Christians to take no part in these abominations, and God forbid that curiosity should lead anybody to explore them."[53]

At Forfar, in 1661, Helen Guthrie and four other witches exhumed the body of an unbaptised infant, which was buried in the churchyard near the south-east door of the church, "and took severall peices thereof, as the feet, hands, a pairt of the head, and a pairt of the buttock, and they made a py thereof, that they might eat of it, that by this meanes they might never make a confession (as they thought) of their witchcraftis."[54]

The belief of 1022 and 1661 is the same, because it is the same organization. The very name of the Vaudois, stout heretics, survives in Voodoo worship, which is, in effect, African fetishism or Witchcraft transplanted to America soil.

In 1028 Count Alduin burned a number of Manichees at Angoulême, and the chronicle runs: "Interea iussu Alduini flammis exustæ sunt mulieres maleficæ extra urbem."[55] (About this time certain evil women, heretics, were burned without the city by the command of Alduin.) The Templars, whose Order was suppressed and the members thereof executed on account of their sorceries, were clearly a Society of Gnostic heretics, active propagandists, closely connected with the Bogomiles and the Mandæans or Johannites.[56]

It is true that in his recent study *The Religion of the Manichees*,[57] Dr. F. G. Buskitt, with a wealth of interesting detail and research, has endeavoured to show that the Bogomiles, the Cathari, the Albigenses, and other unclean bodies only derived fragments of their teaching from Manichæan sources, and he definitely states "I think it misleading to call these sects, even the Albigensians, by the name of Manichees." But in spite of his adroit special pleading the historical fact remains; although we may concede that the abominable beliefs of these various Gnostics were perhaps a deduction from, or a development of, the actual teaching of Mani. Yet none the less their evil was contained in his heresy and a logical consequence of it.

In the early years of this century important discoveries of Manichæan MSS. have been made. Three or four scientific expeditions to Chinese Turkestan brought back some thousands of fragments, especially from the neighbourhood of a town called Turfan. Many of these screeds are written in the peculiar script of the Manichees, some of which can be deciphered, although unfortunately the newly found documents are mere scraps, bits of torn books and rolls, and written in languages as yet imperfectly known. Much of the new doctrine is of the wildest and most fantastic theosophy, and the initiate were, as we know, sufficiently cunning not to commit the esoteric and true teachings to writing, but preferred that there should be an oral tradition. One important piece, the *Khuastuanift*, i.e. "Confession," has been recovered almost in its entirety. It is in the old Turkestan Turkish language, and seems full of the most astounding contradictions or paradoxes, a consensus of double meanings and subtleties.

The question is asked whether we ought to consider Manichæism as an independent religion or a Christian heresy? Eznih of Kolb, the Armenian writer of the fifth century, when attacking Zoroastrianism, obviously treats Manichæism as a variety of Persian religion. The orthodox documents, however, from Mark the Deacon onwards treat Manichæism as in the main a Christian heresy and this is assuredly the correct view. There is in existence a polemical fragment, a single ill-preserved pair of leaves, in which the Manichæan writer pours forth horrid blasphemies and vilely attacks those who call Mary's Son (*Bar Maryam*) the Son of Adonay.

It may be worth while here to say just a word correcting a curious old-fashioned misapprehension which once prevailed in certain quarters concerning the Albigenses, an error of which we occasionally yet catch the echoes, as when Mrs. Grenside wrote that the Albigenses were "a sect of the 14th century which, owing to their secret doctrine, endured much ecclesiastical persecution."[58] The impression left, and it is one which was not altogether uncommon some seventy years ago, is that the Albigensian was a stern old Protestant father, Bible and sword in hand, who defended his hearth and home against the lawless brigands spurred on to attack him by priestly machinations. Nothing, of course, could be further from the truth. The Albigensian was a Satanist, a worshipper of the powers of evil, and he would have found short shrift indeed, fire and the stake, in Puritan England under Cromwell, or in Calvinistic Scotland had his practices been even dimly guessed at by the Kirk. As Dr. Arendzen well says[59]: "Albigensianism was not really a heresy against Christianity and the Catholic Church, it was a revolt against nature, a pestilential perversion of human instinct."

Towards the end of the nineteenth century a *Neo-Gnostic Church* was formed by Fabre des Essarts, but that great pontiff Leo XIII promptly condemned it with fitting severity as a recrudescence of the old Albigensian heresy, complicated by the addition of new false and impious doctrines. It is said still to have a number of unhappy adherents. These Neo-Gnostics believe that the world is created by Satan, who is a powerful rival to the omnipotence of God. They also preach a dangerous communism, speciously masqued under some such titles as the "Brotherhood of Man" or the "Brotherhood of Nations."

In 1900, after a letter from Joanny Bricaud,[60] the patriarch of universal Gnosticism at Lyons, where, in 1913, he was residing at 8, rue Bugeaud, the Neo-Gnostics joined with the Valentinians, a union approved by their pseudo-Council of Toulouse in 1903. But some years later Dr. Fugairon of Lyons, who adopted the name of Sophronius, amalgamated all the branches, with the exception of the Valentinians, under the name of the *Gnostic Church of Lyons*. These, however, although excluded, continued to follow their own way of salvation, and in 1906 formally addressed a legal declaration to the Republican Government defending their religious rights of association. Truly might Huysmans tell us that Satanism flourished at Lyons, "où toutes les hérésies survivent," "where every heresy pullulates and is green." These Gnostic assemblies are composed of "perfected ones," male and female. The modern Valentinians, it is said, have a form of spiritual marriage, bestowing the name of Helen upon the mystic bride. The original founder of this sect, Valentinus, was, according to S. Epiphanius (*Hæresis* XXXI) born in Egypt, and educated at Alexandria. His errors led to excommunication and he died in Cyprus, about A.D. 160–161. His heresy is a fantastic medley of Greek and Oriental speculation, tinged with some vague colouring of Christianity. The Christology of Valentinus is especially confused. He seems to have supposed the existence of three redeemers, but Christ, the Son of Mary, did not have a real body and did not suffer. Even his more prominent disciples, Heracleon, Ptolemy, Marcos, and Bardesanes, widely differed from their master, as from one another. Many of the writings of these Gnostics, and a large number of excerpts from Valentinus's own works yet survive.

One or two writers of the nineteenth century remarked that there seemed to be some connexion between certain points of the Sabbat ceremonial and the rites of various pagan deities, which is, of course, a perfectly correct observation. For we have seen that Witchcraft as it existed in Europe from the eleventh century was mainly the spawn of Gnostic heresy, and heresy by its very nature embraced and absorbed much of heathendom. In some sense Witchcraft was a descendant of the old pre-Christian magic, but it soon assumed a slightly different form, or rather at the advent of Christianity it was exposed and shown in its real foul essence as the worship of the Evil Principle, the Enemy of Mankind, Satan.

It may freely be acknowledged that there are certain symbols common to Christianity itself and to ancient religions. It would in truth be very surprising if, when seeking to propagate her doctrines in the midst of Græco-Roman civilization, the Church had adopted for her intercourse with the people a wholly unknown language, and had systematically repudiated everything that until then had served to give expression to religious feeling.

Within the limits imposed by the conventions of race and culture, the method of interpreting the emotions of the heart cannot be indefinitely varied, and it was natural that the new religion should appropriate and incorporate all that was good in a ritual much of which only required to be rightly interpreted and directed to become the language of the Christian soul aspiring to the one True God. Certain attitudes of prayer and reverence, the use of incense and of lamps burning day and night in the sanctuary, the offering of ex-votos as a testimony to benefits received, all these are man's natural expressions of piety and gratitude towards a divine power, and it would be strange indeed if their equivalents were not met with in all religions.

Cicero tells us that at Agrigentum there was a much-venerated statue of Hercules, of which the mouth and chin were worn away by the many worshippers who pressed their lips to it.[61] The bronze foot of the statue of the first Pope, S. Peter, in Rome has not withstood any better the pious kisses of the faithful. Yet he were a very fool who imagined that modern Christians have learned anything from the Sicilian contemporaries of Verres. What is true is that the same thought in analogous circumstances has found natural expression after an interval of centuries in identical actions and attitudes.

Among the Greeks, heroes, reputed to be the mortal sons of some divinity, were specially honoured in the city with which they were connected by birth and through the benefits they had conferred upon it. After death they became the patrons and protectors of these towns. Every country, nay, almost every village, had such local divinities to whom monuments were raised and whom the people invoked in their prayers. The centre of devotion was generally the hero's tomb, which was often erected in the middle of the agora, the nave of public life. In most cases it was sheltered by a building, a sort of chapel known as ἡρῷον. The celebrated temples, too, were not infrequently adorned with a great number of cenotaphs of heroes, just as the shrines of Saints are honoured in Christian churches.[62] More, the translations of the bones or ashes of heroes were common in Greece. Thus in the archonship of Apsephion, 469 B.C., the remains of Theseus were brought from Scyros to Athens, and carried into the city amid sacrifices and every demonstration of triumphal joy.[63] Thebes recovered from Ilion the bones of Hector, and presented to Athens those of Œdipus, to Lebadea those of Arcesilaus, and to Megara those of Aigialeus.[64]

The analogy between these ancient practices and Christianity may be pushed further yet. Just as, in our own churches, objects that have belonged to the Saints are exposed for the veneration of the faithful, so in the old temples visitors were shown divers curiosities whose connexion with a god or a hero would command their respect. At Minihi Tréguier we may reverence a fragment of the Breviary of S. Yves, at Sens the stole of S. Thomas of Canterbury, at Bayeux the chasuble of S. Regnobert, in S. Maria Maggiore the cincture and veil of S. Scholastica; so in various localities of Greece were exhibited the cittara of Paris, the lyre of Orpheus, portions of the ships of Agamemnon and Æneas. Can anything further be needed to prove that the veneration of Holy Relics is merely a pagan survival?

Superficially the theory seems plausible enough, and yet it will not stand a moment before the judgement of history. The cultus of the Saints and their Relics is not an outcome of ancient hero-worship, but of reverence for the Martyrs, and this can be demonstrated without any possibility of question. So here we have two very striking parallels, each of which has an analogous starting-point, two cults which naturally develop upon logical and similar lines, but without any interdependence whatsoever. Needless to say, the unbalanced folklorist, who is in general far too insufficiently equipped for any such inquiry, has rushed in with his theories —to his own utter undoing. And so, with regard to Witchcraft, there appear in the rites of the Sabbat and other hellish superstitions to be ceremonies which are directly derived from heathendom, but this, as a matter of fact, is far from the case. Accordingly we recognize that the thesis of Miss M. A. Murray in her anthropological study *The Witch-*

Cult in Western Europe,[65] although worked out with nice ingenuity and no little documentation, is radically and wholly erroneous. Miss Murray actually postulates that "underlying the Christian religion was a cult practised by many classes of the community" which "can be traced back to pre-Christian times, and appears to be the ancient religion of Western Europe." We are given a full account of the chief festivals of this imaginary cult, of its hierarchy, its organization, and many other details. The feasts and dances —the obscene horrors of the Sabbat—"show that it was a joyous religion"! It is impossible to conceive a more amazing assertion. Miss Murray continues to say that "as such it must have been quite incomprehensible to the gloomy Inquisitors and Reformers who suppressed it." The Reformers, for all their dour severity, perfectly well appreciated with what they were dealing, and the Inquisitors, the sons of S. Dominic who was boundless in his charity and of S. Francis, whose very name breathes Christ-like love to all creation, were men of the profoundest knowledge and deepest sympathies, whose first duty it was to stamp out the infection lest the whole of Society be corrupted and damned. Miss Murray does not seem to suspect that Witchcraft was in truth a foul and noisome heresy, the poison of the Manichees. Her "Dianic cult," which name she gives to this "ancient religion" supposed to have survived until the Middle Ages and even later and to have been a formidable rival to Christianity, is none other than black heresy and the worship of Satan, no primitive belief with pre-agricultural rites, in latter days persecuted, misinterpreted, and misunderstood. It is true that in the Middle Ages Christianity had—not a rival but a foe, the eternal enemy of the Church Militant against whom she yet contends to-day, the dark Lord of that city which is set contrariwise to the City of God, the Terrible Shadow of destruction and despair.

Miss Murray with tireless industry has accumulated a vast number of details by the help of which she seeks to build up and support her imaginative thesis. Even those that show the appropriation by the cult of evil of the more hideous heathen practices, both of lust and cruelty, which prevailed among savage or decadent peoples, afford no evidence whatsoever of any continuity of an earlier religion, whilst by far the greater number of the facts she quotes are deflected, although no doubt unconsciously, and sharply wrested so as to be patent of the signification it is endeavoured to read into them. Miss Murray speaks, for example, of witches "who, like the early Christian martyrs, rushed headlong on their fate, determined to die for their faith and their God."[66] And later, discussing the "Sacrifice of the God," a theme which it is interesting and by no means impertinent to note, folklorists have elaborated in the most fanciful manner, basing upon the scantiest and quite contradictory evidence an abundant sheaf of wildly extravagant theories and fables, she tells us that the burning of witches at the hands of the public executioner was a "sacrifice of the incarnate deity."[67] One might almost suppose that the condemned went cheerfully and voluntarily to the cruellest and most torturing punishment, for the phrase "Self-devotion to death" is used in this connexion. On the contrary, we continually find in the witch-trials that the guilty, as was natural, sought to escape from their doom by any and every means; by flight, as in the case of Gilles de Sillé and Roger de Bricqueville, companions of Gilles de Rais; by long and protracted defences, such as was that of Agnes Fynnie, executed in Edinburgh in 1644; by threats and blackmail of influential patrons owing to which old Bettie Laing of Pittenween escaped scot-free in 1718; by pleading pregnancy at the trial as did Mother Samuel, the Warbois witch, who perished on the gallows 7 April, 1593; by suicide as the notorious warlock John Reid, who hanged himself in prison at Paisley, in 1697.

Of the theoretical "Sacrifice of the incarnate deity" Miss Murray writes: "This explanation accounts for the fact that the bodies of witches, male or female, were always burnt and the ashes scattered; for the strong prejudice which existed, as late as the eighteenth century, against any other mode of disposing of their bodies; and for some of the otherwise inexplicable occurrences in connexion with the deaths of certain of the victims."[68] Three instances are cited to prove these three statements, but it will be seen upon examination that not one of these affords the slightest evidence in support of the triple contention. In the first place we are informed that "in the light of this theory much of the mystery which surrounds the fate of Joan of Arc is explained." How is not divulged, but this is capped by the astounding and indecorous assertion that S. Joan of Arc "belonged to the ancient religion, not to the Christian." It is superfluous to say that there is not a tittle of evidence for such an amazing hypothesis in reference to the Saint.

Gilles de Rais, whose execution is next quoted by Miss Murray in support of her postulate, proves a singularly unfortunate example. We are told that "like Joan he was willing to be tried for his faith," by which is meant the imaginary "Dianic cult." This is a purely gratuitous assertion, not borne out in any way by his behaviour at his trial, nor by the details of any authoritative account or report of the proceedings. Gilles de Rais was hanged on a gibbet above a pyre, but when the heat had burned through the rope the body was quickly taken up from the blazing wood, and afterwards buried in the neighbouring Carmelite church. One may compare the execution of Savonarola and his two fellow friars on 25 May, 1498. They were strangled at the gallows, their bodies committed to the flames, and their ashes carefully gathered and thrown into the Arno. Gilles de Rais was condemned by three distinct courts; by the Holy Inquisition, the presidents being Jean de Malestroit, Bishop of Nantes, and Jean Blouyn, vice-inquisitor, O.P., S.T.M., on charges of heresy and sorcery; by the episcopal court on charges of sacrilege and the violation of ecclesiastical rights; by the civil court of John V, Duke of Brittany, on multiplied charges of murder.

The third case quoted by Miss Murray is that of Major Weir, who "offered himself up and was executed as a witch in Edinburgh." Thomas Weir, who was a hypocritical Puritan, a leader "among the Presbyterian strict sect," and regarded as a Saint throughout Edinburgh, had all the while secretly led a life of hideous debauchery and was stained with the most odious and unnatural crimes. In 1670, which was the seventieth year of his age, he appears to have been stricken with terrible fits of remorse and despair; the pangs of his guilty conscience drove him to the verge of madness and his agony could only be eased by a full, ample, and public confession of his misdeeds. For a few months his party, in order to avoid the scandal and disgrace, contrived to stifle the matter, but a minister "whom they esteemed more forward than wise" revealed the secret to the Lord Provost of the city, and an inquiry was instituted. The wretched old man, insistently declaring that "the terrors of God which were upon his soul urged him to confess and accuse himself," was arrested, together with his crazy sister Jean, who was implicated in his abominations. "All the while he was in prison he lay under violent apprehension of the heavy wrath of God, which put him into that which is properly called despair," and to various ministers who visited him he declared, "I know my sentence of damnation is already sealed in Heaven . . . for I find nothing within me but blackness, darkness, Brimstone, and burning to the bottom of Hell."[69] The whole account gives a complete and perfectly comprehensible psychological study. So sudden a revulsion of feeling, the loathing of foul acts accompanied by the sheer inability to repent of them, is quite understandable in a septuagenarian, worn out in body by years of excess and enfeebled in mind owing to the heavy strain of hourly acting an artificial and difficult rôle. The intense emotionalism of the degenerate has not infrequently been observed eventually to give way to a state of frenzied anguish, for which the alienist Magnan coined the name "Anxiomania," a species of mental derangement that soon drives the patient to hysterical confession and boundless despair. "I am convinced," says one writer with regard to Major Weir, "of the prisoner having been delirious at the time of his trial."[70] His sister frantically accused her brother of Witchcraft, but it is remarkable that in his case this charge was not taken up and examined. I do not say that Weir was not supposed to be a warlock; as a matter of fact he was notoriously reputed such, and strange stories were told of his magic staff and other enchantments, but Witchcraft was not the main accusation brought against him in the official courts. He was found guilty of adultery, fornication, incest, and bestiality, and on these several counts sentenced to be strangled at a stake betwixt Edinburgh and Leith, on Monday, 11 April, 1670, and his body to be burned to ashes. Jean Weir was condemned for incest and Witchcraft and hanged on 12 April in the Grassmarket at Edinburgh. To the last this miserable lunatic placed "a great deal of confidence in her constant adherence to the Covenant, which she called *the cause and interest of Christ*."[71]

It will be seen that Miss Murray's citation is incorrect and therefore impertinent. Major Weir was not executed "as a witch." Moreover, both he and Gilles de Rais were actually strangled, and such examples must entirely fail to account "for the fact that the bodies of witches, male or female, were always burnt and the ashes scattered," especially since in the latter case, as we have noticed, the body was honourably buried in the church of the Whitefriars. In fine, to endeavour to connect, however ingeniously, the fate of S. Joan of Arc, the execution of Gilles de Rais and Major Weir, with the folklorists' theory of "the sacrifice of the incarnate deity" is merest fantasy.

The gist of the whole matter lies elsewhere. Death at the stake was the punishment reserved for heretics. As we have already noticed, Diocletian ruthlessly burned the Manichees: "We order then that the professors and teachers be punished with the utmost penalties, which is to say they are to be burned with fire together with all their execrable books and writings."[72] The Visigoth code condemned pagans or heretics who had committed sacrilege to the flames, and together with them it grouped all Manichees: "It is known that many Proconsuls have thrown blasphemers to the beasts, ray, have even burned some alive."[73] The Visigoth code of Rekeswinth (652–672) punishes Judaizers with death, "aut lapide puniatur, aut igne cremetur." (Let them be stoned or burned with fire.) But it was actually in the eleventh century that the civil power first generally ordained the penalty of the stake for the heretics, who were, it must always be remembered, mad anarchists endeavouring to destroy all social order, authority, and decency. "In Italy even many adherents of this pestilential belief were found, and these wretches were slain with the sword or burned at the stake,"[74] writes Adhémar de Chabannes, a monk of Angoulême, about the middle of the eleventh century. In a letter of Wazon, Bishop of Liège, there is an allusion to similar punishments which were being inflicted in Flanders.

A striking example of the heretical anarchists who troubled Europe about the beginning of the twelfth century may be seen in Tanchelin[75] and his followers. This fanatic, who was originally a native of Zealand, journeyed throughout Flanders preaching his monstrous doctrines everywhere he could find listeners and especially concentrating upon the city of Antwerp. In 1108 and 1109 he appeared at Arras and Cambrai, persuading many evil and ignorant persons to accept his abominable tenets. The tares were thickly sown, and it is terribly significant that some three centuries later, about 1469, there was a fearful epidemic of sorcery throughout the whole district of the Artois, in reference to which the anonymous author—probably an Inquisitor—of a contemporary work entitled *Erreurs des Gazariens ou de ceux que l'on prouve chevaucher sur un balai ou un bâton* expressly identified such heretics as the Gazariens, who are Cathari, and the Vaudois (Poor Lombards) with warlocks and sorcerers. In 1112 Tanchelin, who had actually visited Rome itself, was upon his return arrested and thrown into prison at Cologne, whence, however, he managed to escape, and accompanied by an apostate priest Everwacher and a Jew Manasses, who had formerly been a blacksmith, at the head of a formidable band of three thousand ruffians, outlaws, cast gamesters, brigands, murderers, beggars and thieves, the parbreak of every slum and stew, he terrorized the whole countryside, the people being afraid, the bishops and secular princes seemingly unable to resist him.

The teaching of Tanchelin was, as might be expected, largely incoherent and illogical, the ravings of a frantic brain, but none the less dangerous and wholly abominable. The Church was, of course, directly attacked and blasphemed. With abuse and foul language, extraordinarily like the language of the so-called Reformers in the sixteenth century, the hierarchy and all ecclesiastical order were repudiated and contemned, priests and religious in particular were to be persecuted and exterminated since the priesthood was a fiction and a snare; the Sacrifice of Holy Mass was a mockery, all Sacraments were void and empty forms, useless for salvation[76]; the churches themselves were to be accounted as brothels and markets of shame. "This very spawn of Satan and black angel of woe declared that the churches, dedicated to God's worship, were bawdy-houses. That, at Holy Mass there was no Sacrifice at the hands of the priest; the Service of the Altar was filth, not a Sacrament."[77]

Tanchelin declared himself to be the Messiah, God, the Son of God, the Perfect Man, the sum of all the divine emanations in one system, upon whom had descended and in whom abode the pleroma of the Holy Spirit. "This miserable wretch advanced from evil to evil and at length proceeded to such an extremity of unheard-of wickedness that he gave himself out to be God, asserting that if Christ be God because the Holy Ghost dwelt in Him, he himself was not less than and of the same nature as God, seeing that he enjoyed the plenitude of the Holy Ghost."[78] Here the Gnostic character of his teaching is very apparent. He even caused a temple to be erected in his honour where he was worshipped with sacrifice and hymns. His followers, indeed, regarded this lunatic wretch with such an excess of veneration that the dirty water from his bath was actually collected in phials and solemnly distributed among them, whereof they partook as of a sacrament.

It must be borne in mind that Tanchelin's programme did not solely comprise a negation of Christian dogma; this we find in most of the innovators at the time of the so-called Reformation, but his ultimate aim was to effect a social revolution, to overturn the existing order of things and produce communistic chaos with himself as overlord and dictator. The way for anarchy could only have been paved by the destruction of the Church, the supreme representative of authority and order throughout the world, and it was accordingly against the Church that this superman launched his fiercest diatribes. To further his ends he encouraged, nay, commanded, the open practice of the foulest vices; incest, adultery, fornication were declared to be works of spiritual efficacy; unmentionable abominations flaunted themselves in the face of day; virtue became an offence; men were driven to vice and crime, and anon they gradually sank in a stupor of infamy and sheer boneless degradation.

The unfortunate town of Antwerp came directly under Tanchelin's influence. Here he reigned as king, surrounded by vile and obsequious satellites who ground the miserable citizens to the dust and filled each street and corner with orgies of lust and blood. There is a strange and striking parallel between the details of his foul career and the Russian tyranny to-day. Little wonder that in 1116 a priest, maddened by the outrages and profanities of this hellish crew, scattered the heretic's brains upon the deck of his royal barge as one afternoon he was sailing in pompous state down the river Schelde: "After a life of infamy, bloodshed, and heresy, whilst he was sailing on the river he was struck on the head by a certain priest and falling down died there."[79] All unfortunately, however, the pernicious errors of Tanchelin did not expire with their author. Antwerp remained plunged in dissipation and riot, and although strenuous efforts were made to restore decency and order, at first these seemed to be entirely nugatory and fruitless. Burchard, the Bishop of Cambrai, at once sent twelve of his most revered and learned canons under the conduct of Hidolphe, a priest of acknowledged sagacity and experience, to endeavour to reform the town by word and example, but it seemed as though their efforts were doomed to failure and ill-success. At length, almost in despair, the good prelate begged S. Norbert,[80] who some three years before had founded his Order at Prémontré, to essay the thankless and wellnigh impossible task. Without demur or hesitation the Saint cheerfully undertook so difficult a mission and accompanied only by S. Evermonde,[81] and Blessed Waltman, together with a few more of his most fervent followers he arrived at Antwerp without delay to begin his work there towards the end of 1123. Success at once crowned his efforts; in an incredibly short space of time the people confessed their errors, abuses were reformed, the leprous town cleansed of its foulness, public safety, order, and decorum once again established, and, what is extremely striking to notice, the old chroniclers draw attention to the fact that a large number both of men and women in deepest penitence brought to S. Norbert quantities of consecrated Hosts which they had purloined from the tabernacles and kept concealed in boxes and other hiding-places to utilize for charms and evil invocations, to profane in devil-worship and at the Sabbat. So marvellous was the change from darkness to light that year by year the Premonstratensian Order upon the Saturday[82] after the Octave of Corpus Christi solemnly observes a fitting memorial thereof in the glad Feast of the Triumph of Holy Father Norbert.

In this incident of the stolen Hosts the connexion between

Gnostic heresy and Satanism is clearly seen. It was in such soil as the antinomianism of Tanchelin that the poisoned weeds of sorcery would thrive apace. The authorities recognized that drastic measures must be employed, and at Bonn a company of impure fanatics who attempted to disseminate his ideas were incontinently sent to the stake.

The other arguments brought forward by Miss Murray to support her thesis of the continuity of a primitive religion are mainly "the persistence of the number thirteen in the Covens, the narrow geographical range of the domestic familiar, the avoidance of certain forms in the animal transformations, the limited number of personal names among the women-witches, and the survival of the names of some of the early gods."[83] Even if these details could be proved up to the hilt and shown to be pertinent the evidence were not convincing; it would at best point to some odd survivals, such as are familiar in an hundred ways to every student of hagiography, history, myths and legends, old religions, geography, iconography, topography, etymology, anthropology, and antiquarian lore in a myriad branches. If we examine the matter broadly we shall find that these circumstances are for the most part local, not general, that in many instances they cannot be clearly substantiated, for the evidence is conflicting and obscure.

"The 'fixed number' among the witches of Great Britain," Miss Murray notes, "seems to have been thirteen,"[84] and certainly in many cases amongst the English trials the coven appears to have consisted of thirteen members, although it may be borne in mind that very probably there were often other associates who were not traced and involved and so escaped justice. Yet Miss Murray does not explain why the number thirteen should form any link with an earlier ritual and worship. On the other hand, the demonologists are never tired of insisting that Satan is the ape of God in all things, and that the worshippers of evil delight to parody every divine ordinance and institution. The explanation is simple. The number thirteen was adopted by the witches for their covens in mockery of Our Lord and His Apostles.

"The narrow geographical range of the domestic familiar" is not at all apparent, and it were futile to base any presumption upon so slender a line of argument. "The avoidance of certain forms in the animal transformation" is upon a general view of Witchcraft found to be nothing other than the non-occurrence of the lamb and the dove, and these two were abhorred by sorcerers, seeing that Christ is the Lamb of God, Agnus Dei, whilst the Dove is the manifestation of the Holy Ghost.[85] There is one instance, the trail of Agnes Wobster at Aberdeen in 1597, when the Devil is said to have appeared to the witch "in the liknes of a lamb, quhom thou callis thy God, and bletit on the, and thaireftir spak to the."[86] But this rare exception must be understood to be a black and deformed lamb, not the snow-white Agnus Dei. In pictures of the Doctors of the Church, particularly perhaps S. Gregory the Great and S. Alphonsus de Liguori, the Dove is seen breathing divine inspiration into the ear of the Saint who writes the heavenly message, thus directly given by God the Holy Ghost. So in a Franco-German miniature of the eleventh century in the *Hortus Deliciarum* we see a black hideous bird breathing into the ear of a magician thoughts evil and dark. This cloudy and sombre spirit, violent in its attitude and lean in body stretches its meagre throat towards the ear of the wicked man, who, seated at a desk, transcribes upon a parchment the malevolent and baleful charms which it dictates. It is in fact the Devil.[87]

With reference to the argument based upon "the limited number of personal names among the women-witches" this simply resolves itself into the fact that in the sixteenth and seventeenth centuries there were in general use (particularly amongst the peasantry) far fewer personal names than have been employed of more recent years. To assert "that the name *Christian* clearly indicates the presence of another religion"[88] is simple nonsense. It may be noticed, too, how many of the names which Miss Murray has catalogued in such conscientious and alas! impertinent detail are those of well-known Saints whose cult was universal throughout Europe: Agnes, Alice, Anne, Barbara, Christopher, Collette, Elizabeth, Giles, Isabel, James, John, Katherine, Lawrence, Margaret, Mary, Michael, Patrick, Thomas, Ursula—and the list might be almost indefinitely prolonged.

"The survival of the names of some of the early gods" is also asserted. In connexion with Witchcraft, however, very few examples of this can be traced even by the most careful research. An old charm or two, a nonsense rhyme, may now and again repeat some forgotten meaningless word or refrain. Thus in a spell used by the witches of the Basses-Pyrénées, cited by De Lancre (1609), we find mention of the old Basque deity Janicot: "In nomine patrica, Aragueaco Petrica, Gastellaco Ianicot, Equidæ ipordian pot." Bodin gives a dance-jingle, "Har, har, diable, diable, saute icy, saute là, ioüe icy, ioüe là," to which the chorus was "sabath sabath." Miss Murray tells us that the Guernsey version "which is currently reported to be used at the present day," runs: "Har, har, Hon, Hon, danse ici."[89] Hon was an old Breton god, and there are still remote districts whose local names recall and may be compounded with that of this ancient deity. It is significant that in one case we have a Basque deity, in the other a Breton; for Basque and Breton are nearly, if obscurely, correlated. Such traces are interesting enough, but by no means unique, hardly singular indeed, since they can be so widely paralleled, and it were idle to base any elaborate argument concerning the continuity of a fully organized cult upon slight and unrelated survivals in dialect place-names and the mere doggerel lilt of a peasant-song.

There is in particular one statement advanced by Miss Murray which goes far to show how in complete unconsciousness she is fitting her material to her theory. She writes: "There is at present nothing to show how much of the Witches' Mass (in which the bread, the wine, and the candles were black) derived from the Christian ritual and how much belonged to the Dianic cult [the name given to this hypothetical but universal ancient religion]; it is, however, possible that the witches' service was the earlier form and influenced the Christian."[90] This last sentence is in truth an amazing assertion. A more flagrant case of hysteron-proteron is hardly imaginable. So self-evident is the absurdity that it refutes itself, and one can only suppose that the words were allowed to remain owing to their having been overlooked in the revision of a long and difficult study, a venial negligence. Every prayer and every gesture of Holy Mass, since the first Mass was celebrated upon the first Maundy Thursday, has been studied in minutest detail by generations of liturgiologists and ceremonialists, whose library is almost infinite in its vastness and extent from the humblest pamphlets to the hugest folios. We can trace each inspired development, when such an early phrase was added, when such a hallowed sign was first made at such words in such an orison. The witches' service is a hideous burlesque of Holy Mass, and, briefly, what Miss Murray suggests is that the parody may have existed before the thing parodied. It is true that some topsy-turvy writers have actually proclaimed that magic preceded religion, but this view is generally discredited by the authorities of all schools. Sir James Frazer, Sir A. L. Lyall, and Mr. F. B. Jevons, for example, recognize " a fundamental distinction and even opposition of principle between magic and religion."[91]

In fine, upon a candid examination of this theory of the continuity of some primitive religion, which existed as an underlying organization manifested in Witchcraft and sorcery, a serious rival feared and hated by the Church, we find that nothing of the sort ever survived, that there was no connexion between sorcery and an imaginary " Dianic cult." To write that " in the fifteenth century open war was declared against the last remains of heathenism in the famous Bull of Innocent VIII "[92] is to ignore history. As has been emphasized above, the Bull *Summis desiderantes affectibus* of 1484 was only one of a long series of Papal ordinances directed against an intolerable evil not heathenism indeed, but heresy. For heresy, sorcery, and anarchy were almost interchangeable words, and the first Bull launched directly against the black art was that of Alexander IV, 1258, two hundred and twenty-six years before.

That here and there lingered various old harmless customs and festivities which had come down from pre-Christian times and which the Church had allowed, nay, had even sanctified by directing them to their right source, the Maypole dances, for example, and the Midsummer fires which now honour S. John Baptist, is a matter of common knowledge. But this is no continuance of a pagan cult.

From the first centuries of the Christian era, throughout the Middle Ages, and continuously to the present day there has invariably been an open avowal of intentional evil-doing on the part of the devotees of the witch-cult, and the more mischief they did the more they pleased their lord and master. Their revels were loathly, lecherous, and abominable, a Sabbat where every circumstance of horror and iniquity found expression. This in itself is an argument against Miss Murray's theory, as none of the earlier religions existed for the express purpose of perpetrating evil for evil's sake. We have but to read the eloquent and exquisite description of the Eleusinian Mysteries by that accomplished Greek scholar Father Cyril Martindale, S.J.,[93] to catch no mean nor mistaken glimpse of the ineffable yearning for beauty, for purity, for holiness, which filled the hearts of the worshippers of the goddess Persephoneia, whose stately and impressive ritual prescribing fasts, bathing in the waters of the sea, self-discipline, self-denial, self-restraint, culminated in the Hall of Initiation, hallowed by the Earth-Mother, Demeter, where the symbolic drama of life, death, and resurrection was shown by the Hierophant to those who had wrestled, and endured, and were adjudged worthy. How fair a shadow was this, albeit always and ever a shadow, of the imperishable and eternal realities to come! How different these Mysteries from the foul orgies of witches, the Sabbat, the black mass, the adoration of hell.

In truth it was not against heathenism that Innocent VIII sounded the note of war, but against heresy. There was a clandestine organization hated by the Church, and this was not sorcery nor any cult of witches renewing and keeping green some ancient rites and pagan creed, but a witch-cult that identified itself with and was continually manifested in closest connexion with Gnosticism in its most degraded and vilest shapes.

There is a curious little piece of symbolism, as it may be, which has passed into the patois of the Pyrenees. Wizards are commonly known as *poudouès* and witches *poudouèros*, both words being derived from *putere*, which signifies to have an evil smell. The demonologists report, and it was commonly believed, that sorcerers could often be detected by their foul and fetid odour. Hagiographers tell that S. Philip Neri could distinguish heretics by their smell, and often he was obliged to turn away his head when meeting them in the street. The same is recorded of many other Saints, and this tradition is interesting as it serves to show the close connexion there was held to be between magic and heresy.[94] Saint Pachomius, the cenobite, could distinguish heretics by their insupportable stench; the abbot Eugendis could tell the virtues and vices of those whom he met by the perfume or the stink. Saint Hilarion, as S. Jerome relates, could even distinguish a man's sins by the smell of a warm garment or cloak. Blessed Dominica of Paradise, passing a soldier in the street, knew by the foul smell that he had abandoned the faith, to which, however, her fervid exhortations and prayers eventually restored him. Saint Bridget of Sweden was wellnigh suffocated by the fetor of a notorious sinner who addressed her. Saint Catherine of Siena experienced the same sensations; whilst Saint Lutgarde, a Cistercian nun, on meeting a vicious reprobate perceived a decaying smell of leprosy and disease.

On the other hand, the Saints themselves have diffused sweetest fragrances, and actually "the odour of sanctity" is more than a mere phrase. One day in 1566, when he had entered the church at Somascha, a secluded hamlet between Milan and Bergamo, S. Charles Borromeo exclaimed: "I know by the heavenly fragrance in this sanctuary that a great Servant of God lies buried here!" The church, in fact, contained the body of S. Jerome Emiliani, who died in 1537. S. Herman Joseph could be traced through the corridors of Steinfeld by the rare perfumes he scattered as he walked. The same was the case with that marvellous mystic S. Joseph of Cupertino. S. Thomas Aquinas smelt of male frankincense. I myself have known a priest of fervent faith who at times diffused the odour of incense. Maria-Vittoria of Genoa, Ida of Louvain, S. Colette, S. Humiliana, were fragrant as sweet flowers. S. Francis of Paul and Venturini of Bergamo scattered heavenly aromas when they offered the Holy Sacrifice. The pus of S. John of the Cross gave forth a strong scent of lilies.

Miss Murray has worked out her thesis with no inconsiderable ingenuity, but when details are considered, historically examined, and set in their due proportions, it must be concluded that the theory of the continuity of an ancient religion is baseless. Her book is called *A Study in Anthropology*, and here we can, I think, at once put our finger upon the fundamental mistake. Anthropology alone offers no explanation of Witchcraft. Only the trained theologian can adequately treat the subject. An amount of interesting material has been collected, but the key to the dark mystery could not be found.

Yet, as our investigations have shown, it was not so far to seek. In the succinct phrase of that profound and prolific scholar Thomas Stapleton[95]: Crescit cum magia hæresis, cum hæresi magia." (The weed heresy grows alongside the weed witchcraft, the weed witchcraft alongside the weed heresy.)

NOTES TO CHAPTER I.

[1] *Paris. Jacques du Puys.* 4to. 1580. The preface, addressed to De Thou, is signed: "De *Laon,* ce xx iour de *Decembre,* M.D.LXXIX." There were nine editions before 1604. The most complete is *Paris,* 4to. 1587. In addition to the text it contains ten extra pages only found here giving the trial of a sorcerer, Abel de la Rue, executed in 1582.

[2] The first Papal bull dealing with sorcery was issued by Alexander IV, 13 December, 1258. The last Papal Constitution concerned with this crime is that of Urban VIII, *Inscrutabilis iudiciorum Dei altitudo,* 1 April, 1631. The last regular English trial seems to have been that of an old woman and her son, acquitted at Leicester in 1717. In 1722 the last execution of a Scottish witch took place at Loth; both English and Scottish statutes were repealed in 1735. The Irish Statute was not repealed until 1821. At Kempten in Bavaria, a mad heretic, a woman, was executed for sorcery in 1775. In the Swiss canton of Glaris, a wench named Anna Goeldi, was hanged as a witch, 17 June, 1782. Two hags were burned in Poland on the same charge as late as 1793.

[3] Roland Brévannes. *Les Messes Noires,* Ier tableau, scène VII.

[4] I have actually heard it categorically laid down by a speaker in a Shakespearean debate, a litterateur of professed culture, that the Elizabethans could not, of course, really have believed in witchcraft.

[5] In the Exhibition of this artist's work at the Leicester Galleries, London, in March, 1925.

[6] . . . qu'elle, & sa mère montoient sur vne ramasse, & que sortans le contremont de la cheminée elles alloient par l'air en ceste façon au Sabbat. Boguet, *Discours,* p. 104.

[7] Glanvill, Part II. p. 194.

[8] Julius Wellhausen. *Reste arabischen Heidenthums,* p. 159. Berlin, 1897.

[9] *Apud* Miss Murray's *The Witch-Cult.* (1921). Appendix V. pp. 279–80.

[10] Boguet, *Discours.* XVI. 4.

[11] Benjamin Thorpe, *Monumenta Ecclesiastica,* II. p. 34. London, 1840. The *Liber Poenitentialis* was first published complete by Wasserschleben in 1851; a convenient edition is Migne, *P.L.* XCIX.

[12] *Calendar of State Papers.* Domestic, 1584.

[13] Sir Walter Scott, *Demonology and Witchcraft,* Letter V, gives the narrative of this case, but in the light of later research his version must be slightly corrected.

[14] Pitcairn. I. pt. ii. p. 162.

[15] *Proceedings of the Society of Antiquaries of Scotland,* New Series, vol. X. Edinburgh.

[16] Sir James Melville, *Memoirs.* Bannatyne Club, Edinburgh. pp. 395–6.

[17] London. "for *William Wright.*" N.D. [1591]. The woodcut is on the title-page verso, and signature [c.ij.] verso. The pages are not numbered.

[18] *Flying Ointments. Apud* Miss Murray's *Witch-Cult in Western Europe,* p. 279. It may be noted that the scandals of the Black Mass under Louis XIV were closely concerned with wholesale accusations of poisoning. La Voisin was a notorious vendor of toxic philtres. The possibility of poisoning the King, the Dauphin, Colbert and others was frequently debated.

[19] Dio Cassius. XLIX. 43. p. 756. ed. Sturz.
[20] *Idem.* LII. 36. p. 149.
[21] Suetonius. *Augustus.* 31.
[22] Tacitus. *Annales.* II. 32. *More prisco.* "Ut eum infelici arbori alligatum uirgis cædi, et postremo securi percuti iuberent." Muret.
[23] XII. 32.
[24] Suetonius. *Vitellius.* 14.
[25] Dio Cassius. LXVI. 10.
[26] *La Magie et la Sorcellerie.* Paris. (1912.) I. p. 33.
[27] *Memoirs of Extraordinary Popular Delusions,* II. p. 117.
[28] The dates are as inaccurate as the statements. Giovanni Battista Cibò was elected Pope 29 August, 1484; and the Bull was issued in the December of that year, not in 1488.
[29] *Rise and Influence of Rationalism in Europe,* c. 1.
[30] *Dictionary of Universal Biography.* VIII. (1890).
[31] A more detailed treatment will be found in the present writer's *The Geography of Witchcraft,* where the Bull is given *in extenso.*
[32] *Epist.,* c.n. 1.
[33] *Hom.,* XLVI. c. 1.
[34] *Sententianum,* III. iv. nn. 4–6.
[35] Theodosius II. *Nouellæ,* tit. III. A.D. 438.
[36] Uanissimus [Priscillianus] et plus iusto inflatior profanarum rerum scientia: quin et magicas artes ab adolescentia cum exercuisse creditum est. Sulpicius Severus. II. 47.
[37] H. C. Lea in his *History of the Inquisition in the Middle Ages,* (1888) I. 215, asserts that Leo I justified the act, and that successive edicts against heresy were due to ecclesiastical influence. This is the exact opposite of historical truth, and the writer has not hesitated to transfer words of the Emperor to the Pope.
[38] In a sermon published in 1896 by Dom Morin *Revue benédictine,* c. xiii. p. 205.
[39] *Epistola Elipandi ad Alcuinum,* Migne. Pat. Lat. CXCVI. p. 872. Alcuin. *Opera Omnia.* Migne Pat. Lat. C–CI., especially *Liber Albini contra hæresim Felicis; Libri VII aduersus Felicem; Aduersus Elipandum Libri IV.* Florez, *España sagrada.* V. p. 562. Menendez y Pelayo, *Historia de los heterodoxos españoles,* Madrid, 1880, I. p. 274.
[40] The martyrdom of S. Peter is a well-known subject in art. Titian's masterpiece in the Dominican church of SS. Giovanni e Paolo at Venice was destroyed by a fire on 16 August, 1867. But there are exquisite paintings of the scene by Lorenzo Lotto and Bellini. S. Peter, whose shrine is in San Eustorgio, Milan, was canonized 25 March, 1253, by Innocent IV. Major Feast, 29 April.
[41] Muratori. *Antiquitates italicæ medii æui,* Milan, 1738–42.
[42] Gabriel Rossetti, *Disquisitions,* vol. I. p. 27.
[43] Gervasius Dorobernensis, *Chronicon.*
[44] *Vita S. Romanæ.* n. 10; Acta SS. die, 3 Oct. p. 138. S. Gregorii VII. Lib. I. Epistola 75, *ad Philippum.*
[45] Labbe. *Sacrosancta concilia.* 18 vols. folio. 1671. Vol. X. col. 84.
[46] Quarum rerum rex uester, qui non rex sed tyrannus dicendus est, suadente diabolo, caput et causa est, qui omnem aetatem suam flagitiis et facinoribus polluit. *Idem,* vol. X. col. 72.
[47] Sane . . . prouinciali ordinis prædicatorum in eodem regno dedimus in mandatis, ut aliquibus fratribus suis aptis ad hoc, inquisitionem contra illos committeret in regno præfato . . . fraternitati tuæ . . . mandamus quatenus . . . per alios qui ad hoc idonei uidebuntur, festines . . . procedere in inquisitionis negotio et ad dominicum certamen accingi. Ripoll et Brémond, *Bullarium ordinis S. Dominici,* I. p. 80. (8 vols. Romæ. 1737, *sqq.*).
[48] Fratres . . . qui ad prædicandum crucem uel inquirendum contra prauitatem hæreticam . . . sunt deputati. Wadding. *Annales Minorum.* ed. secunda. 24 vols. Romæ, 1732, *sqq.* III. 144.
[49] *Gnostic Heresies.*
[50] Jules Bois. *Le Satanisme et la Magie,* c. 6.

[51] It is true that S. Augustine does not bring a charge of depravity against the Manichæans, but they veiled their vices with the greatest caution, and S. Augustine was simply a catechumen, one of the Auditors, who would have known nothing of these esoteric abominations.

[52] Extra ciuitatis educti muros in quodam tuguriolo copioso igne accenso . . . cremati sunt. *Gesta synodi Aurelianensis.* Arnould. *L'Inquisition.* (Paris, 1869). VI. p. 46.

[53] Sed antequam ad conflictum ueniamus, de cibo illo, qui cœlestis ab illis dicebatur, quali arte conficiebatur, nescientibus demonstrare curabo. Congregabantur si quidem certis noctibus in domo denominata, singuli lucernas tenentes in manibus, ad instar letaniæ demonum nomina declamabant, donec subito Dæmonem in similitudine cuiuslibet bestiolæ inter eos uiderent descendere. Qui statim, ut uisibilis ille uidebatur uisio, omnibus extinctis luminaribus, quamprimum quisque poterat, mulierem, quæ ad manum sibi ueniebat, ad abutendum arripiebat, sine peccati respectu, et utrum mater, aut soror, aut monacha haberetur, pro sanctitate et religione eius concubitus ab illis æstimabatur; ex quo spurcissimo concubitu infans generatus, octaua die in medio eorum copioso igne accenso probabatur per ignem more antiquorum Paganorum; et sic in igne cremabatur. Cuius cinis tanta ueneratione colligebatur atque custodiebatur, ut Christiana religiositas Corpus Christi custodire solet, ægris dandum de hoc sæculo exituris ad uiaticum. Inerat enim tanta uis diabolicæ fraudis in ipso cinere ut quicumque de præfata hæresi imbutus fuisset, et de eodem cinere quamuis sumendo parum prælibauisset, uix unquam postea de eadem heresi gressum mentis ad uiam ueritatis dirigere ualeret. De qua re parum dixisse sufficiat, ut Christicolæ caueant se ab hoc nefario opere, non ut studeant sectando imitari. Schmidt. *Histoire et doctrine des Cathares ou Albigeois.* Paris. 1849. I. p. 31.

[54] G. R. Kinloch. *Reliquiæ Antiquæ Scoticæ.* Edinburgh, 1848.

[55] Adhémar de Chabannes. (A monk of Angoulême.) *Chronicon, Recueil des historicus,* vol. X. p. 163.

[56] Fabré Palaprat. *Recherches Historiques sur les Templiers,* Paris. 1835.

[57] Cambridge University Press, 1925.

[58] *The Philosopher,* July–August, 1924.

[59] *The Philosopher,* January–March, 1925. *The Albigenses,* pp. 20–25. The whole article, which is written with extraordinary restraint, should be read.

[60] He is the author of *Éléments d'Astrologie ; Un disciple de Cl. de Saint-Martin, Dutoit-Membrini ; Premiers Éléments d'Occultisme ; La petite Église anticoncordataire, son histoire, son état actuel ; J. K. Huysmans et le Satanisme ; Huysmans, Occultiste et Magicien.*

[61] *In Uerrem.* IV. 43.

[62] H. Th. Pyl, *Die griechischen Rundbauten,* 1861, pp. 67, *sqq.*

[63] Plutarch, *Theseus* 36 ; *Cimon* 8.

[64] Pausanias is the chief authority on this point. See Rohde *Psyche,* I. p. 161.

[65] Clarendon Press, 1921.

[66] *The Witch-Cult in Western Europe,* p. 16. It is true that the Brethren of the Free Spirit, anarchists, who vaunted the Adamite heresy, in the Thirteenth century, went to the stake with pæans of joy. But they were probably drugged. J. L. Mosheim, *Ecclesiastical History.* London. 1819. III. p. 278. *sqq.* The Adamites were a licentious sect who called their church Paradise and worshipped in a state of stark nudity. They were Gnostics and claimed complete emancipation from the moral law. They lived in shameful communism. Bohemian Adamites existed as late as 1849. In Russia the *teleschi,* a branch of the sect known as the " Divine Men," performed their religious rites in a state of nature, following the example, as they asserted, of Adam and Eve in Paradise. These assemblies were wont to end in promiscuous debauchery.

[67] *Idem.* p. 161.

[68] *Witch-Cult in Western Europe,* p. 161.

[69] *Additional Notices of Major Weir and his Sister ;* Sinclar's *Satan' Invisible World.* (Reprint. 1875).

[70] *Criminal Trials*, 1536–1784; Hugo Arnot, 4to, 1785.

[71] *Ravillac Rediuius*, Dr. George Hickes, 4to, 1678.

[72] Iubemus namque, auctores quidem et principes, una cum abominandis scripturis eorum seueriori pœnæ subiici, ita ut flammeis ignibus exurantur. Baronius, 287, 4.

[73] Scio multos [Proconsu[esl et ad bestias damnasse sacrilegos, nonnullos etiam uiuos exussisse. *Lex Romana Visigothorum nouella*, XLVIII. tit. xiii. c. 6–7.

[74] Plures etiam per Italiam tunc huius pestiferi dogmatis sunt reperti, qui aut gladiis, aut incendiis perierunt.

[75] Tanchelinus, Tandemus, Tanchelmus. The history of this important revolutionary movement has been carefully studied. The following authoritative books are a few from many of great value and learning. *Corpus documentorum Inquisitionis hereticæ prauitatis neerlandicæ*, ed. Dr. Paul Frédéricq, vol. I, p. 15 *et sqq.* Ghent. 1889; *Tanchelijn* by Janssen in the *Annales de l'académie Royale d'archéologie de Belgique*, vol. XXIII, p. 448 *et sqq.* 1867; Foppens, *Historia Episcopatus Antuerpiensis*, p. 8 and p. 146, Brussells, 1717; Dierxsens, *Antuerpia Christo nascens et crescens*, vol. I, p. 88, Antwerp, 1773; Poncelet, *Saint Norbert et Tanchelin* in the *Analecta bollandiniana*, vol. XIII, p. 441, 1893; Schools, *Saint Norbert et Tanchelin à Anvers* in the *Bibliothèque norbertine*, vol. II, p. 97, 1900; De Schapper, *Réponse à la question: Faites connaître l'hérésiarque Tanchelin et les erreurs qu'il répandit au commencement du XIIIe siècle* [an error for *XIIe siècle*] in the *Collationes Brugenses*, vol. XVII, p. 107, 1912. L. Vander Essen, *De Katterij van Tanchelm in de XIIe eeuw* in *Ons Geloof*, vol. II, p. 354, 1912; *Antwerpen en de H. Norbertus* in the *Bode van Onze Lieve Vrouw van het H. Hert van Averbode*, Nos. 18 and 19, pp. 207–211 and 217–220, 1914.

[76] "That most vile and abandoned scoundrel had become so open and utterly depraved an enemy to the Christian faith and all religious observance that he denied any respect was due to Bishops and priests; moreover, he affirmed that the reception of the most holy Body and Blood of Our Lord availed nothing to eternal life and man's salvation." "Erat quidem ille sceleratissimus et christianæ fidei et totius religionis inimicus in tantum ut obsequium episcoporum et sacerdotum nihil esse diceret, et sacrosancti corporiset sanguinis Domini J. C. perceptionem ad salutem perpetuam prodesse denegeret." *Vita Noberti archiepiscopi Magdeburgensis*, *Vita A. Monument. Germ. Scriptores*, vol. XII. p. 690, ed. G. A. Pertz, Hanover, Berlin.

[77] "Immo uere ipse angelus Sathanæ declamabat eccelsias Dei lupinaria esse reputanda. Nihil esse, quod sacerdotum officio in mensa dominica conficeretur; pollutiones, non sacramenta nominanda." *Lettre des chanoines d'Utrecht au nom de leur diocèse à Frédéric, archevêque de Cologne. Apud* Frédéricq, vol. I. n. 11.

[78] Talibus nequitiæ successibus miscro homini tanta sceleris accessit audacia, ut etiam se Deum diceret, asserens, quia, si Christus ideo Deus est, quia Spiritum Sanctum habuisset, se non inferius nec dissimilius Deum, quia plenitudinem Spiritus Sancti accepisset. *Idem.*

[79] Qui tandem post multos errores et cædes, dum nauigaret, a quodam presbytero percussus in cerebro occubuit. *Sigiberti continuatio.* Apud *Monument. Germ. Scriptores*, vol. VI, p. 449. See also, Johannes Trithemius, *Annales Hirsaugienses*, vol. I, p. 387, Saint-Gall, 1690; Du Plessis d'Argentré, *Collectio iudiciorum*, vol. I, p. 11 *sqq.* Paris, 1728; Schmidt, *Histoire et doctrine des Cathares ou Albigeois*, vol. I, p. 49, Paris, 1849.

[80] There is a contemporary *Uita Norberti* of which two recensions have been published: *Uita A.* by R. Wilmans in the *Mon. Germ. Hag.*, SS., vol. XIII, pp. 663–706, Hanover, 1853; *Uita B.* by Surius, *De probatis Sanctorum historiis*, vol. III, pp. 517–547, Cologne, 1572. Other authoritative works are: J. Van der Sterse, *Uita S. Norberti*, Antwerp, 1622; Du Pré, *La Vic du bienhereux saint Norbert*, Paris, 1627; Ch. Hugo, *La Vie de St. Norbert*, Luxembourg, 1704; G. Madelaine, *Histoire de St. Norbert*, Lille, 1886; B. Wazasek, *Der Hl. Norbert*, Vienna, 1914. An excellent brief but

scholarly account is *The Life of S. Norbert*, London, 1886, by my late revered friend Abbot Geudens, C.R.P.

[81] Feast, 17 February.

[82] Formerly kept upon the Sunday.

[83] *Op. cit.*, pp. 16, 17.

[84] *Op. cit.*, p. 191.

[85] For a full and detailed statement see Didron's great work, *Iconographie chrétienne*, Paris, 1843.

[86] *Spalding Club Miscellany*, I, p. 129. Aberdeen, 1841.

[87] At their black mass the witches of the Basses-Pyrénées (1609) when the host was elevated said "Corbeau noir, corbeau noir." De Lancre, *Tableau de l'Inconstance des mauvais Anges*, Paris, 1613.

[88] *Op. cit.*, p. 255.

[89] *Op. cit.*, p. 165. It is not at all evident that "the word *diable* is clearly Bodin's own interpellation for the name of the god," indeed this assumption is purely gratuitous to support the argument, and cannot be admitted.

[90] *Op. cit.*, pp. 14, 15. I would not dwell upon the offensiveness of this suggestion, since it is, I am sure, unintentional.

[91] *Golden Bough*, Part I. vol. I. p. xx. Third Edition. 1911.

[92] *Op. cit.*, p. 19.

[93] *The Goddess of Ghosts*, pp. 137–158.

[94] Cassiodorus, *Hist. Eccl.*, VII, 11. *fin.* speaks of the *fetidissimus fons* of heresy.

[95] 1535–1598. His works were collected in four folio volumes, Paris, 1620, prefaced by Henry Holland's *Uita Thomæ Stapletoni*. An original portrait is preserved at Douai Abbey, Woolhampton.

CHAPTER II

The Worship of the Witch

In order clearly to understand and fully to realize the shuddering horror and heart-sick dismay any sort of commerce between human beings and evil spirits, which is the very core and kernel of Witchcraft, excited throughout the whole of Christendom, to appreciate why tome after tome was written upon the subject by the most learned pens of Europe, why holiest pontiffs and wisest judges, grave philosopher and discreet scholar, king and peasant, careless noble and earnest divine, all alike were of one mind in the prosecution of sorcery; why in Catholic Spain and in Puritan Scotland, in cold Geneva and at genial Rome, unhesitatingly and perseveringly man sought to stamp out the plague with the most terrible of all penalties, the cautery of fire; in order that by the misreading of history we should not superficially and foolishly think monk and magistrate, layman and lawyer were mere tigers, mad fanatics—for as such have they, too, often been presented and traduced,—it will be not wholly impertinent briefly to recapitulate the orthodox doctrine of the Powers of Darkness, facts nowadays too often forgotten or ignored, but which to the acute mediæval mind were ever fearfully and prominently in view.

And here, as in so many other beliefs, we shall find a little dogma; certain things that can hardly be denied without the note of temerity; and much concerning which nothing definite can be known, upon which assuredly no pronouncement will be made.

In the first place, the name Devil is commonly given to the fallen angels, who are also called Demons. The exact technical distinction between the two terms in ecclesiastical usage may be seen in the phrase used in the decree of the Fourth Lateran Council[1]: " Diabolus enim et alii dæmones." (The devil and the other demons), i.e. all are demons, and the chief of the demons is called the Devil. This distinction is preserved in in the Vulgate New Testament, where *diabolus* represents the Greek διάβολος, and in almost every instance refers to Satan himself, whilst his subordinate angels are described, in accordance with the Greek, as *dæmones* or *dæmonia*. But save in some highly specialized context when the most meticulous accuracy is required, we now use the words "devil," "demon" indifferently, and employ the definite article to denote Lucifer (Satan), chief of the devils, The Devil. So in S. Matthew xxv. 41, is written "the devil and his angels." The Greek word διάβολος means a slanderer, an accuser, and in this sense is it applied to him of whom it is said "the accuser [ὁ κατήγορος] of our brethren is cast forth, who accused them before our God day and night" (Apocalypse xii. 10). Thus it answers to the Hebrew name Satan, which signifies an adversary, an accuser.

Mention is made of the Devil in many passages both of the Old and New Testaments, but much is left in obscurity, and the full Scriptural teaching on the legions of evil can best be ascertained by combining the scattered notices and reading them in the light of patristic and theological tradition. The authoritative teaching of the Church is declared in the Decrees of the Fourth Lateran Church (cap. 1. *Firmiter credimus*), wherein, after setting forth that God in the beginning had created two creatures, the spiritual and corporeal; that is to say, the angelic and the earthly, and lastly man, who was made of both earth and body; the Council continues: "For the Devil and the other demons were created by God naturally good; but they themselves of themselves became evil."[2] The dogma is here clearly laid down that the Devil and the other demons are spiritual or angelic creatures created by God in a state of innocence, and that they became evil by their own free act. It is added that man sinned by suggestion of the Devil, and that in the next world the reprobate and impenitent will suffer punishment with him. This then is the actual dogma, the dry bones of the doctrine, so to speak. But later theologians have added a great deal to this,—the authoritative Doctor Eximius, Francisco Suarez, S.J.,[3] *De Angelis*, VII, is especially valuable —and much of what they deduce cannot be disputed without such rejection incurring the grave censure technically known as "Erroneous."[4]

It is remarkable that for an account of the Fall of the angels, which happened before the creation of the world, we must turn to the last book in the Bible, the Apocalypse of S. John. For although the picture of the past be blended with prophecies of what shall be in the future, thus must we undoubtedly regard the vision of Patmos. "And there was a great battle in heaven, Michael and his angels fought with the dragon, and the dragon fought and his angels: and they prevailed not, neither was their place found any more in heaven. And that great dragon was cast out, that old serpent, who is called the Devil, and Satan, who seduceth the whole world; and he was cast down unto the earth, and his angels were thrown down with him" (Apocalypse xii. 7–9). To this may be added the words of S. Jude: "And the angels who kept not their principality, but forsook their own habitation, he hath reserved under darkness in everlasting chains, unto the judgement of the great day." To these references should be added a striking passage from the prophet Isaiah: "How art thou fallen from heaven, O Lucifer, who didst rise in the morning! how art thou fallen to the earth, that didst wound the nations! And thou saidst in thy heart: I will ascend into heaven, I will exalt my throne above the stars of God, I will sit in the mountain of the covenant, in the sides of the north. I will ascend above the heights of the clouds, I will be like the most High. But yet thou shalt be brought down to hell, into the depth of the pit" (Isaiah xiv. 12–15). The words of the prophet may in one sense, perhaps primarily, be directed against Merodach-baladan, King of Babylon, but all the early Fathers and later commentators are agreed in understanding the passage as applying with deeper significance to the fall of the rebel angel. This interpretation is confirmed by the words of Our Lord to His disciples: "I saw Satan like lightning falling from heaven." (Uidebam Satanam sicut fulgur de cœlo cadentem.) S. Luke x. 18.

An obvious question which next arises and which has been amply discussed by the theologians is: What was the nature of the sin of the rebel angels? This point presents some difficulty, for theology has logically formed the highest estimate of the perfection of the angelic nature, the powers and possibilities of the angelic knowledge. Sins of the flesh are certainly impossible to angels, and from many sins which are purely spiritual and intellectual they would seem to be equally debarred. The great offence of Lucifer appears to have been the desire of independence of God and equality with God.

It is theologically certain that Lucifer held a very high rank in the celestial hierarchy, and it is evident that he maintains some kind of sovereignty over those who followed him in his rebellion: "Si autem," says Our Lord, "et Satanas in seipsum diuisus est quomodo stabit regnum eius?" (If Satan also be divided against himself, how shall his kingdom stand?) And S. Paul speaks of "Principem potestatis æris huius, qui nunc operatur in filios diffidentiæ." (The Prince of the power of this air, who now worketh in the sons of disobedience) Ephesians ii. 2. It may seem strange that those rebellious spirits who rose against their Maker should be subordinate to and obey one of their fellows who led them to destruction, but this in itself is a proof that Lucifer is a superior intelligence, and the knowledge of the angels would show them that they can effect more mischief and evil by co-operation and organization, although their unifying principle is the bond of hate, than by anarchy and division. There can be little doubt that among their ranks are many mean and petty spirits[5]—to speak comparatively—but even these can influence and betray foolish and arrogant men. We shall be on safe ground if we follow the opinion of Suarez, who would allow Lucifer to have been the highest of all angels negatively, i.e. that no one was higher, although many (and among these the three great Archangels, S. Michael, S. Gabriel, S. Raphael) may have been his equals.

It has been argued that the highest of the angels, by reason of their greater intellectual illumination, must have entirely realized the utter impossibility of attaining to equality with God. So S. Anselm, *De Casu Diaboli* (IV), says: "Non enim ita obtusæ mentis [diabolus] erat, ut nihil aliud simile Deo cogitari posse nesciret?" (The devil was surely not so dull of understanding as to be ignorant of the inconceivability of any other entity like to God?) And S. Thomas writes, in answer to the question, whether the Devil desired to be "as God," "if by this we mean equality with God, then the Devil would not desire it, since he knew this to be impossible." But as the Venerable Duns Scotus, Doctor subtilis, admirably points out, we must distinguish between efficacious volition and the volition of complaisance, and by the latter act an angel could desire that which is impossible. In the same way he shows that, though a creature cannot directly will its own destruction, it may do this *consequenter*, i.e. it can will something from which this would inevitably follow.

And although man must realize that he cannot be God, yet there have been men who have caused themselves to be saluted as God and even worshipped as God. Such was Herod Agrippa I, who on a festival day at Cæsarea, had himself robed in a garment made wholly of silver, and came into the crowded theatre early in the morning, so that his vesture shone out in the rays of the sun with dazzling light, and the superstitious multitude, taught by his flatterers, cried out that he was a god, and prayed to him as divine, saying: "Be thou merciful unto us, for although we have hitherto reverenced thee only as a man yet henceforth we own thee to be god."[6] Caligula, also, arrogated to himself divinity. "Templum etiam numini suo proprium, et sacerdotes et excogitatissimas hostias instituit."[7] (He also built a temple in honour of his own godhead, and consecrated priests to offer him most splendid sacrifices.) This emperor, moreover, set up his statue in the Temple at Jerusalem, and ordered victims to be sacrificed to him. Domitian, with something more than literary compliment, is addressed by Martial as "Dominus Deusque noster"[8] (Our Lord and our God), and he lived up to his title. Heliogabalus identified himself in some mystic way with the deity of Edessa, and ordered no god save himself to be worshipped at Rome, nay, throughout the wide world: "Taking measures that at Rome no god should be honoured save Heliogabalus alone. . . . Nor did he wish to stamp out only the various Roman cults, but his desire was that all the whole wide world through, only one god, Heliogabalus, should everywhere be worshipped."[9] To cite further examples, and they are numerous, from Roman history were superfluous.[10] Perhaps the most astounding case of all was that of the Persian king, Khosroes (Khusrau) II, who in the seventh century sacked Jerusalem and carried off the True Cross to his capital. Intoxicated with success he announced by solemn proclamation that he was Almighty God. He built an extraordinary palace or tower, in which there were vast halls whose ceilings were painted with luminous suns, moons, and stars to resemble the firmament. Here he sat upon a lofty throne of gold, a tiara upon his head, his cope so sewn with diamonds that the stuff could not be seen, sceptre and orb in his hands, upon one side the Cross, upon the other a jewelled dove, and here he bade his subjects adore him as God the Father, offering incense and praying him "Through the Son." This insane blasphemy was ended when the Persians were vanquished by the Emperor Heraclius, and in the spring of 629 the Cross was restored to Jerusalem.[11]

Montanus, the Phrygian heretic of the second century, who had originally, as S. Jerome tells us, been a priest of Cybele, actually claimed to be the Trinity. "I am the Father, the Word, and the Paraclete,"[12] he said, and again, "I am the Lord God omnipotent who have descended into a man . . . neither an angel, nor an ambassador, but I, the Lord, the Father, am come."[13] Elipandus of Toledo in the eighth century spoke of Christ as "a God among gods," inferring that there were many others who had been divine. One may compare the incarnate gods adored in China and Tibet to-day. A Bohemian woman named Wilhelmina, who died in Milan, 1281, declared herself to be an incarnation of the Third Person of the Blessed Trinity, and was actually worshipped by crowds of fanatics, who caused great scandal and disorder. The Khlysti in Russia have not only prophets but "Christs" and "Redeemers," and they pray to one another. About 1830 there appeared in one of the American states bordering upon Kentucky an impostor who declared himself to be Christ. He threatened the world with immediate judgement, and a number of ill-balanced and hysterical subjects were much affected by his denunciations. One day, when he was addressing a large gathering in his usual strain, a German standing up humbly asked him if he would repeat his warnings in German for the benefit of those present who only knew that tongue. The speaker answered that he had never been able to learn that language, a reply which seemed so ludicrous in one claiming divinity that many of the auditors were convulsed with laughter and so profane a charlatan soon lost all credit. Monsignor Flaget, Bishop of Bardstoun, wrote an account of this extraordinary imposture in a letter dated 4 May, 1833,[14] where he says the scene took place some three years before. About 1880 at Patiala in the Punjaub, a fanatic of filthy appearance named Hakim Singh gave himself out to be Christ, and in a short time had a following of more than four thousand persons, but within a few months they melted away.[15] Many "false Christs" have organized Russian sects. In 1840 a man drained the peasants of Simboisk and Saratov of their money by declaring himself to be the Saviour; about 1880 the founder of the *bojki*, an illiterate fanatic named Sava proclaimed that he was the Father, and his kinsman, Samouil, God the Son. Ivan Grigorieff, founder of the "Russian Mormons," taught that he was divine; and other frenzied creatures, Philipoff, Loupkin, Israil of Selengisk, have all claimed to be the Messiah and God.

It is apparent then, that although rationally it should be inconceivable that any sentient creature could claim divinity, actually the contrary is the case. The sin of Satan would appear to have been an attempt to usurp the sovereignty of God. This is further borne out by the fact that during the Temptation of our Lord the Devil, showing Him "omnia regna mundi, et gloriam eorum" (all the kingdoms of the world and the glory of them), said, "Hæc omnia tibi dabo, si cadens adoraueris me." (All these will I give Thee, if Thou wilt fall down and worship me.) And he is rebuked: "Uade Satana: Scriptum est enim: Dominum Deum tuum adorabis, et illi soli seruies." (Begone, Satan: for it is written: The Lord thy God shalt thou adore, and Him only shalt thou serve.) It should be remarked that Lucifer was telling a lie. The kingdoms of this world are not his to offer, but only its sins and follies, disappointment and death. But here the Devil is demanding that divine honours should be paid him. And this claim is perpetuated throughout the witch trials. The witches believed that their master, Satan, Lucifer, the fiend, the principle of evil, was God, and as such they worshipped him with latria, they adored him, they offered him homage, they addressed prayer to him, they sacrificed. So Lambert Danéau, *Dialogue of Witches* (trans. 1575), asserts: "The Diuell comaundeth them that they shall acknowledge him for their god, cal vpõ him, pray to him, and trust in him.—Then doe they all repeate the othe which they haue geuen vnto him; in acknowledging him to be their God." Cannaert records that the accusation against Elisabeth Vlamynex of Alost, 1595, was "You were not even ashamed to kneel before Belzebuth, whom you worshipped."[16] De Lancre, in his *Tableau de l'Inconstance des mauvais Anges* (1613), informs us that when the witches presented a young child they fell on their knees before the demon and said: "Grand Seigneur, lequel i'adore." (Great Lord, whom I worship.) The novice joining the witches made profession in this phrase: "I abandon myself wholly to thy power and I put myself in thy hands, acknowledging no other god; and this since there art my god."[17] The words of Silvain Nevillon, tried at Orleans in 1614, are even plainer: "We say to the Devil that we acknowledge him as our master, our god, our creator."[18] In America[19] in 1692, Mary Osgood confessed that "the devil told her he was her God, and that she should serve and worship him."

There are numberless instances of prayer offered to the Devil by his servants. Henri Boguet, in his *Discours des Sorciers* (Lyons, 1608), relates that Antide Colas, 1598, avowed that "Satan bade her pray to him night and morning, before she set about any other business."[20] Elizabeth Sawyer, the notorious witch of Edmonton (1621), was taught certain invocations by her familiar. In her confession to the Rev. Henry Goodcole, who visited her in Newgate, upon his asking "Did the Diuell at any time find you praying when he came unto you, and did not the Diuell forbid you to pray to Iesus Christ, but to him alone? and did he not bid you to pray to him, the Diuell as he taught you?" She replied: "He asked of me to whom I prayed, and I answered him to Iesus Christ, and he charged me then to pray no more to Iesus Christ, but to him the Diuell, and he the Diuell taught me this prayer, *Sanctibecetur nomen tuum, Amen.*"[21] So as Stearne reports in *Confirmation and Discovery of Witchcraft* (1648), of the Suffolk witches: "*Ellen*, the wife of *Nicholas Greenleife* of *Barton* in *Suffolke*, confessed, that when she prayed she prayed to the Devill and not to God."

In imitation of God, moreover, the Devil will have his miracles, although these are θαύματα, mere delusive wonders which neither profit nor convince. Such was the feat of Jannes and Mambres, the Egyptian sorcerers, who in emulation of Moses changed their rods to serpents. To this source we can confidently refer many tricks of Oriental jugglers. "I am satisfied," wrote an English officer of rank and family, "that the performances of the native 'wise-men' are done by the aid of familiar spirits. The visible growth of a mango tree out of an empty vessel into which a little earth is placed, a growth which spectators witness, and the secret of which has never been discovered, may not be unreasonably referred to the same occult powers which enabled the Egyptian magicians of old to imitate the miraculous acts which Moses, by God's command, openly wrought in the face of Pharaoh and his people."[22] In the basket-trick, which is performed without preparation in any place or spot—a greensward, a paved yard, a messroom—a boy is placed under a large wicker basket of conical shape, which may be examined and handled by all, and this is then stabbed through and through by the fakir with a long sword that pierces from side to side. Screams of pain follow each thrust, and the weapon is discerned to be covered with fresh blood. The cries grow fainter and at length cease altogether. Then the juggler uttering cries and incantations dances round the basket, which he suddenly removes, and no sign of the child is to be seen, no rent in the wicker-work, no stain on the steel. But in a few seconds the boy, unharmed and laughing, appears running forward from some distant spot. In this connexion we may well recall the words of Suarez: "[The Devil] can deceive and trick the senses so that a head may appear to be cut off and blood to flow, when in truth no such thing is taking place."[23]

The wizards of Tartary and Tibet, *bokte*, upon certain special days will with great ceremony appear in the temples, which are always thronged on these occasions, and whilst their disciples howl and shriek out invocations, they suddenly throw aside their robes and with a sharp knife seem to rip open their stomachs from top to bottom, whilst blood pours from the gaping wound. The worshippers, lashed to frenzy, fall prostrate before them and grovel frantically upon the floor. The wizard appears to scatter his blood over them, and after some five minutes he passes his hands rapidly over the wound, which instantly disappears, not leaving even the trace of a scar. The operator is noticed to be overcome with intense weariness, but otherwise all is well. Those who have seen this hideous spectacle assure us that it cannot be explained by any hallucination or legerdemain, and the only solution which remains is to attribute it to the glamour cast over the deluded crowd by the power of discarnate evil intelligences.[24]

The portentous growth of Spiritism,[25] which within a generation passed beyond the limits of a popular and mountebank movement and challenged the serious attention and expert inquiry of the whole scientific and philosophical world, furnishes us with examples of many extraordinary phenomena, both physical and psychical, and these, in spite of the most meticulous and accurate investigation, are simply inexplicable by any natural and normal means. Such phenomena have been classified by Sir William Crookes, in his *Researches in the Phenomena of Spiritualism*. They include the movement of heavy bodies without contact, or with contact altogether insufficient to explain the movement; the alteration of weight of bodies; the rising of tables and chairs off the ground without contact with any human person; the levitation of human beings; "apports," objects such as flowers, coins, pieces of stone conveyed into a hermetically closed room without any visible agency to carry them; luminous appearances; more or less distinct phantom faces and forms. In spite of continual and most deliberate trickery, repeated and most humiliating exposure, and this not only in the case of cheap charlatans but also of famous mediums such as William Eglinton, there occur and have always occurred phenomena which are vouched for upon the evidence of names whose authority cannot be gainsaid. Do such manifestations proceed from the spirits of the departed or from intelligences which have never been in human form? Even avowed believers in a beneficent Spiritism, anxious to establish communication with dead friends, are forced to admit the frequent and irresponsible action of non-human intelligences. This conclusion is based upon lengthy and detailed evidence which it is only possible very briefly to summarize. It proves almost impossible satisfactorily to establish spirit identity, to ascertain whether the communicator is actually the individual he or it purports to be; the information imparted is not such as would naturally be expected from those who have passed beyond this life but trivial and idle to a degree; the statements which the spirits make concerning their own condition are most contradictory and confused; the moral tone which pervades these messages, at first vague and unsatisfactory, generally becomes repulsive and even criminally obscene. All these particulars unmistakably point to demoniac intervention and deceit.[26] The Second Plenary Council of Baltimore (1866) whilst making due allowance for fraudulent practice and subtle sleights in Spiritism declares that some at least of the manifestations are to be ascribed to Satanic intervention, for in no other manner can they be explained. (*Decreta*, 33–41.) A decree of the Holy Office, 30 March, 1898, condemns Spiritistic practices, even though intercourse with evil spirits be excluded and intercourse sought only with good angels.

Not only with miracles but also in prophecies does Lucifer seek to emulate that God Whose Throne he covets. This point is dealt with by Bishop Pierre Binsfeld, who in his *De Maleficis* (1589) writes: "Nunc uidendum est an dæmones præscientiam habeant futurorum et secretorum, ita ut ex eorum reuelatione possit homo prognosticare[27] et occulta cognoscere? . . . Prima conclusio: Futura, si in seipsis considerentur, anullo præterquam a solo Deo cognosci possunt." (Next we will inquire whether devils can have any foreknowledge of future events or of hidden things so that a man might from their revelations to him foretell the future and discover the unknown? . . . First conclusion: The future, precisely considered, can be known to none save to God alone.) But it must be borne in mind that the intelligence of angels, though fallen, is of the acutest order, as Simon Maiolo in his *Dies caniculares* explains: "Astutia, sapientia, acumine longe superant homines, et longius progrediuntur ratiocinando." (In shrewdness, knowledge, perspicuity, they far excel mankind, and they can look much further into the future by logical deduction.) And it is in this way that a demon will often rightly divine what is going to happen, although more often the response will either be a lie or wrapped up in meaningless and ambiguous phrase, such as were the pagan oracles. A notable example of false prophets may be found in the Camisards (probably from *camise*, a black blouse worn as a uniform), a sect of evil fanatics who terrorized Dauphiné, Vivarais, and chiefly the Cévennes at the beginning of the eighteenth century. Their origin was largely due to the Albigensian spirit, which had never been wholly stamped out in that district, and which was fanned to flame by the anarchical preaching and disordered pamphlets of the French Calvinists, such as Jurieu's *Accomplissement des prophéties*. Pope Clement XI styles the Camisards "that execrable race of ancient Albigenses." De Serre, a rank old Calvinist of Dieulefit in Dauphiné, became suddenly inspired and a wave of foul hysteria spread far and wide. In 1702 the saintly abbé de Chaila was treacherously murdered by these wretches, who seized arms and formed themselves into offensive bands under such ruffians as Séguier, Laporte, Castanet, Ravenal, and Cavalier. Louis XIV sent troops to subdue them, but the Catholic leaders at first do not seem to have appreciated the seriousness of the position, and a desultory guerilla warfare dragged on for some years. Cavalier escaped to England,[28] whence he returned in 1709, and attempted to kindle a revolt in Vivarais. On 8 March, 1715, by a proclamation and medals, Louis XIV announced that these demoniacs were entirely extinct.

A number of these prophets fled to England, where they created great disturbances, and Voltaire, *Siècle de Louis XIV*, XXXVI, tells us that one of the leading refugees, a notorious rebel, Elie Marion, became so obnoxious on account of his *avertissements prophétiques* and false miracles, that he was expelled the country as a common nuisance.[29]

The existence of evil discarnate intelligences having been orthodoxly established, a realm which owns one chief, and it is reasonable to suppose, many hierarchies, a kingdom that is at continual warfare with all that is good, ever striving to do evil and bring man into bondage; it is obvious that if he be so determined man will be able in some way or another to get into touch with this dark shadow world, and however rare such a connexion may be it is, at least, possible. It is this connexion with its consequences, conditions, and attendant circumstances, that is known as Witchcraft. The erudite Sprenger in the *Malleus Maleficarum* expressly declares that in his opinion a denial of the possibility of Witchcraft is heresy. " After God Himself hath spoken of magicians and sorcerers, what infidel dare doubt that they exist ? " writes Pierre de Lancre in his *L'Incredulité et Mescreance du Sortilège* (Paris, 1622)[30]. That eminent lawyer Blackstone, in his *Commentaries* (1765), IV, 4, asserts : " To deny the possibility, nay, actual existence of Witchcraft and Sorcery, is at once flatly to contradict the revealed Word of God in various passages both of the Old and New Testament ; and the thing itself is a truth to which every Nation in the World hath in its turn borne testimony, either by examples seemingly well attested, or by prohibitory laws, which at least suppose the possibility of commerce with evil spirits." Even the ultra-cautious—I had almost said sceptical—Father Thurston acknowledges : " In the face of Holy Scripture and the teaching of the Fathers and theologians the abstract possibility of a pact with the Devil and of a diabolical interference in human affairs can hardly be denied." Imposture, trickery, self-deception, hypnotism, a morbid imagination have, no doubt, all played an important part in legends of this kind. It is not enough quite sincerely to claim magical powers to possess them in reality. Plainly, a man who not only firmly believes in a Power of evil but also that this Power can and does meddle with and mar human affections and human destinies, may invoke and devote himself to this Power, may give up his will thereunto, may ask this Power to accomplish his wishes and ends, and so succeed in persuading himself that he has entered into a mysterious contract with evil whose slave and servant he is become.[31] Moreover, as we should expect, the records teem with instances of common charlatanry, of cunning villainies and crime masquerading under the cloak of superstition, of clever fraud, of what was clearly play acting and mumming to impress the ignorant and vulgar, of diseased vanity, sick for notoriety, that craved the name and reputation of witch, of quackery and cozening that proved lucrative and comfortable enough.

But when every allowance has been made, as we examine in detail the long and bloody history of Witchcraft, as we recognize the fearful fanaticism and atrocious extravagances of the witch mania, as we are enabled to account for in the light of ampler knowledge, both psychological and physical, details and accidents which would have inevitably led to the stake without respite or mercy, as we can elucidate case after case—one an hysterical subject, a cataleptic, an epileptic, a sufferer from some obscure nervous disorder even to-day not exactly diagnosed; another, denounced by the malice of private enemies, perhaps on political grounds; a third, some doting beldame the victim of idlest superstition or mere malignity; a fourth, accused for the sake of gain by a disappointed blackmailer or thief; others, silly bodies, eccentrics, and half-crazed cranks; and the even greater number of victims who were incriminated by poor wretches raving in the agonies of the rack and boots;—none the less after having thus frankly discounted every possible circumstance, after having completely realized the world-wide frenzy of persecution that swept through those centuries of terror, we cannot but recognize that there remain innumerable and important cases which are not to be covered by any ordinary explanation, which fall within no normal category. As a most unprejudiced writer has well said: "The underlying and provocative phenomena had really been present in a huge number of cases."[32] And there is no other way of accounting for these save by acknowledging the reality of Witchcraft and diabolic contracts. It must be steadily remembered that the most brilliant minds, the keenest intelligences, the most learned scholars, the noblest names, men who had heard the evidence at first hand, all firmly believed in Witchcraft. Amongst them are such supreme authorities as S. Augustine, "a philosophical and theological genius of the first order, dominating, like a pyramid, antiquity and the succeeding ages"[33]; Blessed Albertus Magnus, the "Universal Doctor" of encyclopædic knowledge; S. Thomas Aquinas, Doctor Angelicus, one of the profoundest intellects the world has ever seen; the Seraphic S. Bonaventura, most loving of mystics; Popes not a few, Alexander IV, the friend of the Franciscans, prudent, kindly, deeply religious, "assiduous in prayer and strict in abstinence"[34]; John XXII, "a man of serious character, of austere and simple habits, broadly cultivated"[35]; Benedict XII, a pious Cistercian monk, most learned in theology; Innocent VIII, a magnificent prelate, scholar and diplomatist; Gregory XV, an expert in canon and civil law, most just and merciful of pontiffs, brilliantly talented. We have the names of learned men, such as Gerson, Chancellor of Notre-Dame and of the University of Paris, "justly regarded as one of the master intellects of his age"[36]; James Sprenger, O.P., who for all his etymological errors was a scholar of vast attainments; Jean Bodin, "one of the chief founders of political philosophy and political history"[36]; Erasmus; Bishop Jewell, of Salisbury, "one of the ablest and most authoritative expounders of the true genius and teaching of the reformed Church of England"[37]; the gallant Raleigh; Lord Bacon; Sir Edward Coke; Cardinal Mazarin; the illustrious Boyle; Cudworth, "perhaps the most profound of all the great scholars who have adorned the English Church"[36]; Selden; Henry More; Sir Thomas Browne; Joseph Glanvill, who "has been surpassed in genius by few of his successors"[36]; Meric Casaubon, the learned Prebendary of Canterbury; Sir Matthew Hale; Sir George Mackenzie; William Blackstone; and many another divine, lawyer, scholar, of lesser note. It is inconceivable that all these, mistaken as they might be in some details, should have been wholly deluded and beguiled. The learned Sinistrari in his *De Dæmonialitate*,[38] upon the authoritative sentence of Francesco-Maria Guazzo, an Ambrosian, (*Compendium Maleficarum*, Liber I. 7), writes: "Primo, ineunt pactum expressum cum Dæmone aut alio Mago seu Malefico uicem Dæmonis gerente, et testibus præsentibus de seruitio diabolico suscipiendo: Dæmon uero uice uersa honores, diuitias, et carnales delectationes illis pollicetur." (Firstly, the Novices have to conclude with the Demon, or some other Wizard or Magician acting in the Demon's place, an express compact by which, in the presence of witnesses, they enlist in the Demon's service, he giving them in exchange his pledge for honours, riches, and carnal pleasures.)

It is said that the formal pact was sometimes verbal, sometimes a signed document. In every case it was voluntary, and as Görres points out, the usual initiation into these foul mysteries was through some secret society at an asseblym of which the neophyte bound himself with terrific oathsnd a blasphemy to the service of evil. But there are cases which can only be explained by the materialization of a dark intelligence who actually received a bond from the worshipper. These are, of course, extremely rare; but occasionally the judges were able to examine such parchments and deeds. In 1453 Guillaume Edelin, Prior of S. Germain-en-Laye, signed a compact with the Devil, and this was afterwards found upon his person. Pierre de Lancre relates that the witch Stevenote de Audebert, who was burned in January, 1619, showed him "le pacte & conuention qu'elle auoit faict auec le Diable, escrite en sang de menstrues, & si horrible qu'on auoit horreur de la regarder."[39] In the library at Upsala is preserved the contract by which Daniel Salthenius, in later life Professor of Hebrew at Köningsberg, sold himself to Satan.

In the archives of the Sacred Office is preserved a picture of the Crucifixion of which the following account is given: A young man of notoriously wicked life and extreme impiety having squandered his fortune, and being in desperate need, resolved to sell himself body and soul to Lucifer on condition that he should be supplied with money enough to enable him to indulge in all the luxuries and lusts he desired. It is said the demon assumed a visible form, and required him to write down an act of self-donation to hell. This the youth consented to do on one proviso. He asked the demon if he had been present on Calvary, and when he was answered in the affirmative he insisted that Lucifer should trace him an exact representation of the Crucifixion, upon which he would hand over the completed document. The fiend after much hesitation consented, and shortly produced a picture. But at the sight of the racked and bleeding Body stretched on the Cross the youth was seized with such contrition that falling upon his knees he invoked the help of God. His companion disappeared, leaving the fatal contract and picture. The penitent, in order to gain absolution for so heinous guilt, was obliged to have recourse to the Cardinal Penitentiary, and the picture was taken in charge by the Holy Office. Prince Barberini afterwards obtained permission to have any exact copy made of it, and this eventually he presented to the Capuchins at S. Maria della Concezione.

A contract with Satan was said always to be signed in the blood of the executor. "The signature is almost invariably subscribed with the writer's own blood. . . . Thus at Augsburg Joseph Egmund Schultz declared that on the 15 May, 1671, towards midnight, when it was betwixt eleven and twelve of the clock, he threw down, where three cross-roads met, an illuminated parchment, written throughout in his own blood and wrapped up in a fair kerchief, and thus he sealed the compact . . . Widmann also tells us how that unhappy wretch Faust slightly cut his thumb and with the drops of blood which trickled thence devoted himself in writing body and soul to the Devil, utterly repudiating God's part in him."[40] From the earliest times and in many nations we find human blood used inviolably to ratify the pledged word.[41] Rochholz, I, 52, relates that it is a custom of German University freshmen (Burschen) for the parties to write "mutually with their own blood leaves in each other's albums." The parchment is still said to be in existence on which with his own blood Maximilian, the great and devout Bavarian elector, religiously dedicated himself to the Most Holy Mother of God. Blood was the most sacred and irrevocable of seals, as may be seen in the custom of blood-brotherhood when friendship was sworn and alliances concluded. Either the blood itself was drunk or wine mixed with blood. Herodotus (IV, 70) tells us that the Scythians were wont to conclude agreements by pouring wine into an earthen vessel, into which the contracting parties having cut their arms with a knife let their blood flow and mingle. Whereupon both they and the most distinguished of their following drank of it. Pomponius Mela, *De Situ Orbis*, II, 1, records the same custom as still existing among them in his day: "Not even their alliances are made without shedding of blood: the partners in the compact wound themselves, and when the blood gushes out they mingle the stream and taste of it when it is mixed. This they consider to be the most assured pledge of eternal loyalty and trust."[42] Gyraldus, *Topographia Hibernorum*, XXII, p. 743, says: "When the Ireni conclude treaties the one drinks the blood of the other, which is shed voluntarily for this purpose." In July, 1891, a band of brigands which had existed for three years was discovered and broken up in South Italy. It was reported that in the ritual of these outlaws, who were allied to the "Mala Vita" of Bari, "the neophytes drank blood-brotherhood with the captain of the band by sucking out and drinking the blood from a scratch wound, which he had himself made in the region of his heart."

In several grimoires and books of magic, such as *The Book of Black Magic and of Pacts, The Key of Solomon the King, Sanctum Regnum,* may be found goetic rituals as well as invocations, and if these, fortunately for the operators, are occasionally bootless, it can only be said that Divine Power holds in check the evil intelligences. But, as Suarez justly observes, even if no response be obtained from the demon "either because God does not allow it, or for some other reason we may not know,"[43] the guilt of the experimenter in this dark art and his sin are in no wise lightened.[44] Towards the end of the eighteenth century a certain Juan Perez, being reduced to the utmost misery, vowed himself body and soul to Satan if he were revenged upon those whom he suspected of injuring him. He consulted more than one magician and witch, he essayed more than one theurgic ceremonial, but all in vain. Hell was deaf to his appeal. Whereupon he openly proclaimed his disbelief in the supernatural, in the reality of devils, and mocked at Holy Scripture as a fairy tale, a nursery fable. Naturally this conduct brought him before the Tribunal of the Holy Office, to whom at his first interrogation he avowed the whole story, declaring himself ready to submit to any penance they might seem fit to inflict.

Any such pact which may be entered into with the demon is not in the slightest degree binding. Such is the authoritative opinion of S. Alphonsus, who lays down that a necromancer or person who has had intercourse with evil spirits now wishing to give up his sorceries is bound : "1. Absolutely to abjure and to renounce any formal contract or any sort of commerce whatsoever he may have entered into with demonic intelligences ; 2. To burn all such books, writings, amulets, talismans, and other instruments as appertain to the black art (i.e. crystals, planchettes, ouija-boards, pagan periapts, and the like) ; 3. To burn the written contract if it be in his possession, but if it be believed that it is held by the demon, there is no need to demand its restoration since it is wholly annulled by penitence; 4. To repair any harm he has done and make good any loss."[45] It may be remarked that these rules have been found exceedingly useful and entirely practical in dealing with mediums and others who forsake spiritism, its abominations and fearful dangers.

There are examples in history, even in hagiography, of sorcerers who have been converted. One of the most famous of these is S. Theophilus the Penitent;[46] and even yet more renowned is S. Cyprian of Antioch who, with S. Justina, suffered martyrdom during the persecution of Diocletian at Nicomedia, 26 September, 304.[47] Blessed Gil of Santarem, a Portuguese Dominican, in his youth excelled in philosophy and medicine. Whilst on his way from Coimbra to the University of Paris he fell into company with a courteous stranger who offered to teach him the black art at Toledo. As payment the stranger required that Gil should make over his soul to the Devil and sign the contract with his blood. After complying with the conditions he devoted seven years to magical studies, and then proceeding to Paris easily obtained the degree of doctor of medicine. Gil, however, repented, burned his books of spells, and returned to Portugal, where he took the habit of S. Dominic. After a long life of penitence and prayer he died at Santarem, 14 May, 1205, and here his body is still venerated.[48] His cult was ratified by Benedict XIV, 9 March, 1748. His feast is observed 14 May.

The contract made by the witch was usually for the term of her life, but sometimes it was only for a number of years, at the end of which period the Devil was supposed to kill his votary. Reginald Scot remarks: "Sometimes their homage with their oth and bargaine is receiued for a certeine terme of yeares; sometimes for ever."[49] Magdalena de la Cruz, a Franciscan nun, born at Aquilar in 1487, entered the convent of Santa Isabel at Cordova in 1504. She acquired an extraordinary reputation for sanctity, and was elected abbess in 1533, 1536, and 1539. Scarcely five years later she was a prisoner of the Inquisition, with charges of Witchcraft proven against her. She confessed that in 1499 a spirit who called himself by the grotesque name Balbar, with a companion Pithon, appeared to her at the tender age of twelve, and she made a contract with him for the space of forty-one years. In 1543 she was seized with a serious illness, during which she confessed her impostures and demonic commerce. She was confined for the rest of her life as a penitent in a house of the utmost austerity. Joan Williford, a witch of Faversham, acknowledged "that the Devil promised to be her servant about twenty yeeres, and that the time is now almost expired."[50] In 1646 Elizabeth Weed, a witch of Great Catworth in Huntingdonshire, confessed that "the Devill then offer'd her that hee would doe what mischiefe she should require him; and said she must covenant with him that he must have her soule at the end of one and twenty years which she granted."[51] In 1664, a Somerset sorceress, Elizabeth Style, avowed that the Devil "promised her Mony, and that she should live gallantly, and have the pleasure of the World for Twelve years, if she would with her Blood sign his Paper, which was to give her Soul to him."[52]

Satan promises to give his votaries all they desire; knowledge, wealth, honours, pleasure, vengeance upon their enemies; and all that he can give is disappointment, poverty, misery, hate, the power to hurt and destroy. He is ever holding before their eyes elusive hopes, and so besotted are they that they trust him and confide in him until all is lost. Sometimes in the case of those who are young the pact is for a short while, but he always renews it. So at Lille in 1661 Antoinette Bourignon's pupils confessed: "The Devil gives them a Mark, which Marks they renew as often as those Persons have any desire to quit him. The Devil reproves them the more severely, and obligeth them to new Promises, making them also new Marks for assurance or Pledge, that those Persons should continue faithful to him."[53]

The Devil's Mark to which allusion is here made, or the Witches' Mark, as it is sometimes called, was regarded as perhaps the most important point in the identification of a witch, it was the very sign and seal of Satan upon the actual flesh of his servant, and any person who bore such a mark was considered to have been convicted and proven beyond all manner of doubt of being in league with and devoted to the service of the fiend. This mark was said to be entirely insensible to pain, and when pricked, however deeply, it did not bleed. So Mr. John Bell, minister at Gladsmuir, in his tract *The Trial of Witchcraft; or Witchcraft Arraigned and Condemned*, published early in the eighteenth century, explains: "The witch mark is sometimes like a blew spot, or a little tate, or reid spots, like flea biting; sometimes also the flesh is sunk in, and hollow, and this is put in secret places, as among the hair of the head, or eye-brows, within the lips, under the arm-pits, and in the most secret parts of the body." Robert Hink, minister at Aberfoill, in his *Secret Commonwealth* (1691), writes: "A spot that I have seen, as a small mole, horny, and brown-coloured; throw which mark, when a large pin was thrust (both in buttock, nose, and rooff of the mouth), till it bowed and became crooked, the witches both men and women, nather felt a pain nor did bleed, nor knew the precise time when this was doing to them, (their eyes only being covered)." This mark was sometimes the complete figure of a toad or a bat; or, as Delrio says, the slot of a hare, the foot of a frog, a spider, a deformed whelp, a mouse.[54] The same great authority informs us on what part of the body it was usually impressed: "In men it may often be seen under the eyelids, under the lips, under the armpits, on the shoulders, on the fundament; in women, moreover, on the breast or on the pudenda."[55]

In his profound treatise *De Dæmonialitate* that most erudite Franciscan Ludovico Maria Sinistrari writes: "[Sagæ seu Malefici] sigillantur a Dæmone aliquo charactere, maxime ii, de quorum constantia dubitat. Character uero non est semper eiusdem formæ, aut figuræ: aliquando enim est simile lepori, aliquando pedi bufonis, aliquando araneæ, uel catello, uel gliri; imprimitur autem in locis corporis magis occultis: uiris quidem aliquando sub palpebris, aliquando sub axillis, aut labiis, aut humeris, aut sede ima, aut alibi: mulieribus autem plerumque in mammis, seu locis muliebribus. Porro sigillum, quo talia signa imprimuntur, est unguis Diaboli." (The Demon imprints upon [the Witches or Wizards] some mark, especially on those whose constancy he suspects. That mark, moreover, is not always of the same shape or figure: sometimes it is the image of a hare, sometimes a toad's leg, sometimes a spider, a puppy, a dormouse. It is imprinted on the most hidden parts of the body: with men, under the eye-lids, or the armpits, or the lips, on the shoulder, the fundament, or somewhere else:

with women it is usually on the breasts or the privy parts. Now, the stamp which imprints these marks is none other but the Devil's claw.)

This Mark was made by the Devil, or by the Devil's vicegerent at the Sabbats upon the admission of a new witch. "The Diuell giveth to euerie nouice a marke, either with his teeth or his clawes," says Reginald Scot, *Discoverie of Witchcraft*, 1584. The young witches of Lille in 1661 confessed that "the Devil branded them with an iron awl upon some part of the body."[56] In Scotland, Geillis Duncane, maid-servant to the deputy bailiff of Tranent, one David Seaton, a wench who was concerned in the celebrated trial of Doctor Fian, Agnes Sampson, Euphemia McCalyan, Barbara Napier, and their associates, would not confess even under torture, "whereuppon they suspecting that she had been marked by the devill (as commonly witches are) made diligent search about her, and found the enemies mark to be in her fore crag, or fore part of her throate; which being found, shee confessed that all her doings was done by the wicked allurements and entisements of the devil, and that she did them by witchcraft."[57] In 1630 Catharine Oswald of Niddrie was found guilty of sorcery, "the advocate for the instruction of the assyze producing the declaration of two witnesses, that being in the tolbuith, saw Mr. John Aird, minister, put a pin in the pannell's shoulder, (where she carries the devill's mark) up to the heid, and no bluid followed theiron, nor she shrinking thereat; which was againe done in the justice-depute his own presence." In 1643 Janet Barker at Edinburgh confessed to commerce with the demon, and stated that he had marked her between the shoulders. The mark was found "and a pin being thrust therein, it remained for an hour unperceived by the pannell."[58]

On 10 March, 1611, Louis Gaufridi, a priest of Accoules in the diocese of Marseilles, was visited in prison, where he lay under repeated charges of foulest sorcery, by two physicians and two surgeons who were appointed to search for the Devil's mark. Their joint report ran as follows: "We, the undersigned doctors and surgeons, in obedience to the directions given us by Messire Anthoine de Thoron, sieur de Thoron, Councillor to the King in his Court of Parliament, have visited Messire L. Gaufridy, upon whose body we observed three little marks, not very different in colour from the natural skin. The first is upon his right thigh, about the middle towards the lower part. When we pierced this with a needle to the depth of two fingers breadth he felt no pain, nor did any blood or other humour exude from the incision.

"The second is in the region of the loins, towards the right, about an inch from the spine and some four fingers breadth above the femoral muscles. Herein we drove the needle for three fingers breath, leaving it fixed in this spot for some time, as we had already done in the first instance, and yet all the while the said Gaufridy felt no pain, nor was there any effluxion of blood or other humour of any kind.

"The third mark is about the region of the heart. At first the needle was introduced without any sensation being felt, as in the previous instances. But when the place was probed with some force, he said he felt pain, but yet no moisture distilled from this laceration. Early the next morning we again visited him, but we found that the parts which had been probed were neither swollen nor red. In our judgement such callous marks which emit no moisture when pierced, cannot be due to any ancient affection of the skin, and in accordance with this opinion we submit our report on this tenth day of March, 1611.

Fontaine, Grassy, Doctors;
Mérindol, Bontemps, Surgeons."[59]

On 26 April, 1634, during the famous Loudun trials, Urbain Grandier, the accused was examined in order to discover the witch-mark. He was stripped naked, blindfolded, and in the presence of the officials, René Mannoury, one of the leading physicians of the town, conducted the search. Two marks were discovered, one upon the shoulder-blade and the other upon the thigh, both of which proved insensible even when pierced with a sharp silver pin.

Inasmuch as the discovery of the devil-mark was regarded as one of the most convincing indications—if not, indeed, an infallible proof—that the accused was guilty since he bore indelibly branded upon his flesh Satan's own sign-manual, it is easy to see how the searching for, the recognition and the probing of, such marks actually grew to be a profession in which not a few ingenious persons came to be recognized as experts and practical authorities. In Scotland, especially, the "prickers," as they were called, formed a regular gild. They received a good fee for every witch they discovered, and, as might be expected, they did not fail to reap a golden harvest. At the trial of Janet Peaston, in 1646, the magistrates of Dalkeith "caused John Kincaid of Tranent, the common pricker, to exercise his craft upon her. He found two marks of the Devil's making; for she could not feel the pin when it was put into either of the said marks, nor did the marks bleed when the pin was taken out again. When she was asked where she thought the pins were put into her, she pointed to a part of her body distant from the real place. They were pins of three inches in length."[60] Another notorious pricker was John Bain, upon whose unsupported evidence a large number of unfortunate wretches were sentenced to death. About 1634 John Balfour of Corhouse was feared over all the countryside for his exploits; whilst twenty years later one John Dick proved a rival to Kincaid himself. The regular trade of these "common prickers" came to be a serious nuisance, and confessedly opened the door to all sorts of roguery. The following extraordinary incident shows how dangerous and villainous in mountebank hands the examinations could become, which, if conducted at all, ought at least to be safeguarded by every precaution and only entrusted to skilled physicians, who should report the result to grave and learned divines. "There came then to Inverness one Mr. Paterson, who had run over the kingdom for triall off witches, and was ordinarily called the Pricker, because his way of triall was with a long brass pin. Stripping them naked, he alledged that the spell spot was seen and discovered. After rubbing over the whole body with his palms he slips in the pin, and, it seemes, with shame and fear being dasht, they felt it not, but he left it in the flesh, deep to the head, and desired them to find and take it out. It is sure some witches were discovered but many honest men and women were blotted and break by this trick. In Elgin there were two killed; in Forres two; and one Margret Duff, a rank witch, burned in Inverness. This Paterson came up to the Church of Wardlaw, and within the church pricked 14 women and one man brought thither by the Chisholm of

Commer, and 4 brought by Andrew Fraser, chamerlan of Ferrintosh. He first polled all their heads and amassed the heap of haire together, hid in the stone dich, and so proceeded to pricking.[61] Severall of these dyed in prison never brought to confession. This villan gaind a great deale off mony, haveing two servants; at last he was discovered to be a woman disguished in mans cloathes. Such cruelty and rigure was sustained by a vile varlet imposture."[62] No doubt in very many, in the majority of instances, these witch-marks were natural malformations of the skin, thickened tissue, birthmarks—I myself have known a subject who was by prenatal accident stamped upon the upper part of the arm with the complete figure of a rat—moles, callous warts, or spots of some kind. But this explanation will not cover all the cases, and even the sceptical Miss Murray who writes: "Local anæsthesia is vouched for in much of the evidence, which suggests that there is a substratum of truth in the statements," is bound candidly to confess, "but I can at present offer no solution of this problem."[63] Moreover, as before noticed, this mark was not infrequently branded upon the novice at admission, often by the Witch-Master, who presided over the rout, sometimes—it must be admitted—by non-human agency.

The "little Teat or Pap," so often found on the body of the wizard or witch, and said to secrete milk which nourished the familiar, must be carefully distinguished from the insensible devil-mark. This phenomenon, for no explainable reason, seems to occur only in the records of England and New England, where, however, it is of exceedingly frequent occurrence. It is worth remarking that in the last act of Shadwell's play, *The Lancashire Witches* (1681), the witches are searched by a woman, who reports "they have all great Biggs and Teats in many Parts, except Mother *Madge*, and hers are but small ones." Shadwell, who in his voluminous notes hás citations from nearly fifty authors, on this point writes: "The having of Biggs and Teats all modern Witch-mongers in *England* affirm."[64] In 1597 at the trial of a beldame, Elizabeth Wright, of Stapenhill, near Burton-on-Trent: "The old woman they stript, and found behind her right sholder a thing much like the vdder of an ewe that giueth sucke with two teates, like vnto two great wartes, the one behinde vnder her armehole, the other a hand off towardes the top of her shoulder. Being demanded how long she had those teates, she answered she was borne so."[65] In the case of the Witch of Edmonton, Elizabeth Sawyer, who was in spite of her resistance searched upon the express order of the Bench, it was found by Margaret Weaver, a widow of an honest reputation, and two other grave matrons, who performed this duty that there was upon her body "a thing like a Teate the bignesse of the little finger, and the length of half a finger, which was branched at the top like a teate, and seemed as though one had suckt it."[66] John Palmer of St. Albans (1649) confessed that "upon his compact with the Divel, hee received a flesh brand, or mark, upon his side, which gave suck to two familiars."[67] The Kentish witch, Mary Read of Lenham (1652), "had a visible Teat, under her Tongue, and did show it to many."[68] At St. Albans about 1660 there was a wizard who "had like a Breast on his side."[69] In the same year at Kidderminster, a widow, her two daughters, and a man were accused; "the man had five teats, the mother three, and the eldest daughter, one."[70] In 1692 Bridget Bishop, one of the Salem witches, was brought to trial: "A Jury of Women found a preternatural Teat upon her Body: But upon a second search, within 3 or 4 hours, there was no such thing to be seen."[71] There is similar evidence adduced in the accounts of Rose Cullender and Amy Duny, two Suffolk witches, executed in 1664; Elizabeth Horner, a Devon witch (1696); Widow Coman, an Essex witch, who died in her bed (1699); and, indeed, innumerable other examples might be quoted affording a whole catena of pertinent illustrations. No doubt many of these are explicable by the cases of polymastia (*mammæ erraticæ*) and polythelia (supernumerary nipples) of which there are continual records in recent medical works. It must be freely admitted that these anatomical divagations are commoner than is generally supposed; frequently they are so slight that they may pass almost unnoticed; doubtless there is exaggeration in many of the inexactly observed seventeenth-century narratives. However, it has to be said, as before, that when every most generous allowance is made, the facts which remain, and the details are very ample, cannot be covered by physical peculiarities and malformations.

There is far more truth in the records of the old theologians and witch finders than many nowadays are disposed to allow.

NOTES TO CHAPTER II.

1 Under Innocent III, 1215.

2 Diabolus enim et alii dæmones a Deo quidem natura creati sunt boni, sed ipsi per se facti sunt mali.

3 Bossuet says that the writings of Suarez contain the whole of Scholastic Philosophy.

4 Since it contradicts a definite (*certa*) theological conclusion or truth clearly consequent upon two premises, of which one is an article of faith (*de fide*), the other naturally certain.

5 Which explains much of the trifling and silliness in Spiritism; the idle answers given through the mediums of the influences at work.

6 Josephus, *Antiquities*, XIX. 8. 2.

7 Suetonius, *Caligula*, XXII. Here ample details of Caligula's worship may be read.

8 *Epigrammatum*, V. 8. 1. See also IX. 4, *et sæpius*.

9 . . . id agens ne quis Romæ deus nisi Heliogabalus coleretur. . . . Nec Romanas tantum extinguere uoluit religiones, sed per orbem terræ unum studens ut Heliogabalus deus unus ubique coleretur. Ælius Lampridius, *Antoninus Heliogabalus*, 3; 6.

10 Even the Christian (Arian) Constantius II suffered himself to be addressed as "Nostra Æternitas."

11 Now commemorated on 14 September, the Feast of the Exaltation of Holy Cross. Shortly after the Restoration of the Cross to Jerusalem, the wood was cut up (perhaps for greater safety) into small fragments which were distributed throughout the Christian world.

12 Didymus, *De Trinitate*, III. xli.

13 Epiphanius, *Hær.*, xlviii. 11.

14 *Annales de la Propogation de la Foi*, VII (1834), p. 84.

15 D. C. J. Ibbetson, *Outlines of Punjaub Ethnography*, Calcutta. 1883. p. 123.

16 . . . vous n'avez pas eu honte de vous agenouiller devant votre Belzebuth, que vous avez adoré. J. B. Cannaert, *Olim procès des Sorcières en Belgique*, Gand, 1847.

17 Ie me remets de tout poinct en ton pouuoir & entre tes mains, ne recognois autre Dieu : si bien que tu es mon Dieu.

18 On dit au Diable nous vous recognoissons pour nostre maistre, nostre Dieu, nostre Createur.

19 John Hutchinson, *History of the Province of Massachusett's Bay*, 1828, II. p. 31.

20 Satan luy commãda de le prier soir & matin, auant qu'elle s'addonat à faire autre œuure.

21 *Wonderful Discoverie of Elizabeth Sawyer*, London, 1621.

22 Rev. F. G. Lee, *More Glimpses of the World Unseen*, 1878, p. 12.

23 Potest [diabolus] eludere sensus et facere ut appareat caput abcisum, *De Religione*, l. 2, c. 16, n. 13, t. 13, p. 578.

24 Huc. *Voyage dans la Tartarie, le Thibet et la Chine*, I, ix, p. 308. The author remarks : Ces cérémonies horribles se renouvellent assez souvent dans les grandes lamaseries de la Tartarie et du Thibet. Nous ne pensons nullement qu'on puisse mettre toujours sur le compte de la supercherie des faits de ce genre : car d'après tout ce que nous avons vu et entendu parmi les nations idolâtres, nous sommes persuadé que le démon y joue un grand rôle. (These horrible ceremonies frequently occur in the larger lamaseries of Tartary and Tibet. I am very certain that we cannot always ascribe happenings of this sort to mere juggling or trickery; for, after all that I have seen and heard among heathen people, I am confident that the powers of evil are very largely concerned therein.)

[25] I use this term rather than the more popular "Spiritualism." Spiritism obtains in Italy, France and Germany. "Spiritualism" is correctly a technical name for the doctrine which denies that the contents of the universe are limited to matter and the properties and operations of matter.

[26] For fuller, and, indeed, conclusive details see Godfrey Raupert's *Modern Spiritism*, London, 1904; and Monsignor Benson's *Spiritualism*, *Dublin Review*, October, 1909, and reprinted by the Catholic Truth Society.

[27] *Prognosticare* is a late word. Strictly to prognosticate is to deduce from actual signs, to prophesy is to foretell the future without any such sign or token.

[28] The Camisards were agreeably satirized by D'Urfey in his comedy *The Modern Prophets ; or, New Wit for a Husband*, produced at Drury Lane, 5 May, 1709, (*Tatler*, 11), and printed quarto, 1709, (no date). One of the principal characters is "*Marrogn*, A Knavish French Camizar and Priest," created by Bowen. This is a portrait of Elie Marion. In his preface D'Urfey speaks of "the abominable Impostures of those craz'd Enthusiasts" whom he lashes. The play had been composed in 1708, but production was postponed owing to the death of the Prince Consort, 28 October of that year. Swift, *Predictions for the Year 1708*, has: "*June*. This month will be distinguished at home, by the utter dispersing of those ridiculous deluded enthusiasts, commonly called the *prophets ;* occasioned chiefly by seeing the time come, when many of their prophecies should be fulfilled, and then finding themselves deceived by contrary events."

[29] See also Fléchier's *Récit fidèle* in *Lettres choisies*, Lyons, 1715; and Brueys' *Histoire du fanatisme de notre temps*, Montpellier, 1713.

[30] Après que Dieu a parlé de sa propre bouche des magiciens et sorciers, qui est l'incredule qui on peut justement douter ?

[31] In the fourteenth century bas-reliefs on cathedrals frequently represent men kneeling down before the Devil, worshipping him, and devoting themselves to him as his servants. Martonne, *Piété au Moyen Âge*, p. 137.

[32] George Ives, *A History of Penal Methods*, p. 75. His admirable and documented chapter II, "The Witch Trials," should be carefully read.

[33] Philip Schaff, *History of the Christian Church.*

[34] Matthew Paris, *Chronica Maiora.*

[35] J. P. Kirsch.

[36] All these quotations are from W. H. Lecky, *History of Rationalism in Europe*. c. 1.

[37] Rev. Peter Lorimer, D.D.

[38] First published by Isidore Liseux, 1875. p. 21. XIII. Ludovico Maria Sinistrari, Minorite, was born at Ameno (Novara) 26 February, 1622. He was Consultor to the Supreme Tribunal of the Holy Office; Vicar-general of the Archbishop of Avignon, and Theologian Advisory to the Archbishop of Milan. He is described as "omnium scientiarum uir." He died 6 March, 1701.

[39] *L'Incredulité et Mescreance du Sortilege*, Paris, 1622, p. 38.

[40] Subscriptio autem sæpissime peragitur proprio sanguine. . . . Sic Augustæ referebat Joseph Egmund Schultz, se anno 1671. d. 15. Maji sanguine proprio tinctum manuscriptum, in membrana, nomine picto, obuolutoque muccinio, in media nocte, cum hora undecima & duodecima agebatur, in compitum iecisse, atque pactum sic corroborasse . . . Sic de infausto illo Fausto *Widmannus* refert, proprio sanguine ex leuiter uulnerato pollice emisso illum se totum diabolo adscripsisse, Deoque repudium misisse. *De Sagis*, Christian Stridtheckh, Lipsiæ, 1691. (XXII).

[41] See Götz, *De subscriptionibus sanguine humano firmatis*, Lübeck, 1724. Also Scheible, *Die Sage vom Faust*. Stuttgart, 1847. So far as I am aware this point has been neglected by writers on Witchcraft.

[42] Ne fœdora quidem incruenta sunt: sauciant se, qui paciscuntur, exemtumque sanguinem, ubi permiscuere, degustant. Id putant mansuræ fidei pignus certissimum.

[43] . . . uel quia Deus non permittit, uel propter alias rationes nobis occultas. *De Superstitione*, VIII. i. 13.

[44] Tunc autem propria culpa diuinationis iam commissa est ab homine,

etiamsi effectus desideratus non fuerit subsecutus. (For the sin of divination is actually committed by the sinner and that willingly, although he obtain not the desired effect of his action.) *Idem.*

45 *Theologia moralis*, l. iii. n. 28. Monendi sunt se teneri 1. Pactum expressum, si quod habent cum dæmone, aut commercium abiurare et dissoluere; 2. Libros suos, schedas, ligaturas, aliaque instrumenta artis comburere; 3. Comburere chirographum, si habeat: si iuro solus dæmon id habeat, non necessario cogendus est ut reddat, quia pactum sufficienter soluitur per pœnitentiam; 4. Damna illata resarcire.

46 Bollandists, 4 February.

47 *Breuiarium Romanum*, Paris Autumnalis, 26 September, lectio iii. of Matins. Upon this history Calderon has founded his great drama *El Magico Prodigioso.*

48 Bollandists, 14 May. *Breuiarium iuxta S. Ordinis Prædicatorum.* 14 May. In Nocturno, Lectiones ii, iij. Touron *Histoire des hommes illustres de l'ordre de Saint Dominique.* (Paris, 1743.)

49 *Discoverie of Witchcraft*, Book III.

50 *Examination of Joane Williford*, London, 1643.

51 John Davenport, *Witches of Huntingdon*, London, 1646.

52 Glanvill, *Sadducismus Triumphatus.*

53 Antoinette Bourignon, *La Vie exterieure*, Amsterdam, 1683.

54 Delrio. *Disquisitiones magicæ*, l. v. sect. 4. t. 2. Non eadem est forma signi; aliquando est simile leporis uestigio, aliquando bufonis pedi, aliquando araneæ, uel catello, uel gliri.

55 *Idem.* In uirorum enim corpore sæpe uisitur sub palpebris, sub labiis, sub axillis, in humeris, in sede ima: feminis etiam, in mammis uel muliebribus locis.

56 . . . le Diable leur fait quelque marque comme avec une aleine de fer en quelque partie du corps.

57 *Newes from Scotland*, London. (1592.) Roxburgh Club reprint, 1816.

58 *Abbreviate of the Justiciary Record.*

59 Nous, medecins et chirurgiens soussignés, suivant le commandement à nous fait par messire Anthoine de Thoron, sieur de Thoron, conseiller du roy en sa cour de parlement, avons visité messire L. Gaufridy au corps duquel avons remarqué trois petites marques peu differentes en couleur du reste du cuir. L'une en sa cuisse sénestre sur le milieu et en la partie inferieure, en laquelle ayant enforcé une aiguille environ deux travers de doigts n'a senti aucune douleur, ni de la place n'est sorti point de sang ni autre humidité.

La seconde est en la region des lombes en la partie droite, un poulce près de l'épine du dos et quatre doigts au-dessus les muscles de la fesse, en laquelle nous avons enfoncé l'aiguille trois travers de doigts, la laissons comme avions fait à la première plantée en cette partie quelque espace de temps, sans toutefois que le dit Gaufridy ait senti aucune douleur et que sang ni humeur quelconque en soit sorti.

La troisième est vers la région du cœur. Laquelle, au commencement qu'on mit l'aiguille parut comme les autres sans sentiment; mais à mesure que l'on enfonçait fort avant, il dit sentir quelque douleur; ne sortant toutefois aucune humidité, et l'ayant visité le lendemain au matin, n'avons reconnu aux parties piquées ni tumeur, ni rougeur. A cause de quoi nous disons telles marques insensibles en rendant point d'humidité étant piquées, ne pouvoir arriver par aucune maladie du cuir précédante, et tel faisons notre rapport ce 10 mars, 1611. *Fontaine, Grassy*, médecins; *Mérindol, Bontemps*, chirurgiens.

So great was the importance attached to the discovery of a witch-mark upon the body of the accused that when the above medico-legal report was read in court, Father Sebastian Michaelis, a learned Dominican, who was acting as consultor in the case, horror-struck, involuntarily exclaimed: "Good sooth, were we at Avignon this man would be executed to-morrow!" Gaufridi confessed: "J'advoue que les dites marques sont faites pour protestation qu'on sera toujours bon et fidèle serviteur du diable toute la vie." (I confess that these marks were made as a sign that I shall be a good and faithful servant to the Devil all my life long.)

[60] Pitcairn, *Records of Justiciary.* In 1663 Kincaid was thrown into jail, where he lay nine weeks for "pricking" without a magistrate's warrant. He was only released owing to his great age and on condition that he would "prick" no more.

[61] This shaving of the head and body was the usual procedure before the search for the devil-mark. We find it recorded in nearly every case. Generally a barber was called in to perform the operation: e.g. the trials of Gaufridi and Grandier, where the details are very ample.

[62] *The Wardlaw Manuscript*, p. 446. Scottish History Society publication, Edinburgh.

[63] *The Witch-Cult in Western Europe*, p. 86.

[64] Angelica in *Love for Love* (1695), II, mocking her superstitious old uncle, Foresight, and the Nurse, cries: "Look to it, Nurse; I can bring Witness that you have a great unnatural Teat under your Left Arm, and he another; and that you Suckle a young Devil in the shape of a Tabby-Cat by turns, I can."

[65] *The most wonderfull . . . storie of a . . . Witch named Alse Gooderidge.* London. 1597.

[66] Goodcole's *Wonderfull Discoverie of Elizabeth Sawyer*, London, 1621. There is an allusion in Ford and Dekker's drama, IV:

Sawyer. My dear *Tom-boy*, welcome . . .
Comfort me: thou shalt haue the teat anon.
Dog. Bow, wow! I'll haue it now.

[67] W. B. Gerish. *The Devil's Delusions*, Bishops Stortford, 1914.

[68] *Prodigious and Tragicall Histories*, London, 1652.

[69] W. B. Gerish, *Relation of Mary Hall of Gadsden*, 1912

[70] T. B. Howell, *State Trials*, London, 1816.

[71] Cotton Mather, *Wonders of the Invisible World.*

CHAPTER III

Demons and Familiars

One of the most authoritative of the older writers upon Witchcraft, Francesco-Maria Guazzo, a member of the Congregation of S. Ambrose ad Nemus,[1] in his encyclopædic *Compendium Maleficarum*, first published at Milan, 1608, has drawn up under eleven heads those articles in which a solemn and complete profession of Witchcraft was then held to consist:

First: The candidates have to conclude with the Devil, or some other Wizard or Magician acting in the Devil's stead, an express compact by which, in the presence of witnesses they devote themselves to the service of evil, he giving them in exchange his pledge for riches, luxury, and such things as they desire.

Secondly: They abjure the Catholic Faith, explicitly withdraw from their obedience to God, renounce Christ and in a particular manner the Patronage and Protection of Our Lady, curse all Saints, and forswear the Sacraments. In Guernsey, in 1617, Isabel Becquet went to Rocquaine Castle, "the usual place where the Devil kept his Sabbath: no sooner had she arrived there than the Devil came to her in the form of a dog, with two great horns sticking up: and with one of his paws (which seemed to her like hands) took her by the hand: and calling her by her name told her that she was welcome: then immediately the Devil made her kneel down: while he himself stood up on his hind legs; he then made her express detestation of the Eternal in these words: *I renounce God the Father, God the Son, and God the Holy Ghost;* and then caused her to worship and invoke himself."[2] De Lancre tells us that Jeannette d'Abadie, a lass of sixteen, confessed that she was made to "renounce & deny her Creator, the Holy Virgin, the Saints, Baptism, father, mother, relations, Heaven, earth, & all that the world contains."[3]

In a very full confession made by Louis Gaufridi on the second of April, 1611, to two Capuchins, Father Ange and Father Antoine, he revealed the formula of his abjuration of the Catholic faith. It ran thus: "I, Louis Gaufridi, renounce all good, both spiritual as well as temporal, which may be bestowed upon me by God, the Blessed Virgin Mary, all the Saints of Heaven, particularly my Patron S. John-Baptist, as also S. Peter, S. Paul, and S. Francis, and I give myself body and soul to Lucifer, before whom I stand, together with every good that I may ever possess (save always the benefit of the sacraments touching those who receive them). And according to the tenour of these terms have I signed and sealed."[4] Madeleine de la Palud, one of his victims, used a longer and more detailed declaration in which the following hideous blasphemies occurred: "With all my heart and most unfeignedly and with all my will most deliberately do I wholly renounce God, Father, Son, and Holy Ghost; the most Holy Mother of God; all the Angels and especially my Guardian Angel, the Passion of Our Lord Jesus Christ, His Precious Blood and the merits thereof, my lot in Paradise, all the good inspirations which God may give me in the future, all prayers which are made or may be made for me."[5]

Thirdly: They cast away with contempt the most Holy Rosary, delivered by Our Lady to S. Dominic;[6] the Cord of S. Francis; the cincture of S. Augustine; the Carmelite scapular bestowed upon S. Simon Stock; they cast upon the ground and trample under their feet in the mire the Cross, Holy Medals, *Agnus Dei*,[7] should they possess such or carry them upon their persons. S. Francis girded himself with a rough rope in memory of the bonds wherewith Christ was bound during His Passion, and a white girdle with three knots has since formed part of the Franciscan habit. Sixtus IV, by his Bull *Exsupernæ dispositionis*, erected the Archconfraternity of the Cord of S. Francis in the basilica of the Sacro Convento at Assisi, enriching it with many Indulgences, favours which have been confirmed by pontiff after pontiff. Archconfraternities are erected not only in Franciscan but in many other churches and aggregated to the centre at Assisi. The Archconfraternity of Our Lady of Consolation, or of the Black Leathern Belt of S. Monica,

S. Augustine and S. Nicolas of Tolentino, took its rise from a vision of S. Monica, who received a black leathern belt from Our Lady. S. Augustine, S. Ambrose, and S. Simplicianus all wore such a girdle, which forms a distinctive feature of the dress of Augustinian Eremites. After the canonization of S. Nicolas of Tolentino it came into general use as an article of devotion, and Eugenius IV in 1439 erected the above Archconfraternity. A Bull of Gregory XIII *Ad ea* (15 July, 1575) confirmed this and added various privileges and Indulgences. The Archconfraternity is erected in Augustinian sanctuaries, from the General of which Order leave must be obtained for its extension to other churches.

Fourthly: All witches vow obedience and subjection into the hands of the Devil; they pay him homage and vassalage (often by obscene ceremonies), and lay their hands upon a large black book which is presented to them. They bind themselves by blasphemous oaths never to return to the true faith, to observe no divine precept, to do no good work, but to obey the Demon only and to attend without fail the nightly conventicles. They pledge themselves to frequent the midnight assemblies.[8] These conventicles or covens[9] (from *conuentus*) were bands or companies of witches, composed of men and women, apparently under the discipline of an officer, all of whom for convenience'sake belonged to the same district. Those who belonged to a coven were, it seems from the evidence at trials, bound to attend the weekly Esbat. The arrest of one member of a coven generally led to the implication of the rest. Cotton Mather remarks, "The witches are organized like Congregational Churches."

Fifthly: The witches promise to strive with all their power and to use every inducement and endeavour to draw other men and women to their detestable practices and the worship of Satan.

The witches were imbued with the missionary spirit, which made them doubly damnable in the eyes of the divines and doubly guilty in the eyes of the law. So in the case of Janet Breadheid of Auldearne, we find that her husband "enticed her into that craft."[10] A girl named Bellot, of Madame Bourignon's academy, confessed that her mother had taken her to the Sabbat when she was quite a child. Another girl alleged that all worshippers of the Devil "are constrained to offer him their Children." Elizabeth Francis of Chelmsford, a witch tried in 1566, was only about twelve years old when her grandmother first taught her the art of sorcery.[11] The famous Pendle beldame, Elizabeth Demdike "brought vp her owne Children, instructed her Graundchildren, and tooke great care and paines to bring them to be Witches."[12] At Salem, George Burroughs, a minister, was accused by a large number of women as "the person who had Seduc'd and Compell'd them into the snares of Witchcraft."

Sixthly: The Devil administers to witches a kind of sacrilegious baptism, and after abjuring their Godfathers and Godmothers of Christian Baptism and Confirmation they have assigned to them new sponsors—as it were—whose charge it is to instruct them in sorcery: they drop their former name and exchange it for another, generally a scurrilous and grotesque nickname.

In 1609 Jeanette d'Abadie, a witch of the Basses-Pyrénées, confessed "that she often saw children baptized at the Sabbat, and these she informed us were the offspring of sorcerers and not of other persons, but of witches who are accustomed to have their sons and daughters baptized at the Sabbat rather than at the Font."[13] June 20, 1614, at Orleans, Silvain Nevillon amongst other crimes acknowledged that he had frequented assemblies of witches, and "that they baptize babies at the Sabbat with Chrism. . . . Then they anoint the child's head therewith muttering certain Latin phrases."[14] Gentien le Clerc, who was tried at the same time, "said that his mother, as he had been told, presented him at the Sabbat when he was but three years old, to a monstrous goat, whom they called l'Aspic. He said that he was baptized at the Sabbat, at Carrior d'Olivet, with fourteen or fifteen other children. . . ."[15]

Among the confessions made by Louis Gaufridi at Aix in March, 1611, were: "I confess that baptism is administered at the Sabbat, and that every sorcerer, devoting himself to the Devil, binds himself by a particular vow that he will have all his children baptized at the Sabbat, if this may by any possible means be effected. Every child who is thus baptized at the Sabbat receives a name, wholly differing from his own name. I confess that at this baptism water, sulphur, and salt are employed: the sulphur renders the recipient the Devil's slave whilst salt confirms his baptism in the Devil's service. I confess that the form and intention are to baptize in the name of Lucifer, Belzebuth and other demons making the sign of the cross beginning backwards and then tracing from the feet and ending at the head."[16]

A number of Swedish witches (1669) were baptized: "they added, that he caused them to be baptized too by such Priests as he had there, and made them confirm their Baptism with dreadful Oaths and Imprecations."[17]

The giving of a new name seems to have been very general. Thus in May, 1569, at S. Andrews "a notabill sorceres callit Nicniven was condemnit to the death and burnt." Her Christian name is not given merely her witch's name bestowed by the demon. In the famous Fian case it was stated that when at the meeting in North Berwick kirk Robert Grierson was named great confusion ensued for the witches and warlocks "all ran hirdie-girdie, and were angry, for it was promised that he should be called Robert the Comptroller, for the expriming of his name."[18] Euphemia McCalyan of the same coven was called Cane, and Barbara Napier Naip. Isabel Goudie of Auldearne (1662) stated that many witches known to her had been baptized in their own blood by such names as "Able-and-Stout," "Over-the-dike-with-it," "Raise-the-wind," "Pickle-nearest-the-wind," "Batter-them-down-Maggy," "Blow-Kate," and similar japeries.

Seventhly: The witches cut off a piece of their own garments, and as a token of homage tender it to the Devil, who takes it away and keeps it.

Eighthly: The Devil draws on the ground a circle wherein stand the Novices, Wizards, and Witches, and there they confirm by oath all their aforesaid promises. This has a mystical signification. "They take this oath to the Demon standing in a circle described upon the ground, perchance because a circle is the Symbol of Divinity, & the earth God's footstool and thus he assuredly wishes them to believe that he is the lord of Heaven and earth."[19]

Ninthly: The sorcerers request the Devil to strike them out of the book of Christ, and to inscribe them in his own. Then is solemnly brought forward a large black book, the same as that on which they laid their hands when they did their first homage, and they are inscribed in this by the Devil's claw.

These books or rolls were kept with great secrecy by the chief officer of the coven or even the Grand Master of a district. They would have been guarded as something as precious as life itself, seeing that they contained the damning evidence of a full list of the witches of a province or county, and in addition thereto seems to have been added a number of magic formulæ, spells, charms, and probably, from time to time, a record of the doings of the various witches. The signing of such a book is continually referred to in the New England trials. So when Deliverance Hobbs had made a clean breast of her sorceries, " She now testifi'd, that this *Bishop* [Bridget Bishop, condemned and executed as a long-continued witch] tempted her to sign the *Book* again, and to deny what she had confess'd." The enemies of the notorious Matthew Hopkins made great capital out of the story that by some sleight of sorcery he had got hold of one of these Devil's memorandum-books, whence he copied a list of witches, and this it was that enabled him to be so infallible in his scent. The Witch-Finder General was hard put to it to defend himself from the accusation, and becomes quite pitiful in his whining asseverations of innocence. There is a somewhat vague story, no dates being given, that a Devil's book was carried off by Mr. Williamson of Cardrona (Peebles), who filched it from the witches whilst they were dancing on Minchmoor. But the whole coven at once gave chase, and he was glad to abandon it and escape alive.

Sometimes the catalogue of witches was inscribed on a separate parchment, and the book only used to write down charms and spells. Such a volume was the Red Book of Appin known to have actually been in existence a hundred years ago. Tradition said it was stolen from the Devil by a trick. It was in manuscript, and contained a large number of magic runes and incantations for the cure of cattle diseases, the increase of flocks, the fertility of fields. This document, which must be of immense importance and interest, when last heard of was (I believe) in the possession of the now-extinct Stewarts of Invernahyle. This strange volume, so the story ran, conferred dark powers on the owner, who knew what inquiry would be made ere the question was poised;

and the tome was so confected with occult arts that he who read it must wear a circlet of iron around his brow as he turned those mystic pages.

Another volume, of which mention is made—one that is often confused[20] with, but should be distinguished from, these two—is what we may term the Devil's Missal. Probably this had its origin far back in the midst of the centuries among the earliest heretics who passed down their evil traditions to their followers, the Albigenses and the Waldenses or Vaudois. This is referred to by the erudite De Lancre, who in his detailed account of the Black Mass as performed in the region of the Basses-Pyrénées (1609) writes: "Some kind of altar was erected upon the pillars of infernal design, and hereon, without reciting the *Confiteor* or *Alleluya*, turning over the leaves of a certain book which he held, he began to mumble certain phrases of Holy Mass."[21] Silvain Nevillon (Orleans, 1614) confessed that "the Sabbat was held in a house. . . . He saw there a tall dark man opposite to the one who was in a corner of the ingle, and this man was perusing a book, whose leaves seemed black & crimson, & he kept muttering between his teeth although what he said could not be heard, and presently he elevated a black host and then a chalice of some cracked pewter, all foul and filthy."[22] Gentien le Clerc, who was also accused, acknowledged that at these infernal assemblies "Mass was said, and the Devil was celebrant. He was vested in a chasuble upon which was a broken cross. He turned his back to the altar when he was about to elevate the Host and the Chalice, which were both black. He read in a mumbling tone from a book, the cover of which was soft and hairy like a wolf's skin. Some leaves were white and red, others black."[23] Madeleine Bavent, who was the chief figure in the trials at Louviers (1647), acknowledged: "Mass was read from the book of blasphemies, which contained the canon. This same volume was used in processions. It was full of the most hideous curses against the Holy Trinity, the Holy Sacrament of the Altar, the other Sacraments and ceremonies of the Church. It was written in a language completely unknown to me."[24] Possibly this blasphemous volume is the same as that which Satanists to-day use when performing their abominable rites.

Tenthly: The witches promise the Devil sacrifices and

offerings at stated times; once a fortnight, or at least once a month, the murder of some child, or some mortal poisoning, and every week to plague mankind with evils and mischiefs, hailstorms, tempest, fires, cattle-plagues and the like.

The *Liber Pœnitentialis* of S. Theodore, Archbishop of Canterbury 668–690, the earliest ecclesiastical law of England, has clauses condemning those who invoke fiends, and so cause the weather to change "si quis emissor tempestatis fuerit." In the *Capitaluria* of Charlemagne (died at Aachen, 28 January, 814), the punishment of death is declared against those who by evoking the demon, trouble the atmosphere, excite tempests, destroy the fruits of the earth, dry up the milk of cows, and torment their fellow-creatures with diseases or any other misfortune. All persons found guilty of employing such arts were to be executed immediately upon conviction. Innocent VIII in his celebrated Bull, *Summis desiderantes affectibus*, 5 December, 1484, charges sorcerers in detail with precisely the same foul practices. The most celebrated occasion when witches raised a storm was that which played so important a part in the trial of Dr. Fian and his coven, 1590–1, when the witches, in order to drown King James and Queen Anne on their voyage from Denmark, "tooke a Cat and christened it," and after they had bound a dismembered corpse to the animal "in the night following the said Cat was convayed into the middest of the sea by all these witches, sayling in their riddles or cives, . . . this doone, then did arise such a tempest in the sea, as a greater hath not bene seene."[25] The bewitching of cattle is alleged from the earliest time, and at Dornoch in Sutherland as late as 1722, an old hag was burned for having cast spells upon the pigs and sheep of her neighbours, the sentence being pronounced by the sheriff-depute, Captain David Ross of Little Dean. This was the last execution of a witch in Scotland.

With regard to the sacrifice of children there is a catena of ample evidence. Reginald Scot[26] writes in 1584: "This must be an infallible rule, that euerie fortnight, or at the least euerie month, each witch must kill one child at the least for hir part." When it was dangerous or impossible openly to murder an infant the life would be taken by poison, and in 1645 Mary Johnson, a witch of Wyvenhoe, Essex, was tried for poisoning two children, no doubt as an act of sorcery.[27] It is unknown how many children Gilles de Rais devoted to death in his impious orgies. More than two hundred corpses were found in the latrines of Tiffauges, Machecoul, Champtocé. It was in 1666 that Louis XIV was first informed of the abominations which were vermiculating his capital "des sacrilèges, des profanations, des messes impies, des sacrifices de jeunes enfants." Night after night in the rue Beauregard at the house of the mysterious Catherine la Voisin the abbé Guibourg was wont to kill young children for his hideous ritual, either by strangulation or more often by piercing their throats with a sharp dagger and letting the hot blood stream into the chalice as he cried: "Astaroth, Asmodée, je vous conjure d'accepter le sacrifice que je vous présente!" (Astaroth! Asmodeus! Receive, I beseech you, this sacrifice I offer unto you!) A priest named Tournet also said Satanic Masses at which children were immolated; in fact the practice was so common that la Chaufrein, a mistress of Guibourg, would supply a child for a crown[28] piece.

Eleventhly: The Demon imprints upon the Witches some mark. . . . When this has all been performed in accordance with the instructions of those Masters who have initiated the Novice, the latter bind themselves by fearful oaths never to worship the Blessed Sacrament; to heap curses on all Saints and especially to abjure our Lady Immaculate; to trample under foot and spit upon all holy images, the Cross and Relics of Saints; never to use the Sacraments or Sacramentals unless with some magical end in view; never to make a good confession to the priest, but always to keep hidden their commerce with hell. In return the Demon promises that he will at all times afford them prompt assistance; that he will accomplish all their desires in this world and make them eternally happy after their death. This solemn profession having been publicly made each novice has assigned to him a several demon who is called *Magistellus* (a familiar). This familiar can assume either a male or a female shape; sometimes he appears as a full-grown man, sometimes as a satyr; and if it is a woman who has been received as a witch he generally assumes the form of a rank buck-goat.

It is obvious that there is no question here of animal familiars, but rather of evil intelligences who were, it is believed, able to assume a body of flesh. The whole question is, perhaps, one of the most dark and difficult connected with Witchcraft and magic, and the details of these hideous connexions are such—for as the Saints attain to the purity of angels, so, on the other hand, will the bond slaves of Satan defile themselves with every kind of lewdness—that many writers have with an undue diffidence and modesty dismissed the subject far too summarily for the satisfaction of the serious inquirer. In the first place, we may freely allow that many of these lubricities are to be ascribed to hysteria and hallucinations, to nightmare and the imaginings of disease, but when all deductions have been made—when we admit that in many cases the incubus or succubus can but have been a human being, some agent of the Grand Master of the district,—none the less enough remains from the records of the trials to convince an unprejudiced mind that there was a considerable substratum of fact in the confessions of the accused. As Canon Ribet has said in his encyclopædic *La Mystique Divine*, a work warmly approved by the great intellect of Leo XIII: "After what we have learned from records and personal confessions we can scarcely entertain any more doubts, and it is our plain duty to oppose, even if it be but by a simple affirmation on our part, those numerous writers who, either through presumption or rashness, treat these horrors as idle talk or mere hallucination."[29] Bizouard also in his authoritative *Rapports de l'homme avec le démon* writes of the incubus and succubus: "These relations, far from being untrue, bear the strongest marks of authenticity which can be given them by official proceedings regulated and approved with all the caution and judgement brought to bear upon them by enlightened and conscientious magistrates who, throughout all ages, have been in a position to test plain facts."[30]

It seems to me that if unshaken evidence means anything at all, if the authority of the ablest and acutest intellects of all ages in all countries is not to count for merest vapourings and fairy fantasies, the possibility—I do not, thank God, say the frequency—of these demoniacal connexions is not to be denied. Of course the mind already resolved that such things cannot be is inconvincible even by demonstration, and one can only fall back upon the sentence of S. Augustine: "Hanc assidue immunditiam et tentare et efficere, plures talesque asseuerant, ut hoc negare impudentiæ uideatur."[31] In which place the holy doctor explicitly declares: "Seeing it is so general a report, and so many aver it either from their own experience or from others, that are of indubitable honesty and credit, that the sylvans and fawns, commonly called incubi, have often injured women, desiring and acting carnally with them: and that certain devils whom the Gauls call *Duses*, do continually practise this uncleanness, and tempt others to it, which is affirmed by such persons, and with such confidence that it were impudence to deny it."

The learned William of Paris, confessor of Philip le Bel, lays down: "That there exist such beings as are commonly called incubi or succubi and that they indulge their burning lusts, and that children, as it is freely acknowledged, can be born from them, is attested by the unimpeachable and unshaken witness of many men and women who have been filled with foul imaginings by them, and endured their lecherous assaults and lewdness."[32]

S. Thomas[33] and S. Bonaventura,[34] also, speak quite plainly on the subject.

Francisco Suarez, the famous Jesuit theologian, writes with caution but with directness: "This is the teaching on this point of S. Thomas, who is generally followed by all other theologians. . . . The reason for their opinion is this: Such an action considered in its entirety by no means exceeds the natural powers of the demon, whilst the exercise of such powers is wholly in accordance with the malice of the demon, and it may well be permitted by God, owing to the sins of some men. Therefore this teaching cannot be denied without many reservations and exceptions. Wherefore S. Augustine has truly said, that inasmuch as this doctrine of incubi and succubi is established by the opinion of many who are experienced and learned, it were sheer impudence to deny it."[35] The Salmanticenses—that is to say, the authors of the courses of Scholastic philosophy and theology, and of Moral theology, published by the lecturers of the theological college of the Discalced Carmelites at Salamanca—in their weighty *Theologia Moralis*[36] state: "Some deny this, believing it impossible that demons should perform the carnal act with human beings," but they affirm, " None the less the opposite opinion is most certain and must be followed."[37] Charles René Billuart, the celebrated Dominican, in his *Tractatus de Angelis* expressly declares: " The same evil spirit may serve as a succubus to a man, and as an incubus to a woman."[38] One of the most learned—if not the most learned—of the popes, Benedict XIV, in his erudite work *De Seruorum Dei Beatificatione,* treats this whole question at considerable length with amplest detail and solid references, Liber IV, Pars i. c. 3.[39] Commenting upon the passage " The sons of God went unto the daughters of men " (Genesis vi. 4), the pontiff writes: " This passage has reference to those Demons who are known as incubi and succubi. . . . It is true that whilst nearly all authors admit the fact, some writers deny that there can be offspring. . . . On the other hand, several writers assert that connexion of this kind is possible and that children may be born from it, nay, indeed, they tell us that this has taken place, although it were done in some new and mysterious way which is ordinarily unknown to man."[40]

S. Alphonsus Liguori in his *Praxis confessariorum,* VII, n.111, writes: " Some deny that there are evil spirits, incubi and succubi; but writers of authority for the most part assert that such is the case."[41]

In his *Theologia Moralis* he speaks quite precisely when defining the technical nature of the sin witches commit in commerce with incubi.[42] [43] This opinion is also that of Martino Bonacina,[44] and of Vincenzo Filliucci, S.J.[45] "Busembaum has excellently observed that carnal sins with an evil spirit fall under the head of the technical term *bestialitas.*"[46] This is also the conclusion of Thomas Tamburini, S.J. (1591–1675); Benjamin Elbel, O.F.M. (1690–1756);[47] Cardinal Cajetan, O.P. (1469–1534) " the lamp of the Church "; Juan Azor, S.J. (1535–1603); " in wisdom, in depth of learning and in gravity of judgement taking deservedly high rank among theologians " (Gury); and many other authorities.[48] What a penitent should say in confession is considered by Monsignor Craisson, sometime Rector of the Grand Seminary of Valence and Vicar-General of the diocese, in his Tractate *De Rebus Uenereis ad usum Confessariorum.*[49] Jean-Baptiste Bouvier (1783–1854) the famous bishop of Le Mans, in his *Dissertatio in Sextum Decalogi Præceptum*[50] (p. 78) writes: "All theologians speak of . . . evil spirits who appear in the shape of a man, a woman, or even some animal. This is either a real and actual presence, or the effect of imagination. They decide that this sin . . . incurs particular guilt which must be specifically confessed, to wit an evil superstition whereof the essence is a compact with the Devil. In this sin, therefore, we have two distinct kinds of malice, one an offence against chastity; the other against our holy faith."[51] Dom Dominic Schram,[52] O.S.B., in his *Institutiones Theologiæ Mysticæ* poses the following: "The inquiry is made whether a demon . . . may thus attack a man or woman, whose obsession would be suffered if the subject were wholly bent upon obtaining perfection and walking the highest paths of contemplation. Here we must distinguish the true and the false. It is certain that—whatever doubters may say—there exist such demons, incubi and succubi: and S. Augustine asserts (*The City of God*, Book XV, chapter 23) that it is most rash to advance the contrary. . . . S. Thomas, and most other theologians maintain this too. Wherefore the men or women who suffer these impudicities are sinners who either invite demons . . . or who freely consent to demons when the evil spirits tempt them to commit such abominations. That these and other abandoned wretches may be violently assaulted by the demon we cannot doubt . . . and I myself have known several persons who although they were greatly troubled on account of their crimes, and utterly loathed this foul intercourse with the demon, were nevertheless compelled sorely against their will to endure these assaults of Satan."[53]

It will be seen that great Saints and scholars and all moral theologians of importance affirm the possibility of commerce with incarnate evil intelligences. The demonologists also range themselves in a solid phalanx of assent. Hermann Thyraus, S.J.,[54] in his *De Spirituum apparitione* says: "It is so rash and inept to deny these (things) that so to adopt this attitude you must needs reject and spurn the most weighty and considered judgements of most holy and authoritative writers, nay, you must wage war upon man's sense and consciousness, whilst at the same time you expose your ignorance of the power of the Devil and the empery evil spirits may obtain over man."[55] Delrio, in his *Dis-*

quisitiones Magicæ, is even more emphatic : "So many sound authors and divines have upheld this belief that to differ from them is mere obstinacy and foolhardiness; for the Fathers, theologians, and all the wisest writers on philosophy agree upon this matter, the truth of which is furthermore proved by the experience of all ages and peoples."[56] The erudite Sprenger in the *Malleus Maleficarum* has much the same.[57] John Nider, O.P. (1380–1438) in his *Formicarius*, which may be described as a treatise on the theological, philosophical, and social problems of his day, with no small acumen remarks : "The reason why evil spirits appear as incubi and succubi would seem to be that . . . they inflict a double hurt on man, both in his soul and body, and it is a supreme joy to devils thus to injure humankind."[58] Paul Grilland in his *De Sortilegio* (Lyons, 1533) writes : "A demon assumes the form of the succubus. . . . This is the explicit teaching of the theologians."[59]

"It has often been known by most certain and actual experience that women in spite of their resistance have been overpowered by demons." Such are the words of the famous Alfonso de Castro, O.F.M.,[60] whose authoritative pronouncements upon Scripture carried such weight at the Council of Trent, and who was Archbishop-elect of Compostella when he died. Pierre Binsfeld, *De confessione maleficarum*, sums up : "This is a most solemn and undoubted fact not only proved by actual experience, but also by the opinion of all the ages, whatever some few doctors and legal writers may suppose."[61]

Gaspar Schott, S.J. (1608–66), physicist, doctor, and divine, "one of the most learned men of his day, his simple life and deep piety making him an object of veneration to the Protestants as well as to the Catholics of Augsburg," where his declining years were spent, lays down : "So many writers of such high authority maintain this opinion, that it were impossible to reject it."[62] Bodin, de Lancre, Boguet, Görres, Bizouard,[63] Gougenot des Mousseaux,[64] insist upon the same sad facts. And above all sounds the solemn thunder of the Bull of Innocent VIII announcing in no ambiguous phrase : "It has indeed come to our knowledge and deeply grieved are we to hear it, that many persons of both sexes, utterly forgetful of their souls' salvation and straying far from the Catholic Faith, have (had commerce) with evil spirits, both incubi and succubi."[65]

I have quoted many and great names, men of science, men of learning, men of authority, men to whom the world yet looks up with admiration, nay, with reverence and love, inasmuch as to-day it is difficult, wellnigh inconceivable in most cases, for the modern mind to credit the possibility of these dark deeds of devilry, these foul lusts of incubi and succubi.[66] They seem to be some sick and loathly fantasy of dim mediæval days shrieked out on the rack by a poor wretch crazed with agony and fear, and written down in long-forgotten tomes by fanatics credulous to childishness and more ignorant than savages. "Even if such horrors ever could have taken place in the dark ages,"—those vague Dark Ages!—men say, "they would never be permitted now." And he who knows, the priest sitting in the grated confessional, in whose ears are poured for shriving the filth and folly of the world, sighs to himself, "Would God that in truth it were so!" But the sceptics are happier in their singleness and their simplicity, happy that they do not, will not, realize the monstrous things that lie only just beneath the surface of our cracking civilization.

It may not impertinently be inquired how demons or evil intelligences, since they are pure spiritual beings, can not only assume human flesh but perform the peculiarly carnal act of coition. Sinistrari, following the opinion of Guazzo, says that either the evil intelligence is able to animate the corpse of some human being, male or female, as the case may be, or that, from the mixture of other materials he shapes for himself a body endowed with motion, by means of which he is united to the human being: "ex mixtione aliarum materiarum effingit sibi corpus, quod mouet, et mediante quo homini unitur."[67] In the first instance, advantage might be taken, no doubt, of a person in a mediumistic trance or hypnotic sleep. But the second explanation seems by far the more probable. Can we not look to the phenomena observed in connexion with ectoplasm as an adequate explanation of this? It must fairly be admitted that this explanation is certainly borne out by the phenomena of the materializing séance where physical forms which may be touched and handled are built up and disintegrated again in a few moments of time. Miss Scatcherd, in a symposium, *Survival*,[68] gives certain of her own experiences that go far to prove the partial re-materialization of the dead by the utilization of the material substance and ectoplasmic emanations of the living. And if disembodied spirits can upon occasion, however rare, thus materialize, why not evil intelligences whose efforts at corporeality are urged and aided by the longing thoughts and concentrated will power of those who eagerly seek them ?

This explanation is further rendered the more probable by the recorded fact that the incubus can assume the shape of some person whose embraces the witch may desire.[69] Brignoli, in his *Alexicacon*, relates that when he was at Bergamo in 1650, a young man, twenty-two years of age, sought him out and made a long and ample confession. This youth avowed that some months before, when he was in bed, the chamber door opened and a maiden, Teresa, whom he loved, stealthily entered the room. To his surprise she informed him that she had been driven from home and had taken refuge with him. Although he more than suspected some delusion, after a short while he consented to her solicitations and passed a night of unbounded indulgence in her arms. Before dawn, however, the visitant revealed the true nature of the deceit, and the young man realized he had lain with a succubus. None the less such was his doting folly that the same debauchery was repeated night after night, until struck with terror and remorse, he sought the priest to confess and be delivered from this abomination. "This monstrous connexion lasted several months; but at last God delivered him by my humble means, and he was truly penitent for his sins."[70]

Not infrequently the Devil or the familiar assigned to the new witch at the Sabbat when she was admitted must obviously have been a man, one of the assembly, who either approached her in some demoniacal disguise or else embraced her without any attempt at concealment of his individuality, some lusty varlet who would afterwards hold himself at her disposition. For we must always bear in mind that throughout these witch-trials there is often much in the evidence which may be explained by the agency of human beings; not that this essentially meliorates their offences, for they were all bond-slaves of Satan, acting under his direction and by the inspiration of hell. When the fiend has ministers devoted to his service there is, perhaps, less need for his interposition *in propria persona.* Howbeit, again and again in these cases we meet with that uncanny quota, by no means insignificant and unimportant, which seemingly admits of no solution save by the materialization of evil intelligences of power. And detailed as is the evidence we possess, it not unseldom becomes a matter of great difficulty, when we are considering a particular case, to decide whether it be an instance of a witch having had actual commerce and communion with the fiend, or whether she was cheated by the devils, who mocked her, and allowing her to deem herself in overt union with them, thus led the wretch on to misery and death, duped as she was by the father of lies, sold for a delusion and by profitless endeavour in evil. There are, of course, also many cases which stand on the border-line, half hallucination, half reality. Sylvine de la Plaine, a witch of twenty-three, who was condemned by the Parliament of Paris, 17 May, 1616, was one of these.[71] Antoinette Brenichon, a married woman, aged thirty, made a confession in almost exactly the same words. Sylvine, her husband Barthélemi Minguet, and Brenichon were hanged and their bodies burned.

Henri Boguet, a Judge of the High Court of Burgundy, in his *Discours des Sorciers*, devotes chapter xii to "The carnal connexion of the Demons with Witches and Sorcerers." He discusses: 1. The Devil knows all the Witches, & why. 2. He takes a female shape to pleasure the Sorcerers, & why. 3. Other reasons why the Devil (has to do) with warlocks and witches.[72] Françoise Secretain, Claude Ianprost, Iaquema Paget, Antoine Tornier, Antoine Gandillon, Clauda Ianguillaume, Thieuenne Paget, Rolande du Vernois, Ianne Platet, Clauda Paget, and a number of other witches confessed "their dealings with the Devil."[73] Pierre Gandillon and his son George also confessed to commerce with the Demon. Under his third division Boguet lays down explicit statements on the matter.[74] [75]

This unnatural physical coldness of the Demon is commented upon again and again by witches at their trials in every country of Europe throughout the centuries. I have already suggested that in some cases there was a full materialization due to ectoplasmic emanations. Now, ectoplasm is described[76] as being to the touch a cold and viscous mass comparable to contact with a reptile, and this certainly seems to throw a flood of light upon these details. It may be that here indeed we have a solution of the whole mystery. In 1645 the widow Bash, a Suffolk witch, of Barton, said that the Devil who appeared to her as a dark swarthy youth "was colder than man."[77] Isobel Goudie and Janet Breadheid, of the Auldearne coven, 1662, both asserted that the Devil was "a meikle, blak, rock man, werie cold; and I fand his nature als cold, a spring-well-water."[78] Isabel, who had been rebaptized at a Sabbat held one midnight in Auldearne parish church, and to whom was assigned a familiar named the Red Riever, albeit he was always clad in black, gave further details of the Devil's person: "He is abler for ws that way than any man can be, onlie he ves heavie lyk a malt-sek; a hudg nature, uerie cold, as yce."[79]

In many of the cases of debauchery at Sabbats so freely and fully confessed by the witches their partners were undoubtedly the males who were present; the Grand Master, Officer, or President of the Assembly, exercising the right to select first for his own pleasures such women as he chose. This is clear from a passage in De Lancre: "The Devil at the Sabbat performs marriages between the warlocks and witches, and joining their hands, he pronounces aloud

Esta es buena parati
Esta parati lo toma."[80]

And in many cases it is obvious that use must have been made of an instrument, an artificial phallus employed.[81]

The artificial penis was a commonplace among the erotica of ancient civilizations; there is abundant evidence of its use in Egypt, Assyria, India, Mexico, all over the world. It has been found in tombs; frequently was it to be seen as an ex-voto; in a slightly modified form it is yet the favourite mascot of Southern Italy.[82] Often enough they do not trouble to disguise the form. Aristophanes mentions the object in his *Lysistrata* (411 B.C.), and one of the most spirited dialogues (VI) of Herodas (*circa* 300–250 B.C.) is that where Koritto and Metro prattle prettily of their *βαύβων*, whilst (in another mime, VII) the ladies visit Kerdon the leather-worker who has fashioned this masterpiece. Truly Herodas is as modern to-day in London or in Paris as he ever was those centuries ago in the isle of Cos. *Fascinum*, explains the *Glossarium Eroticum Linguæ Latinæ*,[83] "Penis fictitius ex corio, aut pannis lineis uel sericis, quibus mulieres uirum mentiebantur. Antiquissima libido, lesbiis et milesiis feminis præsertim usitatissima. *Fascinis* illis abutebantur meretrices in tardos ascensores." As one might expect Petronius has something to say on the subject in a famous passage where that savage old hag[84] Œnothea fairly frightened Encolpius with her *scorteum fascinum*, upon which an erudite Spanish scholar, Don Antonio Gonzalez de Salas, glosses: "Rubrum penem coriaceum ut Suidas exsertim tradit uoce φαλλόι. Confecti & ex uaria materia uarios in usus olim *phalli* ex ligno, *ficu* potissimum qui *ficulnei* sæpius adpellati, ex *ebore*, ex *auro*, ex *serico*, & ex *lineo panno*, quibus Lesbiæ tribades abutebantur."[85] And Tibullus, speaking of the image of Priapus, has:[86]

> Placet Priape? qui sub arboris coma
> Soles sacrum reuincte pampino caput
> Ruber sedere cum rubente fascino.

The Church, of course, condemned with unhesitating voice all such practices, whether they were connected (in however slight a degree) with Witchcraft or not. Arnobius, who regards all such offences as detestable, in his *Aduersus Nationes*, V (*circa* A.D. 296), relates a curiously obscene anecdote which seems to point to the use of the fascinum by the Galli, the priests of Berecynthian Cybele,[87] whose orgies were closely akin to those of Dionysus. And the same story is related by Clement of Alexandria Προτρεπτικὸς πρὸς Ἕλληνας (*circa* A.D. 190); by Julius Firmicus Maternus, *De Errore profanarum Religionum* (A.D. 337–350); by Nicetas (*ob. circa* A.D. 414) in a commentary on S. Gregory of Nanzianzus, oratio XXXIX; and by Theodoret (*ob. circa* A.D. 457) *Sermo octaua de Martyribus*. Obviously some very primitive rite is in question.

Lactantius, in his *De Falsa Religione* (*Diuinarum Institutionum*, I, *circa* A.D. 304), speaks of a phallic superstition, akin to the fascinum, as favoured by the vestals, and implies it was notoriously current in his day. That eminent father, S. Augustine, *De Ciuitate Dei*, VII, 21, gives some account of the fascinum as used in the rites of Bacchus, and when he is detailing the marriage ceremonies (VI, 9), he writes: "Sed quid hoc dicam, cum tibi sit et Priapus nimius masculus, super cuius immanissimum et turpissimum fascinum sedere nona nupta iubeatur, more honestissimo et religiosissimo matronarum." The historian, Evagrius Scholasticus (*ob.* post A.D. 504), in his *Historia Ecclesiastica* (XI, 2), says that the ritual of Priapus was quite open in his day, and the fascinum widely known. Nicephorus Calixtus, a later Byzantine, who died about the middle of the fourteenth century but whose Chronicle closed with the death of Leo Philosophus, A.D. 911, speaks of phallic ceremonies and of the use of ithy-phalli.[88]

Council after council forbade the use of the fascinum, and their very insistence of prohibition show how deeply these abominations had taken root. The Second Council of Châlon-sur-Saône (813) is quite plain and unequivocal; so are the synods of de Mano (1247) and Tours (1396). Burchard of Worms (died 25 Aug., 1025) in his famous *Decretum* has: "Fecisti quod quædam mulieres facere solent, ut facere quoddam molimen aut mechinamentum in modum uirilis membri, ad mensuram tuæ uoluptatis, et illud loco uerendorum tuorum, aut alterius, cum aliquibus ligaturis colligares, et fornicationem faceres cum aliis mulierculis, uel aliæ eodem instrumento, siue alio, tecum? Si fecisti, quinque annos per legitimas ferias pœniteas." And again: "Fecisti quod quædam mulieres facere solent, ut iam supra dicto molimine uel alio aliquo machinamento, tu ipsa in te solam faceres fornicationem? Si fecisti, unum annum per legitimas ferias pœniteas."

Other old Penitentials have: "Mulier qualicumque molimine aut per seipsum aut cum altera fornicans, tres annos pœniteat; unum ex his in pane et aqua."

"Cum sanctimoniali per machinam fornicans annos septem pœniteat; duos ex his in pane et aqua."

"Mulia qualicumque molimine aut seipsam polluens, aut cum altera fornicans, quatuor annos. Sanctimonialis femina cum sanctimoniali per machinamentum polluta, septem annos."

It is demonstrable, then, that artificial methods of coition, common in pagan antiquity, have been unblushingly practised throughout all the ages, as indeed they are at the present day, and that they have been repeatedly banned and reprobated by the voice of the Church. This very fact would recommend them to the favour of the Satanists, and there can be no doubt that amid the dark debaucheries which celebrated the Sabbats such practice was wellnigh universal. Yet when we sift the evidence, detailed and exact, of the trials, we find there foul and hideous mysteries of lust which neither human intercourse nor the employ of a mechanical property can explain. Howbeit, the theologians and the inquisitors are fully aware what unspeakable horror lurks in the blackness beyond.

The animal familiar was quite distinct from the familiar in human shape. In England particularly there is abundance of evidence concerning them, and even to-day who pictures a witch with nut-cracker jaws, steeple hat, red cloak, hobbling along on her crutch, without her big black cat beside her? It is worth remark that in other countries the domestic animal familiar is rare, and Bishop Francis Hutchinson even says: "I meet with little mention of *Imps* in any Country but ours, where the Law makes the feeding, suckling, or rewarding of them to be Felony."[89] Curiously enough this familiar is most frequently met with in Essex, Suffolk, and the Eastern counties. We find that animals of all kinds were regarded as familiars; dogs, cats, ferrets, weasels, toads, rats, mice, birds, hedgehogs, hares, even wasps, moths, bees, and flies. It is piteous to think that in many cases some miserable creature who, shunned and detested by her fellows, has sought friendship in the love of a cat or a dog, whom she has fondled and lovingly fed with the best tit-bits she could give, on the strength of this affection alone was dragged to the gallows or the stake. But very frequently the witch did actually keep some small animal which she nourished on a diet of milk and bread and her own blood in order that she might divine by its means. The details of this particular method of augury are by no means clear. Probably the witch observed the gait of the animals, its action, the tones of its voice easily interpreted to bear some fanciful meaning, and no doubt a dog, or such a bird as a raven, a daw, could be taught tricks to impress the simplicity of inquirers.

The exceeding importance of blood in life has doubtless been evident to man from the earliest times. Man experienced a feeling of weakness after the loss of blood, therefore blood was strength, life itself, and throughout the ages blood has been considered to be of the greatest therapeutic, and the profoundest magical, value. The few drops of blood the witch gave her familiar were not only a reward, a renewal of strength, but also they established a closer connexion between herself and the dog, cat, or bird as the case might be. Blood formed a psychic copula.

At the trial of Elizabeth Francis, Chelmsford, 1556, the accused confessed that her familiar, given to her by her grandmother, a notorious witch, was "in the lykenesse of a whyte spotted Catte," and her grandmother "taughte her to feede the sayde Catte with breade and mylke, and she did so, also she taughte her to cal it by the name of Sattan and to kepe it in a basket. Item that euery tyme that he did any thynge for her, she sayde that he required a drop of bloude, which she gaue him by prycking herselfe, sometime in one place and then in another."[90] It is superfluous to multiply instances; in the witch-trials of Essex, particularly whilst Matthew Hopkins and his satellite John Stearne were hot at work from 1645 to 1647 the animal familiar is mentioned again and again in the records. As late as 1694 at Bury St. Edmunds, when old Mother Munnings of Hartis, in Suffolk, was haled before Lord Chief Justice Holt, it was asserted that she had an imp like a polecat. But the judge pooh-poohed the evidence of a pack of clodpate rustics and directed the jury to bring a verdict of Not Guilty.[91] "Upon particular Enquiry," says Hutchinson, "of several in or near the Town, I find most are satisfied it was a very right Judgement." In 1712 the familiar of Jane Wenham, the witch of Walkerne, in Hertfordshire, was, at her trial, stated to be a cat.

In Ford and Dekker's *The Witch of Edmonton* the familiar appears upon the stage as a dog. This, of course, is directly taken from Henry Goodcole's pamphlet *The Wonderfull Discouerie of Elizabeth Sawyer* (London, 4to, 1621), where in answer to this question the witch confesses that the Devil came to her in the shape of a dog, and of two colours, sometimes of black and sometimes of white. Some children had informed the Court that they had seen her feeding imps, two white ferrets, with white bread and milk, but this she steadfastly denied. In Goethe's *Faust*, Part I, Scene 2, Mephistopheles first appears to Faust outside the city gates as a black poodle and accompanies him back to his study, snarling and yelping when *In Principio* is read. This is part of the old legend. Manlius (1590), in the report of his conversation with Melanchthon, quotes the latter as having said: "He [Faust] had a dog with him, which was the devil." Paolo Jovio relates[92] that the famous Cornelius Agrippa always kept a demon attendant upon him in the shape of a black dog. But John Weye, in his well-known work *De Præstigiis Dæmonum*,[93] informs us that he had lived for years in daily attendance upon Agrippa and that the black dog, *Monsieur*, respecting which such strange stories were spread was a perfectly innocent animal which he had often led about himself in its leash. Agrippa was much attached to his dog, which used to eat off the table with him and of nights lie in his bed. Since he was a profound scholar and a great recluse he never troubled to contradict the idle gossip his neighbours clacked at window and door. It is hardly surprising when one considers the hermetic works which go under Agrippa's name that even in his lifetime this great man should have acquired the reputation of a mighty magician.

Grotesque names were generally given to the familiar: Lizabet; Verd-Joli; Maître Persil (parsley); Verdelet; Martinet; Abrahel (a succubus); and to animal familiars in England, Tissy; Grissell; Greedigut; Blackman; Jezebel (a succubus); Ilemanzar; Jarmara; Pyewackett.

The familiar in human shape often companied with the witch and was visible to clairvoyants. Thus in 1324 one of the accusations brought against Lady Alice Kyteler was that a demon came to her "quandoque in specie cuiusdam æthiopis cum duobus sociis." The society met with at Sabbats is not so easily shaken off as might be wished.

NOTES TO CHAPTER III.

1 Two local Milanese Orders, the Apostolini of S. Barnabas and the Congregation of S. Ambrose *ad Nemus*, were united by a Brief of Sixtus V, 15 August, 1589. 11 January, 1606, Paul V approved the new Constitutions. The Congregation retaining very few members was dissolved by Innocent X in 1650. The habit was a tunic, broad scapular, and capuche of chestnut brown.

They were calced, and in the streets a wide cloak of the same colour as the habit.

[2] E. Goldsmid, *Confessions of Witches under Torture*, Edinburgh, 1886.

[3] . . . renoncer & renier son Createur, la saincte Vierge, les Saincts, le Baptesme, pere, mere, parens, le ciel, la terre & tout ce qui est au monde. *Tableau de l'Inconstance des mauvais Anges*, Paris, 1613.

[4] Je, Louis Gaufridi, renonce à tous les biens tant spirituels que temporels qui me pouvraient être conferés de la part de Dieu, de la Vierge Marie, de tous les Saints et Saintes du Paradis, particulièrement de mon patron Saint Jean-Baptiste, Saints Pierre, Paul, et François, et me donne corps et âme à vous Lucifer ici présent, avec tous les biens que je posséderai jamais (excepté la valeur des sacrements pour le regard de ceux qui les recurent). Ainsi j'ai signé et attesté. *Confession faicte par messire Loys Gaufridi, prestre en l'église des Accoules de Marseille, prince des magiciens . . à deux pères capucins du couvent d'Aix, la veille de Pasques le onzième avril mil six cent onze.* A Aix, par Jean Tholozan, MVCXI.

[5] Je renonce entièrement de tout mon cœur, de toute ma force, et de toute ma puissance à Dieu le Père, au Fils et au Saint-Esprit, à la très Sainte Mère de Dieu, à tous les anges et spécialement à mon bon ange, à la passion de Notre Seigneur Jésus Christ, à Son Sang, à tous les mérites d'icelle, à ma part de Paradis, à toutes les inspirations que Dieu me pourrait donner à l'avenir, à toutes les prières qu'on a faites et pourrait faire pour moi.

[6] S. Pius V, Bull *Consueuerunt*, 17 September, 1569: Bl. Francisco de Possadas, *Vida di Santo Domingo*, Madrid, 1721.

[7] In England at this date it was felony to possess an *Agnus Dei*.

[8] *Spondent quod . . . ad conuentus nocturnos diligenter accedent.*

[9] Coven, coeven, covine, curving, covey, are among the many spellings of this word.

[10] R. Pitcairn, *Criminal Trials*, Edinburgh, 1833.

[11] *Examination of Certain Witches*, Philobiblion Society, London, 1863–4.

[12] Thomas Potts, *Discoverie of Witches*.

[13] . . . qu'elle a veu souuent baptiser des enfans au sabbat, qu'elle nous expliqua estre des enfans des sorcieres & non autres, lesquelles ont accoutumé faire plustost baptiser leurs enfans au sabbat qu'en l'église. Pierre de Lancre, *Tableau de l'Inconstance des mauvais Anges*, Paris, 1613.

[14] . . . qu'on baptise des enfans au Sabbat auec du Cresme, que des femmes apportent, & frottent la verge de quelque homme, & en font sortir de la semence qu'elles amassent, and la meslent auec le Cresme, puis mettant cela sur la teste de l'enfant en prononçant quelques paroles en Latin. Contemporary tract, *Arrest & procedure faicte par le Lieutenant Criminel d'Orleans contre Siluain Neuillon.*

[15] . . . dit que sa mère le presenta (dit-on) en l'aage de trois ans au Sabbat, à vn bouc, qu'on appelloit l'Aspic. Dit qu'il fut baptisé au Sabbat, au Carrior d'Oliuet, auec quatorze ou quinze autres, & que Jeanne Geraut porta du Chresme qui estoit jaune dans vn pot, & que ledit Neuillon ietta de la semence dans ledit pot, & vn nommé Semelle, & brouilloient cela auec vne petite cuilliere de bois, & puis leur en mirent à tous sur la teste.

[16] J'advoue comme on baptise au Sabath et comme chacun sorcier fait vœu particulièrement se donnant au diable et faire baptiser tous ses enfants au Sabath (si faire se peut). Comme aussi l'on impose des noms à chacun de ceux qui sont au Sabath, différents de leur propre nom. J'advoue comme au baptême on se sert de l'eau, du soufre et du sel: le soufre rend esclave le diable et le sel pour confirmer le baptême au service du diable. J'advoue comme la forme et l'intention est de baptiser au nom de Lucifer, de Belzebuth et autres diables faisant le signe de la croix en le commençant par le travers et puis le poursuivant par les pieds et finissant à la tête. Contemporary tract, *Confession faicte par messire Loys Gaufridi, prestre en l'église des Accoules de Marseille, prince des magiciens*, MVCXI.

[17] Anthony Hornech's appendix to Glanvill's *Sadducismus Triumphatus*, London, 1681.

[18] *Newes from Scotland*, London, W. Wright, 1592.

[19] Præstant Dæmoni . . . iuramentum super circulo in terram sculpto fortasse quia cum circulus sit Symbolum Divinitatis, & terra scabellum Dei sic certe uellet eos credere se esse Dominum cœli & terræ. Guazzo, *Compendium*, I. 7, p. 38. I have corrected the text, which runs "uellet eos credere eum esset . . ."

[20] Even by so industrious a searcher as Miss M. A. Murray.

[21] Dressant quelque forme d'autel sur des coloñes infernales, & sur iceluy sans dire le *Confiteor*, ny l'*Alleluya*, tournant les feuillets d'vn certain liure qu'il a en main, il commence à marmotér quelques mots de la Messe. De Lancre, *Tableau*, p. 401.

[22] . . . que le Sabbat se tenoit dans vne maison . . . Vit aussi vn grand homme noir à l'opposite de celuy de la cheminée, qui regardoit dans vn liure, dont les feuillets estoient noirs & bleuds, & marmotait entre ses dents sans entendre ce qu'il disoit, leuoit vne hostie noire, puis vn calice de meschant estain tout crasseux.

[23] On dit la Messe, & que c'est le Diable qui la dit, qu'il a vne Chasuble qui a vne croix : mais qu'elle n'a que trois barres : & tourne le dos à l'Autel quand il veut leuer l'Hostie & le Calice, qui sont noirs, & marmote dans vn liure, duquel le couuerture est toute velue comme d'vne peau de loup, auec des feuillets blancs & rouges, d'autres noirs.

[24] On lisait la messe dans le livre des blasphèmes, qui servait de canon et qu'on employait aussi dans les processions. Il renfermait les plus horribles malédictions contre la sainte Trinité, le Saint Sacrement de l'autel, les autres sacrements et les cérémonies de l'Eglise, et il était écrit dans une langue qui m'était inconnue. Görres, *La Mystique Divine*, trad., Charles Sainte-Foi, V. p. 230. There is a critical recension of *Die christliche Mystik* by Boretius and Krause, Hanover, 1893–7.

[25] *Newes from Scotland*, London, W. Wright (1592).

[26] Book III. p. 42.

[27] T. B. Howell, *State Trials*, London, 1816. IV, 844, 846.

[28] S. Caleb, *Les Messes Noires*, Paris, s.d.

[29] Après ce que nous ont appris les livres et les âmes, il ne nous est pas permis de douter, et notre devoir est de combattre, ne fût-ce que par un simple affirmation, les nombreux auteurs qui, effrontément ou témérairement, traitent ces horreurs de fables ou d'hallucinations. *La Mystique Divine*, nouvelle édition, Paris, 1902. III, pp. 269, 270.

[30] Ces histoires, loin d'être fabuleuses, ont toute l'authenticité que peut leur donner une procédure instruite avec tout le zèle et le talent que pouvaient y apporter des magistrats éclairés et consciencieux, auxquels, à toutes les époques, les faits ne manquaient pas. Libre III. c. 8.

[31] *De Ciuitate Dei*, xv. 23. I quote Healey's translation, 1610.

[32] Esse eorum (qui usualiter incubi uel succubi nominantur) et concupiscentiam eorum libidinosam, necnon et generationem ab eis esse famosam atque credibilem fecerunt testimonia uirorum et mulierem qui illusiones ipsorum, molestiasque et improbitates, necnon et uiolentias libidinis ipsorum, se passos fuisse testificati sunt et adhuc asserunt. *De Universitate*, Secunda Pars, III. 25.

[33] Si tamen ex coitu dæmonum aliqui interdum nascuntur, hoc non est per semen ab eis decisum, aut a corporibus assumptis; sed per semen alicuius hominis ad hoc acceptum, utpote quod idem dæmon qui est succubus ad uirum, fiat incubus ad mulierem. *Summa*, Pars Prima, quæstio 1, a 3. at 6.

[34] Succumbunt uiris in specie mulieris, et ex eis semen pollutionis suscipiunt, et quadam sagacitate ipsum in sua uirtute custodiunt, et postmodum, Deo permittente, fiunt incubi et in uasa mulierum transfundunt. *Sententiarum*, Liber II, d. viii, Pars Prima, a 3. q. 1.

[35] Docet S. Thomas . . . et consentiunt communiter reliqui theologi. . . . Ratio huius sententiæ est quia tota illa actio non excedit potestatem naturalem dæmonis, usus autem talis potestatis est ualde conformis prauæ uoluntati dæmonis, et iuste a Deo permitti potest propter aliquorum hominum peccata. Ergo non potest cum fundamento negari, et ideo non immerito dixit Augustinus, cum de illo usu multis experientiis et testimoniis constet, non sine impudentia negari. *De Angelis*, l. iv. c. 38. nn. 10, 11.

[36] Begun in 1665 by Fra Francisco de Jésus-Maria (*ob.* 1677).

[37] Negant aliqui, credentes impossible esse quod dæmones actum carnalem cum hominibus exercere ualent. Sed tenenda est ut omnino certa contraria sententia. *Theologia moralis*, Tr. xxi. c. 11. p. 10. nn. 180, 181.

[38] Idem dæmon qui est succubus ad uirum potest fieri incubus ad mulierem. In his monumental *Summa S. Thomæ hodiernis Academiarum moribus accommodata*, 19 vols. Liège, 1746–51.

[39] *De Seruonem Dei Beatificatione*, Romæ, MDCCXC, Cura Aloysii Salvioni. Tom. VII. pp. 30–33.

[40] Quæ leguntur de Dæmonibus incubis et succubis. . . . Quamuis enim prædicti concubitus communiter admittantur, sed generatis a nonnullis excludetur . . . alii, tamen, tum concubitum, tum generationem fieri posse, et factam fuisse existimauerunt, modo quodam nouo et inusitate, et hominibus incognito. Sancho de Avila, bishop of Murcia, Jaen, and Siguenza, S. Teresa's confessor (*ob.* December, 1625), in a commentary on Exodus discusses the curious question : *An Angeli de se generare possint* ?

[41] Quidam hos dæmones incubos uel succubos dari negarunt ; sed communiter id affirmant auctores.

[42] Ad bestialitatem autem reuocatur peccatum cum dæmone succubo, uel incubo ; cui peccato superadditur malitia contra religionem ; et præterea etiam sodomiæ, adulterii, uel incestus, si affectu uiri, uel mulieris, sodomitico, adulterino uel incestuoso cum dæmone coeat. Lib. III, Tract iv. c. 2. Dubium 3.

[43] The word *bestialitas* has theologically a far wider signification than the word *bestiality*. In 1222 a deacon, having been tried before Archbishop Langton, was burned at Oxford on a charge of bestiality. He had embraced Judaism in order to marry a Jewess. Professor E. P. Evans remarks : "It seems rather odd that the Christian lawgivers should have adopted the Jewish code against sexual intercourse with beasts, and then enlarged it so as to include the Jews themselves. The question was gravely discussed by jurists whether cohabitation of a Christian with a Jewess, or *vice versa*, constitutes sodomy. Damhouder (*Prax. rer. crim.* c. 96 n. 48) is of the opinion that it does, and Nicolaus Boer (*Decis.*, 136, n. 5) cites the case of a certain Johannes Alardus, or Jean Alard, who kept a Jewess in his house in Paris and had several children by her : he was convicted of sodomy on account of this relation and burned, together with his paramour, 'since coition with a Jewess is precisely the same as if a man should copulate with a dog' (*Dopl. Theat.* ii, p. 157). Damhouder includes Turks and Saracens in the same category." *The Criminal Prosecution and Capital Punishment of Animals*, p. 152. London, 1906.

[44] An oblate of S. Charles, d. 1631.

[45] 1566–1622. His *Synopsis Theologiæ Moralis* is a posthumous work, published 1626.

[46] Bene ait Busembaum quod congressus cum dæmone reducitur ad peccatum bestialitatis. Hermann Busembaum, S.J., 1600–1668.

[47] *Theologia moralis decalogalis et sacramentalis*. Venice, 1731.

[48] Præter autem crimen bestialitatis accedit scelus superstitionis. An autem, qui coit cum dæmone apparente in forma conjugatæ, monialis, aut consanguiniæ, peccet semper affective peccato adulterii, sacrilegii, aut incestus ? Uidetur uniuerse affirmare Busembaum cum aliis ut supra.

[49] Paris, 1883.

[50] A private manual only delivered to priests.

[51] Omnes theologi loquuntur de congressu cum dæmone in forma uiri, mulieris aut alicuius bestiæ apparente, uel ut præsente per imaginationem repræsentato, dicuntque tale peccatum ad genus bestialitatis reuocandum esse, et specialem habere malitiam in confessione declarandam, scilicet superstitionem in pacto cum dæmone consistentem. In hoc igitur scelere duæ necessario reperiuntur malitiæ, una contra castitatem, et altera contra uirtutem religionis. Si quis ad dæmonem sub specie uiri apparentem affectu sodomitico accedat, tertia est species peccati, ut patet. Item si sub specie consanguineæ aut mulieris conjugatæ fingatur apparere, adest species incestus uel adulterii ; si sub specie bestiæ, adest bestialitas.

[52] 1722–1797. He was a monk of Bans, near Bamberg.

[53] Quæri potest utrum dæmon per turpem concubitum possit uiolenter opprimere marem uel feminam cuius obsessio permissa sit ob finem perfectionis et contemplationis acquirendæ. Ut autem uera a falsis separemus, sciendum est quod dæmones (incubi et succubi, quidquid dicant increduli) uere dantur: immo hoc iuxta doctrinam Augustini (lib. 15, *de Ciuit. Dei*, cap. 23) sine aliqua impudentia negari nequit: . . . Hoc idem asserit D. Thomas, aliique communiter. Hic uero, qui talia patiuntur, sunt peccatores qui uel dæmones ad hos nefandos concubitus inuitant, uel dæmonibus turpia hæc facinora intentantibus ultro assentiuntur. Quod autem hi aliique praui homines possint per uiolentiam a dæmone opprimi non dubitamus: . . . et ego ipse plures inueni qui quamuis de admissis sceleribus dolerent; et hoc nefarium diaboli commercium exsecrarentur, tamen illud pati cogebantur inuiti. D. Schram, *Theologia Mystica*, I. 233, scholium 3, p. 408. Paris, 1848.

[54] 1532–1591. Provincial of the Jesuit province of the Rhine.

[55] Congressus hos dæmonum cum utriusque sexus hominibus negare, ita temerarium est, ut necessarium sit simul conuellas et sanctissimorum et grauissimorum hominum grauissimas sententias, et humanis sensibus bellum indicas, et te ignorare fatearis quanta sit illorum spirituum in hæc corpora uis utque potestas. C. x. n. 3.

[56] Placuit enim affirmatio axiomatis adeo multis, ut uerendum sit ne pertinaciæ et audaciæ sit ab eis discedere; communis namque hæc est sententia Patrum, theologorum et philosophorum doctiorum, et omnium fere sæculorum atque nationum experientia comprobata. Liber II, quæstio 15.

[57] Asserere per incubos et succubos dæmones homines interdum procreari in tantum est catholicum, quod eius oppositum asserere est nedum dictis Sanctorum, sed et traditioni sacræ Scripturæ contrarium. *Pars prima, quæstio* 3.

[58] Causa autem quare dæmones se incubos faciunt uel succubos esse uidetur, ut per luxuriæ uitium hominis utramque naturam lædant, corporis uidelicet et animæ, qua in læsione præcipue delectari uidentur. This divine was a prominent figure at the Council of Bâle. I have used the Douai edition, 5 vols. 1602.

[59] Dæmon in forma succubi se transformat, et habet coitum cum uiro . . .; accedit ad mulierem in forma scilicet uiri. . . . Ita firmant communiter Theologi.

[60] Certissima experientia sæpe cognitum est fœminas etiam inuitas a dæmonibus fuisse compressas. *De justa hæreticorum punitione*, Lib. I. c. xviii. Salamanca, 1547.

[61] Hæc est indubitata ueritas quam non solum experientia certissima comprobat, sed etiam antiquitas confirmat, quidquid quidam medici et iurisperiti opinentur. *Conclusio quinta.*

[62] Affirmatiuam sententiam tam multi et graues tuentur auctores, ut sine pertinaciæ nota ab illa discedi non posse uidatur.

[63] *Rapports de l'homme avec le démon.*

[64] *Les hauts phenomènes de la magic.*

[65] Sane ad nostrum, non sine ingenti molestia, peruenit auditum quod . . . complures utriusque sexus personæ, propriæ salutis immemores et a fide catholica deuiantes, cum dæmonibus incubis et succubis abuti.

[66] The Dean of S. Paul's (*Christian Mysticism*, 1899, p. 265) urbanely dismisses the whole subject with a quotation from Lucretius:

> Hunc igitur terrorem animi, tenebrasque necessest
> Non radii solis, neque lucida tela diei
> Discutiant, sed naturæ species ratioque. (I. 147–49.)
>
> These Fears, that darkness that o'erspreads our Souls,
> Day can't disperse, but those *eternal* rules
> Which from firm Premises true *Reason* draws,
> And a deep insight into *Natures* laws. (*Creech.*)

[67] *De Dæmonialitate*, 24.

[68] *Survival*, by various authors. Edited by Sir James Marchant, K.B.E., LL.D. London and New York.

[69] So in Middleton's *The Witch*, when the young gallant Almachildes visits Hecate's abode, she exclaims :

'Tis Almachildes—the fresh blood stirs in me—
The man that I have lusted to enjoy :
I've had him thrice in incubus already.

And in a previous scene Hecate has said :

What young man can we wish to pleasure us,
But we enjoy him in an incubus ?

[70] Ce commerce monstreux dura plusiers mois ; mais Dieu le délivra enfin par mon entremise et il fit pénitence de ses péchés.

[71] Auoir esté au Sabbat ; ne sçait comme elle y fut transportée . . . qu'au Sabbat le Diable cogneust charnellement toutes les femmes qui y estoient, & elle aussi la marqua en deux endroicts. . . . Que le Diable la cogneu vne autrefois, & qu'il a le membre faict comme un cheual, en entrant est froid comme glace, iette la semence fort froide, & en sortant la brusse comme si c'estoit du feu. Qu'elle receut tout mescontentement que lors qu'il eut habité auec elle au Sabbat, vn autre homme qu'elle ne cognoist fit le semblable en presence de tous, que son mary s'appercut quand le Diable eut affaire auec elle, & que le Diable se vint coucher auprez d'elle fort froid, luy mit la main sur le bas du ventre, dont elle effrayée en ayant aduerty son mary, il luy dict ces mots, Taise-toy folle, taise-toy. Que son mary vit quand le Diable la cogneust au Sabbat, ensemble cet autre qui la cogneust après.

[72] L'accouplement du Demon avec la Sorciere et le Sorcier. . . . 1. Le Demon cognoit toutes les Sorcieres, & pourquoy. 2. Il se met aussi en femme pour les Sorciers, & pourquoy. 3. Autres raisons pour lesquelles le Demon cognoit les Sorciers, & Sorcieres.

[73] . . . qui Satan l'auoit cogneue charnellement. . . . Et pource que les hommes ne cedent guieres aux femmes en lubricité.

[74] Il y a encor deux autres raisons pour lesquelles le Diable s'accouple auec le Sorcier : La premiere, que l'offense est de tant plus grande : Car si Dieu a en si grande haine l'accouplement du fidelle auec l'infidele (Exodus xxxiv., Deuteronomy xxxvii.), à combien plus forte raison detesterait celuy de l'homme auec le Diable. La seconde raison est, que parce moyen la semence naturelle de l'homme se pert, d'où vient que l'amitié qui est entre l'homme & la femme, se conuertit le plus souuent en haine, qui est l'vn des plus grands mal-heurs, qui pourroient arriuer au mariage.

[75] In chapter xiii Boguet decides : l'accouplement de Satan auec le Sorcier est réel & non imaginaire. . . . Les vns donc s'en mocquēt . . . mais les confessions des Sorciers qui j'ay eu en main, me font croire qu'il en est quelque chose ! dautant qu'ils ont tout recogneu, qu'ils auoient esté couplez auec le Diable, & que la semence qu'il iettoit estoit fort froide . . . Iaquema Paget adioustoit, qu'elle auoit empoigné plusiers fois auec la main le mēbre du Demon, qui la cognoissoit, & que le membre estoit froid comme glace, lōg d'vn bon doigt, & moindre en grosseur que celuy d'vn homme : Tieuenne Paget, & Antoine Tornier adioustoient aussi, que le membre de leurs Demons estoit long, & gros comme l'vn de leurs doigts.

[76] Heuze, *Do the Dead Live ?* 1923.

[77] John Stearne's *Confirmation and Discovery of Witchcraft.*

[78] Robert Pitcairn, *Criminal Trials*, Edinburgh, 1833, III. pp. 603, 611, 617.

[79] *Idem.*

[80] Le Diable faict des mariages au Sabbat entre les Sorciers & Sorcieres, & leur joignant les mains, il leur dict hautement

Esta es buena parati
Esta parati lo toma.

Mais auant qu'ils couchent ensemble, il s'accouple auec elles, oste la virginité des filles. Lancre, *Tableau de l'Inconstance*, p. 132.

[81] This has been emphasized by Miss Murray in *The Witch-Cult in Western Euròpe* (" The Rites "), but she did not realize that the fascinum was well-known to demonologists, and the use thereof severely reprobated *sub mortali* by the Church.

[82] See G. Belluci, *Amuletti Italiani antichi e contemporanei*; also *Amuletti italiani contemporanei*. Perugia, 1898.

[83] Auctore P.P. Parisiis, MDCCCXXVI.

[84] Crudelissima anus. *Petronii Satirae*. 138. p. 105. Tertium edidit Buecheler. Berlin. 1895.

[85] *Titi Petronii Satyricon*, Concinnante Michaele Hadrianide. Amstelodami, 1669. Amongst the figures on the engraved title-page is a witch mounted on her broomstick.

[86] *Priapeia*. LXXXIV.

[87] For whose impudicities see S. Augustine, *De Ciuitate Dei*, VII. 26.

[88] Priapi lignei in honorem Bacchi.

[89] Francis Hutchinson, *Historical Essay*, London, 1718.

[90] *Witches at Chelmsford*, Philobiblion Society, VIII.

[91] Francis Hutchinson, *Historical Essay on Witchcraft*, 1718.

[92] *Elogia Doctorum Uirorum*, c. 101.

[93] Liber II.; c. v.; 11, 12.

CHAPTER IV

THE SABBAT

THE Assemblies of the witches differed very much from each other in an almost infinite number of ways. On certain ancient anniversaries the meeting was always particularly solemn, with as large an attendance as possible, when all who belonged to the infernal cult would be required to present themselves and punishment was meted out to those who proved slack and slow; at other times these gatherings would be occasional, resorted to by the company who resided within a certain restricted area, it might be by only one coven of thirteen, it might be by a few more, as opportunity served. There were also, as is to be expected, variations proper to each country, and a seemingly endless number of local peculiarities. There does not clearly appear to be any formal and fair order in the ceremonies throughout, nor should we look for this, seeing that the liturgy of darkness is of its essence opposed to the comely worship of God, wherein, as the Apostle bids, all things are to be done "decently and in order."[1] The ceremonial of hell, sufficiently complex, obscure, and obscene, is even more confused in the witches' narratives by a host of adventitious circumstances, often contradictory, nay, even mutually exclusive, and so although we can piece together a very complete picture of their orgies, there are some details which must yet remain unexplained, incomprehensible, and perhaps wholly irrational and absurd. "Le burlesque s'y mêle à l'horrible, et les puérilités aux abominations." (Ribet, *La Mystique Divine*, III. 2. Les Parodies Diaboliques.) (Mere clowning and japery are mixed up with circumstances of extremest horror; childishness and folly with loathly abominations.) In the lesser Assemblies much, no doubt, depended upon the fickle whim and unwholesome caprice of the officer or president at the moment. The conduct of the more important Assemblies was to a certain extent regularized and more or less loosely ran upon traditional lines. The name Sabbat may be held to cover every kind of gathering,[2] although it must continually be borne in mind that a Sabbat ranges from comparative simplicity, the secret rendezvous of some half a dozen wretches devoted to the fiend, to a large and crowded congregation presided over by incarnate evil intelligences, a mob outvying the very demons in malice, blasphemy, and revolt, the true face of pandemonium on earth.

The derivation of the word Sabbat does not seem to be exactly established. It is perhaps superfluous to point out that it has nothing to do with the number seven, and is wholly unconnected with the Jewish festival. Sainte-Croix and Alfred Maury[3] are agreed to derive it from the debased Bacchanalia. Sabazius (Σαβάζιος) was a Phrygian deity, sometimes identified with Zeus, sometimes with Dionysus, but who was generally regarded as the patron of licentiousness and worshipped with frantic debaucheries. He is a patron of the ribald old Syrian eunuch in Apuleius: "omnipotens et omniparens Dea Syria et sanctus Sabadius et Bellona et Mater Idaea (ac) cum suo Adone Venus domina"[4] are the deities whom Philebus invokes to avenge him of the mocking crier. Σαβαζεῖν is found in the Scholiast on Aristophane (*Birds*, 874), and σαβαî, a Bacchic yell, occurs in a fragment of the *Baptæ* of Eupolis; the fuller phrase εὐοî Σαβôι being reported by Strabo the geographer. The modern Greeks still call a madman ζαβός. But Littré entirely rejects any such facile etymology. "Attempts have been made to trace the etymology of the Sabbat, the witches' assembly, from *Sabazies*; but the formation of the word does not allow it; besides, in the Middle Ages, what did they know about *Sabazies*?"[5]

Even the seasons of the principal Assemblies of the year differ in various countries. Throughout the greater part of Western Europe one of the chief of these was the Eve of May Day, 30 April;[6] in Germany[7] famous as Die Walpurgis-Nacht. S. Walburga (Walpurgis; Waltpurde; at Perche Gauburge; in other parts of France Vaubourg or Falbourg) was born in Devonshire *circa* 710. She was the daughter of S. Richard, one of the under-kings of the West Saxons, who married a sister of S. Boniface. In 748 Walburga, who was then a nun of Wimbourne, went over to Germany to found claustral life in that country. After a life of surpassing holiness she died at Heidenheim, 25 February, 777. Her cultus began immediately, and about 870 her relics were translated to Eichstadt, where the Benedictine convent which has charge of the sacred shrine still happily flourishes. S. Walburga was formerly one of the most popular Saints in England, as well as in Germany and the Low Countries. She is patroness of Eichstadt, Oudenarde, Furnes, Groningen, Weilburg, Zutphen, and Antwerp, where until the Roman office was adopted they celebrated her feast four times a year. In the Roman martyrology she is commemorated on 1 May, but in the Monastic Kalendar on 25 February. The first of May was the ancient festival of the Druids, when they offered sacrifices upon their sacred mountains and kindled their May-fires. These magic observances were appropriately continued by the witches of a later date. There was not a hill-top in Finland, so the peasant believed, which at midnight on the last day of April was not thronged by demons and sorcerers.

The second witches' festival was the Eve of S. John Baptist, 23 June. Then were the S. John's fires lit, a custom in certain regions still prevailing.[8] In olden times the Feast was distinguished like Christmas with three Masses; the first at midnight recalled his mission as Precursor, the second at dawn commemorated the baptism he confessed, the third honoured his sanctity.

Other Grand Sabbat days, particularly in Belgium and Germany, were S. Thomas' Day (21 December) and a date, which seems to have been movable, shortly after Christmas. In Britain we also find Candlemas (2 February), Allhallowe'en (31 October), and Lammas (1 August), mentioned in the trials. Wright, *Narratives of Sorcery and Magic* (I. p. 141), further specifies S. Bartholomew's Eve, but although a Sabbat may have been held on this day, it would seem to be an exceptional or purely local use.

During a famous trial held in the winter of 1610 at Logrono, a town of Old Castille, by the Apostolic Inquisitor, Alonso Becerra Holguin, an Alcantarine friar, with his two assessors Juen Valle Alvarado and Alonso de Salasar y Frias, a number of Navarrese witches confessed that the chief Sabbats were usually held at Zugarramurdi and Berroscoberro in the Basque districts, and that the days were fixed, being the vigils of the "nine principal feasts of the year," namely, Easter, Epiphany, Ascension Day, the Purification and Nativity of Our Lady, the Assumption, Corpus Christi, All Saints, and the major festival of S. John Baptist (24 June). It is certainly curious to find no mention of Christmas and Pentecost in this list, but throughout the whole of the process not one of the accused—and we have their evidence in fullest detail—named either of these two solemnities as being chosen for the infernal rendezvous.[9]

Satan is, as Boguet aptly says, "Singe de Dieu en tout,"[10] and it became common to hold a General Sabbat about the time of the high Christian festivals in evil mockery of these holy solemnities, and he precisely asserts that the Sabbat "se tient encor aux festes les plus solemnelles de l'année."[11] (Is still held on the greatest festivals of the year.) So he records the confession of Antide Colas (1598), who "auoit esté au Sabbat à vn chacun bon iour de l'an, comme à Noel, à Pasques, à la feste de Dieu." The Lancashire witches met on Good Friday; and in the second instance (1633) on All Saints' Day; the witches of Kinross (1662) held an assembly on the feast of Scotland's Patron, S. Andrew, 30 November, termed "S. Andrew's Day at Yule," to distinguish it from the secondary Feast of the Translation of S. Andrew, 9 May. The New England witches were wont to celebrate their chief Sabbat at Christmas. In many parts of Europe where the Feast of S. George is solemnized with high honour and holiday the vigil (22 April) is the Great Sabbat of the year. The Huzulo of the Carpathians believe that then every evil thing has power and witches are most dangerous. Not a Bulgarian or Roumanian farmer but closes up each door and fastens close each window at nightfall, putting sharp thorn-bushes and brambles on the lintels, new turf on the sills, so that no demon nor hag may find entry there.

The Grand Sabbats were naturally held in a great variety of places, whilst the lesser Sabbats could be easily assembled in an even larger number of spots, which might be convenient to the coven of that district, a field near a village, a wood, a tor, a valley, an open waste beneath some blasted oak, a cemetery, a ruined building, some solitary chapel or semi-deserted church, sometimes a house belonging to one of the initiates.

It was advisable that the selected locality should be remote and deserted to obviate any chance of espionage or casual interruption, and in many provinces some wild ill-omened gully or lone hill-top was shudderingly marked as the notorious haunt of witches and their fiends. De Lancre says that the Grand Sabbat must be held near a stream, lake, or water of some kind,[12] and Bodin adds: "The places where Sorcerers meet are remarkable and generally distinguished by some trees, or even a cross."[13] These ancient cromlechs and granite dolmens, the stones of the Marais de Dol, the monolith that lies between Seny and Ellemelle (Candroz), even the market-crosses of sleepy old towns and English villages, were among the favourite rendezvous of the pythons and warlocks of a whole countryside. On one occasion, which seems exceptional, a Sabbat was held in the very heart of the city of Bordeaux. Throughout Germany the Blocksburg or the Brocken, the highest peak of the Hartz Mountains, was the great meeting-place of the witches, some of whom, it was said, came from distant Lapland and Norway to forgather there. But local Blocksburgs existed, or rather hills so called, especially in Pomerania, which boasted two or three such crags. The sorcerers of Corrières held their Sabbat at a deserted spot, turning off the highway near Combes; the witches of la Mouille in a tumbledown house, which had once belonged to religious; the Gandillons and their coven, who were brought to justice in June, 1598, met at Fontenelles, a forsaken and haunted spot near the village of Nezar. Dr. Fian and his associates (1591) "upon the night of Allhollen-Even" assembled at "the kirke of North-Berrick in Lowthian." Silvain Nevillon, who was executed at Orleans, 4 February, 1615, confessed "que le Sabbat se tenoit dans vne maison," and the full details he gave shows this to have been a large château, no doubt the home of some wealthy local magnate, where above two hundred persons could assemble. Isobel Young, Christian Grinton, and two or three other witches entertained the Devil in Young's house in 1629. Alexander Hamilton, a "known warlock" executed at Edinburgh in 1630, confessed that "the pannel took him one night to a den betwixt Niddrie and Edmiston, where the devill had trysted hir." Helen Guthrie, a Forfar witch, and her coven frequented a churchyard, where they met a demon, and on another occasion they " went to Mary Rynd's house, and sat doune together at the table . . . and made them selfes mirrie, and the divell made much of them all " (1661). The Lancashire witches often held their local Sabbat at Malking Tower. From the confession of the Swedish witches (1670) at Mohra and Elfdale they assembled at a spot called *Blockula* " scituated in a delicate large Meadow . . . The place or house they met at, had before it a Gate painted with divers colours ; . . . In a huge large Room of this House, they said, there stood a very long Table, at which the Witches did sit down ; And that hard by this Room was another Chamber in which there were very lovely and delicate Beds."[14] Obviously a fine Swedish country house, perhaps belonging to a wealthy witch, and in the minds of the poorer members of the gang it presently became imaginatively exaggerated and described.

Christian Stridtheckh *De Sagis* (XL) writes : " They have different rendezvous in different districts ; yet their meetings are generally held in wooded spots, or on mountains, or in caves, and any places which are far from the usual haunts of men. Mela, Book III, chapter 44, mentions Mount Atlas ; *de Vaulx*, a warlock executed at Etaples in 1603, confessed that the witches of the Low Countries were wont most frequently to meet in some spot in the province of Utrecht. In our own country, the Mountain of the Bructeri, which some call Meliboeus, in the duchy of Brunswick, is known and notorious as the haunt of witches. In the common tongue this Mountain is called the *Blocksberg* or *Heweberg, Brockersburg* or *Vogelsberg*, as *Ortelius* notes in his *Thesaurus Geographicus*."[15] The day of the week whereon a Sabbat was held differed in the various districts and countries, although Friday seems to have been most generally favoured. There is indeed an accumulation of evidence for every night of the week save Saturday and Sunday. De Lancre records that in the Basses-Pyrénées " their usual rendezvous is the spot known as Lane du Bouc, in the Basque tongue *Aquelarre de verros, prado del Cabron*, & there the Sorcerers assemble to worship their master on three particular nights, Monday, Wednesday, Friday."[16] Boguet says that the day of the Sabbat varied, but usually a Thursday night was preferred.[17] In England it was stated that the "Solemn appointments, and meetings . . . are ordinarily on Tuesday or Wednesday night." [18] Saturday was, however, particularly avoided as being the day sacred to the immaculate Mother of God.

It is true that the hysterical and obscene ravings of Maria de Sains, a witness concerned in the trial of Louis Gaufridi and who was examined on 17–19 May, 1614, assert that the Sabbat used to be held on every day of the week. Wednesday and Friday were the Sabbats of blasphemy and the black ass. To the other days the most hideous abominations of which humanity is capable were allotted. The woman was obviously sexually deranged, affected with mania blasphematoria and coprolalia.

Night was almost invariably the time for the Sabbat, although, as Delrio says, there is no actual reason why these evil rites should not be performed at noon, for the Psalmist speaks of "the terror of the night," the "business that walketh about in the dark," and of "the noonday devil."[19] ("Non timebis a timore nocturno . . . a negotio perambulante in tenebris; ab incursu et dæmonio meridiano.") And so Delrio very aptly writes: "Their assemblies generally are held at dead of night when the Powers of Darkness reign; or, sometimes, at high noon, even as the Psalmist saith, when he speaks of 'the noonday devil.' The nights they prefer are Monday and Thursday."[20]

The time at which these Sabbats began was generally upon the stroke of midnight. "Les Sorciers," says Boguet, "vont enuiron la minuict au Sabbat."[21] It may be remembered that in the *Metamorphoseon* of Apuleius, I, xi, the hags attack Socrates at night "circa tertiam ferme uigiliam." Agnes Sampson, "a famous witch"—as Hume of Godscroft in his Account of Archibald, ninth Earl of Angus, calls her—commonly known as the wise wife of Keith, who made a prominent figure[22] in the Fian trials, 1590, confessed that the Devil met her, "being alone, and commanded her to be at North-Berwick Kirk the next night," and accordingly she made her way there as she was bid "and lighted at the Kirk-yard, or a little before she came to it, about eleven hours at even."[23] In this case, however, the Sabbat was preceded by a dance of nearly one hundred persons, and so probably did not commence until midnight. Thomas Leyis, Issobell Coky, Helen Fraser, Bessie Thorn, and the rest of the Aberdeen witches, thirteen of whom were executed in 1597, and seven more banished, generally met " betuixt tuell & ane houris at nycht."[24] Boguet notes that in 1598 the witch Françoise Secretain "adioustoit qu'elle alloit tousiours au Sabbat enuiron la minuit, & beaucoup d'autres sorciers, que i'ay eu en main, ont dit le mesme." In 1600 Anna Mauczin of Tubingen confessed that she had taken part in witch gatherings which she dubbed *Hochzeiten*. They seem to have been held by a well just outside the upper gate of Rotenburg, and her evidence insists upon " midnight dances " and revelling. A Scotch witch, Marie Lamont, " a young woman of the adge of Eighteen Yeares, dwelling in the parish of Innerkip " on 4 March, 1662, confessed most ingenuously " that when shee had been at a mietting sine Zowle last, with other witches, in the night, the devill convoyed her home in the dawing."[25]

The Sabbat lasted till cock-crow, before which time none of the assembly was suffered to withdraw, and the advowal of Louis Gaufridi, executed at Aix, 1610, seems somewhat singular : " I was conveyed to the place where the Sabbat was to be held, and I remained there sometimes one, two, three, or four hours, for the most part just as I felt inclined."[26] That the crowing of a cock dissolves enchantments is a tradition of extremest antiquity. The Jews believed that the clapping of a cock's wings will make the power of demons ineffectual and break magic spells. So Prudentius sang : " They say that the night-wandering demons, who rejoice in dunnest shades, at the crowing of the cock tremble and scatter in sore affright."[27] The rites of Satan ceased because the Holy Office of the Church began. In the time of S. Benedict Matins and Lauds were recited at dawn and were actually often known as *Gallicinium*, Cock-crow. In the exquisite poetry of S. Ambrose, which is chanted at Sunday Lauds, the praises of the cock are beautifully sung :

Light of our darksome journey here,
  With days dividing night from night!
Loud crows the dawn's shrill harbinger,
  And wakens up the sunbeams bright.

Forthwith at this, the darkness chill
  Retreats before the star of morn;
And from their busy schemes of ill
  The vagrant crews of night return.

Fresh hope, at this, the sailor cheers;
  The waves their stormy strife allay;
The Church's Rock at this, in tears,
  Hastens to wash his guilt away.

Arise ye, then, with one accord!
  No longer wrapt in slumber lie;
The cock rebukes all who their Lord
  By sloth neglect, by sin deny.

At his clear cry joy springs afresh;
  Health courses through the sick man's veins;
The dagger glides into its sheath;
  The fallen soul her faith regains.[28]

A witch named Latoma confessed to Nicolas Remy that cocks were most hateful to all sorcerers. That bird is the herald of dawn, he arouses men to the worship of God; and many an odious sin which darkness shrouds will be revealed in the light of the coming day. At the hour of the Nativity, that most blessed time, the cocks crew all night long. A cock crew lustily at the Resurrection. Hence is the cock placed upon the steeple of churches. Pliny and Ælian tell us that a lion fears the cock; so the Devil "leo rugiens" flees at cock-crow.

"Le coq," says De Lancre, "s'oyt par fois es Sabbats sonnât la retraicte aux Sorciers."[29]

The witch resorted to the Sabbat in various manners. If it were a question of attending a local assembly when, at most, a mile or two had to be traversed, the company would go on foot. Very often the distance was even less, for it should be remembered that in the sixteenth and seventeenth centuries, and indeed, as a matter of fact, up to a quite recent date, when the wayfarer had gone a few steps outside the gates of a town or beyond the last house in the village he was enfolded in darkness, entirely solitary, remote, eloined. If footmen with flambeaux, at least the humbler linkboy, were essential attendants after nightfall in the streets of the world's great cities, London, Rome, Paris,

Madrid,[30] how black with shadows, dangerous, and utterly lonesome was the pathless countryside! Not infrequently the witches of necessity carried lanterns to light them on their journey to the Sabbat. The learned Bartolomeo de Spina, O.P.,[31] in his *Tractatus de Strigibus et Lamiis* (Venice, 1533), writes that a certain peasant, who lived at Clavica Malaguzzi, in the district of Mirandola, having occasion to rise very early one morning and drive to a neighbouring village, found himself at three o'clock, before daybreak, crossing a waste tract of considerable extent which lay between him and his destination. In the distance he suddenly caught sight of what seemed to be numerous fires flitting to and fro, and as he drew nearer he saw that these were none other than large lanthorns held by a bevy of persons who were moving here and there in the mazes of a fantastic dance, whilst others, as at a rustic picnic, were seated partaking of dainties and drinking stoups of wine, what time a harsh music, like the scream of a cornemuse, droned through the air. Curiously no word was spoken, the company whirled and pirouetted, ate and drank, in strange and significant silence. Perceiving that many, unabashed, were giving themselves up to the wildest debauchery and publicly performing the sexual act with every circumstance of indecency, the horrified onlooker realized that he was witnessing the revels of the Sabbat. Crossing himself fervently and uttering a prayer he drove as fast as possible from the accursed spot, not, however, before he had recognized some of the company as notorious evil-doers and persons living in the vicinity who were already under grave suspicion of sorcery. The witches must have remarked his presence, but they seem to have ignored him and not even to have attempted pursuit. In another instance Fra Paolo de Caspan, a Dominican of great reputation for piety and learning, reports that Antonio de Palavisini, the parish priest of Caspan in the Valtellina, a territory infected with warlocks, most solemnly affirmed that when going before daybreak to say an early Mass at a shrine hard by the village he had seen through clearings in the wood an assembly of men and women furnished with lanterns, who were seated in a circle and whose actions left no doubt that they were witches engaged in abominable rites. In both the above cases the lanterns were not required in the ceremonies of the Sabbat, and they must have been carried for the purely practical purpose of affording light.

Very often when going to a local Sabbat the coven of witches used to meet just beyond the village and make their way to the appointed spot in a body for mutual help and security. This is pointed out by Bernard of Como, a famous scholar, who says: " When they are to go to some spot hard by they proceed thither on foot cheerily conversing as they walk."[32] The fact that the dark initiates walked to the Sabbat is frequently mentioned in the trials. Boguet, who is most exact in detail, writes: " Sorcerers, nevertheless, sometimes walk to the Sabbat, and this is generally the case when the spot where they are to assemble does not lie very far from their dwellings."[33] And in the interrogatory, 17 May, 1616, of Barthélemi Minguet of Brécy, a young fellow of twenty-five, accused with seventeen more, we have: " He was then asked in what place the Sabbat was held the last time he was present there.

" He replied that it was in the direction of Billcron, at a cross-road which is on the high-road leading to Aix, in the Parish of Saint Soulange. He was asked how he proceeded thither. He replied that he walked to the place."[34]

When Catharine Oswald of Niddrie (1625) one night took Alexander Hamilton " a known warlock " " to a den betwixt Niddrie and Edmiston, where the devill had trysted hir," it is obvious that the couple walked there together.

On one occasion the truly subtle point was raised whether those who walked to the Sabbat were as guilty as those who were conveyed thither by the Devil. But De Lancre decides: " It is truly as criminal & abominable for a Sorcerer to go to the Sabbat on foot as to be voluntarily conveyed thither by the Devil."[35]

Major Weir and his sister seem to have gone to a meeting with the Devil in a coach and six horses when they thus drove from Edinburgh to Musselburgh and back again on 7 September, 1648. So the woman confessed in prison, and added " that she and her brother had made a compact with the devil."[36]

Agnes Sampson, the famous witch of North Berwick (1590), confessed " that the *Devil* in mans lickness met her going out to the fields from her own house at *Keith*, betwixt five and six at even, being alone and commanded her to be at *North-berwick* Kirk the next night. To which place she came on horse-back, conveyed by her Good-son, called Iohn Couper."[37] The Swedish witches (1669) who carried children off to Blockula "set them upon a *Beast* of the *Devil's* providing, and then they rid away." One boy confessed that "to perform the Journey, he took his own Fathers horse out of the Meadow, where it was feeding."[38] Upon his return one of the coven let the horse graze in her own pasture, and here the boy's father found it the next day.

In the popular imagination the witch is always associated with the broomstick, employed by her to fly in wild career through mid-air. This belief seems almost universal, of all times and climes. The broomstick is, of course, closely connected with the magic wand or staff which was considered equally serviceable for purposes of equitation. The wood whence it was fashioned was often from the hazel-tree, witch-hazel, although in De Lancre's day the sorcerers of Southern France favoured the "Souhandourra"—*Cornus sanguinea*, dog-wood. Mid hurricane and tempest, in the very heart of the dark storm, the convoy of witches, straddling their broomsticks, sped swiftly along to the Sabbat, their yells and hideous laughter sounding louder than the crash of elements and mingling in fearsome discord with the frantic pipe of the gale.

There is a very important reference to these beliefs from the pen of the famous and erudite Benedictine Abbot, Regino of Prüm (A.D. 906), who in his weighty *De ecclesiasticis disciplinis* writes: "This too must by no means be passed over that certain utterly abandoned women, turning aside to follow Satan, being seduced by the illusions and phantasmical shows of demons firmly believe and openly profess that in the dead of night they ride upon certain beasts along with the pagan goddess Diana and a countless horde of women, and that in those silent hours they fly over vast tracts of country and obey her as their mistress, whilst on certain other nights they are summoned to do her homage and pay her service."[39] The witches rode sometimes upon a besom or a stick, sometimes upon an animal, and the excursion through the air was generally preceded by an unction with a magic ointment. Various recipes are given for the ointment, and it is interesting to note that they contain deadly poisons: aconite, belladonna, and hemlock.[40] Although these unguents may in certain circumstances be capable of producing definite physiological results, it is Delrio who best sums up the reasons for their use: "The Demon is able to convey them to the Sabbat without the use of any unguent, and often he does so. But for several reasons he prefers that they should anoint themselves. Sometimes when the witches seem afraid it serves to encourage them. When they are young and tender they will thus be better able to bear the hateful embrace of Satan who has assumed the shape of a man. For by this horrid anointing he dulls their senses and persuades these deluded wretches that there is some great virtue in the viscid lubricant. Sometimes too he does this in hateful mockery of God's holy Sacraments, and that by these mysterious ceremonies he may infuse, as it were, something of a ritual and liturgical nature into his beastly orgies."[41]

Although the witch is universally credited with the power to fly through the air[42] to the Sabbat mounted upon a besom or some kind of stick, it is remarkable in the face of popular belief to find that the confessions avowing this actual mode of aerial transport are extraordinarily few. Paul Grilland, in his tractate *De Sortilegiis* (Lyons, 1533), speaks of a witch at Rome during whose trial, seven years before, it was asserted she flew in the air after she had anointed her limbs with a magic liniment. Perhaps the most exactly detailed accounts of this feat are to be found in Boguet,[43] than whom scarcely any writer more meticulously reports the lengthy and prolix evidence of witches, such evidence as he so laboriously gathered during the notorious prosecutions throughout Franche-Comté in the summer of 1598. He records quite plainly such statements as: "Françoise Secretain disoit, que pour aller au Sabbat, elle mettoit un baston blanc entre ses iambes & puis prononçait certaines paroles & dés lors elle estoit portée par l'air iusques en l'assemblée des Sorciers." (Françoise Secretain avowed that in order to go to the Sabbat she placed a white stick between her legs & then uttered certain words & then she was borne through the air to the sorcerers' assembly). In another place she confessed "qu'elle avoit esté vne infinité de fois au Sabbat . . . & qu'elle y alloit sur vn baston blanc, qu'elle mettoit entre ses iambes." (That she had been a great number of times to the Sabbat . . . and that she went there on a white stick which she placed between her legs.) It will be noticed that in the second instance she does not explicitly claim to have been borne through the air. Again: "Françoise Secretain y estoit portée [au Sabbat] sur vn baston blanc. Satan y trãsporta Thieuenne Paget & Antide Colas estant en forme d'vn homme noir, sortans de leurs maison le plus souuent par la cheminée." "Claudine Boban, ieune fille confessa qu'elle & sa mère montoient sur vne ramasse, & que sortans le contremont de la cheminée elles alloient par l'air en ceste façon au Sabbat." (Françoise Secretain was carried [to the Sabbat] on a white stick. Satan, in the form of a tall dark man conveyed thither Thieuenne Paget & Antide Colas, who most often left their house by way of the chimney. . . . Claudine Boban, a young girl, confessed that both she and her mother mounted on a besom, & that flying out by the chimney they were thus borne through the air to the Sabbat.) A marginal note explains *ramasse* as "autrement balai, & en Lyonnois coiue."

Glanvill writes that Julian Cox, one of the Somerset coven (1665), said "that one evening she walkt out about a Mile from her own House and there came riding towards her three persons upon three Broom-staves, born up about a yard and a half from the ground. Two of them she formerly knew, which was a Witch and a Wizzard." It might easily be that there is some exaggeration here. We know that a figure in one of the witch dances consisted of leaping as high as possible into the air, and probably the three persons seen by Julian Cox were practising this agile step. A quotation from Bodin by Reginald Scot is very pertinent in this connexion. Speaking of the Sabbat revels he has: "And whiles they sing and dance, euerie one hath a broome in his hand, and holdeth it vp aloft. Item he saith, that these night-walking or rather night-dansing witches, brought out of *Italie* into *France*, that danse which is called *La Volta*."[44] Sir John Davies in his *Orchestra or A Poeme on Dauncing* (18mo, 1596) describes the lavolta as "A loftie iumping, or a leaping round." De Lancre observes that after the regular country dance at the Sabbat the witches sprang high into the air. "Après la dance ils se mettent par fois à sauter."[45] At their assembly certain of the Aberdeen witches (1597) "danced a devilish dance, riding on trees, by a long space." In an old representation of Dr. Fian and his company swiftly pacing round North Berwick church withershins the witches are represented as running and leaping in the air, some mounted on broomsticks, some carrying their besoms in their hands.

There was discovered in the closet of Dame Alice Kyteler of Kilkenny, who was arrested in 1324 upon the accusation of nightly meeting a familiar Artisson and multiplied charges of sorcery, a pipe of ointment, wherewith she greased a staff "upon which she ambolled and gallopped thorough thicke and thin, when and what manner she listed."[46] In the trial of Martha Carrier, a notorious witch and "rampant hag" at the Court of Oyer and Terminer, held by adjournment at Salem, 2 August, 1692, the eighth article of the indictment ran: "One *Foster*, who confessed her own share in the Witchcraft for which the Prisoner stood indicted, affirm'd, that she had seen the prisoner at some of their *Witch-meetings*, and that it was this *Carrier*, who perswaded her to be a Witch. She confessed that the Devil carry'd them on a pole, to a Witch-meeting: but the pole broke, and she hanging about *Carriers* neck, they both fell down, and she then received an hurt by the Fall, whereof she was not at this very time recovered."[47]

In many of these instances it is plain that there is no actual flight through the air implied; although there is a riding a-cock-horse of brooms or sticks, in fact, a piece of symbolic ritual.

It is very pertinent, however, to notice in this connexion the actual levitation of human beings, which is, although perhaps an unusual, yet by no means an unknown, phenomenon in the séances of modern spiritism, where both the levitation of persons, with which we are solely concerned, and the rising of tables or chairs off the ground without contact with any individual or by any human agency have occurred again and again under conditions which cannot possibly admit of legerdemain, illusion, or charlatanry. From a mass of irrefutable evidence we may select some striking words by Sir William Crookes, F.R.S., upon levitation. "This has occurred," he writes, "in my presence on four occasions in darkness; but . . . I will only mention cases in which deductions of reason were confirmed by the sense of sight. . . . On one occasion I witnessed a chair, with a lady sitting on it, rise several inches from the ground. . . . On another occasion the lady knelt on the chair in such manner that the four feet were visible to us. It then rose about three inches, remained suspended for about ten seconds, and then slowly descended. . . .

"The most striking case of levitation which I have witnessed has been with Mr. Home. On three separate occasions have I seen him raised completely from the floor of the room. . . . On each occasion I had full opportunity of watching the occurrence as it was taking place. There are at least a hundred recorded instances of Mr. Home's rising from the ground."[48]

Writing in July, 1871, Lord Lindsay said: "I was sitting with Mr. Home and Lord Adare and a cousin of his. During the sitting Mr. Home went into a trance, and in that state was carried out of the window in the room next to where we were, and was brought in at our window. The distance between the windows was about seven feet six inches, and there was not the slightest foothold between them, nor was there more than a twelve-inch projection to each window, which served as a ledge to put flowers on. We heard the window in the next room lifted up, and almost immediately after we saw Home floating in air outside our window."[49]

William Stainton Moses writes of his levitation in August, 1872, in the presence of credible witnesses: "I was carried up . . . when I became stationary I made a mark [with a lead pencil] on the wall opposite to my chest. This mark is as near as may be six feet from the floor. . . . From the position of the mark on the wall it is clear that my head must have been close to the ceiling. . . . I was simply levitated and lowered to my old place."[50]

When we turn to the lives of the Saints we find that these manifestations have been frequently observed, and it will suffice to mention but a few from innumerable examples.

S. Francis of Assisi was often "suspended above the earth, sometimes to a height of three, sometimes to a height of four cubits"; the same phenomenon has been recorded by eye-witnesses in many instances throughout the centuries. Among the large number of those who are known to have been raised from the ground whilst wrapt in prayer are the stigmatized S. Catherine of Siena; S. Colette; Rainiero de Borgo San-Sepolcro; S. Catherine de Ricci; S. Alphonsus Rodriguez, S.J.; S. Mary Magdalen de Pazzi; Raimond Rocco; Bl. Charles de Sezze; S. Veronica Giuliani the Capuchiness; S. Gerard Majella, the Redemptorist thaumaturge; that wondrous mystic Anne Catherine Emmerich; Dominica Barbagli (died in 1858), the ecstatica of Montesanto-Savino (Florence), whose levitations were of daily occurrence. S. Ignatius Loyola whilst deeply contemplative was seen by John Pascal to be raised more than a foot from the pavement; S. Teresa and S. John of the Cross were levitated in concurrent ecstasies in the shady locutorio of the Encarnacion, as was witnessed by Beatriz of Jesus and the whole convent of nuns;[51] S. Alphonsus Liguori whilst preaching in the church of S. John Baptist at Foggia was lifted before the eyes of the whole congregation several feet from the ground;[52] Gemma Galgani of Lucca, who died 11 April, 1903, was observed whilst praying one evening in September, 1901, before a venerated Crucifix, to rise in the air in a celestial trance and to remain several minutes at some distance from the floor.[53] Above all, S. Joseph of Cupertino (1603–63), one of the most extraordinary mystics of the seventeenth century, whose whole life seemed one long series of unbroken raptures and ecstasies, was frequently lifted on high to remain suspended in mid-air. Such notice was attracted by this marvel that his superiors sent him from one lonely house of Capuchins or Conventuals to another, and he died at the little hill town of Osimo, where his remains are yet venerated. For many years he was obliged to say Mass at a private altar so inevitable were the ecstasies that fell upon him during the Sacrifice. There are, I think, few sanctuaries more sweet and more fragrant with holiness than this convent at Osimo. During a most happy visit to the shrine of S. Joseph I was deeply touched by the many memorials of the Saints, and by the kindness of the Fathers, his brethren to-day. S. Philip Neri and S. Francis Xavier were frequently raised from the ground at the Elevation, and of the ascetic S. Paul of the Cross the Blessed Strambi writes: "Le serviteur de Dieu s'éleva en l'air à la hauteur de deux palmes, et cela, à deux reprises, avant et après la consecration."[54] (The servant of God during Holy Mass was twice elevated in the air to a height of two hand-breadths from the ground both before and after the Consecration.) It is well known that in a certain London church a holy religious when he said Mass was not unseldom levitated from the predella, which manifestation I have myself witnessed, although the father was himself unconscious thereof until the day of his death.

But, as Görres most aptly remarks,[55] although many examples may be cited of Saints who have been levitated in ecstasy, and although it is not impossible that this phenomenon may be imitated by evil powers—as, indeed, it undoubtedly is in the cases of spiritistic mediums—yet nowhere do we find in hagiography that a large number of Saints were in one company raised from the earth together or conveyed through the air to meet at some appointed spot. Is it likely, then, that the demons would be allowed seemingly to excel by their power a most extraordinary and exceptional manifestation? It must be remembered, also, that save in very rare and singular instances, such as that of S. Joseph of Cupertino, levitation is only for a height of a foot or some eighteen inches, and even this occurs seldom save at moments of great solemnity and psychic concentration.

A question which is largely discussed by the demonologists then arises: Do the witches actually and in person attend the Sabbat or is their journey thither and assistance thereat mere diabolic illusion? Giovanni Francesco Ponzinibio, in his *De Lamiis*,[56] wholly inclines to the latter view, but this is superficial reasoning, and the celebrated canonist Francisco Peña with justice takes him very severely to task for his temerity. Peña's profound work, *In Bernardi Comensis Dominicani Lucernam inquisitorum notæ et eiusdem tractatum de strigibus*,[57] a valuable collection of most erudite glosses, entirely disposes of Ponzinibio's arguments, and puts the case in words of weighty authority.

Sprenger in the *Malleus Maleficarum*, I, had already considered "How witches are bodily transported from one place to another," and he concludes "It is proven, then, that sorcerers can be bodily transported."[58] Paul Grilland inquires: "Whether magicians & witches or Satanists are bodily & actually conveyed to and fro by the Devil, or whether this be merely imaginary?" He freely acknowledges the extraordinary difficulty and intricacy of the investigation, beginning his answer with the phrase "Quaestio ista est multum ardua et famosa."[59] (This is a very difficult and oft-discussed question.) But S. Augustine, S. Thomas, S. Bonaventure, and a score of great names are agreed upon the reality of this locomotion, and Grilland, after balancing the evidence to the nicety of a hair wisely concludes: "Myself I hold the opinion that they are actually transported."[60]

In his *Compendium Maleficarum* Francesco Maria Guazzo discusses (Liber I. 13) "Whether Witches are actually and bodily conveyed from place to place to attend their Sabbats"; and lays down: "The opinion which many who follow Luther & Melancthon hold is that Witches only assist at these assemblies in their imagination, & that they are choused by some trick of the devil, in support of which argument the objectors assert that the Witches have very often been seen lying in one spot and not moving thence. Moreover, what is related in the life of S. Germain is not impertinent in this connexion, to wit, when certain women declared that they had been present at a banquet, & yet all the while they slumbered and slept, as several persons attested. That women of this kind are very often deceived in such a way is certain; but that they are always so deceived is by no means sure. . . . The alternative opinion, which personally I hold most strongly, is that sometimes at any rate Witches are actually conveyed from one place to another by the Devil, who under the bodily form of a goat or some other unclean & monstrous animal himself carries them, & that they are verily and indeed present at their foul midnight Sabbats. This opinion is that generally held by the authoritative Theologians and Master Jurisprudists of Italy and Spain, as also by the Catholic divines and legalists. The majority of writers, indeed, advance this view, for example, Torquemada in his commentary on Grilland, Remy, S. Peter Damian, Silvester of Abula, Tommaso de Vio Gaetani, Alfonso de Castro, Sisto da Siena, O.P., Père Crespet, Bartolomeo Spina in his glosses on Ponzinibio, Lorenzo Anania, and a vast number of others, whose names for brevity's sake I here omit."[61]

This seems admirably to sum up the whole matter. In the encyclopædic treatise *De Strigibus*[62] by an earlier authority, Bernard of Como, the following remarkable passage occurs: "The aforesaid abominable wretches actually & awake & in full enjoyment of their normal senses attend these assemblies or rather orgies, and when they are to go to some spot hard by they proceed thither on foot, cheerily conversing as they walk. If, however, they are to meet in some distant place then are they conveyed by the Devil, yet by whatsoever means they proceed to the said place whether it be on foot or whether they are borne along by the Devil, it is most certain that their journey is real and actual, and not imaginary. Nor are they labouring under any delusion when they deny the Catholic Faith, worship and adore the Devil, tread upon the Cross of Christ, outrage the Most Blessed Sacrament, and give themselves up to filthy and unhallowed copulations, fornicating with the Devil himself who appears to them in a human form, being used by the men as a succubus, & carnally serving the woman as an incubus."[63]

The conclusion then is plain and proven. The witches do actually and individually attend the Sabbat, an orgy of blasphemy and obscenity. Whether they go thither on foot, or horseback, or by some other means is a detail, which in point of fact differs according to the several and infinitely varied circumstances.

It is not denied that in some cases hallucination and self-deception played a large part, but such examples are comparatively speaking few in number, and these, moreover, were carefully investigated and most frequently recognized by the judges and divines. Thus in the *Malleus Maleficarum* Sprenger relates that a woman, who had voluntarily surrendered herself to be examined as being a witch, confessed to the Dominican fathers that she nightly assisted at the Sabbat, and that neither bolts nor bars could prevent her from flying to the infernal revels. Accordingly she was shut fast under lock and key in a chamber whence it was impossible for her to escape, and all the while carefully watched by lynx-eyed officers through a secret soupirail. These reported that immediately the door was closed she threw herself on the bed where in a moment she was stretched out perfectly rigid in all her members. Select members of the tribunal, grave and acute doctors, entered the room. They shook her, gently at first, but presently with considerable roughness. She remained immobile and insensible. She was pinched and pulled sharply. At last a lighted candle was brought and placed near her naked foot until the flesh was actually scorched in the flame. She lay stockish and still, dumb and motionless as a stone. After a while her senses returned to her. She sat up and related in exact detail the happenings at the Sabbat she had attended, the place, the number of the company, the rites, what was spoken, all that was done, and then she complained of a hurt upon her foot. Next day the fathers explained to her all that had passed, how that she had never stirred from the spot, and that the pain arose from the taper which to ensure the experiment had been brought in contact with her flesh. They admonished her straightly but with paternal charity, and upon the humble confession of her error and a promise to guard against any such ill fantasies for the future, a suitable penance was prescribed and the woman dismissed.

In the celebrated cases investigated by Henri Boguet, June, 1598, young George Gandillon confessed to having walked to the Sabbat at a deserted spot called Fontenelles, near the village of Nezar, and also to having ridden to the Sabbat. Moreover, in his indictment the following occurs: "George Gandillon, one Good Friday night, lay in his bed, rigid as a corpse, for the space of three hours, & then on a sudden came to himself. He has since been burned alive here with his father & his sister."[64]

Since Boguet, who is one of our chief authorities, discusses the Sabbat with most copious details in his *Discours des Sorciers* it will not be impertinent to give here the headings and subdivisions of his learned and amply documented chapters.[65]

Chapter XVI. How, & in what way Sorcerers are conveyed to the Sabbat.

1. *They are sometimes conveyed there mounted on a stick, or a broom, sometimes on a sheep or a goat, & sometimes by a tall black man.*
2. *Sometimes they anoint themselves with ointment, & sometimes not.*

3. *There are some people, who although they are not Sorcerers, if they are anointed, are none the less carried off to the Sabbat. The reason for this.*
4. *The unguent, & the ointment are actually of no use to the Sorcerers, and do not in effect carry them to the Sabbat.*
5. *Sorcerers are sometimes conveyed to the Sabbat by a blast of wind & a sudden storm.*

Chapter XVII. Sorcerers may sometimes walk to the Sabbat on foot.

Chapter XVIII. Is the journey of Sorcerers to the Sabbat merely imagination ?

1 & 3. *Reasons for supposing this to be the case, & examples.*
2. *Indications, owing to which it may be supposed, that a certain woman paid a purely imaginary visit to the Sabbat.*
4. *Reasons for supposing that the journey of Sorcerers to the Sabbat, is a real expedition and not imaginary.*
5. *How we are to understand what is related concerning Erichtho, & Apollonius ; the first of whom raised a soldier to life, & the latter a young girl.*
6. *Sorcerers cannot raise the dead to life. Examples.*
7. *Neither can heretics perform miracles. Examples.*
8. *The Author's opinion concerning the subject of this chapter.*
9. *Satan most frequently deceives mankind. Examples.*

Chapter XIX.

1. *Sorcerers go to the Sabbat about midnight.*
2. *The reason why the Sabbat is generally held at night.*
3. *Satan delights in darkness & blackness, which are opposite to the whiteness and light that please Heaven.*
4. *At the Sabbat Sorcerers dance back to back. For the most part they wear masks.*

5 & 8. *When the cock crows the Sabbat immediately comes to an end, and vanishes away. The reason for this.*

6. *The voice of the cock frightens Satan in the same way as it terrifies lions & serpents.*
7. *Several authors relate that demons fear a naked sword.*

Chapter XX. The days on which the Sabbat is held.

1. *The Sabbat may be held on any day of the week, but particularly on a Friday.*
2. *It is also held on the greatest festivals of the year.*

Chapter XXI. The places where the Sabbat is held.

1. *According to many writers the place where the Sabbat is held is distinguished by a clump of trees, or sometimes by a cross. The Author's opinion on this point.*
2. *A remarkable account of a place where the Sabbat was held.*
3. *There must be water near the place where the Sabbat is held. The reason for this.*
4. *If there is no water in the place, the Sorcerers dig a hole in the ground and urinate in this.*

Chapter XXII. The proceedings at the Sabbat.

1. *The Sorcerers worship the Devil who appears under the form of a tall black man, or as a goat. They offer him candles & kiss his posterior.*
2. *They dance. A description of their dances.*
3. *They give themselves up to every kind of filthy abomination. The Devil transforms himself into an Incubus & into a Succubus.*
4. *The hideous orgies & foul copulations practised by the Euchites, & Gnostics.*
5. *The Sorcerers feast at the Sabbat. Their meat & their drink. The way in which they say grace before and after table.*
6. *However, this food never satisfies their appetites, & they always arise from table as hungry as before.*
7. *When they have finished their meal, they give the Devil a full account of all their actions.*
8. *They again renounce God, their baptism, &c. How Satan incites them to do evil.*
9. *They raise dark storms.*
10. *They celebrate their mass. Of their vestments, & holy water.*
11. *Sometimes to conclude the Sabbat Satan seems to be consumed in a flame of fire, & to be completely reduced*

to ashes. All present take a small part of these ashes, which the Sorcerers use for their charms.

12. *Satan is always the Ape of God in everything.*

As the procedure in the various Sabbats differed very greatly according to century, decade, country, district, nay, even in view of the station of life and, it would seem, the very temperaments of the assembly, it is only possible to outline in a general way some of the most remarkable ceremonies which took place on the occasions of these infernal congregations. An intimate and intensive study of the Sabbat would require a large volume, for it is quite possible to reconstruct the rites in every particular, although the precise order of the ritual was not always and everywhere the same.

Dom Calmet, it is true, has very mistakenly said: "To attempt to give a description of the Sabbat, is to attempt a description of what does not exist, & what has never existed save in the fantastic & disordered imagination of warlocks & witches: the pictures which have been drawn of these assemblies are merely the phantasy of those who dreamed that they had actually been borne, body & soul, through the air to the Sabbat."[66] Happy sceptic! But unfortunately the Sabbat did—and does—take place; formerly in deserted wastes, on the hill-side, in secluded spots, now, as often as not, in the privacy of vaults and cellars, and in those lone empty houses innocently placarded "To be Sold."

The President of the Sabbat was in purely local gatherings often the Officer of the district; in the more solemn assemblies convened from a wider area, the Grand Master, whose dignity would be proportionate to the numbers of the company and the extent of his province. In any case the President was officially known as the "Devil," and it would seem that his immediate attendants and satellites were also somewhat loosely termed "devils," which formal nomenclature has given rise to considerable confusion and not a little mystification in the reports of witch trials and the confessions of offenders. But in many instances it is certain—and orthodoxy forbids us to doubt the possibility—that the Principle of Evil, incarnate, was present for the hideous adoration of his besotted worshippers. Such is the sense of the Fathers, such is the conclusion of the theologians who have dealt with these dark abominations. Metaphysically it is possible; historically it is indisputable.

When a human being, a man, occupied the chief position at these meetings and directed the performance of the rites, he would sometimes appear in a hideous and grotesque disguise, sometimes without any attempt at concealment. This masquerade generally took the shape of an animal, and had its origin in heathendom, whence by an easy transition through the ceremonial of heretics, it passed to the sorcerer and the witch. As early as the *Liber Pœnitentialis* of S. Theodore, Archbishop of Canterbury, 668–690, we have a distinct prohibition of this foul mummery. Capitulum xxvii denounces the man who "in Kalendas Ianuarii in ceruulo et in uitula uadit." "If anyone at the kalends of January goes about as a stag or a bull; that is making himself into a wild animal and dressing in the skin of a herd animal, and putting on the head of beasts; those who in such wise transform themselves into the appearance of a wild animal, penance for three years because this is devilish."

Among the many animal forms which the leader of the Sabbat (the "Devil") assumed in masquerade the most common are the bull, the cat, and above all the goat. Thus the Basque term for the Sabbat is "Akhelarre," "goat pasture." Sometimes the leader is simply said to have shown himself in the shape of a beast, which possibly points to the traditional disguise of a black hairy skin, horns, hoofs, claws, and a tail, in fact the same dress as a demon wore upon the stage.[67] In an old German ballad, *Druten Zeitung*, printed at Smalcald in 1627, "to be sung to the tune of *Dorothea*," it is said that the judges, anxious to extort a confession from a witch, sent down into her twilight dungeon the common hangman dressed in a bear's skin with horns, hoofs, and tail complete. The miserable prisoner thinking that Lucifer had indeed visited her at once appealed to him for help:

Man shickt ein Henkersnecht
Zu ihr in Gefängniss n'unter,
   Den man hat kleidet recht,
Mit einer Bärnhaute,
   Als wenns der Teufel wär;
Als ihm die Drut anschaute
   Meints ihr Bühl kam daher.

Here we have a curious and perhaps unique example of the demoniac masquerade subtly used to obtain evidence of guilt by a trick. The Aberdeen witch Jonet Lucas (1597) said that the Devil was at the Sabbat "beand in likenes of ane beist." But Agnes Wobster of the same company declared that "Satan apperit to them in the likenes of a calff," so possibly two masquerades were employed. Gabriel Pellé (1608) confessed that he attended a Sabbat presided over by the Devil, and "le Diable estoit en vache noire."[68] Françoise Secretain, who was tried in August, 1598, saw the Devil "tantost en forme de chat." Rolande de Vernois acknowledged "Le Diable se presenta pour lors au Sabbat en forme d'vn groz chat noir."[69] To the goat there are innumerable allusions. In the Basses-Pyrénées (1609): "Le Diable estoit en forme de bouc ayant vne queue & audessous vn visage d'homme noir." (The Devil appeared in the form of a goat having a tail & his fundament was the face of a black man.) Iohannis d'Aguerre said that the Devil was "en forme de bouc."[70] "Marie d'Aguerre said that there was in the midst of the ring an immense pitcher whence the Devil issued in the form of a goat." Gentien le Clerc, who was tried at Orleans in 1614, "said that, as he was told, his mother when he was three years old presented him at the Sabbat to a goat whom they saluted as l'Aspic."[71] "Sur le trône," writes Görres, "est assis un bouc, ou du moins la forme d'un bouc, car le démon ne peut cacher ce qu'il est."[72]

In 1630 Elizabeth Stevenson, *alias* Toppock, of Niddrie, avowed to her judges that in company with Catharine Oswald, who was tried for being by *habite and repute* a witch, and Alexander Hamilton, "a known warlock," she went "to a den betwixt Niddrie and Edmiston, where the devill had trysted hir, where he appeared first to them like a foall, and then like a man, and appointed a new dyet at Salcott Muire." When one of Catharine Oswald's intimates, Alexander Hunter, *alias* Hamilton, *alias* Hattaraick, a "Warlok Cairle" who "abused the Countrey for a long time,"[73] was apprehended at Dunbar he confessed that the Devil would meet him riding upon a black horse, or in the shape of a *corbie*, a cat, or a dog. He was burned upon Castle Hill, Edinburgh, 1631.

Sometimes those who are present at the Sabbat are

masked. Canon Ribet writes: "Les visiteurs du sabbat se cachent quelquefois sous des formes bestiales, on se couvrent le visage d'un masque pour demeurer inconnus."[74] (Those who attend the Sabbat sometimes disguise themselves as beasts, or cover their faces to conceal their identities.)

At the famous Sabbat of one hundred and forty witches in North Berwick churchyard on All Hallow e'en, 1590, when they danced "endlong the Kirk-yard" "John Fian, missellit [masked] led the ring." The Salamanca doctors mention the appearance at the Sabbats of persons "aut aperta, aut linteo uelata facie,"[75] "with their faces sometimes bare, sometimes shrouded in a linen wimple." And Delrio has in reference to this precaution: "Facie interdum aperta, interdum uelata larua, linteo, uel alio uelamine aut persona."[76] (Sometimes their faces are bare, sometimes hidden, either in a vizard, a linen cloth, or a veil, or a mask.)

In the latter half of the eighteenth century the territory of Limburg was terrorized by a mysterious society known as "The Goats." These wretches met at night in a secret chapel, and after the most hideous orgies, which included the paying of divine honours to Satan and other foul blasphemies of the Sabbat, they donned masks fashioned to imitate goats' heads, cloaked themselves with long disguise mantles, and sallied forth in bands to plunder and destroy. From 1772 to 1774 alone the tribunal of Foquemont condemned four hundred Goats to the gallows. But the organization was not wholly exterminated until about the year 1780 after a regime of the most repressive measures and unrelaxing vigilance.

Among certain tribes inhabiting the regions of the Congo there exists a secret association of Egbo worshippers. Egbo or Ekpé is the evil genius or Satan. His rites are Obeeyahism, the adoration of Obi, or the Devil, and devil-worship is practised by many barbarous races, as, for instance, by the Coroados and the Tupayas, in the impenetrable forests between the rivers Prado and Doce in Brazil, by the Abipones of Paraguay, as well as by the Bachapins, a Caffre race, by the negroes on the Gold Coast and the negroes of the West Indies. In the ju-ju houses of the Egbo sorcerers are obscene wooden statues to which great veneration is paid, since by their means divination is solemnly practised. Certain festivals are held during the year, and at these it is interesting to note that the members wear hideous black masks with huge horns which it is death for the uninitiated to see.

The first ceremony of the Sabbat was the worship of, and the paying homage to the Devil. It would seem that sometimes this was preceded by a roll-call of the evil devotees. Agnes Sampson confessed that at the meeting in North Berwick, when the whole assembly had entered the church, "The *Devil* started up himself in the *Pulpit* like a mickle black man, and calling the Row, every one answered *Here. Mr. Robert Grierson* being named, they all ran *hirdie girdie*, and were angry: for it was promised he should be called *Robert* the *Comptroller, alias Rob* the *Rower*, for expriming of his name. The first thing he demanded was whether they had been good servants, and what they had done since the last time they had convened."

The witches adored Satan, or the Master of the Sabbat who presided in place of Satan, by prostrations, genuflections, gestures, and obeisances. In mockery of solemn bows and seemly courtesies the worshippers of the Demon approach him awkwardly, with grotesque and obscene mops and mows, sometimes straddling sideways, sometimes walking backwards, as Guazzo says: Cum accedunt ad dæmones eos ueneraturi terga obuertunt & cessim eum cancrorum more supplicaturi manus inuersas retro applicant.[77] But their chief act of homage was the reverential kiss, *osculum infame*. This impious and lewd ritual is mentioned in detail by most authorities and is to be found in all lands and centuries. So Delrio writes: "The Sabbat is presided over by a Demon, the Lord of the Sabbat, who appears in some monstrous form, most generally as a goat or some hound of hell, seated upon a haughty throne. The witches who resort to the Sabbat approach the throne with their backs turned, and worship him . . . and then, as a sign of their homage, they kiss his fundament." Guazzo notes: "As a sign of homage witches kiss the Devil's fundament." And Ludwig Elich says: "Then as a token of their homage—with reverence be it spoken—they kiss the fundament of the Devil."[78] "Y al tiempo que le besan debajo de la cola, da una ventosidad de muy horrible olor," adds the Spanish *Relacion*, "fetid, foul, and filthy."

To cite other authorities would be but to quote the same words. Thomas Cooper, indeed, seems to regard this ceremony as a part of the rite of admission, but to confine it to this occasion alone is manifestly incorrect, for there is continual record of its observance at frequent Sabbats by witches of many years standing. "Secondly," he remarks, "when this acknowledgement is made, in testimoniall of this subiection, Satan offers his back-parts to be kissed of his vassall."[79] But in the dittay of the North Berwick witches, all of whom had long been notorious for their malpractices, "*Item*, the said Agnis Sampson confessed that the divell being then at North Barrick Kerke, attending their comming, in the habit or likenesse of a man,[80] and seeing that they tarried over long, hee at their comming enjoyned them all to a pennance, which was, that they should kisse his buttockes, in sign of duety to him, which being put over the pulpit bare, every one did as he had enjoyned them."[81]

One of the principal charges which was repeatedly brought against the Knights Templars during the lengthy ecclesiastical and judicial processes, 1307–1314, was that of the *osculum infame* given by the juniors to their preceptors. Even so prejudiced a writer as Lea cannot but admit the truth of this accusation. In this case, however, it has nothing to do with sorcery but must be connected with the homosexuality which the Order universally practised.

There are some very important details rehearsed in a Bull, 8 June, 1303, of the noble but calumniated Boniface VIII, with reference to the case of Walter Langton, Bishop of Lichfield and Coventry (1296–1322), and treasurer of Edward I, when this prelate was accused of sorcery and homage to Satan: "For some time past it has come to our ears that our Venerable Brother Walter Bishop of Coventry and Lichfield has been commonly defamed, and accused, both in the realm of England and elsewhere, of paying homage to the Devil by kissing his posterior, and that he hath had frequent colloquies with evil spirits."[82] The Bishop cleared himself of these charges with the compurgators. Bodin refers to Guillaume Edeline, who was executed in 1453 as a wizard. He was a doctor of the Sorbonne, and prior of St. Germain en Laye: "The aforesaid sire Guillaume confessed . . . that he had done homage to the aforesaid Satan, who appeared in the shape of a ram, by kissing his buttocks in token of reverence and homage."[83] A very rare tract of the fourteenth century directed against the Waldenses among other charges brings the following: "Item, in aliquibus aliis partibus apparet eis dæmon sub specie et figura cati, quem sub cauda sigillatim osculantur." (The Devil appears to them as a cat, and they kiss him *sub cauda.*)[84]

Barthélemy Minguet of Brécy, a young man of twenty-five, who was tried in 1616, said that at the Sabbat "he often saw [the Devil] in the shape of a man, who held a horse by its bridle, & that they went forward to worship him, each one holding a pitch candle of black wax in their hands."[85] These candles, as Guazzo tells us, were symbolic and required by the ritual of the Sabbat, not merely of use for the purpose of giving light: "Then they made an offering of pitch black candles, and as a sign of homage kissed his fundament."[86] The candles were ordinarily black, and one taper, larger than the rest, was frequently carried by the Devil himself. At the North Berwick meeting when the witches were all to assemble in the church, "*Iohn Fein* blew up the Kirk doors, and blew in the lights, which wer like *Mickl black candles sticking round about the Pulpit.*"[87] Boguet relates that the witches whom he tried confessed that the Sabbat commenced with the adoration of Satan, "who appeared, sometimes in the shape of a tall dark man, sometimes in the shape of a goat, & to express their worship and homage, they made him an offering of candles, which burned with a blue light."[88] John Fian, also, when doing homage to the Devil "thought he saw the light of a candle . . . which appeared blue lowe." This, of course, was on account of the sulphurous material whence these candles were specially compounded. De Lancre expressly states that the candles or flambeaux used at the Sabbat were made of pitch.

An important feature of the greater Sabbats was the ritual dance, for the dance was an act of devotion which has descended to us from the earliest times and is to be found in every age and every country. Dancing is a natural movement, a primitive expression of emotion and ideals. In the ancient world there can have been few things fairer than that rhythmic thanksgiving of supple limbs and sweet voices which Athens loved, and for many a century was preserved the memory of that day when the young Sophocles lead the choir in celebration of the victory of Salamis.[89] The Mystæ in the meadows of Elysium danced their rounds with the silver clash of cymbals and with madly twinkling snow-white feet. At the solemn procession of the Ark from Cariathiarim (Kirjath Jearim) King David "danced with all his might before the Lord, . . . dancing and leaping before the Lord." S. Basil urges his disciples to dance on earth in order to fit themselves for what may be one of the occupations of the angels in heaven. As late as the seventeenth century the ceremonial dance in church was not uncommon. In 1683 it was the duty of the senior canon to lead a dance of choir-boys in the Paris cathedral. Among the Abyssinian Christians dancing forms no inconsiderable part of worship. Year by year on Whit Tuesday hundreds of pilgrims dance through the streets of Echternach (Luxemburg) to the shrine of S. Willibrod in S. Peter's Church. Formerly the devotees danced three times round the great Abbey Courtyard before proceeding to the sanctuary. But beyond all these the dance has its own place in the ritual of Holy Church even yet. Three times a year in Seville Cathedral—on Holy Thursday, upon Corpus Christi and the Immaculate Conception—Los Seises dance before a specially constructed altar, exquisitely adorned with flowers and lights, erected near the outer door of the grand western entrance of the cathedral. The ceremony in all probability dates from the thirteenth century.

The dresses of the boys, who dance before the improvised altar at Benediction on Corpus Christi, are of the period of Philip III, and consist of short trousers and jackets that hang from one shoulder, the doublets being of red satin, with rich embroidery. Plumed white hats with feathers are worn, also shoes with large scintillating buckles. On Holy Thursday the costume is also red and white, whilst it is blue and white for "the day of the Virgin."

The eight boy choristers—with eight others as attendants—dance, with castanets in their hands, to a soft organ obbligato, down the centre of the cathedral to the decorated altar, advancing slowly and gracefully. Here they remain for about a quarter of an hour, singing a hymn, and accompanying it (as the carols of the olden time) with dance and castanets.

They sing a two-part hymn in front of the altar, forming in two eights, facing each other, the clergy kneeling in a semicircle round them.

Assuredly I cannot do better than quote Mr. Arthur Symons' verdict on this dance as he saw it a few years back in Seville: "And, yes, I found it perfectly dignified, perfectly religious, without a suspicion of levity or indecorum. This consecration of the dance, this turning of a possible vice into a means of devotion, this bringing of the people's art, the people's passion, which in Seville is dancing, into the church, finding it a place there, is precisely one of those acts of divine worldly wisdom which the Church has so often practised in her conquest of the world."

Not too fantastically has a writer suggested that High Mass itself in some sense enshrines a survival of the ancient religious dance—that stately, magnificent series of slow movements which surely may express devotion of the most solemn and reverent kind, as well as can the colour of vestment or sanctuary, or the sounds of melody.

Since the dance is so essentially religious it must needs be burlesqued and buffooned by God's ape. For the dance of the witches is degraded, awkward, foul, and unclean. These very movements are withershins, as Guazzo points out: "Then follow the round dances in which, however, they always tread the measure to the left."[90] "The Sorcerers," says Boguet, "dance a country-dance with their backs turned one to the other."[91] This, of course, being the exact reverse of the natural country-dance. "Sometimes, although seldom," he adds, "they dance in couples, & sometimes one partner is there, another here, for always everything is in confusion."[92] De Lancre writes of witches' revels: "They only dance three kinds of brawls. . . . The first is *à la Bohêmienne* . . . the second with quick trippings: these are round dances."[93] In the third Sabbat measure the dancers were placed one behind another in a straight line.

An old Basque legend reported by Estefanella Hirigaray describes how the witches were wont to meet near an old limekiln to dance their rounds, a ceremony regarded throughout that district as an essential feature of the Sabbat. De Lancre notes the brawls *à la Bohêmienne* as especially favoured by sorcerers in Labourd. Sylvester Mazzolini, O.P.

(1460–1523), Master of the Sacred Palace, and the great champion of orthodoxy against the heresiarch Luther, in his erudite *De Strigimagia*[94] relates that in Como and Brescia a number of children between eight and twelve years old, who had frequented the Sabbat, but had been happily converted by the unsparing patience of the Inquisitors, at the request of the Superiors gave exhibitions of these dances when they showed such extraordinary adroitness and skill in executing the most intricate and fantastic figures that it was evident they had been instructed by no mere human tutelage. Marco de Viqueria, the Dominican Prior of the Brussels monastery, closely investigated the matter, and he was a religious of such known acumen and exceptional probity that his testimony soon convinced many prelates at Rome who were inclined to suspect some trickery or cunning practice. In Belgium this Sabbat dance was known as *Pauana*.

In the Fian trial Agnes Sampson confessed that "They danced along the *Kirk-yeard, Geilic Duncan* playing on a *Trump*, and *John Fein* mussiled led the *Ring*. The said *Agnes* and her daughter followed next. Besides these were *Kate Gray, George Noilis* his wife, . . . with the rest of their Cummers above an hundred Persons."[95] She further added "that this Geillis Duncane did goe before them, playing this reill or daunce uppon a small trumpe, called a Jewe's trumpe, untill they entered into the Kerk of North Barrick."[96] "These confessions made the King [James I, then James VI of Scotland] in a wonderfull admiration, and sent for the saide Geillis Duncane, who, upon the like trumpe, did play the saide daunce before the kinges maiestie."

Music generally accompanied the dancers, and there is ample evidence that various instruments were played, violins, flutes, tambourines, citterns, hautboys, and, in Scotland, the pipes. Those of the witches who had any skill were the performers, and very often they obliged the company awhile with favourite airs of a vulgar kind, but the concert ended in the most hideous discords and bestial clamour; the laws of harmony and of decency were alike rudely violated. In August, 1590, a certain Nicolas Laghernhard, on his way to Assencauria, was passing through the outskirts of a wood when he saw through the trees a number of men and women dancing with filthy and fantastic movements. In amaze he signed himself and uttered the Holy Name, whereupon the company perceiving him took to flight, but not before he had recognized many of these wretches. He was prompt to inform the ecclesiastical tribunals, and several persons being forthwith questioned freely acknowledged their infamies. Amongst these a shepherd named Michael, who enjoyed a considerable reputation for his musical talents and strangely fascinating voice, confessed that he was the piper at the local Sabbat and that his services were in constant requisition. At the lesser Sabbats (*aquelarre*) of Zugarramurdi, a hamlet of Navarre, some six hundred souls, in the Bastan valley, some twelve leagues from Pampluna, one Juan de Goyburu was wont to play upon the flute, and Juan de Sansin the tambourine. These two unhappy wretches, having shown every sign of sincerest contrition, were reconciled to the Church.

Sinclar in his Relation XXXV, "Anent some Prayers, Charms, and Avies, used in the *Highlands*," says: "As the Devil is originally the Author of *Charms*, and *Spells*, so is he the Author of several baudy Songs, which are sung. A reverend Minister told me, that one who was the Devils Piper, a wizzard confest to him, that at a Ball of dancing, the Foul Spirit taught him a Baudy song to sing and play, as it were this night, and ere two days past all the Lads and Lasses of the town were lilting it throw the street. It were abomination to rehearse it." Philip Ludwig Elich precisely sums up the confused scene: "The whole foul mob and stinkard rabble sing the most obscene priapics and abominable songs in honour of the Devil. One witch yells, *Harr, harr;* a second hag, Devil, Devil; jump hither, jump thither; a third, Gambol hither, gambol thither; another, *Sabaoth, Sabaoth*, &c.; and so the wild orgy waxes frantic what time the bedlam rout are screeching, hissing, howling, caterwauling, and whooping lewd wassail."[97] Of all the horrors of the Sabbat the climax was that appalling blasphemy and abominable impiety by which the most Holy Sacrifice of the Altar was mocked and burlesqued in hideous fashion. And since no Christian will receive the Blessed Sacrament save he be duly fasting as the Church so strictly enjoins, the witches in derision of Christ's ordinance satiate their appetites with a wolfish feast and cram themselves to excess with food of all kinds, both meat and drink, before they proceed to the ritual of hell. These orgies were often prolonged amid circumstances of the most beastly gluttony and drunkenness.

Guazzo writes: "Tables are laid and duly furnished, whereupon they set themselves to the board & begin to gobbet piecemeal the meats which the Devil provides, or which each member of the party severally brings with him."[98] De Lancre also says: "Many authors say that sorcerers at the Sabbat eat the food which the Devil lays before them: but very often the table is only dressed with the viands they themselves bring along. Sometimes there are certain tables served with rare dainties, at others with orts and offal." "Their banquets are of various kinds of food according to the district & the quality of those who are to partake."[99] It seems plain that when the local head of the witches, who often presided at these gatherings *absente diabolo*, was a person of wealth or standing, delicacies and choice wines would make their appearance at the feast, but when it was the case of the officer of a coven in some poor and small district, possibly a meeting of peasants, the homeliest fare only might be served. The Lancashire witches of 1613, when they met at Malking Tower, sat down to a goodly spread of "Beefe, Bacon, and roasted Mutton," the sheep having been killed twenty-four hours earlier by James Device; in 1633 Edmund Robinson stated that the Pendle witches offered him "flesh and bread upon a trencher, and drink in a glass," they also had "flesh smoaking, butter in lumps, and milk," truly rustic dainties. Alice Duke, a Somerset witch, tried in 1664, confessed that the Devil "bids them *Welcome* at their *Coming*, and brings them *Wine*, *Beer*, *Cakes*, and *Meal*, or the like."[100] At the trial of Louis Gaufridi at Aix in 1610 the following description of a Sabbat banquet was given: "Then they feasted, three tables being set out according to the three aforesaid degrees. Those who were employed in serving bread had loaves made from wheat privily stolen in various places. They drank malmsey in order to excite them to venery. Those who acted as cup-bearers had filched the wine from cellars where it was stored. Sometimes they ate the tender flesh of little children, who had been slain and roasted at some Synagogue, and sometimes babes were brought there, yet alive, whom the witches had kidnapped from their homes if opportunity offered."[101] In many places the witches were not lucky enough to get bumpers of malmsey, for Boguet notes that at some Sabbats "They not unseldom drink wine but more often water."[102]

There are occasional records of unsavoury and tasteless viands, and there is even mention of putrefying garbage and carrion being placed before his evil worshippers by their Master. Such would appear to have been the case at those darker orgies when there was a manifestation of supernatural intelligences from the pit.

The Salamanca doctors say: "They make a meal from food either furnished by themselves or by the Devil. It is sometimes most delicious and delicate, and sometimes a pie baked from babies they have slain or disinterred corpses. A suitable grace is said before such a table."[103] Guazzo thus describes their wine: "Moreover the wine which is usually poured out for the revellers is like black and clotted blood served in some foul and filthy vessel. Yet there seems to be no lack of cheer at these banquets, save that they furnish neither bread nor salt. Isabella further added that human flesh was served."[104]

Salt never appeared at the witches' table. Bodin gives us the reason that it is an emblem of eternity,[105] and Philip Ludwig Elich emphatically draws attention to the absence of salt at these infernal banquets.[106] "At these meals," remarks Boguet, "salt never appears."[107] Gentien le Clerc, who was tried in Orleans in 1615, confessed: "They sit down to table, but no salt is ever seen."[108] Madeleine de la Palud declared that she had never seen salt, olives, or oil at the Devil's feasts.[109]

When all these wretches are replete they proceed to a solemn parody of Holy Mass.

At the beginning of the eighteenth century Marcelline Pauper of the Congregation of the Sisters of Charity of Nevers was divinely called to offer herself up as a victim of reparation for the outrages done to the Blessed Sacrament, especially by sorcerers in their black masses at the Sabbat. In March, 1702, a frightful sacrilege was committed in the convent chapel. The tabernacle was forced open, the ciborium stolen, and those of the Hosts which had not been carried away by the Satanists were thrown to the pavement and trampled under foot. Marcelline made ceaseless reparation, and at nine o'clock of the evening of 26 April, she received the stigmata in hands, feet, and side, and also the Crown of Thorns. After a few years of expiation she died at Tulle, 25 June, 1708.

The erudite Paul Grilland tells us that the liturgy is burlesqued in every detail: "Those witches who have solemnly devoted themselves to the Devil's service, worship him in a particular manner with ceremonial sacrifices, which they offer to the Devil, imitating in all respects the worship of Almighty God, with vestments, lights, and every other ritual observance, and with a set liturgy in which they are instructed, so that they worship and praise him eternally, just as we worship the true God."[110] This abomination of blasphemy is met with again and again in the confessions of witches, and although particulars may differ here and there, the same quintessence of sacrilege persisted throughout the centuries, even as alas! in hidden corners and secret lairs of infamy it skulks and lurks this very day.

What appears extremely surprising in this connexion is the statement of Cotton Mather that the New England witches "met in Hellish *Randezvous*, wherein the Confessors (i.e. the accused who confessed) do say, they have had their Diabolical Sacraments, imitating the *Baptism* and the *Supper* of our Lord."[111] At the trial of Bridget Bishop, *alias* Oliver, at the Court of Oyer and Terminer, held at Salem, 2 June, 1692, Deliverance Hobbs, a converted witch, affirmed "that this *Bishop* was at a General Meeting of the Witches, in a Field at *Salem*-Village, and there partook of a Diabolical Sacrament in Bread and Wine then administered." In the case of Martha Carrier, tried 2 August, 1692, before the same court, two witnesses swore they had seen her "at a Diabolical Sacrament . . . when they had Bread and Wine Administered unto them." Abigail Williams confessed that on 31 March, 1692, when there was a Public Fast observed in Salem on account of the scourge of sorcery "the Witches had a *Sacrament* that day at an house in the Village, and that they had *Red Bread* and *Red Drink*." This "Red Bread" is certainly puzzling. But the whole thing, sufficiently profane no doubt, necessarily lacks the hideous impiety of the black mass. A minister, the Rev. George Burroughs, is pointed to by accumulated evidence as being the Chief of the Salem witches; "he was Accused by Eight of the Confessing Witches as being an Head Actor at some of their Hellish Randezvouses, and one who had the promise of being a King in Satan's kingdom"; it was certainly he who officiated at their ceremonies, for amongst others Richard Carrier "affirmed to the jury that he saw Mr. George Burroughs at the witch meeting at the village and saw him administer the sacrament," whilst Mary Lacy, senr., and her daughter Mary "affirmed that Mr. George Burroughs was at the witch meetings with witch sacraments."[112]

The abomination of the black mass is performed by some apostate or renegade priest who has delivered himself over to the service of evil and is shamefully prominent amongst the congregation of witches. It should be remarked from this fact that it is plain the witches are as profoundly convinced of the doctrines of Transubstantiation, the Totality, Permanence, and Adorableness of the Eucharistic Christ, and of the power also of the sacrificing priesthood, as is the most orthodox Catholic. Indeed, unless such were the case, their revolt would be empty, void at any rate of its material malice.

One of the gravest charges brought against the Templars and in the trials (1307–1314) established beyond any question or doubt was that of celebrating a blasphemous mass in which the words of consecration were omitted. It has, indeed, been suggested that the liturgy used by the Templars was not the ordinary Western Rite, but that it was an Eastern Eucharist. According to Catholic teaching the Consecration takes place when the words of institution are recited with intention and appropriate gesture, the actual change of the entire substances of bread and wine into the Body and Blood of Christ being effected in virtue of the words *Hoc est enim Corpus meum; Hic est enim Calix sanguinis mei. . . .* This has been defined by a decree of the Council of Florence (1439): "Quod illa uerba diuina Saluatoris omnem uirtutem transsubstantiationis habent." (These divine words of Our Saviour have full power to effect transubstantiation.) But the Orthodox Church holds that an Epiklesis is necessary to valid consecration, the actual words of Our Lord being repeated "as a narrative" [διηγηματικῶς],[113] which would seem logically to imply that Christ's words have no part in the form of the Sacrament. In all Orthodox liturgies the words of Consecration are found together with the Epiklesis, and there are in existence some few liturgies, plainly invalid, which omit the words of Consecration altogether. These are all of them forms which have been employed by heretical sects ; and it may be that the Templars used one of these. But it is far more probable that the words were purposely omitted ; the Templars were corroded with Gnostic doctrines, they held the heresies of the Mandæans or Johannites who were filled with an insane hatred of Christ in much the same way as witches and demonolaters, they followed the tenets of the Ophites who venerated the Serpent and prayed to him for protection against the Creator, they adored and offered sacrifice before an idol, a Head, which, as Professor Prutz holds, represented the lower god whom Gnostic bodies worshipped, that is Satan. At his trial in Tuscany the knight Bernard of Parma confessed that the Order firmly believed this idol had the power to save and to enrich, in fine, flat diabolism. The secret mass of the Templars may have burlesqued an Eastern liturgy rather than the Western rite, but none the less it was the essential cult of the evil principle.

In 1336 a priest who had been imprisoned by the Comte de Foix, Gaston III Phébus, on a charge of celebrating a Satanic mass, was sent to Avignon and examined by Benedict XII in person. The next year the same pontiff appointed his trusty Guillaume Lombard to preside at the trial of Pierre du Chesne, a priest from the diocese of Tarbes, accused of defiling the Host.

Gilles de Sillé, a priest of the diocese of S. Malo, and the Florentine Antonio Francesco Prelati, formerly of the diocese of Arezzo, were wont to officiate at the black masses of Tiffauges and Machecoul, the castles of Gilles de Rais, who was executed in 1440.

A priest named Benedictus in the sixteenth century caused great scandal by the discovery of his assistance at secret and unhallowed rites. Charles IX employed an apostate monk to celebrate the eucharist of hell before himself and his intimates, and during the reign of his brother the Bishop of

Paris burned in the Place de Grève a friar named Séchelle who had been found guilty of participating in similar profane mysteries. In 1597 the Parliament of Paris sentenced Jean Belon, curé of S. Pierre-des-Lampes in the Bourges diocese, to be hanged and his body burned for desecration of the Sacrament and the repeated celebration of abominable ceremonies.[114] The Parliament of Bordeaux in 1598 condemned to the stake Pierre Aupetit, curé of Pageas, near Chalus Limousin. He confessed that for more than twenty years he had frequented Sabbats, especially those held at Mathegoutte and Puy-de-Dôme, where he worshipped the Devil and performed impious masses in his honour.[115] August 14, 1606, a friar named Denobilibus was put to death at Grenoble upon a similar conviction. In 1609 the Parliament of Bordeaux sent Pierre De Lancre and d'Espagnet to Labourd in the Bayonne district to stamp out the sorcerers who infested that region. No less than seven priests were arrested on charges of celebrating Satan's mass at the Sabbat. Two, Migalena, an old man of seventy, and Pierre Bocal, aged twenty-seven, were executed, but the Bishop of Bayonne interfered, claimed the five for his own tribunal and contrived that they should escape from prison. Three other priests who were under restraint were immediately set free, and wisely quitted the country. A twelvemonth later Aix and the whole countryside rang with the confessions of Madeleine de la Palud who "Dit aussi que ce malheureux Loys magicien . . . a controuvé le premier de dire la messe au sabatt et consacrer Véritablement et présenter le sacrifice à Lucifer."[116] It was, of course, mere ignorance on her part to suppose that "that accursed Magician Lewes did first inuent the saying of Masse at the Sabbaths," although Gaufridi may have told her this to impress her with a sense of his importance and power among the hierarchies of evil. Certainly in her evidence the details of the Sabbat worship are exceptionally detailed and complete.

They are, however, amply paralleled, if not exceeded, by the narrative of Madeleine Bavent, a Franciscan sister of the Third Order, attached to the convent of SS. Louis and Elizabeth at Louviers. Her confessions, which she wrote at length by the direction of her confessor, des Marets, an Oratorian, meticulously describe scenes of the most hideous blasphemy in which were involved three chaplains, David, Maturin Picard, the curé of Mesnil-Jourdain, and Thomas Boullé, sometime his assistant. Amongst other enormities they had revived the heresy of the Adamites, an early Gnostic sect, and celebrated the Mass in a state of stark nudity amid circumstances of the grossest indecency. Upon one Good Friday Picard and Boullé had compelled her to defile the crucifix and to break a consecrated Host, throwing the fragments upon the ground and trampling them. David and Picard were dead, but Boullé was burned at Rouen, 21 August, 1647.[117]

During the reign of Louis XIV a veritable epidemic of sacrilege seemed to rage throughout Paris.[118] The horrors of the black mass were said in many houses, especially in that of La Voisin (Catherine Deshayes) who lived in the rue Beauregard. The leading spirit of this crew was the infamous abbé Guibourg, a bastard son—so gossip said—of Henri de Montmorency. With him were joined Brigallier, almoner of the Grande Mademoiselle; Bouchot, director of the convent of La Saussaye; Dulong, a canon of Notre-Dame; Dulausens, vicar of Saint-Leu; Dubousquet; Seysson; Dussis; Lempérier; Lépreux; Davot, vicar of Notre-Dame de Bonne-Nouvelle; Mariette, vicar of Saint-Séverin, skilled in maledictions; Lemeignan, vicar of Saint-Eustache, who was convicted of having sacrificed numberless children to Satan; Toumet; Le Franc; Cotton, vicar of St. Paul, who had baptized a baby with the chrism of Extreme Unction and then throttled him upon the altar; Guignard and Sébault of the diocese of Bourges, who officiated at the black mass in the cellars of a house at Paris, and confected filthy charms under conditions of the most fearful impiety.

In the eighteenth century the black mass persisted. In 1723 the police arrested the abbé Lecollet and the abbé Bournement for this profanity; and in 1745 the abbé de Rocheblanche fell under the same suspicion. At the hotel of Madame de Charolais the vilest scenes of the Sabbat were continued. A gang of Satanists celebrated their monstrous orgies at Paris on 22 January, 1793, the night after the murder of Louis XVI. The abbé Fiard in two of his works, *Lettres sur le diable*, 1791, and *La France Trompée* . . . Paris, 8vo, 1803, conclusively shows that eucharistic blasphemies were yet being perpetrated but in circumstances of almost impenetrable secrecy. In 1865 a scandal connected with these abominations came to light, and the Bishop of Sens, in whose diocese it occurred, was so horrified that he resigned his office and retired to Fontainebleau, where he died some eighteen months later, practically of shock. Similar practices were unmasked at Paris in 1874 and again in 1878, whilst it is common knowledge that the characters of Joris Karl Huysmans' *Là-Bas* were all persons easy of identification, and the details are scenes exactly reproduced from contemporary life.[119] The hideous cult of evil yet endures. Satanists yet celebrate the black mass in London, Brighton, Paris, Lyons, Bruges, Berlin, Milan, and alas! in Rome itself. Both South America and Canada are thus polluted. In many a town, both great and small, they have their dens of blasphemy and evil where they congregate unsuspected to perform these execrable rites. Often they seem to concentrate their vile energies in the quiet cathedral cities of England, France, Italy, in vain endeavour to disturb the ancient homes of peace with the foul brabble of devil-worship and all ill.

They have even been brought upon the public stage. One episode of *Un Soir de Folie*, the revue (1925–6) at the Folies Bergère, Paris, was "Le Sabbat et la Herse Infernale," where in a Gothic cathedral an actor (Mons. Benglia) appeared as Satan receiving the adoration of his devotees.

At the more frequented Sabbats the ritual of Holy Mass was elaborately burlesqued in almost every detail. An altar was erected with four supports, sometimes under a sheltering tree, at others upon a flat rock, or some naturally convenient place, "auprès d'vn arbre, ou parfois auprès d'vn rocher, dressant quelque forme d'autel sur des colonés infernales," says De Lancre.[120] In more recent times and to-day when the black mass is celebrated in houses such an altar is often permanent and therefore the infernal sanctuary can be builded with a display of the full symbolism of the hideous cult of evil. The altar was covered with the three linen cloths the ritual enjoins, and upon it were six black candles in the midst of which they placed a crucifix inverted, or an image of the Devil. Sometimes the Devil himself occupied this central position, standing erect, or seated on some kind of monstrous throne. In 1598, at a celebrated witch-trial before the Parliament of Bordeaux with the Vicar-general of the Bishop of Limoges and a learned councillor Peyrat as assessors, Antoine Dumons of Saint-Laurent confessed that he had frequently provided a large number of candles for the Sabbat, both wax lights to be distributed among those present and the large black tapers for the altar. These were lit by Pierre Aupetit, who held a sacristan's reed, and apparently officiated as Master of the Ceremonies when he was not actually himself saying the Mass.[121]

In May, 1895, when the legal representatives of the Borghese family visited the Palazzo Borghese, which had been rented for some time in separate floors or suites, they found some difficulty in obtaining admission to certain apartments on the first floor, the occupant of which seemed unaware that the lease was about to expire. By virtue of the terms of the agreement, however, he was obliged to allow them to inspect the premises to see if any structural repairs or alterations were necessary, as Prince Scipione Borghese, who was about to be married, intended immediately to take up his residence in the ancestral home with his bride. One door the tenant obstinately refused to unlock, and when pressed he betrayed the greatest confusion. The agents finally pointed out that they were within their rights to employ actual force, and that if access was longer denied they would not hesitate to do so forthwith. When the keys had been produced, the cause of the reluctance was soon plain. The room within was inscribed with the words *Templum Palladicum.* The walls were hung all round from ceiling to floor with heavy curtains of silk damask, scarlet and black, excluding the light; at the further end there stretched a large tapestry upon which was woven in more than life-size a figure of Lucifer, colossal, triumphant, dominating the whole. Exactly beneath an altar had been built, amply furnished for the liturgy of hell: candles, vessels, rituals, missal, nothing was lacking. Cushioned prie-dieus and luxurious chairs, crimson and gold, were set in order for the assistants; the chamber being lit by electricity, fantastically arrayed so as to glare from an enormous human eye. The visitors soon quitted the accursed spot, the scene of devil-worship and blasphemy, nor had they any desire more nearly to examine the appointments of this infernal chapel.[122]

The missal used at the black mass was obviously a manuscript, although it is said that in later times these grimoires of hideous profanity have actually been printed. It is not infrequently mentioned. Thus De Lancre notes that the sorcerers of the Basses-Pyrénées (1609) at their worship saw the officiant " tournant les feuillets d'vn certain liure qu'il a en main."[123] Madeleine Bavent in her confession said: " On lisait la messe dans le livre des blasphèmes, qui servait de canon et qu'on employait aussi dans les processions."[124] The witches' missal was often bound in human skin, generally that of an unbaptized babe.[125] Gentien le Clerc, tried at Orleans, 1614–1615, confessed that " le Diable . . . marmote dans un liure duquel la couuerture est toute veluë comme d'vne peau de loup, auec des feuillets blancs & rouges, d'autres noires."

The vestments worn by the celebrant are variously described. On rare occasions he is described as being arrayed in a bishop's pontificalia, black in hue, torn, squalid, and fusty. Boguet reports that a witch stated: " Celuy, qui est commis à faire l'office, est reuestu d'vne chappe noire sans croix,"[126] but it seems somewhat strange that merely a plain black cope should be used, unless the explanation is to be found in the fact that such a vestment was most easily procurable and no suspicion of its ultimate employment would be excited. The abbé Guibourg sometimes wore a cope of white silk embroidered with fir-cones, which again seems remarkable, as the symbolism is in no way connected with the Satanic rites he performed. But this is the evidence of Marguerite, La Voisin's daughter, who was not likely to be mistaken.[127] It is true that the mass was often, perhaps, partially erotic and not wholly diabolic in the same sense as the Sabbat masses were, but yet Astaroth, Asmodeus, and Lucifer were invoked, and it was a liturgy of evil. On other occasions Guibourg seems to have donned the orthodox eucharistic chasuble, stole, maniple, girdle, alb, and amice. In the thirty-seventh article of his confession Gaufridi acknowledged that the priest who said the Devil's mass at the Sabbat wore a violet chasuble.[128] Gentien le Clerc, tried at Orleans in 1614–1615, was present at a Sabbat mass when the celebrant "wore a chasuble which was embroidered with a Cross; but there were only three bars."[129] Later a contemporary witness points to the use of vestments embroidered with infernal insignia, such as a dark red chasuble, the colour of dried blood, upon which was figured a black buck goat rampant; a chasuble that bore the inverse Cross, and similar robes adorned by some needle with the heraldry of hell.

In bitter mockery of the *Asperges* the celebrant sprinkled the witches with filthy and brackish water, or even with stale. "The Devil at the same time made water into a hole dug in the earth, & used it as holy water, wherewith the celebrant of the mass sprinkled all present, using a black aspergillum."[130] Silvain Nevillon, a sorcerer who was tried at Orleans in 1614–1615, said: "When Tramesabot said Mass, before he commenced he used to sprinkle all present with holy water which was nothing else than urine, saying meanwhile *Asperges Diaboli*."[131] According to Gentien le Clerc: "The holy water is yellow . . . & after it has been duly sprinkled Mass is said."[132] Madeleine de la Palud declared that the sorcerers were sprinkled with water, and also with consecrated wine from the chalice upon which all present cried aloud: *Sanguis eius super nos et super filios nostros.*[133] (His blood be upon us and upon our children.)

This foul travesty of the holiest mysteries began with an invocation of the Devil, which was followed by a kind of general confession, only each one made mock acknowledgement of any good he might have done, and as a penance he was enjoined to utter some foul blasphemy or to break some precept of the Church. The president absolved the congregation by an inverse sign of the Cross made with the left hand. The rite then proceeded with shameless profanity, but De Lancre remarks that the *Confiteor* was never said, not even in a burlesque form, and *Alleluia* never pronounced. After reciting the Offertory the celebrant drew back a little from the altar and the assembly advancing in file kissed his left hand. When the Queen of the Sabbat—the witch who ranked first after the Grand Master, the oldest and most evil of the witches ("en chasque village," says De Lancre, "trouuer vne Royne du Sabbat")—was present she sat on the left of the altar and received the offerings, loaves, eggs, any meat or country produce, and money, so long as the coins were not stamped with a cross. In her hand she held a disc or plate " vne paix ou platine," engraved with a figure of the Devil, and this his followers devoutly kissed. In many places to-day, especially Belgium, during Holy Mass the pax-brede (*instrumentum pacis*) is kissed by the congregation at the Offertory, and universally when Mass is said by a priest in the presence of a Prelate the pax-brede is kissed by the officiant and the Prelate after the *Agnus Dei* and the first appropriate ante-communion prayer.

Silvain Nevillon, who was tried at Orleans in 1614–15, avowed : " The Devil preached a sermon at the Sabbat, but nobody could hear what he said, for he spoke in a growl."[134]

At the Sabbat a sermon is not infrequently delivered, a farrago of impiety and evil counsel.

The hosts are then brought to the altar. Boguet describes them as dark and round, stamped with a hideous design; Madeleine Bavent saw them as ordinary wafers only coloured red ; in other cases they were black and triangular in shape. Often they blasphemed the Host, calling it " Iean le blanc," just as Protestants called it " Jack-in-the-box." The chalice is filled, sometimes with wine, sometimes with a bitter beverage that burned the tongue like fire. At the *Sanctus* a horn sounded harshly thrice, and torches burning with a sulphurous blue flare " qui est fort puante " were kindled. There was an elevation, at which the whole gang, now in a state of hysterical excitement and unnatural exaltation, burst forth with the most appalling screams and maniac blasphemies, rivalling each other in filthy adjurations and crapulous obscenities. The protagonist poured out all the unbridled venom that diabolic foulness could express, a stream of scurrility and pollution ; hell seemed to have vomited its reeking gorge on earth. *Domine adiuua nos, domine adiuua nos*, they cried to the Demon, and again *Domine adiuua nos semper*. Generally all present were compelled to communicate with the sacrament of the pit, to swallow morsels soiled with mud and ordures, to drink the dark brew of damnation. Gaufridi confessed that for *Ite missa est* these infernal orgies concluded with the curse : " Allez-vous-en tous au nom du diable ! " Whilst the abbé Guibourg cried : " *Gloria tibi, Lucifero !* "

The black mass of the Sabbat varied slightly in form according to circumstances, and in the modern liturgy of the Satanists it would appear that a considerable feature is made of the burning of certain heavy and noxious weeds, the Devil's incense. In the sixteenth and seventeenth centuries the use of incense is very rare at the Sabbat, although Silvain Nevillon stated that he had seen at the Sabbat "both holy water and incense. This latter smelled foul, not fragrant as incense burned in church."[135]

The officiant nowadays consecrates a host and the chalice with the actual sacred words of Holy Mass, but then instead of kneeling he turns his back upon the altar,[136] and a few moments later—*sit uenia uerbis!*—he cuts and stabs the Host with a knife, throwing it to the ground, treading upon it, spurning it. A part, at least, of the contents of the chalice is also spilled in fearful profanation, and not infrequently there further has been provided a ciborium of consecrated Hosts, all stolen from churches[137] or conveyed away at Communion in their mouths by wretches unafraid to provoke the sudden judgement of an outraged God. These the black priest, for so the celebrant is called by the Devil worshippers, scatters over the pavement to be struggled and fought for by his congregation in their madness to seize and outrage the Body of Christ.

Closely connected with the black mass of the Satanists and a plain survival from the Middle Ages is that grim superstition of the Gascon peasant, the Mass of S. Sécaire.[138] Few priests know the awful ritual, and of those who are learned in such dark lore fewer yet would dare to perform the monstrous ceremonies and utter the prayer of blasphemy. No confessor, no bishop, not even the Archbishop of Auch, may shrive the celebrant; he can only be absolved at Rome by the Holy Father himself. The mass is said upon a broken and desecrated altar in some ruined or deserted church where owls hoot and mope and bats flit through the crumbling windows, where toads spit their venom upon the sacred stone. The priest must make his way thither late attended only by an acolyte of impure and evil life. At the first stroke of eleven he begins; the liturgy of hell is mumbled backward, the canon said with a mow and a sneer; he ends just as midnight tolls. The host is triangular, with three sharp points and black. No wine is consecrated but foul brackish water drawn from a well wherein has been cast the body of an unbaptized babe. The holy sign of the cross is made with the left foot upon the ground. And the man for whom that mass is said will slowly pine away, nor doctor's skill nor physic will avail him aught, but he will suffer, and dwindle, and surely drop into the grave.[139]

Although there is, no doubt, some picturesque exaggeration here the main details are correct enough. A black, triangular wafer is not infrequently mentioned in the witch-trials as having been the sacramental bread of the Sabbat, whilst Lord Fountainhall[140] in describing the devilish communion of the Loudian witches says: "the drink was sometimes blood, sometimes black moss-water," and many other details may be closely paralleled.

When the blasphemous liturgy of the Sabbat was done all present gave themselves up to the most promiscuous debauchery, only interrupting their lasciviousness to dance or to spur themselves on to new enormities by spiced foods and copious draughts of wine. "You may well suppose," writes Boguet, "that every kind of obscenity is practised there, yea, even those abominations for which Heaven poured down fire and brimstone on Sodom and Gomorrah are quite common in these assemblies."[141] The erudite Dominican, Father Sebastian Michaelis, who on the 19 January, 1611, examined Madeleine de la Palud concerning her participation in Sabbats, writes[142] that she narrated the most unhallowed orgies.[143] The imagination reels before such turpitudes! But Madeleine Bavent (1643) supplied even more execrable details.[144] Gentien le Clerc at Orleans (1614–1615) acknowledged similar debauchery.[145] Bodin relates that a large number of witches whom he tried avowed their presence at the Sabbat.[146] In 1459 "large numbers of men & women were burned at Arras, many of whom had mutually accused one another, & they confessed that at night they had been conveyed to these hellish dances."[147] In 1485 Sprenger executed a large number of sorcerers in the Constance district, and "almost all without exception confessed that the Devil had had connexion with them, after he had made them renounce God and their holy faith."[148] Many converted witches likewise confessed these abominations "and let it be known that whilst they were witches demons had swived them lustily. Henry of Cologne in confirmation of this says that it is very common in Germany."[149] Throughout the centuries all erudite authorities have the same monstrous tale to tell, and it would serve no purpose merely to accumulate evidence from the demonologists. To-day the meetings of Satanists invariably end in unspeakable orgies and hideous debauchery.

Occasionally animals were sacrificed at the Sabbat to the Demon. The second charge against Dame Alice Kyteler, prosecuted in 1324 for sorcery by Richard de Ledrede, Bishop of Ossory, was "that she was wont to offer sacrifices to devils of live animals, which she and her company tore limb from limb and made oblation by scattering them at the cross-ways to a certain demon who was called Robin, son of Artes (Robin Artisson), one of hell's lesser princes."[150]

In 1622 Margaret McWilliam "renounced her baptisme, and he baptised her and she gave him as a gift a hen or cock."[151] In the Voodoo rites of to-day a cock is often the animal which is hacked to pieces before the fetish. Black puppies were sacrificed to Hecate; Æneas offers four jetty bullocks to the infernal powers, a coal-black lamb to Night;[152] at their Sabbat on the Esquiline Canidia and Sagana tear limb from limb a black sheep, the blood streams into a trench.[153] Collin de Plancy states that witches sacrifice black fowls and toads to the Devil.[154] The animal victim to a power worshipped as divine is a relic of remotest antiquity.

The presence of toads at the Sabbat is mentioned in many witch-trials. They seem to have been associated with sorcerers owing to the repugnance they generally excite, and in some districts it is a common superstition that those whom they regard fixedly will be seized with palpitations, spasms, convulsions, and swoons: nay, a certain abbé Rousseau of the eighteenth century, who experimented with toads, avowed that when one of these animals looked upon him for some time he fell in a fainting fit whence, if help had not arrived, he would never have recovered.[155] A number of writers—Ælian, Dioscorides, Nicander, Ætius, Gesner—believe that the breath of the toad is poisonous, infecting the places it may touch. Since such idle stories were credited it is hardly to be surprised at that we find the toad a close companion of the witch. De Lancre says that demons often appeared in that shape. Jeannette d'Abadie, a witch of the Basses-Pyrénées, whom he tried and who confessed at length, declared that she saw brought to the Sabbat a number of toads dressed some in black, some in scarlet velvet, with little bells attached to their coats. In November, 1610, a man walking through the fields near Bazas, noticed that his dog had scratched a large hole in a bank and unearthed two pots, covered with cloth, and closely tied. When opened they were found to be packed with bran, and in the midst of each was a large toad wrapped in green tiffany. These doubtless had been set there by a person who had faith in sympathetic magic, and was essaying a malefic spell. No doubt toads were caught and taken to the Sabbat, nor is the reason far to seek. Owing to their legendary venom they served as a prime ingredient in poisons and potions, and were also used for telling fortunes, since witches often divined by their toad familiars. Juvenal alludes to this when he writes:

> "I neither will, nor can Prognosticate
> To the young gaping Heir, his Father's Fate
> Nor in the Entrails of a Toad have pry'd."[156]

Upon which passage Thomas Farnabie, the celebrated English scholar (1575–1647) glosses thus: "He alludes to the office of the Haruspex who used to inspect entrails & intestines. Pliny says: The entrails of the toad (*Rana rubeta*), that is to say the tongue, tiny bones, gall, heart, have rare virtue for they are used in many medicines and salves. Haply he means the puddock or hop-toad, thus demonstrating that these animals are not poisonous, their entrails being completely inefficacious in confecting poisons."[157] In 1610 Juan de Echalar, a sorcerer of Navarre, confessed at his trial before the Alcantarine inquisitor Don Alonso Becerra Holguin that he and his coven collected toads for the Sabbat, and when they presented these animals to the Devil he blessed them with his left hand, after which they were killed and cooked in a stewpot with human bones and pieces of corpses rifled from new-made graves. From this filthy hotch-potch were brewed poisons and unguents that the Devil distributed to all present with directions how to use them. By sprinkling corn with the liquid it was supposed they could blight a standing field, and also destroy flowers and fruit. A few drops let fall upon a person's garments was believed to insure death, and a smear upon the shed or sty effectually diseased cattle. From these crude superstitions the fantastic stories of dancing toads, toads dressed *en cavalier*, and demon toads at the Sabbat were easily evolved.

There is ample and continuous evidence that children, usually tender babes who were as yet unbaptized, were sacrificed at the Sabbat. These were often the witches' own offspring, and since a witch not unseldom was the midwife or wise-woman of a village she had exceptional opportunities of stifling a child at birth as a non-Sabbatial victim to Satan. "There are no persons who can do more cunning harm to the Catholic faith than midwives," says the *Malleus Maleficarum*, Pars I, q. xi: "*Nemo fidei catholicæ amplius nocet quam obstetrices.*" The classic examples of child-sacrifice are those of Gilles de Rais (1440) and the abbé Guibourg (1680). In the process against the former one hundred and forty children are explicitly named: some authorities accept as many as eight hundred victims. Their blood, brains, and bones were used to decoct magic philtres. In the days of Guibourg the sacrifice of a babe at the impious mass was so common that he generally paid not more than a crown-piece for his victim. "Il avait acheté un écu l'enfant qui fut sacrifié à cette messe." ("The child sacrificed at this mass he had bought for a crown.") These abominable ceremonies were frequently performed at the instance of Madame de Montespan in order that Louis XIV should always remain faithful to her, should reject all other mistresses, repudiate his queen, and in fine raise her to the throne.[158] The most general use was to cut the throat of the child, whose blood was drained into the chalice and allowed to fall upon the naked flesh of the inquirer, who lay stretched along the altar. La Voisin asserted that a toll of fifteen hundred infants had been thus murdered. This is not impossible, as a vast number of persons, including a crowd of ecclesiastics, were implicated. Many of the greatest names in France had assisted at these orgies of blasphemy. From first to last no less than two hundred and forty-six men and women of all ranks and grades of society were brought to trial, and whilst thirty-six of humbler station went to the scaffold, one hundred and forty-seven were imprisoned for longer or shorter terms, not a few finding it convenient to leave the country, or, at any rate, to obscure themselves in distant châteaux. But many of the leaves had been torn out of the archives, and Louis himself forbade any mention of his favourite's name in connexion with these prosecutions. However, she was disgraced, and it is not surprising that after the death of Maria Teresa, 31 July, 1683, the king early in the following year married the pious and conventual Madame de Maintenon.

Ludovico Maria Sinistrari writes that witches "promise the Devil sacrifices and offerings at stated times: once a fortnight, or at least each month, the murder of some child, or an homicidal act of sorcery," and again and again in the trials detailed accusation of the kidnapping and murder of children are brought against the prisoners. In the same way as the toad was used for magical drugs so was the fat of the child. The belief that corpses and parts of corpses constitute a most powerful cure and a supreme ingredient in elixirs is universal and of the highest antiquity. The quality of directly curing diseases and of protection has long been attributed to a cadaver. Tumours, eruptions, gout, are dispelled if the afflicted member be stroked with a dead hand.[159] Toothache is charmed away if the face be touched with the finger of a dead child.[160] Birthmarks vanish under the same treatment.[161] Burns, carbuncles, the herpes, and other skin complaints, fearfully prevalent in the Middle Ages, could be cured by contact with some part of a corpse. In Pomerania the "cold corpse hand" is a protection against fire,[162] and Russian peasants believe that a dead hand protects from bullet wounds and steel.[163] It was long thought by the ignorant country folk that the doctors of the hospital of Graz enjoyed the privilege of being allowed every year to exploit one human life for curative purposes. Some young man who repaired thither for toothache or any such slight ailment is seized, hung up by the feet, and tickled to death! Skilled chemists boil the body to a paste and utilize this as well as the fat and the charred bones in their drug store. The people are persuaded that about Easter a youth annually disappears in the hospital for these purposes.[164] This tradition is, perhaps, not unconnected with the Jewish ritual sacrifices of S. William of Norwich (1144); Harold of Gloucester (1168); William of Paris (1177); Robert of Bury S. Edmunds (1181); S. Werner of Oberwesel (1286); S. Rudolph of Berne (1294); S. Andreas of Rinn (1462); S. Simon of Trent, a babe of two and a half years old (1473); Simon Abeles, whose body lies in the Teyn Kirche at Prague, murdered for Christ's sake on 21 February, 1694, by Lazarus and Levi Kurtzhandel; El santo Niño de la Guardia, near Toledo (1490), and many more.[165]

The riots which have so continually during three centuries broken out in China against Europeans, and particularly against Catholic asylums for the sick, foundling hospitals, schools, are almost always fomented by an intellectual party who begin by issuing fiery appeals to the populace: "Down with the missionaries! Kill the foreigners! They steal or buy our children and slaughter them, in order to prepare magic remedies and medicines out of their eyes, hearts, and from other portions of their dead bodies." Baron Hübner in his *Promenade autour du monde*, II (Paris, 1873) tells the story of the massacre at Tientsin, 21 June, 1870, and relates that it was engineered on these very lines. In 1891 similar risings against Europeans resident in China were found to be due to the same cause. Towards the end of 1891 a charge was brought in Madagascar against the French that they devoured human hearts and for this purpose kidnapped and killed native children. Stern legislation was actually found necessary to check the spread of these accusations.[166]

In the Navarrese witch-trials of 1610 Juan de Echelar confessed that a candle had been used made from the arm of an infant strangled before baptism. The ends of the fingers had been lit, and burned with a clear flame, a "Hand of Glory" in fact. At Forfar, in 1661, Helen Guthrie and four other witches exhumed the body of an unbaptized babe and made portions into a pie which they ate. They imagined that by this means no threat nor torture could bring them to confession of their sorceries. This, of course, is clearly sympathetic magic. The tongue of the infant had never spoken articulate words, and so the tongues of the witches would be unable to articulate.

It is a fact seldom realized, but none the less of the deepest significance, that almost every detail of the old witch-trials can be exactly paralleled in Africa to-day. Thus there exists in Bantu a society called the "Witchcraft Company," whose members hold secret meetings at midnight in the depths of the forest to plot sickness and death against their enemies by means of incantations and spells. The owl is their sacred bird, and their signal call an imitation of its hoot. They profess to leave their corporeal bodies asleep in their huts, and it is only their spirit-bodies that attend the magic rendezvous, passing through walls and over the tree-tops with instant rapidity. At the meeting they have visible, audible, and tangible communication with spirits. They hold feasts, at which is eaten the "heart-life" of some human being, who through this loss of his heart falls sick and, unless "the heart" be later restored, eventually dies. Earliest cock-crow is the warning for them to disperse, since they fear the advent of the morning-star, as, should the sun rise upon them before they reach their corporeal bodies, all their plans would not merely fail, but recoil upon themselves, and they would pine and languish miserably. This hideous Society was introduced by black slaves to the West Indies, to Jamaica and Hayti, and also to the Southern States of America as Voodoo worship. Authentic records are easily procurable which witness that midnight meetings were held in Hayti as late as 1888, when human beings, especially kidnapped children, were killed and eaten at the mysterious and evil banquets. European government in Africa has largely suppressed the practice of the black art, but this foul belief still secretly prevails, and Dr. Norris[167] is of opinion that were white influence withdrawn it would soon hold sway as potently as of old.

A candid consideration will show that for every detail of the Sabbat, however fantastically presented and exaggerated in the witch-trials of so many centuries, there is ample warrant and unimpeachable evidence. There is some hallucination no doubt; there is lurid imagination, and vanity which paints the colours thick; but there is a solid stratum of fact, and very terrible fact throughout.

And as the dawn broke the unhallowed crew separated in haste, and hurried each one on his way homewards, pale, weary, and haggard after the night of taut hysteria, frenzied evil, and vilest excess.

"Le coq s'oyt par fois és sabbats sonnãt le retraicte aux Sorciers."[168] (The cock crows; the Sabbat ends; the Sorcerers scatter and flee away.)

NOTES TO CHAPTER IV

[1] Omnia autem honeste et secundum ordinem fiant. 1 Cor. xiv. 40.

[2] Miss Murray, misled no doubt by the multiplicity of material, postulates two separate and distinct kinds of assemblies: The Sabbat, the General Meeting of all members of the religion; the Esbat "only for the special and limited number who carried out the rites and practices of the cult, and [which] was not for the general public." *The Witch-Cult in Western Europe*, p. 97. Görres had already pointed out that the smaller meetings were often known as *Esbats*. The idea of a "general public" at a witches' meeting is singular.

[3] On a voulu trouver l'etymologie du sabbat, réunion des sorciers, dans les *sabazies;* mais la forme ne le permet pas; d'ailleurs comment, au moyen âge aurait on connu les sabazies? Saint-Croix, *Recherches sur les mystères du paganisme;* Maury, *Histoire des religions de la Grèce antique.*

[4] *Metamorphoseon*, VIII. 25.

[5] Miss Murray thinks that Sabbat "is possibly a derivative of *s'esbattre*, 'to frolic,'" and adds "a very suitable description of the joyous gaiety of the meetings"!!

[6] Miss Murray mistakenly says (p. 109) that May Eve (30 April) is called Roodmas or Rood Day. Roodmas or Rood Day is 3 May, the Feast of the Invention of Holy Cross. An early English calendar (702–706) even gives 7 May as Roodmas. The Invention of Holy Cross is found in the Lectionary of Silos and the Bobbio Missal. The date was not slightly altered. The Invention of Holy Cross is among the very early festivals.

[7] Especially in the North and North-East. Bavaria, Wurtemberg, and Baden, knew little of this particular date.

[8] In the *Rituale* we have "Benedictio Rogi, quæ fit a Clero extra Ecclesiam in Uigilia Natiuitatis S. Joannis Baptistæ. (Blessing of a pyre, which the Clergy may give on the Vigil of the Nativity of S. John Baptist, but outside the Church.) This form is especially approved for the Diocese of Tarbes.

[9] *Relacion de las personas que salieron al auto de la fé que los inquisidores apostólicos del reino de Navarra y su distrito, celebraron en la ciudad De Logroño, en* 7 *y* 8 *del mes de noviembre de* 1610 *años*, 1611.

[10] *Discours des Sorciers*, XXII. 12. Tertullian's *Diabolus simia Dei.*

[11] *Idem*, XX. 2.

[12] *Tableau*, p. 65.

[13] Les lieux des assemblées des Sorciers sont notables et signalez de quelques arbres, ou croix. *Fleau*, p. 181.

[14] Anthony Horneck; Appendix to Glanvill's *Sadducismus Triumphatus.* London, 1681.

[15] Locus in diuersis regionibus est diuersus; plerumque autem comitia in syluestribus, montanis, uel subterraneis atque ab hominum conuersatione dissitis locis habentur. *Mela. Lib.* 3. *cap.* 44. montem Atlantem nominat; *de Vaulx* Magus Stabuleti decollatus, fatebatur 1603, in Hollandia congregationem frequentissimam fuisse in Ultraiectinæ ditionis aliquo loco. Nobis ab hoc conuentu notus atq; notatus mons Bructerorum, Meliboeus alias dictus in ducatu Brunsuicensi, uulgo *der Blocksberg oder Heweberg*, Peucero, *der Brockersberg*, & Tilemanno Stellæ, *der Vogelsberg*, perhibente *Ortelio in Thesauro Geographico.* For the Bructeri see Tacitus, *Germania*, 33: Velleius Paterculus, II, 105, i. *Bructera natio*, Tacitus, *Historiæ*, IV, 61.

[16] . . . le lieu où on le trouue ordinairement s'appelle Lanne de bouc, & en Basque *Aquelarre de verros, prado del Cabron*, & là des Sorciers

le vont adorer trois nuicts durant, celle du Lundy, du Mercredy, & du Vendredy. De Lancre, *Tableau*, p. 62.

[17] Boguet, *Discours des Sorciers*, p. 124.

[18] *A Pleasant Treatise of Witches*, London, 1673.

[19] Psalm xc.

[20] Conuentus, ut plurimum ineuntur uel noctis mediæ silentio, quando uiget potestas tenebrarum; uel interdiu meridie, quo sunt qui referant illud Psalmistæ notum de dæmonio meridiano. Noctes frequentiores, quæ feriam tertiam et sextam præcedunt. Delrio, *Disquisitiones Magicæ*, Lib. II. xvi.

[21] *Discours*, XIX. 1. "The Sorcerers assemble at the Sabbat about midnight."

[22] Her indictment consists of fifty-three points.

[23] Spottiswoode's *Practicks*.

[24] Spalding Club, *Miscellany*, I.

[25] MS. formerly in the possession of Michael Stewart Nicolson, Esq.

[26] . . . je me trouvais transporté au lieu où le Sabatt se tenait, y demeurant quelquefois une, deux, trois, quatre heures pour le plus souvent suivant les affections.

[27] Ferunt uagantes Dæmonas
Lætas tenebras noctium
Gallo canente exterritos
Sparsim timere et credere.

[28] Nocturna lux uiantibus
A nocte noctem segregans,
Præco diei iam sonat,
Iubarque solis euocat.
Hoc nauta uires colligit,
Pontique mitescunt freta:
Hoc, ipsa petra Ecclesiæ,
Canente, culpam diluit.
Surgamus ergo strenue:
Gallus iacentes excitat,
Et somnolentos increpat,
Gallus negantes arguit.
Gallo canente, spes redit,
Ægris salus refunditur,
Mucro latronis conditur,
Lapsis fides reuertitur.

The translation in text is by Caswall, 1848.

[29] *Tableau*, p. 154.

[30] For London, see Dr. Johnson's *London* (1738):

Prepare for death, if here at night you roam,
And sign your will before you sup from home.

In 1500 Paolo Capello, the Venetian Ambassador, wrote: "Every night they find in Rome four or five murdered men, Prelates and so forth." During the reign of Philip IV (1621–1665) the streets of Madrid, noisome, unpaved, were only lit on the occasion of festal illuminations.

[31] 1475–1546.

[32] Quando uadunt ad loca propinqua uadunt pedestres mutuo se inuicem inuitantes. *De Strigibus*, II.

[33] Les Sorciers neâtmoins vont quelquefois de pied au Sabbat, ce qui leur aduient principalement, lors que le lieu où ils font leur assemblée, n'est pas guieres eslongé de leur habitation. *Discours*, c. xvii.

[34] Enquis en quel lieu se tint le Sabbat le dernier fois qu'il y fut.
Respond que ce fut vers Billeron à un Carroy qui est sur le chemin tendant aux Aix, Parroisse de Saincte Soulange, Iustice de ceans.
Enquis de quelle façon il y va.
Respond qu'il y va de son pied.
De Lancre, *Tableau*, pp. 803–805.

[35] Aussi vilain & abominable est au Sorcier d'y aller de son pied que d'y estre transporté de son consentement par le Diable. *Tableau*, p. 632.

[36] Sinclar, *Satan's Invisible World Discovered* (Reprint 1875), VII.

[37] *Idem*, p. 25.

[38] *Idem*, pp. 175, 178.

[39] Illud etiam non omittendum quod quædam sceleratæ mulieres retro post Satanam conuersæ, dæmonum illusoribus et phantasmatibus seductæ credunt se et profitentur nocturnis horis cum Diana paganorum dea et innumera multitudine mulierum equitare super quasdam bestias et multa terrarum spatia intempestæ noctis silentio pertransire eiusque iussionibus uelut dominæ obedire, et certis noctibus ad eius seruitium euocari. Minge, *Patres Latini*, CXXXII. 352.

[40] See Professor A. J. Clark's note upon "Flying Ointments." *Witch-Cult in Western Europe*, pp. 279–280.

[41] Posset dæmon eas transferre sine unguento, et facit aliquando; sed unguento mauult uti uariis de causis. Aliquando quia timidiores sunt sagæ, ut audeant; uel quia teneriores sunt ad horribilem illum Satanæ contactum in corpore assumpto ferendum; horum enim unctione sensum obstupefacit et miseris persuadet uim unguento inesse maximam. Alias autem id facit ut sacrosancta a Deo instituta sacramenta inimice adumbret, et per has quasi cerimonias suis orgiis reuerentiæ et uenerationis aliquid conciliat. Delrio, *Disquitiones magicæ*, Liber II, q^to xvi.

[42] In antiquity we have the case of Simon Magus, who was levitated in the presence of Nero and his court.

[43] Henri Boguet, the High Justice of the district of Saint-Claude, died in 1616. The first edition (of the last rarity) of his *Discours des Sorciers* is Lyons, 1602; second edition, Lyons 1608; but there is also a Paris issue, 1603. Pp. 64 and 104.

[44] Scot, *Discoverie of Witchcraft* (1584). Book III. p. 42.

[45] De Lancre, *Tableau*, p. 211.

[46] Thomas Wright, *Proceedings against Dame Alice Kyteler*, Camden Society. 1843.

[47] Cotton Mather, *Wonders of the Invisible World*, 1693. (Reprint, 1862. P. 158.)

[48] *Quarterly Journal of Science*, January, 1874.

[49] J. Godfrey Raupert, *Modern Spiritism*. 1904. Pp. 34, 35. See also Sir W. Barrett, *On the Threshold of the Unseen*, p. 70.

[50] Arthur Lillie, *Modern Mystics and Modern Magic*, 1894, pp. 74, 75.

[51] David Lewis, *Life of S. John of the Cross* (1897), pp. 73–4.

[52] See the Saint's own letter (written in 1777) to the Bishop of Foggia. *Lettere di S. Alfonso Maria de' Liguori* (Roma, 1887), II. 456 f.

[53] Philip Coghlan, O.P. *Gemma Galgani* (1923), p. 62. For fuller details see the larger biography by Padre Germano.

[54] *Vie du B. Paul de la Croix*. (French translation.) I. Book ii. c. 3.

[55] *La Mystique Divine*. Traduit par Sainte-Foi. V. viii. 17. p. 193.

[56] Giovanni Francesco Ponzinibio was a lawyer whose *De Lamiis* was published at Venice, 1523–4. It called forth a reply, *Apologiæ tres aduersum Joannem Franciscum Ponzinibium Iurisperitum*, Venice, 1525. The edition of *De Lamiis* I have used is Venice, 1584, in the *Thesaurus Magnorum iuris consultorum*. This reprint was met by Peña's answer and two treatises by Bartolomeo Spina, O.P.

[57] Rome, 1584.

[58] De modo quo localiter transferentur [sagæ] de loco ad locum. . . . Probatur quod possint malefici corporaliter transferri.

[59] An isti Sortilegi & Strigimagæ siue Lamiæ uere & corporaliter deferantur a dæmone uel solum in spiritu? *De Sortilegiis*, VII.

[60] Sum modo istius secundæ opinionis quod deferantur in corpore.

[61] Doctrina multi eorum qui sequuti sunt Lutherum, & Melanctonem, tenuerent Sagas ad conuentus accedere animi duntaxat cogitatione, & diabolica illusione interesse, allegantes quod eorum corpora inuenta sunt sæpe numero eodem loco iacentia, nec inde mora fuisse, ad hoc illud pertinens quod est in uita D. Germani, de mulierculis conuiuantibus, vt uidebantur, & tamē dormierant dormientes. Huiusmodi mulierculas sæpe numero decipi

certum est, sed semper ita fieri non probatur. . . . Altera, quam uerissimam esse duco, est, nonnunquam uere Sagas transferri a Dæmone de loco ad locum, hirco, uel alteri animali fantastico vt plurimum eas simul asportanti corporaliter, & conuentu nefario interesse, & hæc sententia est multo communior Theologorum, imò & Iurisconsultorum Italiæ, Hispaniæ, & Germaniæ inter Catholicos; hoc idem tenent alii quam plurimi. Turrecremata super Grillandum,[1] Remigius,[2] Petrus Damianus,[3] Siluester Abulensis,[4] Caietanus[5] Alphonsus a Castro[6] Sixtus Senensis[7] Crespetus[8] Spineus[9] contra Ponzinibium, Ananias,[10] & alii quam plurimi, quos breuitatis gratia omitto. *Per Fratrem Franciscum Mariam Guaccium Ord. S. Ambrosii ad Nemus Mediolani compilatum.* Mediolani. Ex Collegii Ambrosiani Typographia. 1626.

[62] *De Strigibus*, II. I have used the reprint, 1669, which is given in the valuable collection appended to the *Malleus Maleficarum* of that date, 4 vols. 4to.

[63] Ad quam congregationem seu ludum præfatæ pestiferæ personæ uadunt corporaliter & uigilantes ac in propriis earũ sensibus & quando uadunt ad loca propinqua uadunt pedestres mutuo se inuicem inuitantes. Si autẽ habent congregari in aliquo loco distanti tunc deferuntur a diabolo, & quomodocunque uadant ad dictum locum siue pedibus suis siue adferantur a diabolo uerũ est quod realiter et ueraciter & nõ phãtastice, neque illusorii abnegant fidẽ catholicam, adorant diabolum, conculcant crucem, & plura nefandissima opprobria committunt contra sacratissimum Corpus Christi, ac alia plura spurcissima perpetrant cum ipso diabolo eis in specie humana apparenti, & se uiris succubum, mulieribus autem incubum exhibenti.

[64] George Gandillon, la nuict d'vn Ieudy Sainct, demeura dans son lict, comme mort, pour l'espace de trois heures, & puis reuint à soy en sursaut. Il a depuis esté bruslé en ce lieu auec son père & vne sienne sœur.

[65] Chapitre xvi. Comme, & en quelle façon les Sorciers sont portez au Sabbat.

1. *Ils y sont portez tantost sur un baston, ou ballet, tantost sur un mouton ou bouc, & tantost par un homme noir.*
2. *Quelquefois ils se frottẽt de graisse, & à d'autres non.*
3. *Il y en a, lesquels n'estans pas Sorciers, & s'estans frottez, ne delaissent pas d'estre transportez au Sabbat, & la raison.*
4. *L'onguent, & la graisse ne seruent de rien aux Sorciers, pour leur transport au Sabbat.*
5. *Les Sorciers sont quelquefois portez au Sabbat par un vent & tourbillon.*

Chapitre xvii. Les Sorciers vont quelques fois de pied au Sabbat.

Chapitre xviii. Si les Sorciers vont en ame seulement au Sabbat.

1 & 3. *L'affirmatiue, & exemples.*
2. *Indices, par lesquels on peut coniecturer, qu'vne certaine femme estoit au Sabbat en ame seulement.*
4. *La negatiue.*
5. *Comme s'entend ce que l'on dit d'Erichtho, & d'Apollonius lesquels resusciterent l'un un soldat, & l'autre une ieune fille.*
6. *Les Sorciers ne peuuent resusciter un mort, & exemples.*
7. *Non plus que les heretiques & exemples.*
8. *Opinion de l'Autheur sur le suiect de ce chapitre.*
9. *Satan endort le plus souuent les personnes, & exemples.*

[1] *De haereticis et sortilegiis.* Lugduni. 1536.
[2] Nicolas Remy, *De la démonolâtrie.*
[3] Epistolarum, IV. 17.
[4] Silvester of Avila.
[5] Tommaso de Vio Gaetani, O.P. 1469–1534.
[6] Alfonso de Castro, Friar Minor. (1495–1558). Confessor to Charles V and Philip II of Spain.
[7] Sisto da Siéna, O.P. Bibliotheca Sancta . . . (Liber V). Secunda editio. Francofurti. 1575. folio.
[8] Père Crespet, Celestine monk. *Deux livres de la haine de Satan et des malins esprits contre l'homme.* Paris. 1590.
[9] Bartholomeo Spina, O.P. *De lamiis. De strigibus.* Both folio, Venice, 1584. *Apologiæ tres aduersus Joannem Franciscum Ponzinibium Jurisperitum.* Venice. 1525. Giovanni Francesco Ponzinibio wrote a *Dedamiis* of which I have used a late edition. Venice, 1584.
[10] Giovanni Lorenzo Anania, *De natura dæmonum*: libri iiii. Venetiis. 1581. 8vo.

Chapitre xix.

1. *Les Sorciers vont enuiron la minuict au Sabbat.*
2. *La raison pourquoy le Sabbat si tient ordinairement de nuict.*
3. *Satan se plait aux tenebres, & à la couleur noire, estant au contraire la blancheur agreable à Dieu.*
4. *Les Sorciers dansent doz contre doz au Sabbat, & se masquent pour la plus part.*

5, 8. *Le coq venant à chanter, le Sabbat disparoit aussi tost, & la raison.*

6. *La voix du coq funeste à Satan tout ainsi qu'au lyon, & au serpent.*
7. *Le Demon, selon quelques uns a crainte d'vne espée nue.*

Chapitre xx. Du iour du Sabbat.

1. *Le Sabbat se tient à un chacun iour de la semaine, mais principalement le Ieudy.*
2. *Il se tient encor aux festes les plus solemnelles de l'année.*

Chapitre xxi. Du lieu du Sabbat.

1. *Le lieu du Sabbat est signalé, selon aucuns, de quelques arbres ou bien de quelques croix, & l'opinion de l'autheur sur ce suiect.*
2. *Chose remarquable d'vn lieu pretendu pour le Sabbat.*
3. *Il faut de l'eau au lieu, où se tient le Sabbat, & pourquoy.*
4. *Les Sorciers, à faute d'eau, urinent dans un trou, qu'ils font en terre.*

Chapitre xxii. De ce qui se fait au Sabbat.

1. *Les Sorciers y adorent Satan, estãt en forme d'homme noir, ou de bouc, & luy offrent des chandelles, & le baisent aux parties honteuses de derriere.*
2. *Ils y dansent, & de leurs danses.*
3. *Ils se desbordent en toutes sortes de lubricitez, & comme Satan se fait Incube & Succube.*
4. *Incestes, & paillardises execrebles des Euchites & Gnostiques.*
5. *Les Sorciers banquettent au Sabbat, de leurs viandes, & breuuages, & de la façon qu'ils tiennent à benir la table, & à rendre graces.*
6. *Ils ne prennent cependant point de gout aux Viandes, & sortent ordinairement auec faim du repas.*
7. *Le repas paracheué, ils rendent conte de leurs actions à Satan.*
8. *Ils renoncent de nouueau à Dieu, au Chresme, &c. Et comme Satan les sollicite à mal faire.*
9. *Ils y font la gresle.*
10. *Ils y celebrent messe, & de leurs chappes, & eau benite.*
11. *Satan se consume finalement en feu, & se reduit en cendre, de laquelle les Sorciers prennent tous, & a quel effet.*
12. *Satan Singe de Dieu en tout.*

[66] Vouloir donner une description du Sabbat, c'est vouloir decrire ce qui n'existe point, & n'a jamais subsisté que dans l'imagination creuse & séduite des Sorciers & Sorcieres : les peintures qu'on nous en fait, sont d'après les rêveries de ceux & de celles qui s'imaginent d'être transportés à travers les airs au Sabbat en corps & en ame. *Traité sur les Apparitions des Esprits*, par le R. P. Dom Augustin Calmet, Abbé de Sénones. Paris, 1751, I. p. 138.

[67] See the woodcut upon the title-page of Middleton & Rowley's *The World tost at Tennis*, 4to, 1620.

[68] De Lancre, *L'Incredulité*, p. 769.

[69] Boguet, *Discours des Sorciers.*

[70] De Lancre, *Tableau*, p. 217.

[71] De Lancre, *L'Incredulité*, p. 800.

[72] Görres, *La Mystique Divine*, traduit par Charles Sainte-Foi. V. viii. 19. p. 208.

[73] George Sinclar, *Satan's Invisible World Discovered*, Relation XVII.

[74] *La Mystique Divine*, 1902 (Nouvelle édition). III. p. 381.

[75] *Tractatus*, xxi, c. 11. P. xi. n. 179.

[76] *Disquisitiones Magicæ*, Lib. II. q[to] x.

[77] *Compendium Maleficarum*, p. 78.

[78] Solent ad conuentum delatæ dæmonem conuentus præsidem in solio considentem forma terrifica, ut plurimum hirci uel canis, obuerso ad illum tergo accedentes, adorare . . . et deinde, homagii quod est indicium, osculari eum in podice."[1] Guazzo notes: "Ad signum homagii dæmonem podice osculantur."[2] And Ludwig Elich says: "Deinde quod homagii est indicium (honor sit auribus) ab iis ingerenda sunt oscula Dæmonis podici."[3]

[79] *Mystery of Witchcraft.*

[80] It may be remembered that, as related elsewhere, there is strong reason to suppose Francis Stewart, Earl of Bothwell, grandson of James V, was "the Devil" on this occasion, as he was certainly the Grand Master of the witches and the convener of the Sabbat.

[81] *Newes from Scotland, declaring the damnable Life of Doctor Fian.* London. W. Wright. [1592].

[82] Dudum ad audientiam nostram peruenit, quod uenerabilis frater noster G. Conuentrensis et Lichefeldensis episcopus erat in regno Angliæ et alibi publice defamatur quod diabolo homagium fecerat et eum fuerat osculatus in tergo eique locutus multotius.

[83] Confessa ledit sire Guillaume . . . avoir fait hommage audit ennemy en l'espèce et semblance d'ung mouton en le baisant par le fondement en signe de révérence et d'hommage. Jean Chartier, *Chronique de Charles VII* (ed. Vallet de Viriville). Paris, 1858. III. p. 45. Shadwell, who has introduced this ceremony into *The Lancashire Witches*, II, (The Scene Sir *Edward's* Cellar), in his notes refers to "Doctor *Edlin* . . . who was burn'd for a Witch."

[84] *Reliquiæ Antiquæ*, vol. I. p. 247.

[85] Il a veu [le diable] quelque fois en forme d'homme, tenant son cheval par le frein, & qu'ils le vont adorer tenans vue chandelle de poix noir en leurs mains, le baisent quelque fois au nombril, quelque fois au cul. De Lancre, *L'Incredulité*, p. 25.

[86] Tum candelis piceis oblatis, vel vmbilico infantili, ad signum homagii eum in podice osculantur, Liber I. xiii.

[87] *Satan's Invisible World Discovered*, Relation III.

[88] . . . qui apparait là, tantost en forme d'vn grand homme noir, tantost en forme de bouc, & pour plus grand hommage, ils luy offrent des chandelles, qui rendent vne flamme de couleur bleüe. *Discours des Sorciers*, p. 131.

εἴθε λύρα καλὴ γενοίμην ἐλεφαντίνη,
καί με καλοὶ παῖδες φέροειν Διονύσιον ες χορόν.

(Fain would I be a fair lyre of ivory, and fair boys carrying me to Dionysus' choir.)

[90] Sequuntur his choree quas in girum agitant semper tamen ad læuam progrediendo. *Compendium Maleficarum*, I. xiii.

[91] Les Sorciers, dansent & font leurs danses en rond doz contre doz.

[92] Quelquefois, mais rarement, ils dansent deux à deux, & par fois l'vn çà & l'autre là, & tousiours en confusion.

[93] On n'y dançoit que trois sortes de bransles. . . . La premiere c'est à la Bohemienne. . . . La seconde c'est à sauts: ces deux sont en rond. Sir John Davies in his *Orchestra or A Poeme on Dauncing*, London, 18mo, 1596, describes the seven movements of the Cransles (Crawls) as:

Upward and *downeward, forth* and *back againe,*
To this side and *to that*, and *turning round.*

[94] II. 1.

[95] Sinclar, *Satin's Invisible World Discovered*, III.

[96] *Newes from Scotland*, (1592).

[97] Tota turba colluuiesque pessima fescenninos in honorem dæmonum cantat obscenissimos. Hæc cantat *Harr, harr;* illa Diabole, Diabole, salta huc, salta illuc; altera lude hic, lude illic; alia Sabaoth, Sabaoth, &c.;

1 *Disquisitiones Magicæ*, Lib. II. qto xvi.
Compendium Maleficarum, I. 13.
3 *Dæmonomagia*, Quæstio x.

immo clamoribus, sibilis, ululatibus, propicinis furit ac debacchatur. *Dæmonomagia*, Quæstio x.

[98] Hi habent mensas appositas & instructas accumbunt & incipiunt conuiuari de cibis quos Dæmon suppeditat uel iis quos singuli attulere, *Compendium Maleficarum*, I. xiii.

[99] Les liures disent que les sorciers mangent au Sabbat de ce que le Diable leur a apresté : mais bien souuēt il ne s'y trouue que des viandes qu'ils ont porté eux mesmes. Parfois il y a plusieurs tables seruies de bons viures & d'autres fois de tres meschans. "Les Sorciers . . . banquettent & se festoient," remarks Boguet, "leur banquets estans composez de plusieurs sortes de viandes, selon les lieux & qualitez des personnes." *Tableau*, p. 197. *Discours des Sorciers*, p. 135.

[100] Sinclar, *Invisible World Discovered*, Relation XXIX.

[101] Ils banquêtent, dressant trois tables selon les trois diversités des gens susnommés. Ceux qui ont la charge du pain, ils portent le pain qu'ils font de blé dérobé aux aires invisiblement en divers lieux. Ils boivent de la malvoisie, pour eschauffer la chair à la luxure, que les deputés portent, la dérobant des caves où elle se trouve. Ils y mangent ordinairement de la chair des petits enfants que les députés cuisent à la Synagogue et parfois les y portent tout vifs, les derobant à leurs maisons quand ils trouvent la commodité. Père Sébastien Michaëlis, O.P. *Histoire admirable de la possession*, 1613.

[102] On y boit aussi du vin, et le plus souvent de l'eau.

[103] Conuiuant de cibis a se uel a dæmone allatis, interdum delicatissimis, et interdum insipidis ex infantibus occisis aut cadaueribus exhumatis, præcedente tamen benedictione mensæ tali coetu digna. *Salamanticenses*, Tr. xxi. c. 11. P. 11. n. 179.

[104] Uinum eorum præterea instar atri atque insinceri sanguinis in sordido aliquo scipho epulonibus solitum propinari. Nullam fere copiam rerum illic deesse afferunt præterquā panis et salis. Addit Dominica Isabella apponi etiam humanas carnes. *Compendium Maleficarum*, I. xiii.

[105] *De la Démonomanie*, III. 5.

[106] *Dæmonomagio*, Quæstio vii.

[107] Il n'y a jamais sel en ces repas. *Discours des Sorciers*.

[108] On se met à table, où il n'a iamais veu de sel.

Shadwell draws attention to this detail: *The Lancashire Witches*, II, the Sabbat scene; where Mother Demdike says:

See our Provisions ready here,
To which no Salt must e'er come near!

[109] Père Sébastien Michaëlis, O.P. *Histoire admirable*, 1613.

[110] Isti uero qui expressam professionem fecerunt, reddunt etiam expressum cultum adorationis dæmoni per solemnia sacrificia, quæ ipsi faciunt diabolo, imitantes in omnibus diuinum cultum, cum paramentis, luminaribus, et aliis huiusmodi, ac precibus quibusdam et orationibus quibus instructi sunt, adeo ipsum adorant et collaudant continue, sicut nos uerum Creatorem adoramus. *De Sortilegiis*, Liber II. c. iii. n. 6.

[111] *The Wonders of the Invisible World*. A Hortatory Address. p. 81.

[112] J. Hutchinson, *History of Massachusett's Bay*, II. p. 55. (1828.)

[113] *Euchologion* of the Orthodox Church, ed. Venice, 1898, p. 63.

[114] Baissac, *Les grands jours de la Sorcellerie* (1890), p. 391.

[115] Calmeil, *De la folie*, I. p. 344.

[116] Sébastien Michaëlis, *Histoire admirable*. 1613. Translated as *Admirable Historie*. London, 1613.

[117] Desmarest, *Histoire de Magdelaine Bavent*. Paris. 4to. 1652.

[118] For full details see François Ravaisson, *Archives de la Bastille*, Paris, 1873, where the original depositions are given.

[119] *Là-Bas* appeared in the *Echo de Paris*, 1890–1.

[120] *Tableau*, p. 401. For the full account of these ceremonies I have chiefly relied upon Guazzo; Boguet, *Discours*, XXII, 10; De Lancre, pp. 86, 122, 126, 129; and Görres, *Mystique*, V. pp. 224–227. It hardly seems necessary to give particular citations here for each circumstance.

121 De Lancre, *Tableau*, IV. 4.
122 *Corriere Nazionale di Torino*, Maggio. 1895
123 De Lancre, *Tableau*, p. 401.
124 Görres, *Mystique*, V. p. 230.
125 Roland Brévannes, *L'Orgie Satanique*, IV. Le Sabbat, p. 122.
126 *Discours*, p. 141.
127 S. Caleb, *Messes Noires*, p. 153.
128 *Confession faicte par Messire Loys Gaufridi*, A Aix. MVCXI.
129 A vne Chasuble qui a vne croix; mais qu'elle n'a que trois barres.
130 Le Diable en mesme temps pisse dans vn trou à terre, & fait de l'eau beniste de son vrine, de laquelle celuy, qui dit la messe, arrouse tous les assistants auec vn asperges noir. Boguet, *Discours*, p. 141.
131 . . . lors que Tramesabot disoit la Messe, & qu'auant la commencer li iettoit de l'eau beniste qui estoit faicte de pissat, & faisoit la reverence de l'espaule, & disoit *Asperges Diaboli*. De Lancre, *L'Incredulité*.
132 L'eau beniste est iaune comme du pissat d'asne, & qu'apres qu'on la iettée on dit la Messe.
133 Michaëlis *Histoire admirable*, 1613. Miss Murray, *The Witch-Cult*, p.149, suggests that this sprinkling was "a fertility rite"! An astounding theory. This blasphemy, of course, alludes to the curse of the Jews. S. Matthew xxvii. 25.
134 Que le Diable dit le Sermo au Sabbat, mais qu'on n'entend ce qu'il dit, parce qu'il parle cōme en grōdant. Which suggests the wearing of a mask, or, at least, a voice purposely disguised.
135 Dit qu'il a veu bailler au Sabbat du pain benist & de l'encens, mais il ne sentoit bon comme celuy de l'Eglise.
136 So in the Orleans trial Gentil le Clerc confessed that the Devil "tourne le dos à l'Autel quand il veut leuer l'Hostie & le Calice, qui sont noirs."
137 Silvain Nevillon, (1614–1615). Dit aussi auoir veu des Sorciers & Sorcieres qui apportoient des Hosties au Sabbat, lesquelles elles auoient gardé lors qu'on leur auoit baillé à communier à l'Eglise.
138 Presumably S. Cæsarius of Arles, 470–543, who incidentally was famous for eradicating the last traces of Pagan superstitions and practices. He imposed the penalty of excommunication upon all those who consulted augurs and wore heathen amulets. The Gnostics were especially notorious for their employment of such periapts, talismans, and charms.
139 J. F. Bladé, *Quatorze superstitions populaires de la Gascogne*, pp. 16 *sqq.* Agen. 1883.
140 *Decisions*. Edinburgh, 1759.
141 Ie laisse à penser si l'on n'exerce pas là toutes les especes de lubricités veu encor que les abominations, qui firent foudre & abismer Sodome & Gomorrhe, y font fort communes. Boguet, *Discours*, c. xxii. p. 137.
142 *Histoire admirable*, 1613.
143 Finalement, ils paillardent ensemble: le dimanche avec les diables succubes ou incubes; le jeudi, commettent la sodomie; le samedi la bestialité; les autres jours à la voie naturelle.
144 The Louviers process lasted four years, 1643–7.
145 Après la Messe on dance, puis on couche ensemble, hommes auec hommes, & auec des femmes. Puis on se met à table. . . . Dit qu'il a cognu des hommes & s'est accouplé auec eux; qu'il auoit vne couppe on gondolle par le moyen de laquelle toutes les femmes le suiuoient pour y boire.
146 Apres la danse finie les diables se coucherēt auecques elles, & eurēt leur cōpagnie.
147 . . . grand nombre d'hommes & femmes furent bruslees en la ville d'Arras, accusees les vns par les autres, & cōfesserent qu'elles estoient la nuict transportees aux danses, & puis qu'ils se couploient auecques les diables, qu'ils adoroient en figure humaine.
148 . . . toutes generalement sans exception, confessoient que le diable auoit copulation charnelle auec elles, apres leur auoir fait renoncer Dieu & leur religion.
149 . . . c'est à sçauoir que les diables, tāt qu'elles auoient esté Sorcieres,

auoiĉt eu copulation auec elles. Henry de Cologne confirmant ceste opinion dit, qu'il y a rien plus vulgaire en Alemaigne.

[150] . . . quod sacrificia dabant dæmonibus in animalibus uiuis, quæ diuidebant membratim et offerebant distribuendo in inferne quadruuiis cuidam dæmoni qui se facit appellari Artis Filium ex pauperioribus inferni. *Dame Alice Kyteler*, ed. T. Wright. Camden Society. 1843. pp. 1–2.

[151] *Highland Papers*, III. p. 18.

[152] *Æneid*, VI. 243–251.

[153] Horace, *Sermonum*, I. viii.

[154] *Dictionnaire Infernal*, ed. 1863, p. 590.

[155] Salgues, *Des erreurs et des prejugés*, I. p. 423.

[156] III. 44–45.

[157] Alludit ad Haruspicis officium, qui exta & viscera inspiciebat. Plinius inquit: *Ex ranæ rubetæ uisceribus; id est, lingua, ossiculo, licne, corde, mira fieri posse constat, sunt enin plurimis medicaminibus referta.* Forte intelligit rubetam uel bufonem, indicans se non esse ueneficum, nec rubetarum extis uti ad uenefica. Cf. also Pliny, *Historia Naturalis*, XXXII. 5.

[158] Ravaisson, *Archives de la Bastille*, VI. p. 295 *et alibi*. The interrogatories of these scandals may be found in volumes IV and V of this work.

[159] L. Strackerjan, *Aberglaube und Sagen aus dem Herzogthum Oldenburg* (1867), I. 70.

[160] *Königsberger Hartung'sche Zeitung*, 1866. No. 9.

[161] V. Fossel. *Volksmedicin und medicinischer Aberglaube in Steiermark*, Graz, 1886.

[162] U. Jahn, *Zauber mit Menschenblut und anderen Teilen des menschlichen Körpers*, 1888.

[163] A. Löwenstimm, *Aberglaube und Strafecht*, (*Die Volksmedizin*), 1897.

[164] V. Fossel, *Volksmedicin, ut supra.*

[165] Adrian Kembter, O.R.P., writing in 1745 enumerates 52 instances, and his last is dated 1650. This number might be doubled, and extends until the present century. H. C. Lee, in an article, *El santo nino de la Guardia*, has signally failed to disprove the account. See the series of forty-four articles in the *Osservatore Cattolico* March and April, 1892, Nos. 8438–8473.

[166] *Le Temps*, Paris, 1 Feb. and 23 March, 1892.

[167] *Fetichism in West Africa*, New York, 1904.

[168] De Lancre, *Tableau*, p. 154.

CHAPTER V

The Witch in Holy Writ

In the course of the Holy Scriptures there occur a great number of words and expressions which are employed in connexion with witchcraft, divination, and demonology, and of these more than one authority has made detailed and particular study. Some terms are of general import, one might even venture to say vague and not exactly defined, some are directly specific: of some phrases the signification is plain and accepted; concerning others, scholars are still undecided and differ more or less widely amongst themselves. Yet it is noteworthy that from the very earliest period the attitude of the inspired writers towards magic and related practices is almost wholly condemnatory and uncompromisingly hostile. The vehement and repeated denunciations launched against the professors of occult sciences and the initiate in foreign esoteric mysteries do not, moreover, seem to be based upon any supposition of fraud but rather upon the "abomination" of the magic in itself, which is recognized as potent for evil and able to wreak mischief upon life and limb. It is obvious, for example, that the opponents of Moses, the sorcerers[1] Jannes and Mambres, were masters of no mean learning and power, since when, in the presence of Pharaoh, Aaron's rod became a live serpent, they also and their mob of disciples "fecerunt per incantationes Ægyptiacas et arcana quædam similiter," casting down their rods, which were changed into a mass of writhing snakes. They were able also to bring up frogs upon the land, but it was past their wit to drive them away. We have here, however, a clear acknowledgement of the reality of magic and its dark possibilities, whilst at the same time prominence is given to the fact that when it contests with the miraculous power divinely bestowed upon Moses it fails hopelessly and completely. The serpent, which was Aaron's rod, swallows all the other serpents. The swarms of mosquitoes and gadflies which Aaron caused to rise in myriads from the dust the native warlocks could not produce, nay, they were constrained to cry "Digitus Dei est hic"; whilst a little later they were unable to protect even their own bodies from the pest of blains and swelling sores. None the less a supernatural power was possessed by Jannes and Mambres as truly as by Moses, although not to the same extent, and derived from another, in fact, from an opposite and antagonistic source.

Even more striking is the episode of Balaam, who dwelt at Pethor, a city of Mesopotamia (the Pitru of the cuneiform texts), and who was summoned thence by Balak, King of Moab, to lay a withering curse upon the Israelites, encamped after their victory over the Amorrhites at the very confines of his territory. The royal messengers come to Balaam "with the rewards of divination in their hand," a most illuminating detail, for it shows that already the practice of magical arts is rewarded with gifts of great value.[2] In fact when Balaam refuses, although with reluctance, to accompany the first embassy, princes of the highest rank are then sent to him with injunctions to offer him rank and wealth or whatsoever he may care to ask. "I will promote thee to very great honour, and I will do whatsoever thou sayest unto me; come, therefore, and curse this people," are the king's actual words. After great difficulties, for Balaam is, at first, forbidden to go and only wins his way on condition that he undertakes to do what he is commanded and to speak no more than he is inspired to say, the seer commences his journey and is met by the king at a frontier town, and by him taken up "unto the high places of Baal," to the sacred groves upon the hill-tops, where seven mystic altars are built, and a bullock and a ram offered upon each. Balaam then senses the imminent presence of God, and withdraws swiftly apart to some secret place where "God met" him. He returns to the scene of sacrifice and forthwith blesses the Israelites. Balak in consternation and dismay hurries him to the crest of Pisgah (Phasga), and the same ceremonies are performed. But again Balaam pours forth benisons upon the people. A third attempt is made, and this time was chosen the summit of Peor (Phogor), a peculiarly sacred sanctuary, the centre of the local cult of Baal Peor, whose ancient worship comprised a ritual of most primitive obscenity.[3] Again the sevenfold sacrifice is offered upon seven altars, and this time Balaam deliberately resists the divine control, a vain endeavour, since he passes into trance, and utters words of ineffable benediction gazing down the dim avenues of futurity to the glorious vision of the Madonna, Stella Jacob, and her Son, the Sceptre of Israel. Beating his clenched hands together in an access of ungovernable fury the choused and exasperated king incontinently dismisses his guest.

It must be remarked that throughout the whole of this narrative, the details of which are as interesting as they are significant, there is on the part of the writer a complete recognition of the claims put forth by Balaam and so amply acknowledged and appreciated by Balak. Balaam was a famous sorcerer, and one, moreover, who knew and could launch the mystic Word of Power with deadly effect. Among the early Arabs as among the Israelites the magic spell, the Word of Blessing or the Curse, played a prominent part. In war, the poet, by cursing the enemy in rhythmic runes, rendered services not inferior to the heroism of the warrior himself. So the Jews of Medina used to bring into their synagogues images of their hated enemy Malik b. al-Aglam; and at these effigies they hurled maledictions each time they met. The reality of Balaam's power is clearly the key-note of the Biblical account. Else why should his services be transferred to the cause of Israel? Balak's greeting to the seer is no empty compliment but vitally true: "I wot that he whom thou blessest is blessed, and he whom thou cursest is cursed." Not impertinent is the bitter denunciation in the song of Deborah, Judges v. 23, "Curse ye me Meroz, said the angel of the Lord, curse ye bitterly the inhabitants thereof; because they came not to the help of the Lord against the mighty!" (A.V.) Belief in the potency of the uttered word has existed at all times and in all places, and yet continues to exist everywhere to-day.

Although Balaam prophesied it must be borne in mind that he was not a prophet in the Scriptural sense of the term; he was a soothsayer, a wizard; the Vulgate has *hariolus*,[4] which is derived from the Sanskrit *hira*, entrails, and equivalent to *haruspex*. This term originally denoted an Etruscan diviner who foretold future events by an inspection of the entrails of sacrificial victims. It was from the Etruscans that this practice was introduced to the Romans. It is probable that Balaam employed the seven bullocks and rams in this way, the technical *extispicium*, a method of inquiry and forecasting which seems to have been almost universal, although the exact manner in which the omens were read differed among the several peoples and at various times. It persisted, none the less, until very late, and indeed it is resorted to, so it has been said, by certain occultists even at the present day. It is known to have been practised by Catherine de' Medici, and it is closely connected with the dark Voodoo worship of Jamaica and Hayti. S. Thomas, it is true, has spoken of Balaam as a prophet, but the holy doctor hastens to add "a prophet of the devil." The learned Cornelius à Lapide, glossing upon Numbers xxii and xxiii writes: "It is clear that Balaam was a prophet, not of God, but of the Devil. . . . He was a magician, and he sought for a conference with his demon to take counsel with him."[5] He is of opinion that the seven altars were erected in honour of the Lords of the Seven Planets. Seven is, of course, the perfect number, the mystic number, even as three; and all must be done by odd numbers. The woman in Vergil who tries to call back her estranged lover Daphnis by potent incantations cries: *numero deus impare gaudet.* (Heaven loves unequal numbers.) Eclogue viii. 75 (*Pharmaceutria*). S. Augustine, S. Ambrose, and Theodoret consider that when Balaam on the first occasion withdrew hastily saying "Peradventure the Lord will come to meet me," he expected to meet a demon, his familiar. But "God met Balaam." The very precipitation and disorder seem to point to the design of the sorcerer, for as in the Divine Liturgy all is done with due dignity, grace, and comeliness, so in the functions of black magic all is hurried, ugly, and terrible.

One of the most striking episodes in the Old Testament is concerned with necromancy, the appearance of Samuel in the cave or hut at Endor. Saul, on the eve of a tremendous battle with the Philistines, is much dismayed and almost gives away to a complete nervous collapse as he sees the overwhelming forces of the ruthless foe. To add to his panic, when he consulted the Divine Oracles, no answer was returned, "neither by dreams, nor by Urim, nor by prophets." And although he had in the earlier years of his reign shown himself a determined represser of Witchcraft, in his dire extremity he catches at any straw, and bids his servants seek out some woman "that hath a familiar spirit," and his servants said to him, "Behold there is a woman that hath a familiar spirit at Endor," which is a miserable hamlet on the northern slope of a hill, lying something south of Mount Tabor.

The phrase here used, rendered by the Vulgate "pytho" (Quærite mihi mulierem habentem pythonem) and by the Authorized Version "familiar spirit," is in the original *'ôbh,*[6] which signifies the departed spirit evoked, and also came to stand for the person controlling such a spirit and divining by its aid. The Witch of Endor is described as the possessor of an *'ôbh.* The LXX. translates this word by ἐγγαστράμυθος, which means ventriloquist, either because the real actors thought that the magician's alleged communication with the spirit was a mere deception to impose upon the inquirer who is tricked by the voice being thrown into the ground and being of strange quality—a view which mightily commends itself to Lenormant[7] and the sceptical Renan[8] but which is quite untenable—or rather because of the belief common in antiquity that ventriloquism was not a natural faculty but due to the temporary obsession of the medium by a spirit. In this connexion the prophet Isaias has a remarkable passage: Quærite a pythonibus, et a diuinis qui strident in incantationibus suis. (Seek unto them that have familiar spirits, and unto wizards that peep and that mutter. *A.V.*) Many Greek and Latin poets attribute a peculiar and distinctive sound to the voices of spirits. Homer (*Iliad*, XXIII, 101; *Odyssey*, XXIV, 5, and 9) uses τρίζειν, which is elsewhere found of the shrill cry or chirping of partridges, young swallows, locusts, mice, bats,[9] and of such other sounds as the creaking of a door, the sharp crackling of a thing burned in a fire. Vergil *Æneid*, III, 39, speaks of the cry of Polydorus from his grave as *gemitus lacrimabilis*, and the clamour of the spirits in Hades is *uox exigua.* Horace also in his description of the midnight Esbat on the Esquiline describes the voice as *triste et acutum;* (*Sermonum*, I. viii, 40–1):

> singula quid memorem, quo pacto alterna loquentes
> umbrae cum Sagana resonarent triste et acutum.

Statius, *Thebais*, VII, 770, has "stridunt animæ," upon which Kaspar von Barth, the famous sixteenth-century German scholar, annotates "Homericum hoc est qui corporibus excedentes animas stridere excogitauit." So in Shakespeare's well-known lines, *Hamlet* I, 1:

> the sheeted dead
> Did squeak and gibber in the Roman streets.

When he had been informed of this witch Saul, accordingly, completely divested himself of the insignia of royalty and in a close disguise accompanied only by two of his most trusted followers similarly muffled in cloaks, he painfully made his way at dead of night to her remote and squalid hovel. He eagerly requested her to exercise her powers, and to raise the spirit of the person whom he should name. At first she refused, since some years before the laws had been stringently enforced and the penalty of death awaited all sorcerers and magicians. Not unreasonably she feared that these mysterious strangers might be laying a trap for her, to imperil her life. But the concealed king persuaded her, and bound himself by a mighty oath that she should come to no harm. Whereupon she consented to evoke the soul of the prophet Samuel, as he desired. The charm commenced, and after the vision of various familiars—the woman said: Deos uidi ascendentes de terra—and S. Gregory of Nyssa explains these as demons, *τὰ φαντάσματα*,—Samuel appeared amid circumstances of great terror and awe, and in the same moment the identity of her visitant was recognized (we are not informed how) by the sybil.[10] In a paroxysm of rage and fear the haggard crone turned to him and shrieked out: "Why hast thou deceived me? For thou art Saul." The king, however, tremblingly reassured her for her own safety, and feeling that he was confronted by no earthly figure—he could not see the phantom, although he sensed a presence from beyond the grave—he asked: "What form is he of?" And when the beldame, to whom alone the prophet was visible, described the spirit: "An old man cometh up, and he is covered with a mantle," Saul at once recognized Samuel, and fell prostrate upon the ground, whilst the apparition spake his swiftly coming doom.

Here we have a detailed scene of necromancy proper. There are, it is true, some remarkable, and perhaps unusual, features: the witch alone sees the phantom, but Saul instantly knows who it is from her description; he directly addresses Samuel, and he hears the prediction of the dead prophet. The whole narrative undoubtedly bears the impress of actuality and truth.

There are several interpretations of these incidents. In the first place some writers have denied the reality of the vision, and so it is claimed that the witch deceived Saul by skilful trickery. This hardly seems possible. It is not likely that she would have run so grave a risk as the exercise, or pretended exercise, of magical arts must entail were she a mere charlatan; an accomplice of remarkably quick wit and invention would have been necessary to carry out the details of the plot; it is surely incredible that they should have ventured upon so uncompromising a denunciation of the king and have foretold so evil an end to his house. In fact the whole tenor of the story conflicts with this explanation, which is not allowed by the Fathers. Theodoret, it is true, inclines to suppose that some deception was practised, but he hesitates to maintain an unequivocal opinion in the matter. In his *Quæstiones in I Regum* Cap. xxviii he asks πῶς τὰ κατὰ τὴν ἐγγαστρίμυθον νοητέον;[11] and says that some think that the witch actually evoked Samuel, others believe the Devil took the likeness of the prophet. The first opinion he characterizes as impious, the second foolish.

S. Jerome, whose authority would, of course, be entirely conclusive, does not perhaps pronounce definitely; but his comments sufficiently show, I think, that he regarded the apparition as being really Samuel. In his tractate *In Esaiam*, III, vii, he writes: "Most authors think that a clear sign was given Saul from the earth itself and from the very depths of Hades when he saw Samuel evoked by incantations and magic spells."[12] And again, *In Ezechielem*, Lib. IV; xiii, the holy doctor, speaking of witches, has: "they are inspired by an evil spirit. The Hebrews say that they are well versed in baleful crafts, necromancy and soothsayings, such as was the hag who seemed to raise up the soul of Samuel."[13]

Some authors directly attribute this appearance of Samuel to an evil spirit, who took the form of the prophet in order to dishearten Saul and tempt him to despair. Thus S. Gregory of Nyssa in his letter *De pythonissa ad Theodosium*[14] says that the Devil deceived the witch, who thus in her turn deceived the king. S. Basil expressly lays down (*In Esaiam*, VIII. 218): "They were demons who assumed the appearance of Samuel."[15] And he conjectures that, inasmuch as the denunciation of Saul was strictly true in every detail, the demons having heard the sentence delivered by God merely reported it. Among the Latins Tertullian, more than a century before, had written: "And I believe that evil spirits can deceive many by their lies; for a lying spirit was allowed to feign himself to be the shade of Samuel."[16]

The preponderance of opinion, however, is decidedly in favour of a literal and exact understanding of the event, that it was, in effect, Samuel who appeared to the guilty monarch and foretold his end. Origen argues upon these lines, basing his reasons upon the plain statements of Holy Writ: "But it is distinctly stated that Saul knew it was Samuel."[17] And later he adds: "The Scripture cannot lie. And the words of Scripture are: And the woman saw Samuel."[18] Elsewhere when treating of evil spirits he precisely states: "And that souls have their abiding place I have made known to you from the evocation by the witch of Samuel, when Saul requested her to divine."[19] S. Ambrose also says: "Even after his death Samuel, as Holy Scripture informs us, prophesied of what was to come."[20] We have further the overwhelming witness of S. Augustine, who in more than one place discusses the question at some length, and decides that the phantom evoked by the sibyl was really and truly the soul of the prophet Samuel. Thus in that important treatise *De Doctrina Christiana*, commenced in 397 and finally revised for issue in 427, he has: "The shade of Samuel, long since dead, truly foretold what was to come unto King Saul."[21] Whilst a passage in the even more famous and weighty *De Cura pro mortuis gerenda*, written in 421, asserts: "For the prophet Samuel, who was dead, revealed the future to King Saul, who was yet alive."[22]

Josephus believed the apparition to have been summoned by the witch's necromantic powers, for in his *Jewish Antiquities*, VI, xiv, 2, when dealing with the story of Endor, he chronicles: "[Saul] bade her bring up to him the soul of Samuel. She, not knowing who Samuel was, called him out of Hades,"[23] a remarkable testimony.

Throughout the whole of the Old Testament the sin of necromancy is condemned in the strongest terms, but the very reiteration of this ban shows that none the less evocation of the dead was extensively and continuously practised, albeit in the most clandestine and secret manner. The Mosaic law denounces such arts again and again: "Go not aside after wizards, neither ask any thing of soothsayers, to be defiled by them: I am the Lord your God" (Leviticus xix. 31); "The soul that shall go aside after magicians and soothsayers, and shall commit fornication with them, I will set my face against that soul, and destroy it out of the midst of its people" (Leviticus xx. 6). Even more explicit in its details is the following prohibition: "Neither let there be found among you any one . . . that consulteth soothsayers, or observeth dreams and omens, neither let there be any wizard, nor charmer, nor any one that consulteth pythonic spirits, or fortune tellers, or that seeketh the truth from the dead. For the Lord abhorreth all these things" (Deuteronomy xviii. 10–12). Hence it is obvious that the essential malice of the sin lay in the fact that it was *lèse-majesté* against God, such as is also the sin of heresy.[24] This is, moreover, clearly brought out in the fact that the temporal penalty was death. "A man, or woman, in whom there is a pythonical or divining spirit, dying, let them die" (Leviticus xx. 27). And the famous statute, Exodus xxii. 18, expressly says: "Wizards thou shalt not suffer to live." Nevertheless, necromancy persisted, and on occasion, such as during the reign of Manasses, thirteenth king of Juda (692–638 B.C.),[25] it no longer lurked in dark corners and obscene hiding-holes, but flaunted its foul abomination unabashed in the courts of the palace and at noon before the eyes of the superstitious capital. In the days of this monarch divination was openly used, omens observed, pythons publicly appointed, whilst soothsayers multiplied "to do evil before the Lord, and to provoke Him" (4 Kings [2 Kings] xxi. 6). The ghastly rites of human sacrifice were revived, and it was common knowledge that the sovereign himself, upon the slightest and most indifferent pretexts, resorted to *extispicium*, the seeking of omens from the yet palpitating entrails of boys devoted to this horrid purpose. "Manasses shed also very much innocent blood, till he filled Jerusalem up to the mouth" (4 Kings [2 Kings] xxi. 16). We may parallel the foul sorceries of the Jewish king with the detailed confession of Gilles de Rais, who at his trial "related how he had stolen away children, detailed all his foul cajolements, his hellish excitations, his frenzied murders, his ruthless rapes and ravishments: obsessed by the morbid vision of his poor pitiful victims, he described at length their long-drawn agonies or swift torturings; their piteous cries and the death-rattle in their throats; he avowed that he had wallowed in their warm entrails; he confessed that he had torn out their hearts through large gaping wounds, as a man might pluck ripe fruit."[26] The demonolatry of the sixth century before Christ is the same as that of fourteen hundred years after the birth of Our Lord.

As has been previously noticed, Balaam employed bullocks and rams for *extispicium*, and nine centuries later, in the book of Ezechiel (xxi. 21), Esarhaddon is represented as looking at the liver of an animal offered in sacrifice with a view to divination. "For the king of Babylon stood in the highway, at the head of two ways, seeking divination, shuffling arrows: he inquired of the idols, and consulted entrails. On his right hand was the divination of Jerusalem, to set battering rams, to open the mouth in slaughter." The mode of sortilege by arrows, belomancy, to which allusion is here made was extensively practised among the Chaldeans, as also by the Arabs. Upon this passage S. Jerome comments: "He shall stand in the highway, and consult the oracle after the manner of his nation, that he may cast arrows into a quiver, and mix them together, being written upon or marked with the names of each people, that he may see whose arrow will come forth, and which city he ought first to attack."

Among the three hundred and sixty idols which stood round about the Caaba of Mecca, and which were all destroyed by Mohammed when he captured the city in the eighth year of the Hejira, was the statue of a man, made of agate, who held in one hand seven arrows such as the pagan Arabs used in divination. This figure, which, it is said, anciently represented the patriarch Abraham, was regarded with especial awe and veneration.

The arrows employed by the early Arabs for magical practices were more generally only three in number. They were carefully preserved in the temple of some idol, before whose shrine they had been consecrated. Upon one of them was inscribed "My Lord hath commanded me"; upon another "My Lord hath forbidden me"; and the third was blank. If the first was drawn the inquirer looked upon it as a propitious omen promising success in the enterprise; if the second were drawn he augured failure; if the third, all three were mixed again and another trial was made. These divining arrows seem always to have been consulted by the Arabs before they engaged in any important undertaking, as, for example, when a man was about to go upon a particular journey, to marry, to commence some weighty business.

In certain cases and in many countries rods were used instead of arrows. Small sticks were marked with occult signs, thrown into a vessel and drawn out; or, it might be, cast into the air, the direction they took and the position in which they fell being carefully noted. This practice is known as rhabdomancy. The LXX, indeed, Ezechiel xxi. 21, has *ῥαβδομαντεία* not *βελομαντεία*, and rhabdomancy is mentioned by S. Cyril of Alexandria.

In the Koran, chapter V, The Table or The Chapter of Contracts, "divining arrows" are said to be "an abomination of the work of Satan," and the injunction is given "therefore avoid them that ye may prosper."

It is noticeable that in the early Biblical narrative one form of divination is mentioned, if not with approval, at any rate without overt reproach. Upon the occasion of the second journey of Jacob's sons to Egypt to buy corn in the time of famine, Joseph gave orders that their sacks were to be filled with food, that each man's money was to be put in the mouth of his sack, but that in the sack of Benjamin was also to be concealed the "cup, the silver cup." And the next morning when they had set out homewards and were gone a little way out of the city they were overtaken by a band of Joseph's servants under the conduct of his steward who arrested their progress and accused them of the theft of the cup : " Is not this it in which my lord drinketh, and whereby indeed he divineth ? Ye have done evil in so doing " (*A.V.*). The Vulgate has : " Scyphus quem furati estis, ipse est in quo bibit dominus meus et in quo augurari solet : pessimam rem fecistis " (Genesis xliv. 5). And later when they are brought back in custody and led into the presence of Joseph he asks them : " Wot ye not that such a man as I can certainly divine ? " Vulgate : " An ignoratis quod non sit similis mei in augurandi scientia ? "

In the first place it cannot be for a moment supposed that Joseph's claim, which here he so publicly and so emphatically states, to be a diviner of no ordinary powers was a mere device for the occasion. From the prominence given to the cup in the story it is clear that his steward regarded it as a vessel of especial value and import, dight with mysterious properties.

This cup was used for that species of divination known as hydromantia, a practice almost universal in antiquity and sufficiently common at the present day. The seer, or in some cases the inquirer, by gazing fixedly into a pool or basin of still water will see therein reflected as in a mirror a picture of that which it is sought to know. Strabo, XVI, 2, 39, speaking of the Persians, writes : *παρὰδε τοῖς πέρσαις οἱ Μάγοι καὶ νεκυομάντεις καὶ ἔτι οἱ λεγόμενοι λεκανομάντεις καὶ ὑδρομάντεις.* King Numa, according to one very ancient tradition, divined by seeing gods in a clear stream. " For Numa himself, not being instructed by any prophet or Angel of God, was fain to fall to hydromancy : making his gods (or rather his devils) to appear in water, and instruct him in his religious institutions. Which kind of divination, says Varro, came from Persia and was used by Numa and afterwards by Pythagoras, wherein they used blood also and called forth spirits infernal. Necromancy, the Greeks call it, but necromancy or hydromancy, whether you like, there it is that the dead seem to speak " (*S. Augustine De Ciuitate Dei.* VII. 35).[27]

Apuleius in his *De Magia*,[28] quoting from Varro, says : " Trallibus de euentu Mithridatici belli magica percontatione consultantibus puerum in aqua simulacrum Mercuri contemplantem, quæ futura erant, centum sexaginta uersibus cecinisse." In Egypt to-day the Magic Mirror is frequently consulted. A boy is engaged to gaze into a splash of water, or it may be ink or some other dark liquid poured into the palm of the hand, and therein he will assuredly see pictorially revealed the answers to those questions put to him. When a theft has been committed the Magic Mirror is invariably questioned thus. In Scandinavia the country folk, who had lost anything, would go to a diviner on a Thursday night to see in a pail of water who it was had robbed them.[29] All the world over this belief prevails, in Tahiti and among the Hawaiians, in the Malay Peninsula, in New Guinea, among the Eskimos.

Similar forms of divination are those by things dropped into some liquid, a precious stone or rich amulet is cast into a cup, and the rings formed on the surface of the contents were held to predict the future. Again warm wax or molten lead is poured into a vessel of cold water, and significant letters of the alphabet may be spelled out or objects discerned from the shapes this wax or lead assumes ; or again, the empty tea-cup is tilted and from the leaves, their size, shape, and the manner in which they lie, prognostications are made. This is common in England, Scotland, Ireland, Sweden, Lithuania, whilst in Macedonia coffee-dregs are employed in the same manner.

But whether the seer be Hebrew patriarch or Roman king and the divination dignified by some occult name, Ceromancy (the melting of wax), Lecanomancy (basins of water), Oinomancy (the lees of wine), or whether it be some old plaid-shawled grandam by her cottage fire peering at the leaves of her afternoon tea, the object is the same throughout the ages, for all systems of divination are merely so many methods of obscuring the outer vision, in order that the inner vision may become open.

As was inevitable hydromantia lent itself to much trickery, and Hippolytus of Rome, presbyter and antipope (*ob. circa* A.D. 236), in his important polemic against heretics, *Philosophumena*,[30] IV, 35, explains in detail how persons were elaborately duped by the pseudo-magicians. A room was prepared, the roof of which was painted blue to resemble the sky, there was set therein a large vessel full of water with a glass bottom, immediately under which lay a secret chamber. The inquirer gazed steadfastly into the water, and the actors walking in the secret chamber below would seem as though they were figures appearing in the water itself.

In view of the severe and general condemnation of magical practices found throughout Holy Writ it is remarkable that the Pentateuchal narrative does not censure Joseph's hydromantic arts. Indeed, except in the book Genesis, it is seldom that any forms of presaging or the use of charms are noted save with stern reprobation. In Isaias iii. 2, however, the Kōsēm, magician or diviner, is mentioned with singular respect. "Ecce enim dominator Dominus exercituum auferet a Jerusalem et a Juda ualidum et fortem omne robur panis et omne robur aquæ, fortem, et uirum bellatorem, iudicem, et prophetam, et *hariolum*, et senem." Here the Authorized Version deliberately mistranslates and obscures the sense: "For, behold, the Lord, the Lord of hosts, doth take away from Jerusalem and from Judah, the stay and the staff, the whole stay of bread and the whole stay of water, the mighty man and the man of war, the judge and the prophet, and *the prudent*, and the ancient." "The Prudent" is by no means a rendering of Kōsēm which "hariolus" perfectly represents.

In the thirteenth chapter of Genesis we have a most detailed and striking narrative of sympathetic magic. Jacob, who is serving Laban, is to receive as a portion of his hire all the speckled and spotted cattle, all the brown among the sheep, and the spotted and speckled among the goats. But the crafty old Syrian prevented his son-in-law by removing to a distance, a journey of three days, all such herds as had been specified, "and Jacob fed the rest of Laban's flocks. Thereupon Jacob took rods of green poplar, hazel, and chestnut, and peeled these rods in alternate stripes of white and bark, and he put them in the gutters in the watering-troughs when the flocks came to drink." The animals duly copulated, and "the flocks conceived before the rods, and brought forth cattle, ringstraked, speckled, and spotted." Moreover, it was only when the stronger cattle conceived that Jacob set the rods before their eyes, so that eventually all the best of the herds fell to his share. The names of the trees are in themselves significant. The poplar in Roman folklore was sacred to Hercules,[31] and as it grew on the banks of the river Acheron in Epirus it was connected with Acheron, the waters of woe in the underworld, a confused tradition which is undoubtedly of very early origin. So Pausanias has: *τὴν λευκην ὁ Ἡρακλῆς πεφυκυῖαν παρὰ τὸν Ἀχέροντα εὕρετο ἐν Θεσπρωτιᾳ ποταμόν·* In seventeenth-century England poplar-leaves were accounted an important ingredient in hell-broths and charms. The hazel has been linked with magic from remotest antiquity, and the very name witch-hazel remains to-day. The chestnut-tree and its nuts seem to have been associated with some primitive sexual rites. The connexion is obscure, but beyond doubt traceable. In that most glorious marriage song, the Epithalamium of Catullus, as the boys sang their Fescennines of traditional obscenity nuts were scattered among the crowd.[32] Petronius (Fragmentum XXXIII, ed. Buecheler, Berolini, 1895) mentions chestnuts as an amatory gift:

> aurea mala mihi, dulcis mea Marcia, mittis
> mittis et hirsutae munera castaneae.

In Genesis again is recorded a most interesting and instructive example of the belief in the magic efficacy of plants. "And Reuben went in the days of wheat harvest and found mandrakes in the field and brought them to his mother Leah" (xxx. 14 A.V.). Reuben brings his mother mandrakes (Love Apples), which Rachel desires to have. Whereupon Leah bargains with Rachel, and the latter for a portion of the fruit consents that Jacob shall that night return to the bed of his elder wife, who indeed conceives and in due time she bare Issachar. Leah ate of the mandrake as a charm to induce pregnancy, and no disapproval of such use is expressed.

A similar theme is treated in Machiavelli's famous masterpiece of satirical comedy *La Mandragola*,[33] written between 1513 and 1520, and performed by request before Leo X in the April of the latter year. It had already been acted in Florence. In this play Callimaco is bent upon securing as his mistress Lucrezia, the wife of a gullable doctor of laws, Messer Nicia, whose one wish in life is to get a son. Callimaco is introduced as a physician to Nicia, to whom he explains that a potion of mandragora administered to the lady will remove her sterility, but that it has fatal consequences to the husband. He must perish unless some other man be first substituted whose action will absorb the poison, and leave Lucrezia free to become the mother of a blooming family. This plot is fully worked out, and by the services of his supple confederates Callimaco is introduced to Lucrezia's bedchamber as the necessary victim, and gains his desire.

Mandrakes and mallows were potent in all forms of enchantment, and about the mandrake in particular has grown up a whole library of legend, which it would require much time and space thoroughly to investigate. Western lore is mainly of somewhat a grim character, but not entirely, and by the Orientals mandrake is regarded as a powerful aphrodisiac. So in Canticles VII, 13, we have: Mandragoræ dederunt odorem. (The mandrakes give a fragrant smell.) In antiquity mandrakes were used as an anæsthetic. Dioscorides alludes to the employment of this herb before patients have to be cut or burned; Pliny refers to its odour as causing sleep during an operation; Lucian speaks of it as used before cautery; and both Galen and Isidorus have passages which mention its dormitive quality. The Shakespearean allusions have rendered this aspect familiar to all.

The Arabs and ancient Germans thought that a powerful spirit inhabited the plant, an idea derived, perhaps, from the fancied resemblance of the root to the human form. Ducagne has under Mandragore: "Pomi genus cuius mentio fit, Gen. xxx. 14. nostris etiam notis sub nomine *Mandragores*, quod pectore asseruatum sibi diuitiis acquirendis idoneum somniabunt." And Littré quotes the following from an old chronicle of the thirteenth century: "Li dui compaignon [un couple d'éléphants] vont contre Orient près du paradis terreste, tant que la femelle trouve une herbe que on apele mandragore, si en manjue, et si atize tant son masle qu'il en manjue avec li, et maintenant eschaufe la volenté de chascun, et s'entrejoignent à envers et engendrent un filz sanz plus." In the *Commentaria ad Historiam Caroli VI et VII* it is related that several mandrakes found in the possession of Frère Richard, a Cordelier, were seized and burned as savouring of witchcraft.

It seems certain that the teraphim, which Rachel stole

from her father (Genesis xxxi, 19, and 31–35), and which when he was in pursuit she concealed by a subtle trick, were used for purposes of divination. From the relation of the incident it is obvious that they were regarded of immense value—he who had conveyed them away was, if found, to die the death —and invested with a mysterious sanctity. Centuries later, during the period of drastic reform, King Josias (639–608 B.C.) would no longer tolerate them : " Moreover the workers with familiar spirits, and the wizards, and the images [teraphim], and the idols, and all abominations that were spied in the land of Judah and in Jerusalem did Josiah put away" (2 Kings xxiii. 24. A.V.). The Vulgate has: "Sed et pythones, et hariolos, et figuras idolorum, et immunditias, et abominationes, quæ fuerant in terra Juda et Jerusalem, abstulit Josias." In Ezechiel xxi. 21, Esarhaddon is said to have divined by teraphim as well as by belomancy; and in Zacharias (x. 2) the teraphim are stated on occasion to have deceived their inquirers, "simulacra locuta sunt inutile," "the idols have spoken vanity." Notwithstanding this it is obvious from Osee (Hosea) iii. 4, that divination by teraphim was sometimes permitted: "Dies multos sedebunt filii Israel sine rege, et sine principe, et sine sacrificio, et sine altari, et sine ephod, et sine teraphim." "The children of Israel shall abide many days without a king, and without a prince, and without a sacrifice, and without an image, and without an ephod, and without teraphim."

The learned Cornelius à Lapide glossing on Genesis xxxi writes: "Idola, *teraphim* quod significat statuæ humanæ siue humaneas formas habentes ut patet, I. Reg. xix." The allusion is to the deception practised by Michal on Saul's messengers, when putting one of the teraphim in bed and covering it with quilts she pretended it was David who lay sick. "Secundo," continues à Lapide, "nomen *theraphim* non appropriatum est in eas statuas, quæ opera dæmonorum deposci debent, ut patet Judicum, xviii, 18," the reference being to the history of Micas. Calvin very absurdly says: "Theraphim sunt imagines quales habent papistæ."

Spencer[34] is of opinion that these teraphim were small images or figures, and the point seems conclusively settled by S. Jerome, who in his twenty-ninth Epistle, *De Ephod et Teraphim*, quotes 1 Kings xix. 15, and uses "figuras siue figurationes" to translate *μορφώματα* of Aquila of Pontus. This writer was the author of a Greek version of the Old Testament published *circa* A.D. 128. About eight years before he seems to have been expelled from the Christian community, by whom he was regarded as an adept in magic. The work of Aquila, who studied in the school of Rabbi Akiba, the founder of Rabbinical Judaism, is said by S. Jerome to have attained such exactitude that it was a good dictionary to furnish the meaning of the obscurer Hebrew words. The Targum of Jonathan commenting upon Genesis xxxi. 19, puts forward the singular view that the teraphim, concealed by Rachel, consisted of a mummified human head.

In the book Tobias we have a detailed and important account of exorcism, and one, moreover, which throws considerable light upon the demonology of the time. Tobias, the son of Tobias, is sent under the guidance of the unknown Angel, S. Raphael, to Gabelus in Rages of Media, to obtain the ten talents of silver left in bond by his father. Tobias, whilst bathing in the Tigris is attacked by a monstrous fish, of which he is told by his Angel protector to reserve the heart, liver, and gall; the first two of these are to prevent the devil who had slain seven previous husbands of Sara, the beautiful daughter of Raguel, from attacking him. They arrive at the house of Raguel, and Tobias seeks the hand of Sara. She, however, is so beloved by the demon Asmodeus that seven men who had in turn married her were by him put to death the night of the nuptials, before consummation. Tobias, however, by exorcism, by the odour of the burning liver of the fish, and by the help of S. Raphael, routs Asmodeus, "Then the Angel Raphael took the Devil, and bound him in the desert of upper Egypt." The story which must be accepted as fact-narrative was originally written during the Babylonian exile in the early portion of the seventh century, B.C. It plainly shows that demons were considered to be capable of sexual love, such as was the love of the sons of God for the daughters of men recorded in Genesis (vi. 2). One may compare the stories of the Jinns in Arabian lore. Asmodeus is perhaps to be identified with the Persian *Aēshma daēva,* who in the *Avesta* is next to Angromainyus, the chief of the evil spirits. The introduction of Tobias's dog should be remarked. The dog accompanies his master on the journey and when they return home "the dog, which had been with them in the way, ran before, and coming as if he had brought the news, shewed his joy by his fawning and wagging his tail." Among the Persians a certain power over evil spirits was justly assigned to the faithful dog.

The New Testament evidence for the reality of magic and divination is such that cannot be disregarded by any who accept the Christian revelation.

In the Gospels we continually meet with possession by devils; the miracle wrought in the country of the Gerasenes (Gergesenes) (S. Matthew viii. 28–34), the dumb man possessed by a devil (S. Matthew ix. 32–34), the healing of the lunatic boy who was obsessed (S. Matthew xvii. 14–21), the exorcism of the unclean spirit (S. Mark i. 23–27), the casting out of devils whom Christ suffered not to speak (S. Mark i. 32–34), the exorcism in the name of Jesus (S. Mark ix. 38), the demons who fled our Lord's presence crying out "Thou art Christ, the son of God" (S. Luke iv. 41), the healing of those vexed with unclean spirits (S. Luke vi. 18), and many instances more.

Very early in the Apostolic ministry appears one of the most famous figures in the whole history of Witchcraft, Simon, who is as Simon Magus, sorcerer and heresiarch. At the outbreak of that persecution (*circa* A.D. 37) of the Christian community in Jerusalem which began with the martyrdom of S. Stephen, when Philip the Deacon went down to Samaria, Simon, a native of Gitta, was living in that city. By his magic arts and by his mysterious doctrine, in which he announced himself as "the great power of God," he had made a name for himself and gained many adherents. He listened to Philip's sermons, was greatly impressed by them, he saw with wonder the miracles of healing and the exorcisms of unclean spirits, and like many of his countrymen was baptized and united with the community of believers in Christ. But it is obvious that he only took this step in order to gain, as he hoped, greater magical power and thus increase his influence. For when the Apostles S. Peter and S. John came to Samaria to bestow upon those who had been baptized by Philip the outpouring of the Holy Ghost which was accompanied by heavenly manifestations Simon offered them money, saying, " Give me also this power," which he obviously regarded as a charm or occult spell. S. Peter forthwith sharply rebuked the unholy neophyte, who, alarmed at this denunciation, implored the Apostles to pray for him.

Simon is not mentioned again in the New Testament, but the first Christian writers have much to say concerning him. S. Justin Martyr, in his first *Apologia* (A.D. 153–155) and in his dialogue *Contra Tryphonem* (before A.D. 161), describes Simon as a warlock who at the instigation of demons claimed to be a god. During the reign of the Emperor Claudius, Simon came to Rome, and by his sorceries won many followers who paid him divine honours. He was accompanied by a lewd concubine from Tyre, Helena, whom he claimed was Heavenly Intelligence, set free from bondage by himself the " great power."

In the *Pseudo-Clementine Homilies* (probably second century) Simon appears as the chief antagonist of S. Peter, by whom his devilish practices are exposed and his enchantments dissolved. The apocryphal *Acts of S. Peter*, which are of high antiquity,[35] give in detail the well-known legend of the death of Simon Magus. By his spells the warlock had almost won the Emperor Nero to himself, but continually he was being foiled and thwarted owing to the intercession of the Apostle. At last when Cæsar demanded one final proof of the truth of his doctrines, some miracle that might be performed at midday in the face of all Rome, Simon offered to take his flight into the heavens—a diabolical parody of the Ascension—so that men might know his power was full as mighty as that of Him whom the Christians worshipped as God.

A mighty concourse gathered in the Forum : Vestal Virgins, Senators, Equites, their ladies, and a whole rabble of lesser folk. In the forefront of a new Imperial box sat the Lord Nero Claudius Cæsar Augustus Germanicus, on one side his mother, Agrippina, on the other Octavia his wife. Magic staff in hand the magician advanced into the midst of the arena : muttering a spell he bade his staff await his return, and forthwith it stood upright, alone, upon the pavement. Then with a deep obeisance to the ruler of the known world Simon Magus stretched forth his arms, and a moment more with rigid limbs and stern set face he rose from the ground and began to float high in air toward the Capitol. Like some monstrous bird he rose, and hovered fluttering in space awhile. But among the throng stood S. Peter, and just as the sorcerer had reached the topmost pinnacles of the shrine of Juno Moneta, now Santa Maria in Aracœli, where brown Franciscans sing the praises of God, the first Pope of Rome kneeled down, lifted his right hand and deliberately made a mighty Sign of the Cross towards the figure who usurped the privileges of the Incarnate Son of Mary. Who shall say what hosts of hells fled at that moment? The wizard dropped swift as heavy lead; the body whirled and turned in the air; it crashed, broken and breathless, at the foot of the Emperor's seat, which was fouled and bespattered with black gouts of blood. At the same moment with a ringing sound the staff fell prone on the pavement. The flag upon which S. Peter kneeled may be seen even until this day in the Church of Santa Francesca Romana. For, in order to commemorate the defeat of the warlock, Pope S. Paul I (757–767) built a church upon the site of his discomfiture, and in 850 Pope S. Leo IV reconstructed it as Santa Maria Nova, which gave place to the present fane dedicated in 1612.

But the fame of Simon Magus as a wizard has been swallowed up in his ill repute as a heretic; so early do heresy and magic go hand in hand. He was the first Gnostic, whose disciples the Simonians, an Antinomian sect of the second century, indulged the sickest fantasies. Menander, the successor of Simon, proclaimed himself the Messiah and asserted that by his baptism immortality was conferred upon his followers. He also was regarded as a mighty magician, and the sect which was named after him, the Menandrians, seems to have lasted for no inconsiderable time.

In his missionary journeys S. Paul was continually combating Witchcraft. At Paphos he was opposed by the sorcerer Elymas; in Philippi a medium, "a certain damsel possessed with a spirit of divination," "spiritum pythonem," followed him along the streets crying out and naming him as "a servant of the most high God," until he exorcized the spirit; at Ephesus, a hotbed of sorcery and superstition, he converted many diviners and witches, who cleansed their souls by the Sacrament of Penance, and burned their conjuring books, a library of no mean value. It amounted indeed to fifty thousand drachmas (£2000), and one may suppose that in addition to manuscripts there were amulets of silver and gold, richly wrought and jewelled. In Ephesus, also, had foregathered a large number of vagabond Jews, exorcists. The chief characteristic of a Jewish exorcism was the recitation of names believed to be efficacious, principally names of good angels, which were used either alone, or in combination with El (God); and, indeed, a blind reliance upon the sound of mere names had long been a settled practice with these amateur sorcerers, who considered that the essence of their charms lay in the use of particular names declaimed in a particular order, which differed on several occasions. It was this belief, no doubt, that induced the seven sons of Sceva, who had witnessed S. Paul's exorcisms in the name of Jesus, to try upon their own account the formula "I conjure thee by Jesus whom Paul preacheth," an experiment disastrous to their credit. For in one case the patient cried out "Jesus I know, and Paul I know, but who are ye?" and leaped upon them with infernal strength, beating and wounding them, so that they fled for safety from the house, their limbs bruised and their garments torn, to the great scandal of the neighbourhood.

For the fact of demoniac possession the authority of Christ Himself is plainly pledged; whilst Witchcraft is explicitly ranked by S. Paul with murder, sedition, hatred, and heresy (Galatians v. 20–21). S. John, also, twice mentions sorcerers in a hideous catalogue of sinners. There can be no doubt whatsoever that the reality of Witchcraft is definitely maintained by the New Testament writers,[36] and any denial of this implicitly involves a rejection of the truth of the Christian revelation.

Among the Jews of a later period, and probably even to-day, various diseases are said to be induced by demons, who, it is instructive to notice, haunt marshy places, damp and decayed houses, latrines, squalid alleys, foul atmospheres where sickness is bred and ripened.

Josephus (*ob.* A.D. 100) relates that God taught Solomon how demons were to be expelled, a "science useful and sanitative to men." He also gives an account of Eliezar, a celebrated exorcist of the time, whom, in the presence of the Emperor Vespasian, the historian actually saw casting out evil spirits. The operator applied to the nose of the possessed a ring having attached to it a root which Solomon is said to have prescribed—" Baaras," a herb of magical properties, and one dangerous for the uninitiate to handle. As the devils came forth Eliezar caused them to pass into a basin filled with water, which was at once poured away. It may be noticed also that demonology plays an important part in the Book of Enoch (before 170 B.C.). Even in the Mishna there are undoubted traces of magic, and in the Gemara demonology and sorcery loom very largely. Throughout the Middle Ages Jewish legend played no insignificant part in the history of Witchcraft, and, especially in Spain, until the nineteenth century at least, there were prosecutions, not so much for the observance of Hebrew ceremonies as is often suggested and supposed, but for the practice of the dark and hideous traditions of Hebrew magic. Closely connected with these ancient sorceries are those ritual murders, of which a learned Premonstratensian Canon of Wilthin, Adrian Kembter, writing in 1745, was able to enumerate no less than two-and-fifty,[37] the latest of these having taken place in 1650, when at Cadan in Bohemia, Matthias, a lad of four years old, was killed by certain rabbis with seven wounds. In many cases the evidence is quite conclusive that the body, and especially the blood of the victim, was used for magical purposes. Thus with reference to little S. Hugh of Lincoln, after various very striking details, the chronicler has: " Et cum exspirasset puer, deposuerunt corpus de cruce, et nescitur qua ratione, euiscerarunt corpusculum; dicitur autem, quod ad magicas artes exercendas." In 1261 at Forcheim in Bavaria the blood of a murdered boy was used to sprinkle certain thresholds and doors. In 1285 at Munich a witch was convicted of selling Christian children to the Jews, who carefully preserved the blood in curious vessels for secret rites. In 1494 at Tyrnau twelve vampires were executed for having opened the veins of a boy whom they had snared, and having drunk his warm blood thence whilst he was yet alive. A deed of peculiar horror was discovered at Szydlow in 1597 when the victim was put to death in exquisite tortures, the blood and several members of the body being partaken of by the murderers. In almost every case the blood was carefully collected, there can be no doubt for magical purposes, the underlying idea being the precept of the Mosaic law: Anima enim omnis carnis in sanguine est:[38] For the life of all flesh is in the blood thereof

NOTES TO CHAPTER V

[1] *Khartummim*. The same word is used to describe the magicians whom Pharaoh summoned to interpret his dream, *Genesis* xli. 8, where the Vulgate has *coniectores*. *Exodus* viii. 11, the Vulgate reads: "Uocauit autem Pharao sapientes et maleficos."

[2] It is perhaps worth mentioning that even the most modernistic commentators assign the history of Balaam to the oldest document of the Hexateuch, that they call the Jehovistic.

[3] In his commentary on the ninth chapter of the prophet Osee (Hosea), S. Jerome says: "Ingressi [sunt] ad Beel-Phegor, idolum Moabitarum quem nos PRIAPUM possumus appelare." And Rufinus on the same prophet has: "Beel-Phegor figuram Priapi dixerunt tenere." (They entered in unto Beel-Phegor, the idol of the Moabites, whom we may identify with PRIAPUS. . . . Beel-Phegor is said to have had the same shape as Priapus.)

[4] Balaam hariolus a Domino mittitur ut decipiat Balac filium Beor. *In Ezechielem*, IV. xiv. Migne, *Patres Latini*, XXV. p. 118. (Baalam, a soothsayer, is sent by God to deceive Balac, son of Beor.)

[5] Balaam fuisse prophetam non Dei, sed diaboli constat. . . . Fuit ipse magus, et dæmonis alloquium quærebat, eumque consulere.

[6] The word is usually found with *yidde 'onim* (from *yada*, "to know,") and they are generally considered to be identical in meaning. But W. R. Smith, *Journ. Phil.*, XIV. 127, makes the following distinction: Yidde 'oni is a familiar spirit, one known to him who calls it up; the 'ôbh is any spirit who may be invoked by a spell and forced to answer questions.

[7] *Divination, et la science des présages*, Paris, 1875. p. 161 ff.

[8] *History of the People of Israel*, 3 vols., London, 1888–91. I. p. 347.

[9] Cf. Ovid, *Metamorphoseon*, IV, 412–3, of bats:

Conatæque loqui, minimam pro corpore uocem
Emittunt; peraguntque leues stridore querelas.

[10] Josephus says that Samuel told the witch it was Saul.

[11] Migne, *Patres Græci*, LXXX. p. 589.

[12] Plerique putant Saulem signum accepisse de terra et de profundo inferni quando Samuelem per incantationes et artes magicas uisus est suscitasse. Migne, *Patres Latini*, XXIV. p. 106.

[13] . . . inspirantur diabolico spiritu. Has autem dicunt Hebræi maleficis artibus eruditas per necromantias et pythicum spiritum qualis fuit illa quæ uisa est suscitare animam Samuelis. *Idem*, XXV. p. 114.

[14] Migne, *Patres Græci*, XLV. pp. 107–14.

[15] *Δαίμονες γαρ ἦσαν οἱ κατασχηματίζουτες ἑαυτοὺς εἰς τὸ τοῦ Σαμουὴλ πρόσωπον.* *Idem*, XXX. p. 497.

[16] Et credo quia [spiritus immundi] mendacio possunt; nec enim pythonico tunc spiritui minus liciut animam Samuelis effingere. (*De Anima*, LVII.) Migne, *Patres Latini*, II. p. 749.

[17] *'Αλλὰ γέγραπται, ὁτὶ ἔγνω Σαουλ ὅτι Σαμουὴλ ἔστι.*

[18] *ἐπεὶ οὐ δύναται ψευδέσθαι ἡ Γραφη. τὰ δε ῥήματα τῆς Γραφῆς ἐστὶν· Καὶ εἶδεν ἡ γυνὴ τὸν Σαμουὴλ.* (*In librum Regum.* Homilia II.) Migne, *Patres Græci*, XII. p. 1013.

[19] *καὶ ὅτι μένουσιν αἱ ψυχαί, ἀπέδειξα ὑμῖν ἐκ τôυ καὶ τὴν Σαμουὴλ ψυχὴν κληθῆναι ὑπὸ τῆς ἐγγαστριμμύθου, ὡς ἠξίωσιν ὁ Σαουλ.* (*In I. Regum.* XXVIII.) *Idem*, XII.

[20] Samuel post mortem, secundum Scripturæ Testimonium futura non tacuit. *I. Regum.* XXVIII. 17 *et seq.* (*In Lucam.* I. 33.) Migne, *Patres Latini*. XV. p. 1547.

[21] Imago Samuelis mortui Saul regi uera prænuntiauit. *Idem*, XXXIV. p. 52. And *De Cura*, XL. p. 606.

[22] Nam Samuel propheta defunctus uiuo Sauli etiam regi futura prædixit.

[23] Whiston's translation. Ed. 1825. Vol. I, p. 263.

[24] So 1 *Kings* (*Samuel*) xv. 23 : "Because it is like the sin of witchcraft, to rebel." Heresy and rebellion are fundamentally the same.

[25] Schrader, *Die Keilenscheiften und das alte Testament*, Giessen, 2nd ed., 1883.

[26] . . . raconta ses rapts d'enfants, ses hideuses tactiques, ses stimulations infernales, ses meurtres impétueux, ses implacables viols ; obsédé par la vision des ses victimes, il décrivit leurs agonies ralenties ou hâtées, leurs appels et leurs râles ; il avoua s'être vautré dans les élastiques tiédeurs des intestins ; il confessa qu'il avait arraché des cœurs par des plaies élargies, ouvertes, telles que des fruits mûrs. *Là-Bas*, J. K. Huysmans, c. xviii.

[27] Healey's translation, 1610.

[28] *De Magia*, XLVII.

[29] *The Primitive Inhabitants of Scandinavia*, Sven Nilsson. 3rd edition. 1868. p. 241.

[30] The original title is κατὰ πασῶν αἱρέσεων ἔλεγχος. A Refutation of all Heresies. The first book had long been known ; books IV–X, which had been discovered a short time previously, were first published in 1851 (Oxford) by Miller as the work of Origen, but edited by Duncker and Schneidewin as by Hippolitus, eight years later, Göttingen, 1859. The first chapters of the Fourth, and the whole of the Second and Third Books are still missing.

[31] Theocritus, II. 121. Κρατὶ δ' ἔχων λεύκαν Ἡρακλέος ἱερὸν ἔρνος. Vergil. *Eclogue* VIII, 61 : Populus Alcidæ gratissima. *Æneid*, VIII, 276 : Herculea bicolor quem populus umbra . . .

[32] Pliny (*Historia Naturalis*, XV. 86) says walnuts were thrown, and it appears from an inscription that this custom prevailed on birthdays as well as at weddings. But originally, at any rate, chestnuts were also used. In time the meaning became obscured, and as nuts were used in all kinds of games they merely became synonymous with playthings.

[33] The play is referred to in 1520 as *Messer Nicia*, and the first edition printed at Florence *circa* 1524 has the title *The Comedy of Callimaco and Lucrezia*, but the Prologue definitely gives the name *La Mandragola* (*The Mandrake*), and this is used in all later editions. The story has been imitated by La Fontaine ; the play itself (which is still acted in Italy) has been repeatedly translated, at least six times into French and five times into German, but as yet no English version has been published.

[34] *De Legibus Hebræorum ritualibus earumque rationibus*, 2 vols., Tubingæ, 1732.

[35] Not later than A.D. 200. They were well known to Commodian, who wrote about A.D. 250.

[36] This is, of course, the view of the Fathers, and even later theological writers (e.g. Alfred Edersheim, Delitzsch, Rev. Walter Scott) accept this literal truth.

[37] In his book *Acta pro Ueritate Martyrii corporis, & cultus publici B. Andreæ Rinnensis*, Innsbruck, 1745. Blessed Andrew, a child, was killed at Rinn in the Tyrol, 12 July, 1462. A systematic investigation would, no doubt, wellnigh double the number of instances recorded by Kembter, and there are 15 for the eighteenth, 39 for the nineteenth century. In 1913 Mendil Beiliss was tried upon the charge of ritually murdering a Russian lad, Yushinsky.

[38] Leviticus xvii. 14.

CHAPTER VI

Diabolic Possession and Modern Spiritism

The phenomenon of diabolic possession, the mere possibility of which materialists and modernists in recent years have for the most part stoutly denied, has, nevertheless, been believed by all peoples and at all periods of the earth's history. In truth he who accepts the spiritual world is bound to realize all about him the age-long struggle for empery of discarnate evil ceaselessly contending with a thousand cunning sleights and a myriad vizardings against the eternal unconquerable powers of good. Nature herself bears witness to the contest; disease and death, cruelty and pain, ugliness and sin, are all evidences of the mighty warfare, and it would be surprising indeed if some were not wounded in the fray—for we cannot stand apart, each man, S. Ignatius says, must fight under one of the two standards—if some even did not fall.

The ancient Egyptians, whose religion of boundless antiquity is pre-eminent in the old world for its passionate earnestness, its purity, and lofty idealism certainly held that some diseases were due to the action of evil spirits or demons, who in exceptional circumstances had the power of entering human bodies and of vexing them in proportion to the opportunities consciously or unconsciously given to their malign natures and influences. Moreover, the Egyptians were regarded as being supremely gifted in the art of curing the diseases caused by demoniacal possession, and one noteworthy instance of this was inscribed upon a stele and set up in the temple of the god Khonsu at Thebes so that all men might learn his might and his glory.[1] When King Rameses II was in Mesopotamia the various princes made him many offerings of gold and gems, and amongst other came the Prince of Bekhten, who brought his daughter, the fairest maiden of that land. When the king saw he loved her and bestowed upon her the title of "Royal spouse, chief lady,

Rā-neferu" (the beauties of Ra, the Sun-god), and taking her back to Egypt he married her with great pomp and hallowed solemnity. In the fifteenth year of the king's reign there arrived at his court an ambassador from the Prince of Bekhten, bearing rich presents and beseeching him "on behalf of the lady Bent-ent-resht, the younger sister of the royal spouse Rā-neferu, for, behold, an evil disease hath laid hold upon her body, "wherefore," said the envoy, "I beseech thy Majesty to send a physician[2] to see her." Rameses ordered the books of the "double house of life" to be brought and the wise men to choose from their number one who might be sent to Bekhten. They selected the sage Tehuti-em-heb, who in company with the ambassador forthwith departed on their journey, and when they had arrived the Egyptian priest soon found the lady Bent-ent-resht was possessed of a demon or spirit over which he was powerless. Wellnigh in despair the Prince of Bekhten sent again to the king begging him to dispatch even a god to his help.

When the ambassador arrived a second time Rameses was worshipping in the temple of Khonsu Nefer-hetep at Thebes, and he at once besought that deity to allow his counterpart Khonsu to go to Bekhten and to deliver the daughter of the prince of that country from the demon who possessed her. Khonsu Nefer-hetep granted the request, and a fourfold measure of magical power was imparted to the statue of the god which was to go to Bekhten. The god, seated in his boat, and five other boats with figures of gods in them, accompanied by a noble attendance of horses and chariots upon the right and the left, set out for Bekhten, where in due course they were received with great honour. The god Khonsu was brought to the place where the princess was, magical ceremonies were performed, and the demon incontinently departed. Khonsu remained in Bekhten three years, four months, and five days, being worshipped with the utmost veneration. One night, however, the Prince had a dream in which he saw a hawk of gold issue from the sacred shrine and wing its way towards Egypt. In the morning the Egyptian priests interpreted his dream as meaning that the god now wished to return, and accordingly he was escorted back in superb state, and with him were sent grateful gifts and thank offerings innumerable to be laid in the temple of Khonsu Nefer-hetep at Thebes.

The Greeks of the earlier civilization were inclined generally to attribute all sickness to the gods, who again often by this particular means took almost immediate revenge upon those who had insulted their images, profaned their sanctuaries, or derided their worship. Thus Pentheus who resists the introduction of the mysteries of Dionysus into Thebes is driven mad by the affronted deity.[3] The madness of Ajax, and that of the daughters of Proetus,[4] who imagined themselves changed into cows, shows us that this belief went back to heroic times. In later days Demaratus and his brother Alopecos were driven lunatic (*παραφρονῆσαν*) after having found the statue of Artemis Orthosia, and this was considered to be the power of the goddess.[5] The frenzy which attacked Quintus Fulvius was regarded as a punishment, a possession by evil spirits on account of his sacrilege in having stolen the marble roof of the temple of Juno Lacinia at Locri.[6]

Pythagoras taught that the ailments both of men and of animals are due to demons who throng the regions of the air, and this doctrine does no more than state clearly what had been more or less vaguely believed from the dawn of human history. Wherefore Homer in the *Odyssey*, speaking of a man who is racked by a sore disease, says that a hateful demon is tormenting him: *στυγερὸς δέ οἱ ἔχραε δαίμων*, V, 396. (But a hateful demon griped him fast.) The word *κακοδαιμονία*, possession by an evil spirit, in Aristophanes signifies "raving madness," and the verb *κακοδαιμονάω*, to be tormented by an evil spirit, is used by Xenophon, Demosthenes, Dinarchus, and Plutarch[7] amongst other authors.

Many philosophers believed that each man has a protecting daimon, who in some sense personifies his individuality. It followed that lunatics and the delirious were afflicted with madness by these spirits who guided them, and accordingly the Greek names for those distraught are highly significant: *ἐνεργούμενοι* (in later Greek, persons possessed of an evil spirit), *δαιμονιόληπτοι* (influenced by devils), *θεόληπτοι*, *θεόβλαβες* (stricken of God), *θεόμανες* (maddened by the gods); and so Euripides has *λύσσα θεομανής*, and again *θεομανης πότμος*.[8] The very name *μανία* given by the Greeks to madness was derived from the root-word *man*, *men*,[9] which occurs in the Latin *Manes*, and indeed the Romans thought that a madman was tormented by the goddess Mania, the mother of the Lares, the hallucinations of lunatics being taken to be spectres who pursued them.[10] And so a madman was *laruarum plenus*, *laruatus*,[11] one whom phantoms disturbed; as in Plautus, where the doctor says: "What kind of a disease is this? Explain. Unfold, old sire, I say. Art thou crazed (*laruatus*) or lunatic? Tell me now."[12]

The frantic exaltation which thrilled the Galli, and the Corybantes when they celebrated the Dionysia, seems to have been epidemic, and was universally attributed to divine possession. There are many allusions to the connexion between the rites of Cybele and Dionysus. Apollodorus[13] says Dionysus was purified from madness by Rhea at the Phrygian Cybela, and was then initiated into her rites and took her dress; thence he passed into Thrace with a train of Bacchanals and Satyrs. Strabo,[14] on the other hand, thinks the rites were brought from Thrace by colonists from that country into Phrygia; he even quotes a fragment from the *Edoni* of Æschylus[15] as proving the identity of the cultus of Dionysus and Cybele. So also we have in Euripides, *Bacchæ*, 58,

> Up, and wake the sweet old sound,
> The clang that I and mystic Rhea found,
> The Timbrel of the Mountains.[16]

It is interesting to remark that Nicander of Claros,[17] who was a physician, in his *Alexipharmaca* (Ἀλεξιφάρμακα), speaking of a particular form of lunacy, compares the shrieks uttered by patients with those of a priestess of Rhea, when on the ninth day she makes all whom she encounters in the streets tremble at the hideous howl of the Idæan Mother; κερνοφόρος ζάκορος βωμίστρια Ῥείης is the exact phrase.[18]

In the *Hippolytus* (141 *sqq.*) the Chorus speaking to Phaedra says:

> Is this some spirit, O child of man?
> Doth Hecat hold thee perchance, or Pan?
> Doth She of the Mountains work her ban,
> Or the Dread Corybantes bind thee?[19]

And in the *Medea* (1171–2) we have: "She seemed, I wot, to be one frenzied, inspired with madness by Pan or some other of the gods."[20]

Here *τινὸς θεῶν*, says Paley, alludes to Dionysus or Cybele. Madness was sometimes thought to be sent by Pan for any neglect of his worship, so in the *Rhesus* Hector cries (36–7): "Can it be that you are scared by the fear-causing stroke of Pan of old Kronos's line?"[21]

Aretæus, the medical writer, who is especially celebrated for his accuracy of diagnosis, in his *De signis chronicorum morborum*, VI, describes Corybantic frenzy as a mental malady and says that patients may be soothed and even cured by the strains of soft music.[22] We have here then the same remedy as was applied in the case of Saul, whom, we are told, "an evil spirit from the Lord troubled,"[23] and to whose court David, the sweet harper, was summoned. This seems to be the only instance of demoniac possession in the Old Testament and although the Hebrew word *rûah* need not absolutely imply a personal influence, if we may judge from Josephus[24] the Jews certainly gave the word that meaning in this very passage.

It may be well here clearly to explain the difference between possession and obsession, two technical terms sometimes confounded. By obsession is meant that the demon attacks a man's body from without;[25] by possession is meant that he assumes control of it from within. Thus S. Jerome describes the obsessions which beset S. Hilarion: "Many were his temptations; day and night did the demons change and renew their snares. . . . As he lay down how often did not nude women encircle him? When he was an hungered how often a plenteous board was spread before him?"[26] S. Antony the Great, also was similarly attacked: "The devil did not let to attack him, at night assuming the form of some maiden and imitating a woman's gestures to deceive Antony."[27] These painful phenomena are not uncommon in the lives of the Saints. Very many examples might be cited, but one will suffice, that of S. Margaret of Cortona,[28] the Franciscan penitent,[29] who was long and terribly tormented: "Following her to and fro up and down her humble cell as she wept and prayed [the devil] sang the most filthy songs, and lewdly incited Christ's dear handmaid, who with tears was commending herself to the Lord, to join him in trolling forth bawdy catches . . . but her prayers and tears finally routed the foul spirit and drove him far away."[30] The theologians, however, warn us to be very cautious in dealing with so difficult a matter, and the supreme authority of S. Alphonsus Liguori advises us that by far the greater part of these obsessions are distressing hallucinations, neurasthenia, imagination, hysteria, in a word, pathological: "It is advisable always to be very suspicious of such diabolic attacks, for it cannot be gainsaid that for the most part they are fancy, or the effect of imagination, or weakness, especially when women are concerned."[31] Dom Dominic Schram presses home the same point with equal emphasis: "Very often what are supposed to be demoniacal obsessions are nothing else than natural ailments, or morbid imaginings, or even distractions or actual lunacy. Wherefore it is necessary to deal with these cases most carefully, until the peculiar symptoms clearly show that it is actual obsession."[32]

Demoniac possession is frequently presented to us in the New Testament, and we have the authority of Christ Himself as to its reality. The infidel argument is to deny the possibility of possession in any circumstances, either on the hypothesis that there are no evil spirits in existence, or that they are powerless to influence the human body in the manner described. But whatever view Rationalists may adopt—and they are continually shifting their ground—no reader of the Scriptural narrative can deny that Christ by word and deed showed His entire belief in possession by evil spirits. And if Christ were divine how came He to foster and encourage a delusion? Why did He not correct it? Only two answers can be supposed. Either He was ignorant of a religious truth, or He deliberately gave instructions that He knew to be false, frequently acting in a way which was something more than misleading. To a Christian either of these explanations is, of course, unthinkable. The theory of accommodation formulated by Winer[33] may be accepted by Modernists, but will be instantly condemned by all others. Accommodation is understood as the toleration of harmless illusions of the day having little or no connexion with religion. Even if this fine piece of profanity were allowed, which, of course, must not be the case, the argument could not be applied here, indeed it seems wholly repugnant even in regard to a Saint, but entirely impossible in consideration of the divinity of Christ.

The victims of possession were sometimes deprived of speech and sight: "Then was offered to him one possessed of a devil, blind and dumb: and he healed him, so that he spoke and saw" (S. Matthew xii. 22). Sometimes they had lost speech alone: "Behold, they brought him a dumb man, possessed with a devil, and after the devil was cast out the dumb man spoke" (S. Matthew ix. 32, 33); also "And he was casting out a devil, and the same was dumb: and when he had cast out the devil the dumb spoke" (S. Luke xi. 14). In many cases the mere fact of possession is mentioned without further details: "they presented to him such as were possessed by devils, and lunatics . . . and he cured them" (S. Matthew iv. 24); "and when evening was come, they brought to him many that were possessed with devils, and he cast out the spirits with his word" (S. Matthew viii. 16); "And, behold a woman of Canaan, who came out of those coasts, crying out, said to him: Have mercy on me, O Lord, thou son of David: my daughter is grievously troubled by a devil . . . Then Jesus answering, said to her: O woman, great is thy faith: be it done to thee as thou wilt: and her daughter was cured from that hour" (S. Matthew xv. 22–28); "And when it was evening after sunset they brought to him all that were ill and that were possessed with devils"; "And he cast out many devils, and he suffered them not to speak, because they knew him"; "And he was preaching in their synagogues, and in all Galilee, and casting out devils" (S. Mark i. 32, 34, 39); "And the unclean spirits, when they saw him, fell down before him: and they cried, saying: Thou art the Son of God" (S. Mark iii. 11, 12); "And devils went out from many, crying out and saying: Thou art the Son of God" (S. Luke iv. 41); "And they that were troubled with unclean spirits were cured" (S. Luke vi. 18); "And in that same hour, he cured many of their diseases, and hurts, and evil spirits" (S. Luke vii. 21). The exorcism of the man "who had a devil now a very long time," and who dwelt among the tombs in the country of the Gerasens (Gadarenes) is related by S. Luke (viii. 27–39). The possessed is tormented by so many unclean spirits that they proclaim their name as Legion: he is endowed with supernatural strength so that he breaks asunder bonds and fetters: the devils recognize Christ as God, and Our

Lord converses with them, asking how they are called. Immediately the devils have been cast out the man is clothed, peaceable, reasonable, and quiet, "in his right mind."

At the foot of Mount Tabor a young man is brought by his father to be healed. The youth is possessed of a dumb spirit, "who, wheresoever he taketh him dasheth him, and he foameth, and gnasheth with the teeth, and pineth away." When Jesus approached, "immediately the spirit troubled him; and being thrown down upon the ground, he rolled about foaming." The patient had been thus afflicted "from his infancy, and oftentimes hath he cast him into the fire and into waters to destroy him." Our Lord threatened the spirit, and forthwith expelled it. (S. Mark ix. 14–28.) It should be noticed that it is the demons who are addressed on these occasions, not their victims. In the face of this catena of Biblical evidence and the various circumstances attending these exorcisms it is impossible to maintain that the possessed suffered merely from epilepsy, paralysis, acute mania, or any other such disease. In fact the Evangelists carefully separate natural maladies from diabolic possession: "He cast out the spirits with his word: and all that were sick he healed" (S. Matthew viii. 16); "They brought to him all that were ill and that were possessed with devils . . . and he healed many that were troubled with divers diseases and he cast out many devils" (S. Mark i. 32, 34). In the original Greek the distinction is still more clearly and unmistakably shown: πάντας τοὺς κακῶς ἔχοντας καὶ τοὺς δαιμονιζομένους. Saint Matthew, again, differentiates: "they presented to him all sick people that were taken with divers diseases [ποικίλαις νόσοις] and torments [βασάνοις] and such as were possessed by devils [δαιμονιζομένους] and lunatics [σεληνιαζομένους] and those who had the palsy [παραλυτικούς] and he cured them," iv. 24. Moreover, Our Lord expressly distinguishes between possession and natural disease; "Behold I cast out devils and do cures," are the Divine Words; ἰδοὺ ἐκβάλλω δαιμόνια καὶ ἰάσεις ἀποτελῶ (S. Luke xiii. 32).

That the demoniacs were often afflicted with other diseases as well is highly probable. The demons may have attacked those who were already sick, whilst the very fact of obsession or possession would of itself produce disease as a natural consequence.

According to S. Matthew x. 1, Our Lord gave special powers to the Apostles to exorcize demons: "And having called his twelve disciples together, he gave them power over unclean spirits to cast them out, and to heal all manner of diseases, and all manner of infirmities." And S. Peter, when describing the mission and miracles of Christ, stresses this very point: "Jesus of Nazareth: how God anointed him with the Holy Ghost, and with power, who went about doing good, and healing all that were possessed by the devil," *τοὺς καταδυναστευομένους ὑπὸ τοῦ διαβόλου* (Acts x. 38). Our Lord Himself directly appeals to His power over evil spirits as a proof of His Messiahship: "If I by the finger of God cast out devils; doubtless the kingdom of God is come upon you"; *εἰ δὲ ἐν δακτύλῳ Θεοῦ ἐκβάλλω τά δαιμόνια, ἄρα ἔφθασεν ἐφ' ὑμᾶς ἡ βασιλεία τοῦ Θεοῦ* (S. Luke xi. 20).

Whilst yet on earth Christ empowered the Apostles to cast out demons in His Name, and in His last solemn charge He promised that the same delegated power should be perpetuated: "These signs shall follow them that believe: in my name they shall cast out devils"; *σημεῖα δὲ τοῖς πιστεύσασι ταῦτα παρακολουθήσει· ἐν τῷ ὀνόματί μου δαιμόνια ἐκβαλοῦσι* (S. Mark xvi. 17.) But the efficacy of exorcism was conditional, not absolute as in the case of Our Lord Himself, for He explained, upon an occasion when the Apostles seemed to fail, that certain spirits could only be expelled by prayer and fasting. Moreover, a perfect belief and complete command are necessary for the exorcizer. *τότε προσέλθοντες οἱ μαθηταὶ τῷ Ἰησοῦ κατ ἰδίαν εἶπον, Διατί ἡμεῖς οὐκ ἠδυνήθημεν ἐκβαλεῖν αὐτό; ὁ δὲ Ἰησοῦς λέγει αὐτοῖς, Διὰ τὴν ὀλιγοπιστίαν ὑμῶν· . . . τοῦτο δὲ τὸ γένος οὐκ ἐκπορεύεται εἰ μὴ ἐν προσευχῇ καὶ νηστείᾳ* (S. Matthew xvii. 19–21). S. Paul, and no doubt the other Apostles and Disciples, regularly made use of this exorcizing power. Thus, at Philippi, where the girl "having a pythonical spirit . . . who brought to her masters much gain by divining" (*παιδίσκην τινὰ ἔχουσαν πεῦνμα πύθωνα . . . ἥτις ἐργασίαν πολλὴν παρεῖχε τοῖς κυρίοις αὐτῆς μαντευομένη*)[34] met S. Paul and S. Luke and proclaimed them as servants of the most high God, S. Paul "being grieved, turned, and said to the spirit: I command thee, in the name of Jesus Christ, to go out from her. And he went out the same hour" (Acts xvi. 16–18). And at Ephesus, a hot-bed of magic and necromancy, "God wrought by the hand of Paul more than common miracles. So that even there were brought from his body to the sick, handkerchiefs and aprons, and the diseases departed from them, and the wicked spirits went out of them" (Acts xix. 11, 12). Those who do not imagine that the powers Our Lord perpetually bestowed upon the Apostles and their followers abruptly ceased with the thirty-first verse of the twenty-eighth chapter of The Acts of the Apostles, realize that the charisma of exorcism has continued through the ages, and in truth the Church has uninterruptedly practised it until the present day.

The Exorcist is ordained by the Bishop for this office, ordination to which is the second of the four minor orders of the Western Church. Pope Cornelius (251–252) mentions in his letter to Fabius that there were then in the Roman Church forty-two acolytes, and fifty-two exorcists, readers, and door-keepers, and the institution of these orders together with the organization of their functions, seems to have been the work of the predecessor of Cornelius, Pope Saint Fabian the Martyr (236–251).

The rite of the Ordination of Exorcists, "De Ordinatione Exorcistarum," is as follows: First, the Book of Exorcisms, or in its place the Pontifical or Missal must be ready at hand; *Pro Exorcistis ordinandis paretur liber exorcismorum, cuius loco dari potest Pontificale uel Missale* (A Book of Exorcisms must be prepared for those who are to be ordained Exorcists. Howbeit in place thereof the Pontifical or the Missal may be handed to them) runs the rubric. When the Lectors have been ordained, the Bishop resuming his mitre takes his place upon his seat or faldstool at the Epistle side of the altar, and the Missal with the bugia being brought by his acolytes he proceeds to read the Gradual, or (if it be within the Octave of Pentecost) the *Alleluia*. Meantime the Gradual is sung by the choir. When it is finished, he rises, takes off his mitre, and turning to the altar intones the third collect. He next sits again, resumes his mitre, and the third Lection is read. Two chaplains assist him with bugia and book whence he reads the Lection. The Archdeacon now summons the ordinandi, who approach, holding lighted tapers in their hands, and kneel before the Bishop, who solemnly admonishes them with the prayer:

"Dearest children who are about to be ordained to the office of Exorcists, ye must duly know what ye are about to undertake. For an Exorcist must cast out devils; and announce to the people that those that may not be present at the sacrifice should retire; and at the altar minister water to the priest. Ye receive also the power of placing your hand upon energumens, and by the imposition of your hands and the grace of the Holy Spirit and the words of exorcism unclean spirits are driven out from the bodies of those who are obsessed. Be careful therefore that as ye drive out devils from the bodies of others, so ye banish all uncleanness and evil from your own bodies lest ye fall beneath the power of those spirits who by your ministry are conquered in others. Learn through your office to govern all imperfections lest the enemy may claim a share in you and some dominion over you. For truly will ye rightly control those devils who attack others, when first ye have overcome their many crafts against yourselves. And this may the Lord vouchsafe to grant you through His Holy Spirit."[35] After which the Bishop hands to each severally the Book of Exorcisms (or Pontifical or Missal), saying: "Receive this and commit it to thy memory and have power to place thy hands upon energumens, whether they be baptized, or whether they be catechumens."[36] All kneel, and the Bishop, wearing his mitre, stands and prays:

"Dearest brethren, let us humbly pray God the Father Almighty that He may vouchsafe to bless these his servants to the office of Exorcists that they may have the power to command spirits, to cast forth from the bodies of those who are obsessed demons with every kind of their wickedness and deceit. Through His only begotten Son Jesus Christ Our Lord who with Him liveth and reigneth in the unity of the Holy Spirit, one God, world without end. *R.* Amen."[37] Then, his mitre having been removed, he turns to the altar with "Oremus" to which is given the reply "Flectamus genua" with "Leuate," and the last prayer is said over the kneeling exorcists: "Holy Lord, Almighty Father, Eternal God vouchsafe to bless these thy servants to the office of Exorcists; that by the imposition of our hands and the words of our mouth they may have power and authority to govern and restrain all unclean spirits: that they may be skilful physicians for Thy Church, that they may heal many and be themselves strengthened with all Heavenly Grace. Through Our Lord Jesus Christ Thy Son who with Thee liveth and reigneth in the unity of the Holy Spirit one God world without end. *R.* Amen." And then, at a sign from the Archdeacon, they return to their places.[38]

It should be remarked that the Exorcist is specifically ordained "to cast out demons," and he receives "power to place his (your) hands upon the possessed, so that by the imposition of his (your) hands,[39] the grace of the Holy Ghost, and the words of exorcism, evil spirits are driven out from the bodies of the possessed." The very striking term *spiritualis imperator* is strictly applied to him, and God the Father is earnestly entreated to grant him the grace "to cast out demons from the bodies of the possessed with all their many sleights of wickedness." Nothing could be plainer, nothing could be more solemn, nothing could be more pregnant with meaning and intention. The Order and delegated power of Exorcists cannot be minimized; at least, so to do is clean contrary to the mind of the Church as emphatically expressed in her most authoritative rites. In actual practice the office of Exorcist has almost wholly been taken over by clerics in major orders, but this, of course, in no way affects the status and authority of the second of the four minor orders.

Every priest, more especially perhaps if he be a parish priest, is liable to be called upon to perform his duty as Exorcist. In doing so he must carefully bear in mind and adhere to the prescriptions of the *Rituale Romanum*, and he will do well to have due regard to the laws of provincial or diocesan synods, which for the most part require that the Bishop should be consulted and his authorization obtained before exorcism be essayed.

The chief points of importance in the detailed instructions under twenty-one heads prefixed to the rite in the *Rituale* may thus be briefly summarized: (1) The priest or exorcist should be of mature age, humble, of blameless life, courageous, of experience, and well-attested prudence. It is fitting he should prepare himself for his task by special acts of devotion and mortification, by fervent prayer and by fasting (S. Matthew xvii. 20). (2) He must be a man of scholarship and learning, a systematic student and well versed in the latest trends and developments of psychological science. (3) Possession is not lightly to be taken for granted. Each case is to be carefully examined and great caution to be used in distinguishing genuine possession from certain forms of disease. (4) He should admonish the possessed in so far as the latter is capable, to dispose himself for the exorcism by prayer, fasting, by confession, and Holy Communion, and while the rite is in progress he must excite in his heart a most lively faith in the goodness of God, and perfect resignation to the divine will. (5) The exorcism should take place in the Church, or some other sacred place, if convenient, but no crowd of gazers must be suffered to assemble out of mere curiosity. There should, however, be a number of witnesses, grave and devout persons of standing, eminent respectability, and acknowledged probity, not prone to idle gossip, but discreet and silent. If on account of sickness or for some legitimate reason the exorcism takes place in a private house it is well that members of the family should be present; especially is this enjoined, as a measure of precaution, if the subject be a woman. (6) If the patient seems to fall asleep, or endeavours to hinder the exorcist in any way during the rite he is to continue, if possible with greater insistence, for such actions are probably a ruse to trick him. (7) The exorcist, although humble and having no reliance upon himself alone, is to speak with command and authority, and should the patient be convulsed or tremble, let him be more fervent and more insistent; the prayers and adjurations are to be recited with great faith, a full and assured consciousness of power. (8) Let the exorcist remember that he uses the words of Holy Scripture and Holy Church, not his own words and phrases. (9) All idle and impertinent questioning of the demon is to be avoided, nor should the evil spirit be allowed to speak at length unchecked and unrebuked. (10) The Blessed Sacrament is not to be brought near the body of the obsessed during exorcism for fear of possible irreverence; Relics of the Saints may be employed, but in this case every care must be most scrupulously observed that all due veneration be paid to them; the Crucifix and Holy Water are to be used. (11) If expulsion of the evil spirit, who will often prove obstinate, is not secured at once, the rite should be repeated as often as need be.

It will be seen that the Church has safeguarded exorcism with extraordinary precautions, and that everything which is humanly possible to prevent superstition, indecorum, or abuse is provided for and recommended. Again and again the warning is repeated that so solemn, and indeed terrible, an office must not lightly be undertaken. The actual form in present use is as follows:[40]

THE FORM OF EXORCISING THE POSSESSED

[TRANSLATED FROM THE "ROMAN RITUAL."]

The Priest, having confessed, or at least hating sin in his heart, and having said Mass, if it possibly and conveniently can be done, and humbly implored the Divine help, vested in surplice and violet stole, the end of which he shall place round the neck of the one possessed, and having the possessed person before him, and bound if there be danger of violence, shall sign himself, the person, and those standing by, with the sign of the Cross, and sprinkle them with holy water, and kneeling down, the others making the responses, shall say the Litany as far as the prayers.

At the end the Antiphon. Remember not, Lord, our offences, nor the offences of our forefathers, neither take Thou vengeance of our sins.

Our Father. *Secretly.*

℣ And lead us not into temptation.
℟ But deliver us from evil.

Psalm liii.

Deus, in Nomine.

The whole shall be said with Glory be to the Father.

℣. Save Thy servant,
℟. O my God, that putteth his trust in Thee.
℣. Be unto him, O Lord, a strong tower,
℟. From the face of his enemy.

℣. Let the enemy have no advantage of him,
℟. Nor the son of wickedness approach to hurt him.

℣. Send him help, O Lord, from the sanctuary,
℟. And strengthen him out of Sion.

℣. Lord, hear my prayer,
℟. And let my cry come unto Thee.

℣. The Lord be with you,
℟. And with thy spirit.

Let us pray.

O God, Whose property is ever to have mercy and to forgive: receive our supplications and prayers, that of Thy mercy and loving-kindness Thou wilt set free this Thy servant (or handmaid) who is fast bound by the chain of his sins.

O holy Lord, Father Almighty, Eternal God, the Father of our Lord Jesus Christ: Who hast assigned that tyrant and apostate to the fires of hell; and hast sent Thine Only Begotten Son into the world, that He might bruise him as he roars after his prey: make haste, tarry not, to deliver this man, created in Thine Own image and likeness, from ruin, and from the noon-day devil Send Thy fear, O Lord, upon the wild beast, which devoureth Thy vine. Grant Thy servants boldness to fight bravely against that wicked dragon, lest he despise them that put their trust in Thee, and say, as once he spake in Pharaoh: I know not the Lord, neither will I let Israel go. Let Thy right hand in power compel him to depart from Thy servant N. (or Thy handmaid N.) ✠, that he dare no longer to hold him captive, whom Thou hast vouchsafed to make in Thine image, and hast redeemed in Thy Son; Who liveth and reigneth with Thee in the Unity of the Holy Spirit, ever One God, world without end. Amen.

Then he shall command the spirit in this manner.

I command thee, whosoever thou art, thou unclean spirit, and all thy companions possessing this servant of God, that by the Mysteries of the Incarnation, Passion, Resurrection and Ascension of our Lord Jesus Christ, by the sending of the Holy Ghost, and by the Coming of the same our Lord to judgment, thou tell me thy name, the day, and the hour of thy going out, by some sign: and, that to me, a minister of God, although unworthy, thou be wholly obedient in all things: nor hurt this creature of God, or those that stand by, or their goods in any way.

Then shall these Gospels, or one or the other, be read over the possessed.

The Lesson of the Holy Gospel according to S. John i. 1. *As he says these words he shall sign himself and the possessed on the forehead, mouth, and breast.* In the beginning was the Word . . . full of grace and truth.

The Lesson of the Holy Gospel according to S. Mark xvi. 15. At that time: Jesus spake unto His disciples: Go ye into all the world . . . shall lay hands on the sick, and they shall recover.

The Lesson of the Holy Gospel according to S. Luke x. 17. At that time: The seventy returned again with joy . . . because your names are written in heaven.

The Lesson of the Holy Gospel according to S. Luke xi. 14. At that time: Jesus was casting out a devil, and it was dumb . . . wherein he trusted, and divideth his spoils.

℣. Lord, hear my prayer,
℟. And let my cry come unto Thee.

℣. The Lord be with you,
℟. And with thy Spirit.

Let us pray.

Almighty Lord, Word of God the Father, Jesus Christ, God and Lord of every creature: Who didst give to Thy Holy Apostles power to tread upon serpents and scorpions: Who amongst other of Thy wonderful commands didst vouchsafe to say—Put the devils to flight: by Whose power Satan fell from heaven like lightning: with supplication I beseech Thy Holy Name in fear and trembling, that to me Thy most unworthy servant, granting me pardon of all my faults, Thou wilt vouchsafe to give constancy of faith and power, that shielded by the might of Thy holy arm, in trust and safety I may approach to attack this cruel devil, through Thee, O Jesus Christ, the Lord our God, Who shalt come to judge the quick and the dead, and the world by fire. Amen.

Then defending himself and the possessed with the sign of the Cross, putting part of his stole round the neck, and his right hand upon the head of the possessed, firmly and with great faith he shall say what follows.

℣. Behold the Cross of the Lord, flee ye of the contrary part,

℟. The Lion of the tribe of Judah, the Root of David, hath prevailed.

℣. Lord, hear my prayer,

℟. And let my cry come unto Thee.

℣. The Lord be with you,

℟. And with thy spirit.

Let us pray.

O God, and Father of our Lord Jesus Christ, I call upon Thy Holy Name, and humbly implore Thy mercy, that Thou wouldest vouchsafe to grant me help against this, and every unclean spirit, that vexes this Thy creature. Through the same Lord Jesus Christ.

THE EXORCISM.

I exorcise thee, most foul spirit, every coming in of the enemy, every apparition, every legion; in the Name of our Lord Jesus ✠ Christ be rooted out, and be put to flight from this creature of God ✠. He commands thee, Who has bid thee be cast down from the highest heaven into the lower parts of the earth. He commands thee, Who has commanded the sea, the winds, and the storms. Hear therefore, and fear, Satan, thou injurer of the faith, thou enemy of the human race, thou procurer of death, thou destroyer of life, kindler of vices, seducer of men, betrayer of the nations, inciter of envy, origin of avarice, cause of discord, stirrer-up of troubles: why standest thou, and resistest, when thou knowest that Christ the Lord destroyest thy ways? Fear Him, Who was sacrificed in Isaac, Who was sold in Joseph, was slain in the Lamb, was crucified in man, thence was the triumpher over hell. *The following signs of the Cross shall be made upon the forehead of the possessed.* Depart therefore in the Name of the Father ✠, and of the Son ✠, and of the Holy ✠ Ghost: give place to the Holy Ghost, by this sign of the holy ✠ Cross of Jesus Christ our Lord: Who with the Father, and the same Holy Ghost, liveth and reigneth ever one God, world without end. Amen.

℣. Lord, hear my prayer.
℟. And let my cry come unto Thee.

℣. The Lord be with you.
℟. And with thy spirit.

Let us pray.

O God, the Creator and Protector of the human race, Who hast formed man in Thine own Image: look upon this Thy servant N. (*or* this Thy handmaid N.), who is grievously vexed with the wiles of an unclean spirit, whom the old adversary, the ancient enemy of the earth, encompasses with a horrible dread, and blinds the senses of his human understanding with stupor, confounds him with terror, and harasses him with trembling and fear. Drive away, O Lord, the power of the devil, take away his deceitful snares: let the impious tempter fly far hence: let Thy servant be defended by the sign ✠ (*on his forehead*) of Thy Name, and be safe both in body, and soul. (*The three following crosses shall be made on the breast of the demoniac.*) Do Thou guard his inmost ✠ soul, Thou rule his inward ✠ parts, Thou strengthen his ✠ heart. Let the attempts of the opposing power in his soul vanish away. Grant, O Lord, grace to this invocation of Thy most Holy Name, that he who up to this present was causing terror, may flee away affrighted, and depart conquered; and that this Thy servant, strengthened in heart, and sincere in mind, may render Thee his due service. Through our Lord Jesus Christ. Amen.

THE EXORCISM.

I adjure thee, thou old serpent, by the Judge of the quick and the dead, by thy Maker, and the Maker of the world: by Him, Who hath power to put thee into hell, that thou depart in haste from this servant of God N., who returns to the bosom of the Church, with thy fear and with the torment of thy terror. I adjure Thee again ✠ (*on his forehead*), not in my infirmity, but by the power of the Holy Ghost, that thou go out of this servant of God N., whom the Almighty

God hath made in His Own Image. Yield, therefore, not to me, but to the minister of Christ. For His power presses upon thee Who subdued thee beneath His Cross. Tremble at His arm, which, after the groanings of hell were subdued, led forth the souls into light. Let the body ✠ (*on his breast*) of man be a terror to thee, let the image of God ✠ (*on his forehead*) be an alarm to thee. Resist not, nor delay to depart from this person, for it has pleased Christ to dwell in man. And think not that I am to be despised, since thou knowest that I too am so great a sinner. God ✠ commands thee. The majesty of Christ ✠ commands thee. God the Father ✠ commands thee. God the Son ✠ commands thee. God the Holy ✠ Ghost commands thee. The Sacrament of the Cross ✠ commands thee. The faith of the holy Apostles Peter and Paul, and of all the other Saints ✠, commands thee. The blood of the Martyrs ✠ commands thee. The stedfastness (*continentia*) of the Confessors ✠ commands thee. The devout intercession of all the Saints ✠ commands thee. The virtue of the Mysteries of the Christian Faith ✠ commands thee. Go out, therefore, thou transgressor. Go out, thou seducer, full of all deceit and wile, thou enemy of virtue, thou persecutor of innocence. Give place, thou most dire one: give place, thou most impious one: give place to Christ in Whom thou hast found nothing of thy works: Who hath overcome thee, Who hath destroyed thy kingdom, Who hath led thee captive and bound thee, and hath spoiled thy goods: Who hath cast thee into outer darkness, where for thee and thy servants everlasting destruction is prepared. But why, O fierce one, dost thou withstand? why, rashly bold, dost thou refuse? thou art the accused of Almighty God, whose laws thou hast broken. Thou art the accused of Jesus Christ our Lord, whom thou hast dared to tempt, and presumed to crucify. Thou art the accused of the human race, to whom by thy persuasion thou hast given to drink thy poison. Therefore, I adjure thee, most wicked dragon, in the Name of the immaculate ✠ Lamb, Who treads upon the lion and adder, Who tramples under foot the young lion and the dragon, that thou depart from this man ✠ (*let the sign be made upon his forehead*), that thou depart from the Church of God ✠ (*let the sign be made over those who are standing by*): tremble, and flee away at the calling upon the Name of that Lord, of Whom hell is afraid; to Whom the Virtues, the Powers, and the Dominions of the heavens are subject; Whom Cherubim and Seraphim with unwearied voices praise, saying: Holy, Holy, Holy, Lord God of Sabaoth. The Word ✠ made Flesh commands thee. He Who was born ✠ of the Virgin commands thee. Jesus ✠ of Nazareth commands thee; Who, although thou didst despise His disciples, bade thee go bruised and overthrown out of the man: and in his presence, having separated thee from him, thou didst not presume to enter into the herd of swine. Therefore, thus now adjured in His Name ✠, depart from the man, whom He has formed. It is hard for thee to wish to resist ✠. It is hard for thee to kick against the pricks ✠. Because the more slowly goest thou out, does the greater punishment increase against thee, for thou despisest not men, but Him, Who is Lord both of the quick and the dead, Who shall come to judge the quick and the dead, and the World by fire. ℟. Amen.

℣. Lord, hear my prayer.
℟. And let my cry come unto thee.

℣. The Lord be with you.
℟. And with thy spirit.

Let us pray.

O God of heaven, God of earth, God of the Angels, God of the Archangels, God of the Prophets, God of the Apostles, God of the Martyrs, God of the Virgins, God, Who hast the power to give life after death, rest after labour; because there is none other God beside Thee, nor could be true, but Thou, the Creator of heaven and earth, Who art the true King, and of Whose kingdom there shall be no end: humbly I beseech Thy glorious majesty, that Thou wouldest vouchsafe to deliver this Thy servant from unclean spirits, through Christ our Lord. Amen.

The Exorcism.

I therefore adjure thee, thou most foul spirit, every appearance, every inroad of Satan, in the Name of Jesus Christ ✠ of Nazareth, Who, after His baptism in Jordan, was led into the wilderness, and overcame thee in thine own stronghold: that thou cease to assault him whom He hath formed from the dust of the earth for His own honour and glory: and that thou in miserable man tremble not at human weakness, but at the image of Almighty God. Yield, therefore, to God ✠ Who by His servant Moses drowned thee and thy malice in Pharaoh and his army in the depths of the sea. Yield to God ✠, Who put thee to flight when driven out of King Saul with spiritual song, by his most faithful servant David. Yield thyself to God ✠, Who condemned thee in the traitor Judas Iscariot. For He touches thee with Divine ✠ stripes, when in His sight, trembling and crying out with thy legions, thou saidst: What have I to do with Thee, Jesus, Son of the Most High God? Art Thou come hither to torment us before the time? He presses upon thee with perpetual flames, Who shall say to the wicked at the end of time—Depart from Me, ye cursed, into everlasting fire, prepared for the devil and his angels. For thee, O impious one, and for thy angels, is the worm that dieth not; for thee and thy angels is the fire unquenchable prepared: for thou art the chief of accursed murder, thou the author of incest, thou the head of sacrileges, thou the master of the worst actions, thou the teacher of heretics, thou the instigator of all uncleanness. Therefore go out ✠, thou wicked one, go out ✠, thou infamous one, go out with all thy deceits; for God hath willed that man shall be His temple. But why dost thou delay longer here? Give honour to God the Father ✠ Almighty, before Whom every knee is bent. Give place to Jesus Christ ✠ the Lord, Who shed for man His most precious Blood. Give place to the Holy ✠ Ghost, Who by His blessed Apostle Peter struck thee to the ground in Simon Magus; Who condemned thy deceit in Ananias and Sapphira; Who smote thee in Herod, because he gave not God the glory; Who by his Apostle Paul smote thee in Elymas the sorcerer with a mist and darkness, and by the same Apostle by his word of command bade thee come out of the damsel possessed with the spirit of divination. Now therefore depart ✠, depart, thou seducer. The wilderness is thy abode. The serpent is the place of thy habitation: be humbled, and be overthrown. There is no time now for delay. For behold the Lord the Ruler approaches closely upon thee, and His fire shall glow before Him, and shall go before Him; and shall burn up His enemies on every side. If thou hast deceived man, at God thou canst not scoff: One expels thee, from Whose Sight nothing is hidden. He casts thee out, to Whose power all things are subject. He shuts thee out, Who hast prepared for thee and for thine angels everlasting hell; out of Whose mouth the sharp sword shall go out, when He shall come to judge the quick and the dead, and the World by fire. Amen.

All the aforesaid things being said and done, so far as there shall be need, they shall be repeated, until the possessed person be entirely set free.

The following which are noted down will be of great assistance, said devoutly over the possessed, and also frequently to repeat the Our Father, Hail Mary, *and* Creed.

The Canticle. Magnificat.

The Canticle. Benedictus.

The Creed of S. Athanasius.

Quicunque uult.

Psalm xc. *Qui habitat.*
Psalm lxvii. *Exurgat Deus.*
Psalm lxix. *Deus in adiutorium.*
Psalm liii. *Deus, In Nomine Tuo.*
Psalm cxvii. *Confitemini Domino.*
Psalm xxxiv. *Iudica, Domine.*
Psalm xxx. *In Te, Domine, speraui.*
Psalm xxi. *Deus, Deus meus.*
Psalm iii. *Domine, quid multiplicasti?*
Psalm x. *In Domino confido.*
Psalm xii. *Usquequo, Domine?*
Each Psalm shall be said with Glory be to the Father, &c.

Prayer after being set free.

We pray Thee, O Almighty God, that the spirit of wickedness may have no more power over this Thy servant N. (*or* Thy handmaid N.), but that he may flee away, and never come back again: at Thy bidding, O Lord, let there come into him (*or* her) the goodness and peace of our Lord Jesus Christ, by Whom we have been redeemed, and let us fear no evil, for the Lord is with us, Who liveth and reigneth with Thee, in the Unity of the Holy Ghost, ever one God, world without end. ℟. Amen.

A shorter form of exorcism, which, being general, differs in aim and use, was published by order of Pope Leo XIII and may be found in the later editions of the *Rituale Romanum*, "Exorcismus in Satanam et Angelos apostalicos."[41] After the customary invocation *In nomine . . .* the rite begins with a prayer to S. Michael, the solemn adjuration of some length follows with versicles and responses, a second prayer is next recited, and the whole concludes by three aspirations from the Litany: "From the deceits and crafts of the Devil; O Lord, deliver us. That it may please Thee to rule Thy Church so it shall alway serve Thee in lasting peace and true liberty; We beseech Thee, hear us. That Thou wouldst vouchsafe to beat down and subdue all the enemies of Thy Holy Church; We beseech Thee, hear us." *And the place is sprinkled with Holy Water*,[42] is the final rubric.

The Baptismal Exorcism and exorcisms such as those of water, salt,[43] and oil, it were perhaps impertinent to treat of here. It may, however, be noticed that in the ceremony of the Blessing of the Waters[44] (approved by the Sacred Congregation of Rites, 6 December, 1890), performed on the Vigil of the Epiphany, there occurs a solemn "Exorcismus contra Satanam et Angelos apostalicos," followed by "Exorcismus salis" and "Exorcismus aquæ."

There are recorded throughout history innumerable examples of obsession and demoniacal possession, as also of potent and successful exorcism. It is, of course, quite possible, and indeed probable, that many of these cases were due to natural causes, epilepsy, acute hysteria, incipient lunacy, and the like. But, none the less, when every allowance has been made for incorrect diagnosis, for ill-informed ascriptions of rare and obscure forms of both physical and mental maladies, for credulity, honest mistakes, and exaggerations of every kind, there will yet remain a very considerable quota which it seems impossible to account for and explain save on the score of possession by some evil and hostile intelligence. But nobody is asked to accept all the instances of diabolic possession recorded in the history of the Church, nor even to form any definite opinion upon the historical evidence in favour of any particular case. That is primarily a matter for historical and medical science. And, perhaps, even at the present day and among civilized races this phenomenon is not so rare as is popularly supposed.

The annals of Bedlam, of many a private madhouse, and many an asylum could tell strange and hideous histories. And if we may judge from the accounts furnished by the pioneers of the Faith in missionary countries the evidences of diabolical agency there are as clearly defined and unmistakable as they were in Galilee in the time of Christ.[45]

Demoniacal possession is frequently described and alluded to by the early fathers and apologists in matter-of-fact terms which leave no shadow of doubt as to their belief in this regard. Indeed the success of Christian exorcism is often brought forward as an argument for the acceptance of the Divinity of the founder of Christianity. It would be an easy, but a very lengthy process, to make a catena of such passages from Greek and Latin authors alike.[46] S. Justin Martyr (*ob. circa* A.D. 165) speaks of demons flying from "the touch and breathing of Christians" (*Apologia*, II, 6), "as from a flame that burns them," adds S. Cyril of Jerusalem (*ob.* 385–6: *Catechesis*, XX, 3). Origen (*ob.* 253–4) mentions the laying on of hands to cast out devils, whilst S. Ambrose[47] (*ob.* 397), S. Ephrem Syrus[48] (*ob.* 373), and others used this ceremony when exorcizing. The holy sign of the Cross also is extolled by many Fathers for its efficacy against all kinds of diabolic molestation; thus Lactantius writes: "Nunc satis est, huius signi [Crucis] potentiam, quantum ualeat exponere. Quanto terrori sit dæmonibus hoc signum, sciet, qui uiderit, quatenus adiurati per Christum, de corporibus, quæ obsederint, fugiant,"[49] *Diuinarum Institutionum*, IV, xxvii.[50] S. Athanasius (*ob.* 373), *De Incarnatione Uerbi*, XLVII; S. Basil (*ob.* 379), *In Esaiam*, XI, 249; S. Cyril of Jerusalem, *Catechesis*, XIII; S. Gregory of Nazianzus (*ob. circa* 389), *Carmen aduersus Iram*, 415 *sqq.*, all have passages of no little weight to the same effect. S. Cyril, *Procatechesis*, IX; and S. Athanasius, *Ad Marcellum*, XXIII, recommend that the prayers of exorcism and the adjuration should as far as possible repeat the exact words of Holy Scripture.

In the annals of hagiography we find from the earliest days until our own time very many instances of possession, very many cases where a poor afflicted wretch has been released and relieved by the power and prayer of some Saint or holy servant of God.[51]

Thus in the life of S. Benedict, that noble, calm, dignified, prudent, great-souled, and high-minded hero, there are recorded several occasions upon which he was confronted by extraordinary manifestations of evil spirits who resisted the building of his monastery upon the crest of Monte Cassino, where Satanism had been previously practised. It is not said that there were any visible appearances, save to S. Benedict alone,[52] but a succession of untoward accidents, of abnormal occurrences and constant alarms, plainly showed that the Saint was contending against superhuman difficulties. More than once he found it necessary to exorcize certain of his monks,[53] and so marked was his triumph over these malignant and destructive influences that he has always been venerated in the Church as a most potent "effugator dæmonum," and is confidently invoked in the hour of spiritual peril and deadly attack. Great faith also is placed in the Medal of Saint Benedict. This medal, originally a cross, is dedicated to the devotion in honour of the Patriarch. One side bears the figure of the Saint holding a cross in his right hand, and the Holy Rule in his left. Upon the other is a cross together with the following letters arranged on and around it: C.S.P.B., Crux Sancti Patris Benedicti (The Cross of the holy Father Benedict). C.S.S.M.L., Crux Sacra Sit Mihi Lux (May the holy Cross be my Light). N.D.S.M.D., Non Draco Sit Mihi Dux (Let not the Devil be my guide). U.R.S.: N.S.M.U.: S.M.Q.L.: I.U.B.: Uade Retro Satana: Nunquam Suade Mihi Uana: Sunt Mala Quæ Libas: Ipse Uenena Bibas. (Begone, Satan, never suggest things to me, what thou offerest is evil, drink thou thyself thy poison).[54] The "Centenary" form of the medal (struck at Monte Cassino in 1880 to commemorate the 13th centenary of the birth of S. Benedict in 480) has under the figure the words: *Ex S.M. Cassino MDCCCLXXX.* Upon the same side round the edge runs the inscription: Eius in obitu ñro præsentia muniamur (May we be protected by his presence at the hour of our death), and the word PAX appears above the cross.

It is doubtful when the Medal of S. Benedict originated, but during a trial for Witchcraft at Natternberg, near the abbey of Metten, in Bavaria, during the year 1647, the accused women testified that they had no power over Metten which was under the particular protection of the cross. Upon investigation a number of painted crosses surrounded by the letters which are now engraved upon Benedictine medals were found on the walls of the abbey, but their signification had been wholly forgotten. At length, in an old manuscript, written in 1415, was discovered a picture representing S. Benedict holding in one hand a staff which ended in a cross, and in the other a scroll. On the staff and scroll were written in full the formulas of which the mysterious letters were the initials. Medals with the figure of S. Benedict, a cross, and these letters began now to be struck and rapidly spread over Europe. The medals were first authoritatively approved by Benedict XIV in his briefs of 23 December, 1741, and 12 March, 1742.

In the case of the possessed boys of Illfurt (Alsace) they exhibited the utmost horror and dread of a Medal of S. Benedict.

These medals are hallowed with a proper rite[55] in which the adjuration commences: "Exorcizo uos, numismata, per Deum Patrem ✠ omnipotentem. . . ." "I exorcize ye, medals, through God the Father ✠ Almighty. . . . May the power of the adversary, all the host of the Devil, all evil attack, every spirit and glamour of Satan, be utterly put to flight and driven far away by the virtue of these medals. . . .[56] The prayer runs: "O Lord Jesus Christ . . . by Thy most Holy Passion I humbly pray and beseech Thee, that Thou wouldest grant that whosoever devoutly invoketh Thy Holy Name in this prayer and petition which Thou Thyself hast taught us, may be delivered from every deceit of the Devil and from all his wiles, and that Thou wouldest vouchsafe to bring Thy servant to the harbour of salvation. Who livest and reignest. . . ."[57]

S. Maurus also, the beloved disciple of S. Benedict, was famous for the cures he wrought in cases of possession.[58] Visiting France in 543 he became founder and superior of the abbey of Glanfeuil, Anjou, later known by his name, St. Maur-sur-Loise.[59] The relics of S. Maurus after various translations were finally enshrined at St. Germain-des-Prez. In the eleventh century an arm of the Saint had been with great devotion transferred to Monte Cassino, where by its touch a demoniac was delivered. This is related by Desiderius,[60] who was abbot at that time, and afterwards became Pope, Blessed Victor III (*ob.* 16 September, 1087). Throughout the Middle Ages the tomb of S. Maur at St. Germain was a celebrated place of pilgrimage, and the possessed were brought here in large numbers to be healed.[61]

The Holy Winding Sheet of Besançon, again, was greatly resorted to for the relief and cure of possession. This venerable relic, being one of the linen cloths used at the burial of Christ, was brought to Besançon in 1206 by Otto de la Roche, and the feast of its arrival (*Susceptio*) was ordered to be kept on 11 July. At present it is a double of the first class in the cathedral, St. Jean, and of the second class throughout the diocese.

Novenas made in the church at Bonnet, near Nantes, were popularly supposed to be of especial efficacy in healing possession.

It is, of course, impossible even briefly to catalogue the most important and striking of the numberless cases of possession recorded throughout the centuries in every country and at every era. Of these a great number are, no doubt, to be attributed to disease; very many to a commixture of hysteria and semi-conscious, or more frequently unconscious, fraud; some few to mere chousing; and, if human evidence is worth anything at all, many actually to diabolic influence.

There were some curious episodes in England during Queen Elizabeth's reign, when a third-rate Puritan minister, John Darrel, made a considerable stir owing to his attempts at exorcism. This idea seems to have been suggested to him by the exorcisms of the famous Jesuit missionary priest, William Weston, who after having been educated at Oxford, Paris, and Douai, entered the Society on 5 November, 1575, at Rome. He then worked and taught in Spain, until he was called to his native mission, actually arriving in England, 20 September, 1584. In the course of his labours, which at that dangerous time were carried on in circumstances of extremest peril, he was required to perform the rite of exorcism upon several distressed persons, who were for the most part brought to him at the houses of two zealous Catholics, Sir George Peckham of Denham, near Uxbridge, and Lord Vaux of Hackney, both of which gentlemen had suffered in many ways for their faith. With regard to the patients we can only say that we lack evidence to enable us to decide whether the cases were genuine, or whether they were merely sick and ailing folk; but we can confidently affirm that there is no suspicion of any fraud or cozenage. Father Weston is acknowledged to have been a man of the most candid sincerity, intensely spiritual, and of no ordinary powers. Although the rites, in which several priests joined, were performed with the utmost secrecy and every precaution was taken to prevent any report being spread abroad, somebody gossiped, and in about a year various exaggerated accounts were being circulated, until the matter came before the Privy Council. A violent recrudescence of persecution at once followed, many of the exorcists were seized and butchered for their priesthood, the rest, including Weston, were flung into jail, August, 1586. A long period of imprisonment ensued, and in 1599 Weston was committed to the Tower, where he suffered such hardships that he wellnigh lost his sight. Eventually in 1603 he was banished, and spent the rest of his days at Seville and Valladolid. He was rector of the latter college at the time of his death, 9 June, 1615.[62]

It was in 1586, just when the exorcisms of the Jesuit fathers had unfortunately attracted so widespread attention and foolish comment, that John Darrel, although a Protestant and lacking both appropriate ordination and training, rashly resolved to emulate their achievements. He was young, not much more than twenty, he was foolhardy and he was ignorant, three qualities which even in our own time often win cheap notoriety. It seems that he was first called in to cure a young girl of seventeen, Katherine Wright, who lived at Mansfield, Nottingham. Darrel forthwith pronounced that she was afflicted by an evil spirit, and he prayed over her from four o'clock in the morning till noon, but entirely without result. He then declared that the wench had been bewitched and that the demon, moreover, was sent by one Margaret Roper, with whom the patient had recently quarrelled. The girl backed his story, and the accused woman was at once taken into custody by the constable. When, however, she appeared before Mr. Fouliamb, a justice of the peace, not only was she incontinently discharged, but Darrel received a smart rebuff and found himself in no small danger of arrest.

This mischance sufficiently scared the would-be exorcist, and for some ten years he disappeared from view, only to come before the public again at Burton-upon-Trent, where he was prominent in the sensation and the scandal that centred round Thomas Darling, a young Derbyshire boy. This imaginative juvenal was subject to fits—real or feigned—during which he had visions of green angels and a green cat. Betimes his conversation became larded with true Puritan cant, and he loved to discourse with godly ministers. A credulous physician suggested that the lad was bewitched, and very soon afterwards it was noticed that the reading aloud of the Bible, especially certain verses in the first chapter of S. John's Gospel, threw him into frantic convulsions. He also began a long prattling tale about "a little old woman" who wore "a broad thrimmed hat," which proved amply sufficient to cause two women, Elizabeth Wright, and her daughter, Alse Gooderidge, long vehemently suspected of sorcery, to be examined before two magistrates, who committed Alse to jail. Next those concerned summoned a cunning man, who used various rough methods to induce the prisoner to confess. After having been harried and even tortured the wretched creature made some rambling and incoherent acknowledgements of guilt, which were twisted into a connected story. By now Darling had been ill for three months, and so far from improving, was getting worse.

At this juncture, exactly the dramatic moment, John Darrel, full of bluff and bounce, appeared upon the scene, and forthwith took charge of affairs. According to his own account his efforts were singularly blessed; that is to say the boy got better and the sly Puritan claimed all the credit. Alse Gooderidge was tried at the assizes, convicted by the jury, and sentenced to death by Lord Chief Justice Anderson; "She should have been executed but that her spirit killed her in prison," says John Denison the pamphleteer! The whole affair greatly increased Darrel's reputation.

Not long after a much-bruited case of alleged possession

in Lancashire gave him further opportunity to pose in the limelight. Ann Starchie, aged nine, and John, her brother, aged ten, were seized with a mysterious disorder; "a certaine fearefull starting and pulling together of her body" affected the girl, whilst the boy was "compelled to shout" on his way to school. Both grew steadily worse until their father, Nicholas Starchie, consulted Edmund Hartley, a notorious conjurer of no very fair repute. Hartley seems to have quieted the children by means of various charms, and the father paid him something like a retaining fee of forty shillings a year. This, however, he insisted should be increased, and when any addition was denied, there were quarrels, and presently the boy and girl again fell ill. The famous Dr. Dee was summoned, but he was obviously nonplussed, and whilst he "sharply reproved and straitly examined" Hartley, in his quandary could do or say little more save advise the help of "godlie preachers." The situation in that accursed house now began to grow more serious. Besides the children three young wards of Mr. Starchie, a servant, and a visitor, were all seized with the strange disease. "All or most of them joined together in a strange and supernatural loud whupping that the house and grounde did sounde therwith again." Hartley fell under suspicion, and was haled before a justice of the peace, who promptly committed him to the assizes. Evidence was given that he was continually kissing the Starchie children, in fact, he kept embracing all the possessed, and it was argued that he had thus communicated an evil spirit to them. He was accused of having drawn magic circles upon the ground, and although he stoutly denied the charge, he was convicted of felony and hanged at Lancaster. John Darrel and his assistant, George More, minister of a church in Derbyshire, undertook to exorcize the afflicted, and in a day or two, after long prayers and great endeavours, they managed to expel the devils. Here we have folly, imposture, and hysteria all blended together to make a horrible tale.

At this time Darrel was officiating as a minister at Nottingham, where there happened to be living a young apprenticed musician, a clever and likely lad, William Somers, who some years before had met Darrel at Ashby-de-la-Zouch, where both had been resident. It appears that the boy had once met a strange woman, whom he offended in some way, and suddenly he "did use such strang and idle kinde of gestures in laughing, dancing, and such like lighte behaviour, that he was suspected to be madd." The famous exorcist was sent for on the 5th of November, 1597, and forthwith recognized the signs of possession. The lad was suffering for the sins of Nottingham. Accordingly sermons were delivered and prayers were read in true ranting fashion, and when Darrel named one after the other fourteen signs of possession the patient, who had been most carefully coached, illustrated each in turn.

It is possible that Darrel had to some extent mesmeric control over Somers, whose performance was of a very remarkable nature at least, for "he tore; he foamed; he wallowed; his face was drawn awry; his eyes would stare and his tongue hang out"; together with a thousand other such apish antics which greatly impressed the bystanders. Finally the boy lay as if dead for a quarter of an hour, and then rose up declaring he was well and whole.

However, obsession followed possession. The demon still assailed him, and it was not long before Master Somers accused thirteen women of having contrived his maladies by their sorcery. Darrel, the witch-finder, had by this time attained a position of no small importance in the town, being chosen preacher at S. Mary's, and he was prepared to back his pupil to the uttermost. Yet even his influence for some reason did not serve, and all but two of the women concerned were released from prison. Next certain unbelieving citizens had the bad taste to interfere, and to carry off the chief actor to the house of correction, where he pretty soon confessed his impostures, in which, as he acknowledged, he had been carefully instructed by Darrel. The matter now became a public scandal, and upon the report of the Archdeacon of Derby the Archbishop of York appointed a commission to inquire into the facts. Brought before these ministers, not one of whom could possibly have had any means of forming a correct judgement, Somers retracted his words, asserted that he had been induced to slander Darrel, and thereat fell into such fits, foamings, and contortions that the ignoramuses were convinced of the reality of his demoniac possession.

At the Nottingham assizes, however, things went differently. Summoned to court and encouraged by the Lord Chief Justice, Sir Edmund Anderson,[63] to tell the truth the wretched young man made a clean breast of all his tricks. The case against Alice Freeman, the accused, was dismissed, and Sir Edmund, shocked at the frauds, wrote a weighty letter to Whitgift, the Archbishop of Canterbury. Darrel and More were cited to the Court of High Commission, where Bancroft, Bishop of London, two of the Lord Chief Justices, the Master of Requests, and other high officials heard the case. It is obvious that Bancroft really controlled the examination from first to last, and that he combined the rôles of prosecutor and judge. Somers now told the Court how he had been in constant communication with Darrel, how they had met secretly when Darrel taught him "to doe all those trickes which Katherine Wright did" and later sent him to see and learn of the boy of Burton. In fact Darrel made him go through a whole series of antics again and again in his presence, and it was after all these preliminaries and practice that the lad posed as a possessed person at Nottingham and was prayed over and exhibited. The vulpine Puritan was fairly caught. No doubt the Bishop of London may have been a trifle arbitrary, but after all he was dealing with a rank impostor. Darrel and More were deposed from the ministry, and committed to close prison.

The whole of this case is reported by Samuel Harsnett, chaplain to Bancroft, in a book of three hundred and twenty-four pages, *A Discovery of the Fraudulent Practises of John Darrel, Bacheler of Artes. . . .* London, 1599, and a perfect rain of pamphlets followed. Both Darrel and More answered Harsnett, drawing meantime a number of other persons into the paper fray. We have such works as *An Apologie, or defence of the possession of William Sommers, a young man of the towne of Nottingham. . . . By John Darrell, Minister of Christ Jesus . . .* a black letter brochure which is undated but may be safely assigned to 1599; *The Triall of Maist. Dorrel, or A Collection of Defences against Allegations . . .* 1599;[64] and Darrel's abusive *A Detection of that sinnful, shamful, lying, and ridiculous discours of Samuel Harshnet,* 1600. There are several allusions in contemporary dramatists to the scandal, and Jonson in *The Divell is an Asse*, acted in 1616, V, 3, has:

> It is the easiest thing, Sir, to be done.
> As plaine as fizzling: roule but wi' your eyes,
> And foame at th' mouth. A little castle-soape
> Will do't, to rub your lips: And then a nutshell,
> With toe and touchwood in it to spit fire,
> Did you ner'e read, Sir, little *Darrel's* tricks,
> With the boy o' *Burton*, and the 7 in *Lancashire*,
> Sommers at *Nottingham?* All these do teach it.
> And wee'l give out, Sir, that your wife ha's bewitch'd you.

It is probable that in his books Harsnett is to a large extent the mouthpiece of the ideas of Bancroft,[65] whose opinions must have carried no small weight seeing that in 1604 he became Archbishop of Canterbury. But Harsnett himself was also a man who could well stand alone, a divine marked out for the highest preferments. As Master of Pembroke Hall, Cambridge, Vice-chancellor of that University, Bishop of Chichester, Bishop of Norwich, and finally in 1628 Archbishop of York,[66] he was certainly one of the most prominent men of the day. His views, therefore, are not only of interest, but may be regarded as an expression of recognized Anglican authority. Bancroft, who was a bitter persecutor of Catholics, seems to have turned over a quantity of material he had collected to Harsnett, who in 1603 published a verjuiced attack upon the priesthood in particular and upon the supernatural in general under the title of *A Declaration of Egregious Popish Impostures.*[67] This violent and foolish polemic with its heavy periods of coarse ill-humour and scornful profanity jars upon the reader like the harsh screeching of some cankered scold. True, it has a certain force due to the very vehemence and elaborate gusto of the wrathful ecclesiastic, the force of Billingsgate and deafening vituperation bawled by leathern lungs and raucous tongue. As a sober argument, a reasoned contribution to controversy and debate, the thing is negligible and has been wholly forgotten. Nevertheless, historically Harsnett and Bancroft are important, for it was the latter who drew up, or at least inspired, carried through Convocation, and at once enforced the Canons generally known as those of 1604, of which number 72 lays down: "No minister or ministers shall . . . without the license or direction (*manda-*

tum) of the Bishop . . . attempt upon any pretence whatsoever either of possession or obsession, by fasting or prayer, to cast out any devil or devils, under pain of the imputation of imposture or cozenage, and deposition from the ministry."

This article seems definitely intended to fix the position of the Church of England.[68] The whole question of exorcism had, in common with every other point of Christian doctrine, caused the most acrid disagreement. The Lutherans retained exorcism in the baptismal rite and were both instant and persevering in their exorcisms of the possessed. Martin Luther himself had a most vivid realization of and the firmest belief in the material antagonism of evil. The black stain in the castle of Wartburg still marks the room where he flung his ink-horn at the Devil. The silly body, the blind, the dumb, the idiot, were, as often as not, afflicted by demons; the raving maniac was assuredly possessed. Physicians might explain these evils as natural infirmity, but such physicians were ignorant men; they did not know the craft and power of Satan. Many a poor wretch who was generally supposed to have committed suicide had in truth been seized by the Fiend and strangled by him. The Devil could beget children; had not Luther himself come in contact with one of them?[69] At the close of the sixteenth century, however, an interminable and desperate struggle took place between the believers in exorcism and the Swiss and Silesian sectaries who entirely discarded exorcism,[70] either declaring it to have belonged only to the earliest years of Christianity or else trying to explain away the Biblical instances on purely rationalistic grounds. In England baptismal exorcism was retained in the First Prayer Book of 1549, but by 1552, owing to the authority of Martin Bucer, we find it entirely eliminated. Under Elizabeth the ever-increasing influence of Zurich and Geneva, to which completest deference was paid, thoroughly discredited exorcisms of any kind, and this misbelieving attitude is repeatedly and amply made clear in the sundry "Apologies" and "Defences" of Jewel and his followers.

A letter of Archbishop Parker in 1574[71] with reference to the proven frauds of two idle wenches, Agnes Bridges and Rachel Pinder,[72] shows that he was thoroughly sceptical as to the possibility of possession, and his successor, the stout old Calvinist Whitgift, was certainly of the same mind.

In 1603 five clergymen attempted exorcism in the case of Mary Glover, the daughter of a merchant in Thames Street, who was said to be possessed owing to the sorceries of a certain Elizabeth Jackson. John Swan, "a famous Minister of the Gospel," took the lead in this business, which made considerable noise at the time. The Puritans were not unnaturally anxious to vindicate their powers over the Devil and they seem avidly to have grasped at any such opportunity that offered. Swan did not fail to advertise his supposed triumph in *A True and Breife Report of Mary Glover's Vexation and of her deliverance by the meanes of fastinge and prayer*, 1603; moreover, after her deliverance he took her home to be his servant "least Satan should assault her again." Old Mother Jackson was indicted, committed by Sir John Crook, the Recorder of London, and actually sentenced by Sir Edmund Anderson, the Lord Chief Justice, to be pilloried four times and be kept a year in prison. Unfortunately for the would-be exorcists and their pretensions King James, whose shrewd suspicions were aroused, sent to examine the girl, a physician, Dr. Edward Jorden, who detected her imposture, in which, I doubt not, she had been well coached by the Puritans. Dr. Jorden recounted the circumstance in his pamphlet *A briefe discourse of a disease called the Suffocation of the Mother, Written uppon occasion which hath beene of late taken thereby to suspect possession of an evill spirit* (London, 1603). The ministers were extremely chagrined, and one Stephen Bradwell even took up the cudgels in a tart rejoinder to Jorden, which was singularly futile as his lucubrations remain unpublished.[73] It is not improbable that this performance had its share of influence on Bancroft when he drew up article 72 of the 1604 Canons.

Francis Hutchinson in his *Historical Essay on Witchcraft* (1718)[74] doubts whether any Bishop of the Church of England ever granted a licence for exorcism to any one of his clergy, and indeed the case which is given by Dr. F. G. Lee,[75] who relates how Bishop Seth Ward of Exeter assigned a form under his own signature and seal in January, 1665, to the Rev. John Ruddle, vicar of Altarnon, is probably unique. And even so, this was not strictly speaking an instance of exorcism, at least there was no deliverance of a person possessed. Mr. Ruddle records in his MS. Diary that in a lonely field belonging to the parish of Little Petherick[76] an apparition was seen by a lad aged about sixteen, the son of a certain Mr. Bligh. The ghost, which was that of one Dorothy Durant, who had died eight years before, appeared so frequently to the boy at this same spot which he was obliged to pass daily as he went to and from school, that he fell ill and at last confessed his fears to his family, who treated the matter with ridicule and scolded him roundly when they saw that jest and mockery were of no avail. Eventually Mr. Ruddle was sent for to argue him out of his foolishness. The vicar, however, was not slow to perceive that young Bligh was speaking the truth, and he forthwith accompanied his pupil to the field, where they both unmistakably saw the phantom just as had been described. After a little while Mr. Ruddle visited Exeter to interview his diocesan and obtain the necessary licence for the exorcism. The Bishop, however, asked: "On what authority do you allege that I am entrusted with faculty so to do? Our Church, as is well known, hath abjured certain branches of her ancient power, on grounds of perversion and abuse." Mr. Ruddle quoted the Canons of 1604, and this appears to have satisfied the prelate, who called in his secretary and assigned a form "insomuch that the matter was incontinently done." But the worthy vicar was not permitted to depart without a thoroughly characteristic caution: "Let it be secret, Mr. Ruddle,—weak brethren! weak brethren!" The MS. Diary gives some details of the manner in which the ghost was laid, and it is significant to read that the operator described a circle and a pentacle upon the ground further making use of a rowan "crutch" or wand. He mentions "a parchment scroll," he spoke in Syriac and proceeded to demand as the books advise; he "went through the proper forms of dismissal and fulfilled all, as it was set down and written in my memoranda," and then "with certain fixed rites I did dismiss that troubled ghost." It would be interesting to know what form and ceremonies the Bishop prescribed. It does not sound like the details of a Catholic exorcism, but rather some superstitious and magical ritual. From what is related the form can hardly have been arranged for the nonce.

Although exorcism was not recognized by Protestants

there are instances upon record where an appeal has been made by English country-folk for the ministrations of a Catholic priest. In April, 1815, Father Edward Peach of the Midland District, was implored to visit a young married woman named White, of King's Norton, Worcestershire. She had for two months been afflicted with an extraordinary kind of illness which doctors could neither name nor cure. Her sister declared that a young man of bad repute, whose hand had been rejected, had sworn revenge and had employed the assistance of a reputed wizard at Dudley to work some mischief. However that might be, the unhappy girl seemed to lie at death's door; she raved of being beset day and night by spirits who mocked and moped at her, threatening to carry her away body and soul, and suggesting self-destruction as the only means to escape them. The clergyman of the parish visited and prayed with her, but no good resulted from all his endeavours. It so happened that a nurse who was called in was a Catholic, and horrified at the hideous ravings of the patient she procured a bottle of holy water, with which she sprinkled the room and bed. A few drops fell upon the sufferer, who uttered the most piercing cries, and screamed out, "You have scalded me! You have scalded me!" The paroxysm, however, passed, and she fell for the first time during many weeks into a sound slumber. After some slight improvement for eight and forty hours she was attacked by violent convulsions, and her relatives, in great alarm, on Tuesday in Rogation Week, 2 May, 1815, sent a special messenger to beg Father Peach to come over immediately.

When the priest appeared the girl was being held down in bed by two women who were forced to put forth all their strength, and as soon as she saw him—he was a complete stranger to her nor could his sacred profession be recognized by his attire—so terrible were her struggles that her husband was bound to lend his aid also to master her writhing limbs. Presently she fell into a state of complete exhaustion, and Father Peach, dismissing the rest of the company, was able to talk to her long and seriously. He seems to have been quite satisfied that it was a genuine case of diabolic possession, and his evidence, carefully expressed and marshalled with great moderation, leave no reasonable doubt that this strange sickness owned no natural origin. In the course of conversation it appeared that she had never been baptized. A simple instruction was given and finding her in excellent dispositions Father Peach at once baptized her. During the administration of this sacrament she trembled like a leaf, and as the water fell upon her she winced pitifully, a spasm of agony distorting her countenance. She afterwards averred that it gave her as much pain as if boiling water had been poured upon her bare flesh. Immediately afterwards there followed a truly remarkable change in her health and spirits; her husband and sister were overjoyed and thought it no less than a miracle. The next day Father Peach visited her again and noticed a rapid improvement. Save for a slight weakness she seemed perfectly restored, and, says the good father, writing a twelvemonth later than the event from notes he had taken at the time, there was no return, nor the least lingering symptom of her terrible and distressing malady.

In its issue of 11 October, 1925, *The Sunday Express*, under the heading "Evil Spirit Haunts A Girl," devoted a prominent column to the record of some extraordinary happenings. The account commences:

"Haunted for twelve months and more by a mischievous spirit—called a Poltergeist—driven almost to a state of distraction, threatened with a lunatic asylum, and then cured by the help of a band of spirit Indians, is the extraordinary experience of the nineteen-year-old Gwynneth Morley, who lives with her widowed mother at Keighley, and who was employed in the spinning mills of Messrs. Hay and Wright."

These phenomena were communicated to Sir Arthur Conan Doyle, who informed Mr. Hewet McKenzie, with the result that the girl was brought to London for psychic treatment, Mr. McKenzie being "honorary principal of the British College of Psychic Science," an institution which is advertised as the "Best equipped Centre for the study of Psychic Science in Britain," and announces "Lectures on Practical Healing," "Public Clairvoyance," "A Small Exhibition of notable water colours . . . representing Soul development, or experience of the Soul in ethereal conditions." "The College" is, I am given to understand, a well-known centre for spiritistic séances.

Gwynneth Morley worked in Mr. McKenzie's family for three months " as a housemaid, under close observation, and receiving psychic treatment.

" Day by day the amazing manifestations of her tormenting spirit were noted down. In between the new and full moon the disturbances were worse. Everything in the room in which Gwynneth happened to be would be thrown about and smashed. Tables were lifted and overturned, chairs smashed to pieces, bookcases upset, and heavy settees thrown over.

" In the kitchen of Holland Park the preparation of meals, when Gwynneth was about, was a disconcerting affair. Bowls of water would be spilt and pats of butter thrown on the floor.

" On another occasion when Gwynneth was in the kitchen the housekeeper, who was preparing some grape fruit for breakfast, found that one half had disappeared and could be found neither in the kitchen nor in the scullery. She got two bananas to take its place, and laid them on the table beside her; immediately the missing grape fruit whizzed past her ear and fell before her and the bananas vanished. Some ten minutes later they were found on the scullery table.

" All this time Gwynneth was being treated by psychic experts. Every week the girl sat with Mr. and Mrs. McKenzie and others. It was found that she was easily hypnotised, and that tables moved towards her in the circle.

" At other times during the cure the Poltergeist seemed to accept challenges. One night after a particularly exciting day, Mrs. Barkel magnetised her head and quietened her, and Mrs. McKenzie suggested that she should go to bed, saying ' Nothing happens when you get into bed.' Going up the stairs a small table and a metal vase crashed over, and a little later a great noise of banging and tearing was heard in Gwynneth's room. When Mrs. McKenzie went into the room it looked as if a tornado had swept over it.

" After an active spell from June 21 to June 25 the spirit behaved itself until July 1, when the girl had a kind of fit. Suddenly she fell off her chair with her hands clenched. They laid her on a bed, and she fell into another fit. She gripped her own throat powerfully.

" Since that evening she has had no further attacks, nor have there been any disturbances."

The main cause of this apparent cure is said to be the mediumship of Mrs. Barkel.

"On many occasions Mrs. Barkel gave Gwynneth excellent clairvoyance, describing deceased relatives, friends, and incidents in her past life which the girl acknowledged and corroborated.

"One near relative, says Mr. McKenzie, whose life had been misspent, and who had been a heavy drinker, was clearly seen. The girl feared and hated this personality, in life and beyond death, and had herself often seen him clairvoyantly before the disturbances began at all. Through Mrs. Barkel's spirit guide, Mr. McKenzie got into touch with him, and he promised to carry out any instructions that might be given for the benefit of the girl.

"The request was made that he should withdraw altogether from any contact with her and not return except by request. 'Professor J.,' a worker on the other side, became interested. Mr. McKenzie asked that a band of Indians, who sometimes profess to be able to help, should take Gwynneth in hand and protect her from the assaults of disturbing influences.

"The following day Mrs. Barkel described an Indian who had come to help, and improvements were noted from about this date. The 'professor' encouraged the treatment by suggestion, and told Mr. McKenzie that in a few weeks, with the help of the Indian workers, he would place the medium in an entirely new psychic condition. Mr. McKenzie says that the promise was kept."

I have quoted this case at some length owing to the prominence afforded it in a popular and widely read newspaper. That the facts are substantially true I see no reason at all to doubt. It is an ordinary instance of obsession, and will be easily recognized as such by those priests whose duty has required them to study these distressing phenomena. That the interpretation put upon some of the occurrences is utterly false I am very certain. The clairvoyance is merely playing with fire—I might say, with hell-fire—by those who cannot understand what they are about, what forces they are thus blindly evoking. "Professor J." and "the band of Indians," indeed all these "workers on the other side" are nothing else than evil, or at the least gravely suspect intelligences, masquerading as spirits of light and goodness. If, indeed, the girl is relieved from obsession one cannot but suppose some ulterior motive lurks in the background; it is but part of a scheme organized for purposes of their own by dark and secret powers ever alert to trick and trap credulous man. The girl, Gwynneth Morley, should have been exorcized by a trained and accredited exorcist. These amateurs neither know nor even faintly realize the harm they may do, the dangers they encounter. A bold mind, such as that of Guazzo, might specify their attempts—well-meaning as they are, no doubt—in terms I do not care to use.

At Illfurt, five miles south of Mulhausen in Alsace, is a monument consisting of a stone column thirty feet high surmounted with a statue of the Immaculate Conception, and upon the plinth of the pillar may be read the following remarkable inscription: *In memoriam perpetuam liberationis duorum possessorum Theobaldi et Josephi Burner, obtentæ per intercessionem Beatæ Mariæ Uirginis Immaculatæ, Anno Domini* 1869.

Joseph Burner[77] and Anna Maria, his wife, were poor but intelligent persons, who were not merely respected but even looked up to for their probity and industry by their fellow-villagers of Illfurt. The family consisted of five children, the eldest son, Thiébaut, being born on 21 August, 1855, and the second, Joseph, on 29 April, 1857. They were quiet lads of average ability, who, when eight years old, were sent in the usual course to the local elementary school. In the autumn of 1864 both were seized with a mysterious illness which would not yield to the ordinary remedies. Dr. Levy, of Altkirch, who was called in to examine the case acknowledged himself completely baffled, and a number of other doctors who were afterwards consulted declared themselves unable to diagnose such extraordinary symptoms. From 25 September, 1865, the two boys displayed most abnormal phenomena. Whilst lying on their backs they spun suddenly round like whirling tops with the utmost rapidity. Convulsions seized them, twisting and distorting every limb with unparalleled mobility, or again their bodies would for hours together become absolutely rigid and motionless so that no joint could be bent, whilst they lay motionless as stocks or stones. Fearful fits of vomiting often concluded these attacks. Sometimes they were dumb for days and could only gibber and mow with blazing eyes and slabbering lips, sometimes they were deaf so that even a pistol fired close to their ears had not the slightest effect.[78] Often they became fantastically excited, gesticulating wildly and shouting incessantly. Their voices were, however, not their normal tones nor even those of children at all, but the strong, harsh, hoarse articulation of rough and savage men. For hours together they would blaspheme in the foulest terms, cursing and swearing, and bawling out such hideous obscenities that the neighbours took to flight in sheer terror at the horrible scenes, whilst the distracted parents knew not whence to turn for help or comfort. Not only did the sufferers use the filthy vocabulary of the lowest slums, but they likewise spoke with perfect correctness and answered fluently in different languages, in French, Latin, English, and even in most varied dialects of Spanish and Italian, which could by no possible means have been known to them in their normal state. Nor could they at any time have heard conversation in these languages and subconsciously assimilated it. A famous case is on record where a servant girl of mean education fell ill and during a delirium began to mutter and babble in a language which was recognized as Syriac. This was considered to be accounted for when it was discovered that formerly she had been in service in a house where there was lodging a theological student, who upon the eve of his examinations used to walk up and down stairs and pace his room saying aloud to himself Syriac roots and vocables, which she thus often overheard and which in this way registered themselves in her brain. But there could not be any such explanation in the case of Thiébaut and Joseph Burner, since they did not merely reel out disconnected words and phrases in any one or two tongues, but conversed easily and sensibly in a large variety of languages and even in dialects. This has always been considered one of the genuine signs of diabolic possession, as is stated in the third article of *De Exorcizandis Obsessis a Dæmonio:* "3. In primis, ne facile credat, aliquem a dæmonio obsessum esse, sed nota habeat ea signa, quibus obsessus dignoscitur ab iis, qui uel atra bile, uel morbo aliquo laborant. Signa autem obsidentis dæmonis sunt: ignota lingua loqui pluribus uerbis, uel loquentem intelligere; distantia et occulta patefacere; uires super ætatis seu conditionis naturam ostendere; et id genus alia, quæ cum plurima concurrunt, maiora sunt indicia." Moreover, both Thiébaut and Joseph Burner repeatedly and in exactest detail described events which were happening at a distance, and upon investigation their accounts were afterwards found to be precisely true in every particular. Their strength was also abnormal, and often in their paroxysms and convulsions it needed the utmost exertions of three powerful men severally to hold these lads who were but nine and seven years old.

It was noticed at the very beginning of these maladies that the patients were thrown into the most violent fits and every symptom of disease and disorder exacerbated by the presence of any sacramental such as holy water, or medals, rosaries, and other objects which had been blessed according to the ritual. They seemed particularly enraged by the blessed Medal of S. Benedict and pictures of Our Lady of Perpetual Succour. On one occasion Monsieur Ignace Spies, the *Maire* of Selestat, a man of exceptional devotion and piety, held before their eyes a Relic of S. Gerard Majella,[79] the Redemptorist thaumaturge, when their shrieks and yells were truly terrific, finally dying away in inhuman whines and groans of despair. It so happened that a Corpus Christi procession passed the house, opposite which an Altar of Repose had been erected. The children, who were in bed, knew nothing of this and seemed to lie in a deep stupor. However, as the Blessed Sacrament approached their behaviour is said to have been indescribable. They poured forth torrents of filth and profanity, distorting their limbs into a thousand unnatural postures, their eyes almost starting from their heads, a crisis which was succeeded by a sudden horrible composure, whilst they crept away into the furthest corners of the room moaning, panting, and retching as if in mortal agony. Above all, pictures and Medals of Our Lady and the invocation of Her Most Holy Name filled the possessed with terror and rage. At any mention of "the Great Lady," as they termed Her, they would curse and howl in so monstrous a way that all who had heard them shook and sweated with fear.

The abbé Charles Brey, parish priest of Illfurt, quickly

made up his mind as to the diabolic nature of the phenomena. It was an undoubted case of possession, since in no other way could what was taking place be explained. Accordingly he sent to his diocesan, Monsignor Andreas Räss (1842–87) a full account of such extraordinary and fearful events. The Bishop, however, was far from satisfied that these things could not be accounted for naturally. In fact it was only after three or four years' delay that at the instance of the Dean of Altkirch he decided to order a special ecclesiastical investigation. He finally appointed for this task three acute theologians, Monsignor Stumpf,[80] Superior of his Grand Seminary at Strasburg; Monsignor Freyburger, Vicar-General of the diocese; and Monsieur Sester, rector of Mulhausen. These priests, then, presented themselves unexpectedly at the Burner's house on Tuesday morning, 13 April, 1869, at 10 o'clock. It was found that Joseph Burner had already concealed himself, and it was only after a prolonged search he could with difficulty be dragged from under his bed where he had taken refuge. Thiébaut feigned to be unconscious of the presence of strangers. The inquiry lasted for more than two hours, and it was not until past noon that the investigators left the house. Meanwhile they had witnessed the most hideous scenes, and their minds were quite made up as to the reality of the possession. They shortly presented their report to the Bishop, who then, and not until then, allowed himself to be convinced of the facts.

Even so, the prudent prelate ordered fresh precautions to be taken. At the beginning of September, 1869, Thiébaut was conveyed in the company of his unhappy mother, to the orphanage of S. Charles at Schiltigheim, where he was to be lodged whilst the case was investigated *de nouo* by Monsignor Rapp, Monsignor Stumpf, and Father Eicher, S.J., Superior of the Jesuit house at Strasburg. At the same time Father Hausser, the chaplain of S. Charles, and Father Schrantzer, a well-known scholar and psychologist, were to keep the boy systematically but secretly under the closest observation.

It was decided to proceed to exorcism, and a priest of great reverence and experience, Father Souquat, was commissioned by the Bishop to perform the solemn rite. At two o'clock on Sunday, 3 October, Thiébaut was forcibly brought into the chapel of S. Charles, which hitherto he had always sedulously avoided, and when compelled to enter he uttered without intermission such hoarse yells that it was necessary to remove him for fear of scandal and alarming the other inmates. The lad, however, was now held fast by the abbés Schrantzer and Hausser, assisted by Charles André, the gardener of the establishment, a stalwart and muscular Hercules. The sufferer stood upon a carpet spread just before the communion rails, his face turned towards the tabernacle. He struggled and writhed in the grasp of those who were restraining him; his face was scarlet; his eyes closed; whilst from his swollen and champing lips there flowed down a stream of thick yellowish froth which fell in great viscous gouts to the floor. The Litanies began, and at the words "Sancta Maria, ora pro nobis" a hideous yell burst from his throat. The exorcizer unmoved continued the prayers and gospels of the Ritual. Meanwhile the possessed blasphemed and defied their utmost efforts. It was resolved to recommence upon the following day. Thiébaut, accordingly, was confined in a strait jacket and strapped down in a red arm-chair, around which stood the three guards as before. The evil spirit roared and howled in a deep bass voice, raising a terrific din; the boy's limbs strained and contorted but the bonds held tight; his face was livid; his mouth flecked with the foam of slobbering saliva. In a firm voice the priest adjured the demon; he held the crucifix before his eyes, and finally a statue of Our Lady with the words: "Unclean spirit, disappear before the face of the Immaculate Conception! She commands! Thou must obey! Thou must depart!" The assistants upon their knees fervently recited the *Memorare*, when the air was rent by a yell of hideous agony, the boy's limbs were convulsed in one sharp convulsion, and suddenly he lay still wrapped in a deep slumber. At the end of about an hour he awoke gently and gazed about him with wondering eyes. "Where am I?" he asked. "Do you not know me?" questioned the abbé Schrantzer. "No, father, I do not," was the reply. In a few days Thiébaut was able to return home, worn and weak but bright and happy. Of all that happened during those fateful years he had not the smallest recollection. He returned to school, and was in every respect a normal healthy boy.

Joseph, who had grown steadily worse, was meantime secluded from his brother, pending the preparations for his exorcism. On 27 October he was taken very early in the morning to the cemetery chapel near Illfurt. Only the parents, Mons. Ignace Spies, Professor Lachemann, and some half a dozen more witnesses were present, as the affair was conducted in the utmost privacy. At six o'clock the abbé Charles Brey said Mass, after which he exorcized the unhappy victim. During three successive hours they renewed prayers and adjurations, until at last some present began to feel discouraged. But the glowing faith of the priest sustained them, and at length with a loud groan that sounded like a deep roar the boy, who had been struggling and screeching in paroxysms of frantic fury all the while, fell back into a deep swoon and lay motionless. After no long pause he sat up, opened his eyes as awaking from sleep, and was overcome with amazement to find himself in a church with strange people around him.

Neither Thiébaut nor Joseph ever experienced any recurrence of this strange malady. The former died when he was only sixteen years old on 3 April, 1871. The latter, who obtained a situation at Zillisheim, died there in 1882 at the age of twenty-five.

An even more recent case of possession, which has been authoritatively studied in minutest detail and at first hand, presents many of the same features.[81] Hélène-Joséphine Poirier, the daughter of an artisan family—her father was a mason—was born on 5 November, 1834, at Coullons, a small village some ten miles from Gien in the district of the Loire. Whilst still young she was apprenticed to Mlle Justine Beston, a working dressmaker, and soon became skilful with her needle and a remarkable embroideress. Already she had attracted attention by her sincere and modest piety, and was thought highly of by the parish priest, M. Preslier, a man of unusual discernment and the soundest common sense. On the night of 25 March, 1850, she was suddenly awakened by a series of sharp raps, which soon became violent blows, as if struck upon the walls of the small attic where she slept. In terror she rushed into her parents' room next door, and they returned with her to search. Nothing at all could be discovered, and she was persuaded to go back to bed. Although they could actually see no cause for alarm her parents had heard the extraordinary noises. "From this date," says M. Preslier, "the life of Hélène in the midst of such terrible physical and moral suffering that she might well have given utterance to the complaints of holy Job."[82]

These manifestations to Hélène Poirier may not unfittingly be compared with the famous "Rochester knockings," the phenomenon of the rappings at Hydesville in 1848 at the house of the Fox family, which by many writers is considered to be the beginning of that world-wide movement known as Spiritism or Spiritualism in its modern manifestations and recrudescence.[83]

Some months after this event Hélène suddenly fell rigid to the ground as if she had been thrown down by some strong hands. She was able to get up immediately but only to fall again. It was thought she was epileptic or at any rate seized with some unusual attack, some fit or convulsion. But after a careful observation of her case Dr. Azéma, the local practitioner, shrewdly remarked: "Nobody here but the Priest can cure you." From this time disorders of spirit and physical maladies increased with unprecedented rapidity and violence. "Her physical and mental sufferings, which began on 25 March, 1850, continued until her death on 8 January, 1914, that is to say during a period of sixty-four years. But those of diabolic origin ceased towards the end of 1897. So the diabolic attacks actually lasted for some seven-and-forty years, and for six years of this time she was possessed."[84] It was in January, 1863, it first became undeniably evident that her sufferings, her spasms, and painful trances had a supernatural origin. The abbé Bougaud, Archdeacon of Orleans, having interviewed her, advised that she should be brought to the Bishop, Monsignor Dupanloup, and made arrangements for her to stay at a Visitation convent in the suburbs, promising that a commission of theologians and doctors should examine her case. On Thursday, 28 October, 1865, Hélène accordingly commenced a retreat at the convent, where she was kindly received. M. Bougaud saw her for about two minutes, and she was handed an official order which would allow her access to the Bishop without waiting for a summons from his lordship or any other undue delay. But there was some misunderstanding, for on the Friday a doctor of high repute called at the convent, as he had been requested, interrogated and examined her for some three-quarters of an hour and then roundly informed the Mother Superior that she was mad, stark mad, and had better be sent home at once. He seems to have impressed the Bishop with his report, for Monsignor Dupanloup sent a messenger to direct the nuns to dismiss her forthwith, and accordingly she was perforce taken back to Coullons after a fruitless journey of bitter disappointments and discouragement. Many persons now began to regard her with suspicion, but in the following year, 1866, the Bishop, whilst visiting Coullons for an April confirmation, granted her an interview which caused him very considerably to modify his first opinion, and M. Bougaud, who saw her in September, declared himself convinced of the supernatural origin of the symptoms she displayed.

The most terrible obsessions now attacked her, and more than once she was driven to the verge of suicide and despair. "From 25 March, 1850, until March, 1868, Hélène was *only obsessed.* This obsession *lasted* 18 *years.* At the end of this time she was *both obsessed and possessed* for 13 months. From this double agony of obsession and possession she was completely delivered by the exorcisms, which the Bishop had sanctioned, at Orleans, on 19 April, 1869. Four months' peace followed, until with heroic generosity she voluntarily submitted to new inflictions.

"At the end of August, 1869, she accepted from the hands of Our Lord the agony of a new obsession and possession in order to obtain the conversion of the famous general Ducrot. When he was converted, she was delivered from her torments at Lourdes on 3 September, 1875, the cure being effected by the prayers of 15,000 pilgrims who had assembled there. *The obsession and possession in their new form* had lasted five years. During the forty years which passed before her death, she was never again subject to possession, but she was continually obsessed, the attacks now being of short duration, now long and severe. The sufferings of every kind which she endured as well she offered with the intention of the triumph and good estate of God's priests. Why she was originally thus persecuted by the Devil for nineteen years, and with what intention she offered those torments from which she was delivered by the exorcisms directed by the Bishop, must always remain a secret."[85] On Tuesday, 13 August, 1867, a supernormal impulse came over her to write a paper full of the most hideous blasphemies against Our Lord and His Blessed Mother, and, what is indeed significant, to draw blood from her arm and to sign therewith a deed giving herself over body and soul to Satan. This she happily resisted after a terrible struggle. Upon the following 28 August reliable witnesses saw her levitated from the ground on two distinct occasions. With this phenomenon we may compare the levitation of mediums at spiritistic séances. Sir William Crookes in *The Quarterly Journal of Science*, January, 1874, states that " There are at least a hundred recorded instances of Mr. Home's rising from the ground." Of the same medium he writes: " On three separate occasions have seen him raised completely from the floor of the room."

In March, 1868, it became evident that the poor sufferer was actually possessed. Fierce convulsive fits seized her; she suddenly fell with a maniacal fury and a deep hoarse voice uttered the most astounding blasphemies; if the Holy Names of Jesus and Mary were spoken in her presence she gnashed her teeth and literally foamed at the mouth; she was unable to hear the words *Et caro Uerbum factum est* without an access of insane rage which spent itself in wild gestures and an incoherent howling. She was interrogated in Latin, and answered the questions volubly and easily in the same tongue. The case attracted considerable attention, and was reported by the Comte de Maumigny to Padre Picivillo, the editor of the *Civiltá Cattolica*, who gave an account thereof to the Holy Father. The saintly Pius IX[86] showed himself full of sympathy, and even sent through the Comte de Maumigny a message of most salutary advice recommending great caution and the avoidance of all kinds of curiosity or advertisement.

In February, 1869, when interrogated by several priests Hélène gave most extraordinary details concerning bands of Satanists. " In order to gain admission it is necessary to bring one or more consecrated Hosts, and to deliver these to the Devil, who in a materialized form visibly presides over the assembly. The neophyte is obliged to profane the Sacred

Species in a most horrible manner, to worship the Devil with humblest adoration, and to perform with him and the other persons present the most bestial acts of unbridled obscenity, the foulest copulations. Three towns, Paris, Rome, and Tours, are the headquarters of the Satanic bands."[87] She also spoke of a gang of devil-worshippers at Toulouse. It is obvious that a mere peasant woman could have no natural knowledge of these abominations, the details concerning which were unhappily only too true.

In the following April Hélène was taken to Orleans to be examined and solemnly exorcized. The interrogatories were conducted by Monsieur Desbrosses, a consultor in theology for the diocese, Monsieur Bougaud, and Monsieur Mallet, Superior of the Grand Seminary. They witnessed the most terrible crisis; the sufferer was tortured by fierce cramps and spasms; she howled like a wild beast; but they persisted patiently. Mons. Mallet questioned her on difficult and obscure points in theology and philosophy using now Latin, now Greek. She replied fluently in both tongues, answering his queries concisely, clearly, and to the point, incontestable proof that she was influenced by some supernormal power. Two or three days later the Bishop was present at a similar examination, and forthwith commissioned his own director, Monsieur Roy, a professor at the Seminary, to undertake the exorcisms. With him were associated Monsieur Mallet, the parish priest of Coullons, and Monsieur Gaduel, Vicar-General of the diocese. Two nuns and Mlle Preslier held the patient. It was found necessary to repeat the rite five times upon successive days. On the last occasion the cries of the unhappy Hélène were fearful to hear. She writhed and foamed in paroxysms of rage; she blasphemed and cursed God, calling loudly upon the fiends of hell; she broke free from all restraint, hurling chairs and furniture in every direction with the strength of five men; it was with the utmost difficulty she could be seized and restrained before some serious mischief was done; at last with an unearthly yell, twice repeated, her limbs relaxed, and after a short period of insensibility she seemed to awake, calm and composed, as if from a restful slumber. The possession had lasted thirteen months from March, 1868, to April, 1869.

Into the details of her second possession from 23 August,

1869, until 3 September, 1874, it is hardly necessary to enter at any length. Monsieur Preslier noted : " The second crisis of possession was infinitely more terrible than the first; 1st, owing to the length; the first lasted thirteen months, the second five years. 2nd, the first was relieved was a number of heavenly consolations, but very little solace was obtained during the second. 3rd, there was much bodily suffering in the first, in the second there were far keener mental sufferings and more exquisite pain."[88] She was finally and completely delivered at Lourdes on Thursday, 3 September, 1874. It is not to be supposed that she passed the remaining forty years of her life without occasional manifestations of extraordinary phenomena. After much sickness, cheerfully and smilingly borne, she made a good end in her eightieth year, on 8 January, 1914, and is buried in the little village cemetery of her native place.

We have here the case of a woman who was mediumistic and clairvoyant to an almost unexampled degree, and it is very certain that if these would-be fortune-tellers and mages who so freely advertise their powers in many spiritistic journals to-day truly realized to what terrible dangers and very real psychic perils the use and even the mere possession of such faculties expose them, they would, so far from trafficking in the presumption of abnormal gifts, regard them with caution and indeed shrink from any occult practice at all, lest haply they become the prey of controls and influences so cunning, so potent for evil, as to merge them body and soul in untold miseries and shadows darker even than the bitterness of death.

The modern Spiritistic movement, so strongly supported by recent scientific utterances, is increasingly affecting all classes and conditions of society, and is beginning in every direction to undermine and actually to usurp the religious belief and convictions of thousands of earnest and seriously inclined but not very accurately informed or well-instructed persons. The basis of the movement is the claim that the spirits of the dead are continually seeking to communicate and, indeed, communicating with us through the agency of sensitives, so that it is possible to get into touch and to converse with our dear ones who have passed from this life. It is hardly necessary to emphasize the almost infinite consolation and comfort such a doctrine holds for the bereaved, how eagerly and with what yearning mourners will embrace such teaching, and how perseveringly and with what tender agonies of an hungered love they will devote themselves to the practices they imagine will place them in closest connexion and communion with those whom they have lost awhile, but whose voices they ever long to hear, whose faces they long to see once again. It is a matter of common knowledge that during and since the Great War Spiritism has increased tenfold; many who were wont to laugh at it, who refused to listen to its claims and scorned it as futile nonsense, are now among its most enthusiastic devotees. In truth there must be few of us who cannot appreciate the irresistible influence such beliefs will have upon the mind. Spiritism is seemingly full of joy, and hope, and promise, and happiness. It will wipe all tears of sorrow from poor human eyes; it is balm to the wounded heart; divine solace and sympathy; the barriers of death are broken down; mortality is robbed of its terrors.

Were it true, could we summon to our side the spirits of those whom we have so fondly cherished and converse with them of things holy and eternal, could we learn wisdom from their fuller knowledge, could we be assured in their own sweet accents of their fadeless love, could we now and again be comforted with a sight of their well-known faces, the touch of their hands upon ours, were it God's will that this should be so, then assuredly Spiritism is a most blessed and sacred thing, consolation to the afflicted, succour to the distressed, a shining light upon earth's dark ways, a very ready help to us all. But if on the other hand there is reason and grave reason to suppose that the spirits, with whom it is possible under certain exceptional conditions and by certain remarkable devices to establish a contact, although often claiming to be departed friends or relatives and supporting their contention (we acknowledge) with no little plausibility, are again and again found to be masquerading intelligences, in some cases undoubtedly actors of excellence who play their part for a time with consummate skill, but who have never at any séance whatsoever anywhere been able conclusively to demonstrate their identity, if in fact these manifesting intelligences are deceivers, imposing for purposes of their own a fraudulent impersonation upon those who with breaking hearts are so eagerly longing to communicate with son or husband fallen in battle, it may be, or on some lone shore, if they are proven liars, if their messages are trivial, ambiguous, cryptic, incapable of verification, shifty, ignorant, nay worse, blasphemous and hideously obscene, then are we justified—and we are in point of fact fully and completely justified—in concluding that the spirits are not those of the departed, but evil intelligences who never have been and never will be incarnate, unclean spirits, demons, and then assuredly Spiritism is most foul, most loathly, most dangerous, and most damnable.

The mediums, who of their own will freely open the door to these spirits, who invite them to enter, stand in the most deadly peril. A Spiritist of many years' experience who saw not too late the hazard and abandoned that creed, writes as follows: "Spirit communion soon absorbs all the time, faculties, hopes, fears, and desires of its devotees, and herein lies one of the greatest dangers of spiritualism. Infatuated by communication with the unseen inhabitants of the hidden world, the medium loses his or her interest in the things pertaining to everyday life and interest. A soft and pleasing atmosphere appears to surround them. The realities of flesh and blood are lost in ideal dreaming and there is no incentive to break away from a state of existence so agreeable, no matter how monstrous are the delusions practised by the spirits. Their consciences are so callous as if seared with a hot iron, sin has to them lost its wickedness, and they are willing dupes to unseen beings who delight to control their every faculty. Very seldom has a full-fledged spiritualist been able to comprehend the necessity and blessedness of the religion of Jesus Christ, and to withdraw from the morbid conditions into which he has fallen. . . .

"For about three months I was in the power of spirits, having a dual existence, and greatly tormented by their contradictory and unsatisfactory operations. . . . They tormented me to a very severe extent, and I desired to be freed from them. I lost much of my confidence in them, and their blasphemy and uncleanness shocked me. But they were my constant companions. I could not get rid of them. They tempted me to suicide and murder, and to other sins. I was fearfully beset and bewildered and deluded. There was no human help for me. They led me into some extravagances of action, and to believe, in a measure, a few of their delusions, often combining religion and devilry in a most surprising manner."[89]

In my own experience, I myself, not once, but over and over again, have seen all these symptoms unmistakably marked in those whose sole interest and aim in life seemed to be a constant attendance at séances. I have watched, in spite of every effort unable to check and dissuade, the fearfully rapid development of such characteristics in persons who have begun to dabble with Spiritism, at first no doubt in moods of levity and wanton curiosity, but soon with hectic anxiety and the most morbid absorption. Some fifteen years ago in a well-known English provincial town a circle was formed by a number of friends to experiment with table-turning, psychometry, the planchette, ouija-boards, crystal-gazing, and the like. They were, perhaps, a little tired of the usual round of social engagements, dances, concerts, bridge, the theatre, dinner parties, and all those mildly pleasurable businesses which go to make up life, or at least a great portion of life, for so many. They wanted some new excitement, something a little out of the ordinary. A lady, just returned home from a prolonged visit to London, had (it seems) been taken to some Spiritistic meeting, and she was full of the wonders both witnessed and heard there. The sense of the eerie, the unknown, lent a spice of adventure too. The earlier meetings were informal, first at one house, now at another. They began by being infrequent, almost casual, at fairly long intervals. Next a certain evening each week was fixed for these gatherings, which soon were fully attended by all concerned. No member would willingly miss a single reunion. Before long they met twice, three times, every evening in the week. Professional mediums were engaged who travelled down from London and other great cities, some at no small distance, to give strange exhibitions of their powers. I myself met two of these experts, a man and a woman, both of whose names I have since seen advertised in Spiritistic journals of a very recent date, and I am bound to say that I was most unfavourably impressed in each instance. Not that I for a moment think they were fraudulent, nor do I suspect any vulgar trickery or pose; they were undoubtedly honest, thoroughly convinced and sincere, which makes the matter ten times worse. And so from being mere idle triflers at a new game, incredulous and a little mocking, the whole company became besotted by their practices, fanatics whose thoughts were always and ever centred and concentrated upon their communion with spirits, who talked of nothing else, who seemed only to live for those evenings when they might meet and enter—as it were—another world. Argument, pleading, reproof, authority, official admonishment, all proved useless; one could only stand by and see the terrible thing doing its deadly work. The symptoms were exactly as above described. In two cases, men, the moral fibre was for a while apparently destroyed altogether; in another case, a woman, there was obsession, and persons who either knew nothing of, or had no sort of belief in, Spiritism, whispered of eccentricities, of outbursts of uncontrolled passion and ravings, which pointed to a disordered mind, to an asylum. All sank into a state of apathy; former interests vanished; the amenities of social intercourse were neglected and forgotten; old friendships allowed to drop for no reason whatsoever; a complete change of character for the worse, a terrible deterioration took place; the physical health suffered; their faces became white and drawn, the eyes dull and glazed, save when Spiritism was discussed, and then they lit with hot unholy fires; one heard covert gossip that hinted of crude debauch, of blasphemous speeches, of licence and degradation. Fortunately by a series of providential events the circle was broken up; outside circumstances compelled the principals to fall away, and what was doubtless a more potent factor than any, one or two were suddenly brought to realize the deadly peril and the folly of their proceedings. It proved a hard struggle indeed to rid themselves of the controls to which they had so blindly and so utterly submitted; their wills were weakened, their health impaired; more than once they slid back again into the old danger zone, more than once they were on the verge of giving up the contest in despair. But under direction and availing themselves of those means of grace the Church so bounteously proffers they persevered, and were at length made clean.

There must be many who have had similar experiences, who know intimately, even if they have not actually had to rescue and to guide, those who have been meshed and trapped by Spiritism and are endeavouring to escape. They will appreciate how difficult is the task, they will realize how pernicious, how potent, how evil, such toils may be. Nobody who has had to deal with sensitives, with poor dupes who are eager to abandon their practices, can think lightly of Spiritism.

That Spiritism opens the door to demoniac possession, so often classed as lunacy, is generally acknowledged by all save the prejudiced and superstitious. As far back as 1877 Dr. L. S. Forbes Winslow wrote in *Spiritualistic Madness:* "Ten thousand unfortunate people are at the present time confined in lunatic asylums on account of having tampered with the supernatural." And quoting an American journal he goes on to say: "Not a week passes in which we do not hear that some of these unfortunates destroy themselves by suicide, or are removed to a lunatic asylum. The mediums often manifest signs of an abnormal condition of their mental faculties, and among certain of them are found unequivocal indications of a true demoniacal possession. The evil spreads rapidly, and it will produce in a few years frightful results. . . . Two French authors of spiritualistic works, who wrote *Le Mondè Spirituel* and *Sauvons le genre humain,* died insane in an asylum; these two men were distinguished in their respective professions; one as a highly scientific man, the other as an advocate well learned in the Law. These individuals placed themselves in communication with spirits by means of tables. I could quote many such instances where men of the highest ability have, so to speak, neglected all and followed the doctrines of Spiritualism only to end their days in the lunatic asylum."

Some half a dozen years ago an inquiry was undertaken and there was circulated an interrogatory or *enquête* which invited opinions upon (1) "the situation as regards the renewed interest in psychic phenomena"; (2) whether this "psychic renewal" denoted a "passing from a logical and scientific (deductive) to a spiritual and mystic (inductive) conception of life," or "a reconciliation between the two, that is between science and faith";[90] (3) "the most powerful argument for, or against, human survival" ; (4) "the best means of organizing this (psychic) movement in the highest interest, philosophical, religious and scientific, of the nation, especially as a factor of durable peace." Five-and-fifty of the answers were collected and published under the title *Spiritualism: Its Present-Day Meaning*,[91] a book which certainly makes most interesting and illuminating if extremely varied reading. Being a symposium, all schools of thought are represented, and I would venture to add that among the contributions are some outpourings which evince no thought at all, a fact which is of itself not without considerable significance. We have the unflinching logic and sound common-sense of Father Bernard Vaughan, whose verdict is reiterated by the Rev. James Adderley and the Rev. J. A. V. Magee; the concise, outspoken, pertinent and telling comments of General Booth; the vague hopelessly inadequate flotsam of Dr. Percy Dearmer,[92] vapid stuff which makes a theologian writhe; the sweet sugary sentimentalism of Miss Evelyn Underhill, so anæmic, so obviously popular, and so ingenuously miscalled mysticism; the dull worthless dross of Mr. McCabe's superstitious materialism; the feverish panicky special pleading of the convinced Spiritists. Here, too, we have much that directly bears out our present contention, the medical evidence of such names as Sir Bryan Donkin; Dr. W. H. Stoddart, who treats of "The Danger to Mental Sanity"; with Dr. Bernard Hollander on "The Peril of Spirits"; and Dr. A. T. Schofield on "The Spiritist Epidemic." Thus Dr. Stoddart writes: "In some cases the spiritualistic hallucinations so dominate the whole mental life that the condition amounts to insanity; and I can confirm Sir Bryan Donkin's statement that spiritualistic inquiries tend to induce insanity."[93] Dr. Hollander is even more emphatic: "The practice is a dangerous one. Persons become intoxicated with spirits of that nature as others do with spirits of another kind. And similarly, as not all persons who take alcohol get drunk, so not all spiritualists show the effects of their indulgences. . . . But that is no proof against the harmful nature of these practices, and, as a mental specialist, I confess I have seen victims of both, and that the one addicted to material spirits is the easier to treat."[94] Spiritism, Dr. Schofield points out, "has been known to

Christians for 2000 years. Any benefit derived therefrom is more than neutralized by the very doubtful surroundings and character of the supposed revelation (I say 'supposed' because it has been known so long). If, however, it must be coupled with the dangers, horrors, and frauds that so often in modern Spiritism accompany the knowledge of the unseen, we are almost as well without it, at any rate from such a source. . . . There can be no doubt the epidemic will eventually subside, but before it does, the vast mischief of a spiritual tidal wave of very doubtful origin will be most disastrously done, and thousands of unstable souls will be wrecked in spirit, if not in mind and body as well. . . . To class it as a religion is an insult to the faith of Christ."[95]

Sir William Barrett utters a word of grave import: "All excitable and unbalanced minds need to be warned away from a subject that may cause, and in many cases has caused, serious mental derangement."[96] "Spiritualism," says Father Bernard Vaughan, "only too often means loss of health, loss of morals and loss of faith. Consult not Sir Oliver Lodge or Sir Arthur Conan Doyle or Mr. Vale Owen, but your family medical adviser, and he will tell you to keep away from the séance-room as you would from an opium den. In fact, the drug habit is not more fatal than the practice of Spiritualism in very many cases. Read the warning note sounded by Dr. Charles Mercier, or by Dr. G. H. Robertson or by Colonel R. H. Elliot, and be satisfied that yielding to Spiritualism is qualifying for an asylum. You may not get there but you deserve to be an inmate."[97] The following letter written by Miss Mary G. Cardwell, M.B., Ch.B., from the Oldham Union Infirmary, speaks for itself: "One day recently I admitted a woman of thirty-five years to the hospital of which I have the honour to be resident medical officer. She was sent in as incapable of looking after herself or her family. She told me that she was a medium, having been introduced into Spiritualism by a man, also a medium, who said he could thereby help her over some family worries. As a direct result of this, she has neglected her children, so that the public authorities have removed them from her care, her home is ruined, and she herself is a mental and moral wreck. She had paid the other medium for his services by the sacrifice of her virtue."[98] And this is no isolated, no exceptional, instance. I have myself known precisely similar cases.

Occasionally some particularly shocking incident will find its way into the public Press and we have records such as the following, which was headed "Family of Eleven Mad. Burning Mania after Séance. Child to be Sacrificed.

"The story of an entire family of eleven persons, in the village of Krucktenhofen, Bavaria, going out of their minds after a spiritualistic séance is sent by the Exchange Paris correspondent, quoting the *Berliner Tageblatt*.

"Renouncing the goods of this world, the father, mother, three sons, two elder daughters, and subsequently the remaining four younger members of the family, joined in burning their furniture and bedding.

"Finally, the three-months-old child of one of the daughters was about to be burnt when neighbours interfered. The whole family is now in an asylum." (*Daily Mirror*, 19 May, 1921.)

"Camouflage it as you will, Spiritualism with its kindred superstitions, such as necromancy and occultism, is a recrudescence of the old, old practices cultivated in the days of long ago."[99] In other words this "New Religion" is but the Old Witchcraft. There is, I venture to assert, not a single phenomenon of modern Spiritism which cannot be paralleled in the records of the witch trials and examinations; not a single doctrine which was not believed and propagated by the damnable Gnostic heresies of long ago.

Some of the definitions of Spiritism given by spiritists themselves are sufficiently startling. They frankly tell us that "Spiritualism is the science or art of communion with spirits. . . . It does not follow that because a communication comes from 'the unseen,' it is therefore from God, as a revelation. It may be from the latest dead lounger, as an amusement,"[100] or, I would add, from a demon as a snare. There is something inexpressibly ugly and revolting about this cold-blooded necromancy defined in set categorical terms.

Modern Spiritism is usually considered to have had its origin in America. In the year 1848 there lived at Hydesville, Wayne, New York State, a family of the Methodist persuasion named Fox; a father, mother, and two daughters,

Margaretta and Katie, aged fifteen and twelve respectively. During the month of March all the household began to declare that they were kept awake at night by the most extraordinary noises, loud knockings on the wall, and footsteps. The children amused themselves by trying to imitate the noises; they tapped on the wainscot, and to their great surprise answering taps came back, so that they found they could get into communication with the unknown agency. They would ask a question and invite it to respond with one sharp rap for "no" and three for "yes," and thus it continually replied. They further held actual conversations in this way by repeating the alphabet and establishing a regular code. Mrs. Fox then began to make inquiries concerning the former occupants of the house, and soon discovered that a pedlar named Charles Rayn was said to have been murdered in the very bedroom where her two girls were sleeping, and that his body had been buried in the cellar. Public curiosity was aroused, and it was now generally believed that it was the spirit of the unfortunate victim who haunted the farm-house, endeavouring to convey some message to those whom he had left. Actually no body was found in the cellar, and the alleged murderer whose name was given, appeared at Hydesville and "threw very hot water on the story." Later when the family moved to Rochester—it is said they were practically driven out of Hydesville by the Methodist minister there—the rappings followed them, and the whole town was speedily on the tiptoe of excitement. It was then given out that the noises were communications from the spirits of those recently dead, and that the Fox girls, who apparently attracted them, were gifted with some special faculty which rendered intercourse of this kind possible. People soon began to flock round them asking their assistance in getting messages from their departed relatives and friends; the two girls held regular séances, and netted a fair sum of money. It was not long before other persons discovered that they also possessed this extraordinary faculty of attracting spirit manifestations, and of getting into communication with the other world at will. But the Fox sisters were first in the field, and to them came a continuous stream of persons with well-filled pockets from all parts of America. There was also opposition, which sometimes took a very violent form. As early as November,

1850, an attack was made upon Margaretta Fox, who was staying at West Troy in the house of a Mr. Bouton. A rough mob surrounded the premises, stones were thrown at the windows, and shots fired, whilst both men and women uttered threats and imprecations against the "unholy witch-woman within." At one of the séances Dr. Kane, a famous Arctic explorer was present, and he was so fascinated by the beauty of Margaretta Fox that he never rested until he had taken her away from her sordid and harmful surroundings, had her educated at Philadelphia, and finally, much to the annoyance of his relations, who loathed any connexion with the Fox family, made her his wife.

Dr. Kane died soon after his marriage, but in the book published by his widow there are several references to his abhorrence of Spiritism. "Do avoid spirits," he urges, "I cannot bear to think of you as engaged in a course of wickedness and deception." For ten years Mrs. Kane did indeed abandon it; in fact in August, 1858, she was baptized as a Catholic at New York; but then,[101] owing perhaps to the pinch of poverty, she again took up work as a medium, and was received back with acclamations by the whole Spiritistic community. From that moment dates her steady deterioration, both physical and moral.

Kate Fox, Mrs. Jencken as she had become, the wife of a London barrister, was the mother of a baby whom popular talk credited with mediumistic powers of the most extraordinary kind. The whole Spiritistic following prophesied a brilliant future for the poor child, of whom, however, there is nothing recorded save that he was sadly neglected by his miserable mother, who died of chronic alcoholism in June, 1892. Mrs. Kane survived her sister for nine months, a pitiable and hopeless wreck, craving only for drink. The last few weeks of her life were spent in a derelict tenement house. "This wreck of womanhood has been a guest in palaces and courts. The powers of mind now imbecile were the wonder and the study of scientific men in America, Europe, and Australia. . . . The lips that utter little else now than profanity, once promulgated the doctrine of a new religion."[102] It would, indeed, be difficult to conceive anything more sordid and more miserable than this sad and shocking story of utter degradation. The collapse and moral corruption of the first apostles of modern Spiritism should surely prove a timely warning and a danger signal not to be mistaken.[103]

In the earliest days of Spiritism the subject was investigated by men like Horace Greeley, William Lloyd Garrison, Robert Hare, professor of chemistry in the University of Pennsylvania, and John Worth Edmonds, a judge of the Supreme Court of New York State. Conspicuous among the spiritists we find Andrew Jackson Davis, whose work *The Principles of Nature* (1847), dictated by him in trance, contained theories of the universe closely resembling those of the Swedenborgians. From America the movement filtered through to Europe, and when in 1852 two mediums, Mrs. Haydon and Mrs. Roberts, came to London, not merely popular interest but the careful attention of the leading scientists of the day was attracted. Robert Owen, the Socialist, frankly accepted the Spiritistic explanation of the various phenomena, while Professor De Morgan, the mathematician, in his account of a sitting with Mrs. Haydon declared himself convinced that "somebody or some spirit was reading his thoughts." In the spring of 1855 Daniel Dunglas Home (Hume)—Home was the son of the eleventh Lord Home and a chambermaid at the Queen's Hotel, Southampton, but was brought up in America—who was then a young man of twenty-two, crossed to England from America. In 1856 Home was received into the Church at Rome by Father John Etheridge, S.J., and he then gave a promise to refrain from all exercise of his mediumistic powers, but in less than a year he had broken his pledge and was living as before. This famous medium is almost the only one who, as even Podmore admits, was never clearly convicted of fraud. Sir David Brewster, the scientist, and Dr. J. J. Garth Wilkinson, a scholar of unblemished integrity and one of the leading homœopathic physicians, both avowed that they were incapable of explaining the phenomena they had witnessed by any natural means. It was in 1855 that the first English periodical dealing exclusively with the subject, *The Yorkshire Spiritual Telegraph*, was published at Keighley, in Yorkshire. In 1864 the Davenport brothers visited England, and in 1876 Henry Slade. Amongst English mediums the Rev. William Stainton Moses became prominent in 1872,[104] and about the same year Miss Florence

Cook, so well known for the materializations of "Katie King," which were scrupulously investigated by the late Sir William Crookes. In 1873 and in 1874, however, the trickery of two mediums, Mrs. Bassett and Miss Showers, was definitely exposed.[105] In 1876 and 1877 the sensitive "Dr." Monck was at the height of his reputation, and both Dr. Alfred Russel Wallace, F.R.S., and the late Archdeacon Colley state that in various séances with him they witnessed on several occasions phenomena, including materialization, under rigid test conditions which admitted of no dispute as to their genuineness. It is true that in 1876 Monck had been in trouble and was sentenced to a term of imprisonment under the Vagrant Act. About the same time William Eglinton, who figures in Florence Marryat's work *There is No Death*, appeared on the scenes and for a while loomed largely in the public eye. He became famous for his slate-writing performances as well as his materializations. He was, however, exposed by Archdeacon Colley, who during the discussion which had centred round a medium named Williams, detected in fraudulent practices during séances in Holland, wrote to *The Medium and Daybreak* to say: "It unfortunately fell to me to take muslin and false beard from Eglinton's portmanteau. . . . Some few days before this I had on two several occasions cut pieces from the drapery worn by, and clipped hair from the beard of, the other figure representing Abdullah. I have the pieces so cut off beard and muslin still. But note that when I took these things into my possession I and a medical gentleman (25 years a Spiritualist and well known to the old members of the Movement) found the pieces of muslin cut fit exactly into certain corresponding portions of the drapery thus taken."[106]

The medium Slade, who was famous for slate-writing, was upon one occasion suddenly seized as he was about to put the slate under the table. His hands were held fast, and when the slate was snatched from him it was seen to be already covered with characters. Anna Rothe, who died in 1901, a medium well known for her apports of flowers, suffered a term of imprisonment in Germany on a charge of fraud. When Baily, the Australian sensitive, visited Italy he refused to sit under the strict conditions which were arranged in answer to a challenge of his powers. Charles

Eldred of Clowne, an adept at materialization, employed a chair skilfully made with a double seat, and in this recess were discovered the whole paraphernalia he employed in his performances.

Mrs. Williams, an American medium, who for a long while was a centre of spiritistic attention at Paris, used to materialize a venerable doctor with a flowing beard who was sometimes accompanied by a young girl dressed in white. At one circle Mons. Paul Leymaric gave a prearranged signal. He and a friend each laid hold of one of the apparitions; a third spectator seized Mrs. Williams' assistant; and a fourth turned on the lights. Mons. Leymaric was seen to be struggling with the medium, who had donned a grey wig and a long property beard; the young girl was a mask from which were draped folds of fine white muslin and which she manipulated with her left hand. Miller, a Californian medium, was more than suspected of producing spirits from gauze and nun's veiling.[107] From one of the mediums of Mons. de Rochas, Valentine, there emanated mysterious lights, which moved quickly hither and thither during the séances. Colonel de Rochas, when this manifestation was once at its height, suddenly switched on a powerful electric torch and Valentine was seen to have slipped off his socks and to be waving in the air his feet, which were covered with some preparation of phosphorus.[108] As early as June, 1875, a photographer named Buguet was convicted of selling faked photographs of spirits by which he netted a very pretty sum.[109]

It is notorious that in Spiritistic séances and circles charlatanry and swindling of every kind are rife; that again and again mediums have been convicted of fraud; that not infrequently all kinds of properties, stuffed gloves, gauzes, yards of diaphanous muslin, invisible wires, hooks, beards, wigs, have been discovered; that the use of luminous paint is very effective and far from uncommon; that a sliding trap or panel may on occasion prove of inestimable service; that we must allow for self-deception, delusions, suggestion, hypnotism even; but when all has been said, when we candidly acknowledge the imposture, the adroit legerdemain, the conjurer's clever tricks, the significant *mise en scène*, the verbal wit and quibbling, the deliberate and subtle cozenage contrived by shrewd minds and the full play of dramatic instinct and energy, nevertheless there yet remain numbers of instances when it has been repeatedly proven that acute and trained observers have witnessed phenomena which could not by any possibility whatsoever have been fraudulently produced; that clear-headed, cold-hearted, suspicious, hard men of science with every sense keenly alert at that very moment have conversed with, inspected, nay, actually handled, materialized forms and figures no personation could have devised and manifested.

The proceedings against Monck plainly showed that he had at any rate a firm belief in his own psychic powers, and although Eglinton was detected in a trick upon more than one occasion there is irrefutable evidence to prove that in other instances when he assisted at séances any normal mode of production of the phenomena seen there was quite impossible. A large number of Miller's manifestations also were genuine.[110] The same may be said of very many mediums. This means, in fine, that although the manifestations of almost any medium may in some cases have been artificially contrived, such phenomena are not on any account to be adjudged *always* fraudulent, and even if the charge of imposture could be brought home far more conclusively than has so far been possible as regards the majority of sensitives, yet it were a false inference indeed to deduce therefrom that all phenomena are equally fraudulent and devised. It is only the recklessly illogical mind and the loose thinker who will in the face of absolutely conclusive proof of genuine manifestations continue to maintain that a certain quota of quackery can invalidate the whole. Writers of the temper of Messrs. Edward Clodd, Joseph McCabe, J. M. Robertson must, of course, be expected to condemn Spiritism without knowing the facts or weighing the evidence as an obvious absurdity which calls for no serious refutation. But this, I think, matters little. The superstitious dogmatism of the materialist is gravely discredited nowadays. True, the sort of book he produces is widely circulated and very successful within certain limits. We should expect tenth-rate ideas which could only emanate from a lack of understanding, a total want of imagination, and no training in metaphysics or philosophy, to have a direct appeal to the immature intelligences, the uneducated vulgar and the blatant yet presumptuous ignorance, which alone are eager for this kind of outmoded fare.

In France Spiritism was first proclaimed by a pamphlet of Guillard *Table qui danse et Table qui répond.* The way had been long paved owing to the interest which was generally taken in the doctrines of Emanuel Swedenborg. Balzac had published in 1835 his esoteric hybrid *Séraphita* (*Séraphitus*), a fanciful yet interesting work, in which there are many pages of theosophic philosophy. Perhaps he meant these seriously, but it is impossible to take them as other than flights of romance. In 1848 Cohognet more immediately heralded Guillard by publishing at Paris the first volume of his *Arcanes de la vie future devoilées,* which actually contains what purport to be communications from the dead. In 1853 séances were being held at Bourges, Strasburg, and Paris, and a regular furore ensued. Nothing was talked of but the wonders of Spiritism, which, however, soon met an opponent, Count Agénor de Gasparin, a Swiss Protestant, who carefully investigated table-turning with a circle of his friends and came to the conclusion that the phenomena originated in some physical force of the human body. It must be admitted that his *Des Tables Tournantes* (Paris, 1854) is unconvincing and to some extent superficial, but more perhaps could hardly be expected from a pioneer in so tortuous an investigation. The Baron de Guldenstubbe, on the contrary, declared his firm belief in the reality of these phenomena and spirit intervention in general. His work *La Réalité des Esprits* (Paris, 1857) eloquently argued for his convictions, whilst *Le Livre des Esprits* (Paris, 1853) by M. Rivail or Rival, better known under his pseudonym Allan Kardec, became a world-wide textbook to the whole subject. In these early days the most distinguished men were wont to meet in the rue des Martyrs at Paris for séances. Tiedmen Marthèse, governor of Java; the academician Saint-René-Taillandier; Sardou, with his son; Flammarion; all were constant visitors. The notorious Home was, it is said, expelled from France after a séance at the Tuileries, during which he had touched the arm of the Empress with his naked foot, pretending that it was a caress from the tiny hands of a little child who was about fully to materialize. No one, I think, could be surprised to know that the famous Joris Karl Huysmans, an epicure in the byways of the occult, made many experiments in Spiritism, and séances were frequently held at No. 11 rue de Sèvres where he lived. Extraordinary manifestations took place, and upon one occasion at least the circle effected a materialization of General Boulanger, or an apparition of the General appeared to them.

At the present time Spiritism is as widely spread in France as in England, if indeed not far more widely. Thus *La Science de l'Ame* is a new bi-monthly journal issued under the auspices of *La Revue Spirite*. It has articles on Magnetism and Radio-activity, the analysis of the soul, and vital radiations. In the number of *La Revue Spirite*, which commences the year 1925, Mons. Camille Flammarion prints a signed letter from Heliopolis, which describes a first experience of a séance, where the death of the writer's father was predicted in six months and took place ten days after the allotted time. Elsewhere in the issue are particulars of the International Congress of Spiritism which was to be held at Paris in September, 1925, and would be open to all Federations, Societies, and Groups everywhere. An immense concourse was expected. The President is Mr. George F. Berry, a well-known name in English Spiritistic circles, and the compliment of honorary membership is paid to Léon Denis,[111] Gabriel Delanne, Sir William Barrett, and Ernest Bozzano.

A glance at the pages of any Spiritistic journal in England will show almost endless activities in every direction. In one issue of the weekly *Light* (Saturday, 21 February, 1925) we have amongst other announcements nine " Sunday's Society Meetings " in various districts of London, with addresses on Wednesdays and Thursdays. The following seems sufficiently startling and a close enough imitation : " *St. Luke's Church of the Spiritual Evangel of Jesus the Christ, Queen's-road, Forest Hill, S.E.*—Minister : Rev. J. W. Potter. February 22nd, 6.30, Service, Holy Communion and Address. Healing Service, Wed., Feb. 25th, 7 p.m." In the next column are details of " Rev. G. Vale Owen's Lecture Tour." The " London Spiritualist Alliance, Ltd." has a list of meetings. There are discussion classes and demonstrations of clairvoyance, psychometry, and Mystic Pictures. Among " Books that will Help you " we find *Talks with the Dead*, *Report on*

Spiritualism, The Aquarian Gospel of Jesus the Christ—(is this used at St. Luke's Church of the Spiritual Evangel ?)—*Spirit Identity, Spiritualism,* and many more of similar import. There is a "British College of Psychic Science" where Mr. Horace Leaf, a medium of some repute, lectures on "The Psychology and Practice of Mediumship," Mrs. Barker demonstrates Trance Mediumship, and Mrs. Travers Smith the Ouija-Board and Automatic Writing. There is a "London Spiritual Mission" and a "Wimbledon Spiritualist Mission." At Brighton "St. John's Brotherhood Church" provides "The Spiritual Evangel of Jesus the Christ," "Minister, Brother John." And all this is scarcely a tithe of the various announcements and advertisements.

However grotesque, and indeed often puerile in its bombast and grandiloquence, such a mass of heterogeneous notices may seem we must remember that these people are in deadly earnest, and I doubt not but their meetings and assemblies are well attended by enthusiastic devotees. In a report of an address by the Rev. G. Vale Owen at the "Spiritualist Community Services in the County Hall" on Sunday evening, 15 February, 1925, I read "all seats were filled long before the advertised hour for starting. The doors were closed and many for a time were denied admission. A little later they were allowed to enter and take up positions along the edges of the dais and other odd places about the hall."[112] This, of course, was possibly some exceptional occasion, but there is no indication that such was the case. Mr. Vale Owen may be a very eloquent speaker and able to hold his audience spell-bound with the magic of his words. It must assuredly be his manner and not his matter, for his so-called revelations of the life beyond the grave, written under control and presumed to be directly derived from spirit agency, which appeared in *The Weekly Dispatch* are vapid, inept, idle, and insipid to the last degree. Such banal ramblings would provoke a smile, were it not for the pity that any person can be so self-deluded, and can apparently induce others to give credit to his silliness.

There have been large numbers of mediums in recent years who owing to one cause or another attracted considerable attention from time to time, and there are many well-known contemporary sensitives widely practising to-day.

Mrs. Verrall and Mrs. Holland, who were believed to have obtained spirit messages from the late F. W. H. Myers, occupied the serious attention of the Society of Psychical Research[113] for a considerable period; Mrs. Piper is an automatic writer of no little repute; Mr. Vout Peters specializes in psychometry and clairvoyance; Mr. Vearncombe and Mrs. Deane have recently enjoyed their full share of notoriety;[114] the Rev. Josie K. Stewart (Mrs. Y.), a lady hailing from the United States, has a gift for the production of "writing and drawings on cards held in her hand"; Mrs. Elizabeth A. Tomson, in spite of being detected of fraud at a Spiritistic "Church" in Brooklyn, still has devoted followers; Franek Kluski, Stella C., and Ada Besinnet, are in the forefront of American mediums; whilst the famous Goligher circle at Belfast was carefully and patiently investigated for no less than three months by Dr. Fournier d'Albe, who has published the result of his experiences.[115] The very cream of these occult manifestations is materialization, the most complex problem of all, which has been described as "the exercise of the power of using of the matter of the medium's and the sitters' bodies in the formation of physical structures on a principle totally unknown to ordinary life, although probably present there."[116] Recently (1922) Erto, the Italian medium, appears to have been the subject of careful experiments at the French Metaphysical Institute during a period of several months, those who assisted being pledged to silence until a decision had been reached. The particular phenomena produced by or in his presence were chiefly characterized by the radiation of an extraordinary light about his person. At the end of 1922 two papers appeared in *La Revue Métapsychique* on the part of Dr. Sanguinetti and Dr. William Mackenzie of Genoa indicating their assurance (1) that every scientific precaution had been taken, and (2) that the phenomena were genuine. However, the experiments seem to have continued and later there appeared in *Le Matin* an enthusiastic contribution by Dr. Stephen Chauvet, which caused Dr. Gustave Geley, Director of the Metaphysical Institute, to come forward in confirmation of the testimony. It is only fair to add that immediately afterwards Dr. Geley to a certain extent retracted his statement, as he suggested that the psychic lights could be produced with *ferro-cerium*, and it was thought that traces of this substance could be found on Erto's clothes. The medium protested his innocence of any deception, and offers himself for further experiments. A writer in *Psychica* is inclined to believe that the phenomena were genuine, but that later some fraud may have been practised owing to waning power. This is possibly the case, for that the radiations were at first supernormal cannot, I think, be gainsaid in view of the high testimony adduced. For this phenomenon Mr. Cecil Hush and Mr. Craddock have sat repeatedly; of the extraordinary manifestations of the late Eusapia Palladino there can be no reasonable doubt at all; the materializations of Mlle "Eva Carrère,"[117] although on several occasions not altogether successful, are at other times supported by the strongest evidence; Nino Pecoraro, who is described as "a remarkably muscular young Neapolitan," is famous for "ectoplasmic effects"; and Stanislava P., Willy S., the Countess Castelvicz, and very many more psychics possess these supernormal powers, although, as we might expect, they have to be used with the utmost caution and often prove very exhausting to the subject. After all, it must be remembered that probably under certain conditions materialization cannot take place, whilst under favourable conditions it can be completely effected. For an exhaustive and authoritative discussion of the whole matter the Baron Von Schrenck-Notzing's *Phenomena of Materialization* (Kegan Paul, 1923), should be consulted. The 225 photographic reproductions are of the utmost importance, whilst the investigations were carried on under conditions of such pitiless severity to eliminate any hypothesis of fraud that the mediums cannot but have been subjected to the intensest physical and moral strain.

Among recent psychic phenomena very general attention has been attracted by what is known as "The Oscar Wilde Script," which was widely discussed in 1923–24. Briefly, this purports to be a number of communications which were delivered by the spirit of the late Oscar Wilde at the rate of 1020 words in an hour by means of automatic writing through the mediumship of Mrs. Travers Smith (Mrs. Hester M. Dowden)[118] and a certain Mr. V. True, there were published in *The Sunday Express* pages which had a superficial resemblance to the more flashy characteristics of Wilde's flamboyant style, but it seemed as if the wit and point had vanished, leaving only a somewhat heavy and imitative prose; one had a sense of damp fireworks, and personally I do not for a moment accept this script as being inspired or dictated by Wilde. I hasten to add that I do not suggest there was any conscious fraud or trickery on the part of those concerned; it is quite probable that these psychic messages were conveyed by some intelligence of no very high standing, and the result in fine is not of any value. It is said that a three act play is being or has been communicated through the ouija-board from what purports to be Wilde. This I have not read, and therefore I am not in a position to pronounce upon it.

Spiritism is upheld by many distinguished names. Sir Oliver Lodge, F.R.S., has battled on its behalf, as also have Sir William Barrett, F.R.S., and Sir William Crookes, F.R.S., Professors Charles Richet, Janet, Bernheim, Lombroso, and Flammarion lend it the weight of their authority, whilst Sir Conan Doyle has poured forth his benedictions upon occultism of every kind.[119] He has even presided over the opening of a most attractive bookshop in Victoria Street, Westminster, where Spiritistic publications are sold.

How then are we to regard this mighty movement at which it were folly to sneer, which it is impossible to ignore? The Catholic Church does neither. But none the less she condemns it utterly and entirely. Not because she disbelieves in it, but because she believes in it so thoroughly, because she knows what is the real nature of the moving forces, however skilfully they may disguise themselves, however quick and subtle their shifts and turns, the intelligences which inform and direct the whole. It is a painful subject since (I reiterate) many good people, no doubt many thoughtful seekers after truth, have been fascinated and swept along by Spiritism. They are as yet conscious of neither physical nor moral harm, and, it may be, they have been playing with the fire for years. Nay more, Spiritism has been a sweet solace to many in most poignant hours of bitter sorrow and loss; wherefore it is hallowed in their eyes by tenderest memories. They are woefully deceived. Hard as it may seem, we must get down to the bed-rock of fact.

Spiritism has been specifically condemned on no less than four occasions by the Holy Office,[120] whose decree, 30 March, 1898, utterly forbids all Spiritistic practices although intercourse with demons be strictly excluded, and communication sought with good spirits only. Modern Spiritism is merely Witchcraft revived. The Second Plenary Council of Baltimore (1866), whilst making ample allowance for prestidigitation and trickery of every kind, warns the faithful against lending any support whatsoever to Spiritism and forbids them to attend séances even out of idle curiosity, for some, at least, of the manifestations must necessarily be ascribed to Satanic intervention since in no other manner can they be understood or explained.

NOTES TO CHAPTER VI

1 E. de Rougé, *Étude sur une stèle Égyptienne*, Paris, 1858: E. A. W. Budge, *Egyptian Magic*, VII.

2 *Rekh Khet*, "knower of things."

3 Euripides, *Bacchæ:* passim; Ovid, *Metamorphoses*. III. 513, *sqq.*; Apollodorus, III. v. 2.; Hyginus, *Fabulæ*, 184; Nonnus, *Dionysiaca* (*Bassarica*), XIV, 46.

4 Sophocles, *Ajax;* Pindar, *Nemea*, VII, 25; Ovid, *Metamorphoses*, XIII, 1–398.

5 Pausanias, III, xvi, 6.

6 Valerius Maximus, I, 11, 5. Lacinium was a promontory on the east coast of Bruttium, a few miles south of Croton, and forming the western boundary of the Tarentine gulf. The remains of the temple of Juno Lacinia are still extant, and have given the modern name to the promontory, *Capo delle Colonne* or *Capo di Nao* (*ναός*).

7 Xenophon, *Memorabilia*. II. i. 5; Demosthenes, XCIII, 24; Dinarchus, CI, 41; Plutarch, *Lucullus*, IV.

8 Euripides, *Orestes*, l. 854, and l. 79.

9 Cf. *μάντις*.

10 Cf. Vergil *Æneid*. IV. 471–3:

Agamemnonius scænis agitatus Orestes
armatam facibus matrem et serpentibus atris
cum fugit, ultricesque sedent in limine Diræ.

(Or as the Atridan matricide
Runs frenzied o'er the scene,
What time with snakes and torches plied
He flees the murdered queen,
While at the threshold of the gate
The sister-fiends expectant wait.)

11 Plautus, *Amphitruo*, II. 2. 145. Nam hæc quidem edepol lauarum plenast.

12 Quid esset illi morbi, dixeras ? Narra, senex.
Num laruatus, aut cerritus ? fac sciam.

Menæchmei. V. 1, 2. Apuleuis has *laruans* = a madman: "hunc [pulcherrimam Mercurii imaginem] denique qui laruam putat, ipse est laruans." (*Laruatus* is a poorer reading in this passage.) *Cerritus*. a rare word, is contracted from *cerebritus* (*cerebrum*), and not connected with Ceres, as was formerly suggested. Cf. Horace, *Sermonum*, II, iii. 278.

[13] *Bibl.* III, v, 1.
[14] 471, *sqq.*
[15] 56, Nauck.

[16] *τἀπιχώρί ἐν πόλει φρυγῶν τύμπανα,*
'Ρέας τε μητρὸς ἐμά θ' εὑρήματα.

[17] *Circa* 185–135 B.C.

[18] Professor Leuba, *The Psychology of Religious Mysticism* Kegan Paul, London, 1925, p. 11 *sqq.* has some very important references to the worship of Dionysus.

[19] *σὺ γὰρ ἔνθεος, ὦ κούρα,*
εἴτ' ἐκ Πανὸς εἴθ' Ἑκάτας
ἢ σεμνῶν Κορυβάντων
φοιτᾷς, ἢ ματρὸς ὀρείας.

[20] *δόξασά που*
ἢ Πανὸς ὀργὰς ἢ τινὸς θεῶν μολεῖν.

[21] *ἀλλ' ἢ Κρονίου Πανὸς τρομερᾷ*
μάστιγι φοβεῖ ;

[22] Pythagoras prescribes music for mental disorders, Eunapius *Uita philosophorum*, 67 ; and Cælius Aurelianus by his references shows that this was a common remedy in such cases, *De Morbis Chronicis* (*Tardarum Passionum*) VI. Origen, *Aduersus Celsum*, III, x, and Martianus Capella *De Nuptiis Philologiæ et Mercurii* IX, 925, have similar allusions.

[23] 1 Kings xvi. 14 (A.V. 1 Samuel xvi. 14) : "Exagitabat eum [Saul] spiritus nequam a Domino."

[24] *Antiquitates Iud.*, VI, viii, 2 ; ii, 2.

[25] *La Mystique Divine*, Ribet, II, ix, 4, it is true, speaks of "l'obsession intérieure," but he makes the above distinction, and further says : "L'obsession purement intérieure ne diffère des tentations ordinaires que par la véhémence et la durée."

[26] Multæ sunt tentationes eius, et die noctuque uariæ dæmonum insidiæ . . . Quoties illi nudæ mulieres cubanti, quoties esurienti largissimæ apparuere dapes ? *Uita S. Hilarionis*. VII. Migne. vol. XXIII. col. 32.

[27] Sustinebat miser diabolus uel mulieris formam noctu induere, feminæque gestus imitari, Antonium ut deciperet. S. Athanasius, *Uita S. Antonii*, V. Migne. vol. XXVI. col. 847.

[28] Feast (duplex maius apud Minores), 22 February.

[29] It may perhaps not be amiss to point out that S. Margaret before her conversion was by no means the woman of scandalous life so many biographers have painted her.

[30] Sectando per cellam orantis et flentis, cantauit [diabolus] turpissimas cantationes, et Christi famulam lacrymantem et se Domino commendantem procaciter inuocabat ad cantum . . . ; tentantem precibus et lacrymis repulit ac eiecit. Bollandists, 22 February. Vol. VI.

[31] Ceterum consilium est semper de talibus inuasionibus suspicionem habere, non enim negandum maiorem earum partem esse aut fictiones, aut imaginationes, aut infirmitates, præsertim in mulieribus. *Praxis confessariorum*, n. 120.

[32] Sæpissime, quæ putantur dæmonis obsessiones, non sunt nisi morbi naturales, aut Naturales imaginationes, uel etiam inchoata aut perfecta amentia. Quare caute omnino procedendum, usquedum per specialissima signa de obsessione constet. *Theologia mystica*, I. n. 228.

[33] *Biblisches Realworterbuch*, Leipsig, 1833.

[34] This word is found nowhere else in the New Testament, and wherever it is used in the LXX, it is invariably of the sayings of lying prophets, or those who practised arts forbidden by the Jewish Law. Thus of the witch of Endor (1 Kings (1 Samuel) xxviii. 8) *μάντευσαι δή μοι ἐν τῷ ἐγγαστριομύθῳ*, and (Ezechiel xiii. 6) *βλέπουτες ψευδῆ, μαντευόμενοι μάταια.*

[35] Ordinandi, filii charissimi, in officium Exorcistarum, debitis noscere quid suscipitis. Exorcistam etenim oportet abiicere dæmones ; et dicere populo, ut, qui non communicat, det locum ; et aquam in ministerio fundere. Accipitis itaque potestatem imponendi manum super energumenos, et per

impositionem manuum uestrarum, gratia spiritus sancti, et uerbis exorcismi pelluntur spiritus immundi a corporibus obsessis. Studete igitur, ut, sicut a corporibus aliorum dæmones expellitis, ita a mentibus, et corporibus uestris omnem immunditiam, et nequitiam eiiciatis; ne illis succumbatis, quos ab aliis, uestro ministerio, effugatis. Discite per officium uestrum uitiis imperare; ne in moribus uestris aliquid sui iuris inimicus ualeat uindicare. Tunc etenim recte in aliis dæmonibus imperabitis, cum prius in uobis eorum multimodam nequitiam superatis. Quod nobis Dominus agere concedat per Spiritum suum sanctum.

36 Accipite, et commendate memoriæ, et habete potestatem imponendi manus super energumenos, siue baptizatos, siue catechumenos.

37 Deum Patrem omnipotentem, fratres charissimi, supplices deprecamur, ut hos famulos suos bene ✠ dicere dignetur in officium Exorcistarum; ut sint spirituales imperatores, ad abiiciendos dæmones de corporibus obsessis, cum omni nequitia eorum multiformi. Per unigenitum Filium suum Dominum nostrum Iesum Christum, qui cum eo uiuit et regnat in unitate Spiritus sancti Deus, per omnia sæcula sæculorum. *R.* Amen.

38 Domine sancte, Pater omnipotens, æterne Deus, bene ✠ dicere dignare hos famulos tuos in officium Exorcistarum; ut per impositionem manuum, et oris officium, potestatem, et imperium habeant spiritus immundos coercendi: ut probabiles sint medici Ecclesiæ tuæ, gratia curationum uirtuteque cœlesti confirmati. Per Dominum nostrum Iesum Christum Filium tuum, qui tecum uiuit, et regnat in unitate Spiritus sancti Deus, per omnia sæcula sæculorum. *R.* Amen. *Post hæc, suggerente Archidiacono, redeunt ad loca sua.*

39 Sulpitius Severus (d. 420–5) in his *Dialogues*, III (II), 6; (Migne, *Patres Latini*, XX, 215) tells us that S. Martin of Tours was wont to cast out demons by prayer alone without the imposition of hands or the use of the formulæ recommended to the clergy. Similar instances occur in the lives of the Saints.

40 Translated from the *Rituale Romanum*. There are several forms extant, some authorized, but more, perhaps, unauthorized. There is an authorized form in the Greek *Euchologion*. It commences with the Trisagion, and Psalms, *Domine exaudi* (cxlii.), *Dominus regit me* (xxii.), *Dominus illuminatio mea* (xxvi.), *Esurgat Deus* (lxvii.), *Miserere* (lvi.), *Domine ne in furore* (vi.), *Domine exaudi orationem* (ci.). Then follows the Consolatory Canon, with a long Hymn addressed to Our Lord, Our Lady, and All Saints. Next the priest anoints the patient, saying a prayer over him, and so the office closes.

41 It is also given in the *Horæ Diurnæ O.P.*, Rome, 1903, where an indulgence of 300 days is attached, plenary once a month.

42 Ab insidiis diaboli, libera nos Domine; Ut Ecclesiam tuam secura tibi facias libertate seruire, te rogamus, audi nos; Ut inimicos sanctæ Ecclesiæ humiliare digneris, te rogamus, audi nos. *Et aspergatur locus aqua benedicta.*

43 Holy water, the commonest of the sacramentals, is a mixture of exorcised salt and exorcised water.

44 Of Eastern origin. It should be remembered that the Baptism of Christ in Jordan is commemorated on the Epiphany. In the present Breviary office in Nocturn I the first response for the day, the Octave, and the Sunday within the Octave deal with the Baptism, as does the second response. The antiphon to the Benedictus and the Magnificat antiphon at Second Vespers also make mention of the same mystery. In Rome the Latin rite of the Blessing of the Waters is pontificated by a Cardinal at S. Andrea della Valle on 5 January, about 3.30 p.m., at the church of the Stimmate of S. Francesco at 9.30 a.m. on the Feast itself. On the Vigil the Oriental rite is performed at the Greek church of S. Atanasio, beginning about 3.30 a.m.

45 See Wilson, *Western Africa*; and the article "Possession diabolique" by Waffelaert in the *Dictionnaire apologétique de la foi catholique*, Paris, 1889. The opinion of the Cistercian Dom Robert de la Trappe (Dr. Pierre-Jean-Corneille Debreyne), who, whilst acknowledging that the demoniac possessions as detailed in the New Testament are *de fide*, supposes that all other cases are to be attributed to fraud or disease, must be severely censured as regrettably rash and even culpable. *Essai sur la théologie morale*, IV. p. 356.

[46] S. Justin Martyr, *Apologia*, VI; *Dialogues*, XXX, LXXXV: Minutius Felix, *Octavius*, XXVII; Origen, *Contra Celsum*, I, 25; VII, 4, 67: Tertullian, *Apologia*, XXII, XXIII.

[47] Paulinus, *Uita Ambrosii*, 28, 43.

[48] S. Gregory of Nyssa, *De Uita Ephraem*

[49] Upon this passage Servatius Galle (1627–1709), a Dutch minister at Haarlem, in his edition of Lactantius, 1660, writes the most absurd note I have ever met with in any commentator.

[50] Published between 304–313. De Labriolle, *Histoire de la Littérature Latine Chrétienne*, p. 272.

[51] A very full and scholarly monograph upon this subject may be recommended: *La Réalité des Apparitions Démoniaques*, by Dom Bernard-Marie Maréchaux, Olivetan, O.S.B., Paris, Téqui, 1899.

[52] It is true that on one occasion S. Maurus, who was with S. Benedict, beheld an apparition, and S. Benedict once enabled a monk to see a similar vision.

[53] One of Sodoma's exquisite frescoes at Monte Oliveto (Siena) depicts an exorcism by S. Benedict.

[54] The letters have been thus translated by Dom Benedict McLaughlin of Ampleforth:

Holy Cross be thou my light,
Put the evil one to flight.
Behind me Satan speedily,
Whisper not vain things to me.
You can give but evil, then
Keep it for yourself. Amen.

[55] All English Benedictine priests hold the special faculty to use this (bestowed 23 February, 1915), and it has also been granted to many others, religious and seculars.

[56] Omnis virtus aduersarii, omnis exercitus diaboli, et omnis incursus, omnis phantasma Satanæ, eradicare et effugare ab his numismatibus . . .

[57] Domine Iesu Christe . . . per hanc tuam sanctissimam passionem humiliter exoro; ut omnes diabolicas insidias et fraudes expellas ab eo, qui nomen sanctum tuum, his litteris ac characteribus a te designatis, deuote inuocauerit, et eum ad salutis portum perducere digneris. Qui uiuis et regnas . . .

[58] The *Rituale Romanum* has "Benedictio Infirmorum cum Ligno SS. Crucis, D.N.J.C. *seu* Signum S. Mauri Abbatis." This is a blessing of the sick with a Relic of the Holy Cross and the invocation of S. Benedict and S. Maurus.

[59] The *Uita S. Mauri* (Mabillon, *Acta S.S. O. S.B.*, I, 274) is ascribed to a companion, the monk Faustus of Monte Cassino. Père Delehaye, in his unfortunate and temerarious work *Légendes Hagiographiques* (translation. London, 1907), indecorously attacks this and treats S. Maurus with scant respect. A worthy defence was made by Adlhoch, *Stud. u. Mittheil.*, 1903, 3; 1906, 185. According to Peter the Deacon he also wrote a *Cantus ad B. Maurum*.

[60] Blessed Victor III. *Dialogues*, I, 2.

[61] Abbé Lebeuf. *Histoire du diocèse de Paris*, V. 129 *sqq.*

[62] Portraits of him are preserved at Rome and Valladolid.

[63] A hearty believer in witchcraft. He had sent at least one witch to the gallows, and another to prison.

[64] Apparently the work of Darrel himself, but in the Huth catalogue (V, 1643) ascribed to James Bamford.

[65] Darrel in his *Detection of that sinnful, shamful, lying, and ridiculous discours of Samuel Harshnet*, 1600, writes: "There is no doubt but that S.H. stand for Samuell Harsnet, chapline to the Bishop of London, but whither he alone, or his lord and hee, have discovered this counterfeyting and cosonage there is the question. Some think the booke to be the Bishop's owne doing: and many thinke it to be the joynt work of them both."

[66] On 10 November, 1629, he was sworn of the Privy Council.

[67] Whence Shakespeare derived the names of various evil spirits whom Edgar mentions in *King Lear*.

[68] I do not conceive that at the present time many, if any, Bishops of the Church of England would license exorcism. Certainly the more scientifically minded and modernistic Lords Spiritual of the Anglican bench have rid themselves of such an idle superstition. How they would explain Our Blessed Lord's words and actions I do not pretend to know, but I suppose that according to their wider knowledge Christ—*sit uenia uerbis*—was mistaken in this as in other particulars.

[69] *Colloquia Mensalia*, passim.

[70] It is difficult to see how the teachings of such a Protestant leader as Gaspar von Schwenckfeld (1489–90—1561) are anything save tantamount to mere personal morality and a vague individual pietism. A critical edition of his numerous works is in course of publication under the editorship of Hartranft, Schlutter, and Johnson: *Corpus Schwenckfeldianorum*, I, Leipzig, 1907.

[71] Parker's *Correspondence*, Parker Society, Cambridge, 1856, pp. 465–6.

[72] By vomiting pins and straws they had made many believe that they were bewitched, but the tricks were soon found out and they were compelled to public penance at S. Paul's. There is a black letter pamphlet *The discloysing of a late counterfeyted possession by the devyl in two maydens within the Citie of London* [1574], which describes this case. See also Holinshed, *Chronicles* (ed. London, 1808), IV, 325, and Stow *Annales*, London, 1631, p. 678. But the fact that there are malingerers does not mean there are none sick.

[73] *Marie Glover's late woefull case. . . . A defence of the truthe against D. J. his scandalous Impugnations*, British Museum, Sloane MSS., 831. Sinclar, *Satan's Invisible World Discovered*, Edinburgh, 1685, Relation XII quotes an account of Mary Glover from Lewis Hughes' *Certaine Grievances* (1641–2); and hence Burton, *The Kingdom of Darkness*, and Hutchinson, *Historical Essay concerning Witchcraft*, both assign a wrong date (1642) to the occurrence.

[74] Enlarged edition, 1720.

[75] *The Other World*, London, 1875, I, pp. 59–69. The incident is narrated by Fortescue Hitchins, *The History of Cornwall*, Helston, 1824, II, pp. 548–51; and also in fuller detail by the Rev. R. S. Hawker, *Footprints of Former Men in Far Cornwall*, London, 1870, who quotes from Ruddle's MS. Diary.

[76] Six miles north of S. Columb and three miles due south from Padstow.

[77] A full and documented account of these strange happenings may be found in *Lucifer, or the True Story of the Famous Diabolic Possession in Alsace*, London, 1922, with the Imprimatur of the Bishop of Brentwood. Compiled from original documents by the abbé Paul Sutter and translated by the Rev. Theophilus Borer.

[78] Jesus . . . comminatus est spiritui immundo, dicens illi: Surde et mute spiritus, Ego præcipio tibi, exi ab eo: et amplius ne introeas in eum. *Euan. sec. Marcum*. IX. 25.

[79] 1726–1755. This great Saint was then Venerable; he was beatified by Leo XIII, 29 January, 1893, and canonized by Pius X, 11 December, 1903. His feast is kept on 16 October.

[80] Peter Paul Stumpf succeeded Andreas Räss as Bishop of Strasburg, 1887–1890.

[81] *Une Possédée Contemporaine* (1834–1914). *Hélène Poirier de Coullons (Loiret)*. Paris, Téqui, 1924. An ample study, profusely documented, of 517 pages, edited by M. le Chanoine Champault of the diocese of Orleans.

[82] A partir de cette époque, la vie d'Hélène s'écoulera au milieu de souffrances physiques et morales si grandes, que dans sa bouche les plaintes de Job ne seraient point déplacées.

[83] Mr. G. R. S. Mead, however, in this connexion not impertinently recalls the "controlling" of members of the Shaker communities by what purported to be spirits of North American Indians. This was prior to 1848.

[84] Ses souffrances physiques et morales, commencées le 25 mars, 1850, se poursuivirent jusqu'à sa mort, 8 janvier, 1914, soit pendant soixante-quatre ans.

Toutefois les vexations diaboliques cessèrent vers la fin de 1897. Ces vexations durèrent donc près de quarante-sept années, dont six de possession.

[85] Du 25 mars, 1850, au courant de mars, 1868, Hélène *fut seulement obsédée.* Cette *obsession dùra donc* 18 *années.* Au bout de ce temps et pendant 13 *mois* elle fut *obsédée et possédée tout ensemble.*

De l'obsession et de la possession elle fut complètement délivrée par les exorcismes officiels, à Orléans, le 19 avril, 1869.

Suivirent quatre mois de tranquillité, jusqu'au recommencement volontaire et généreux de ses peines.

A la fin d'août, 1869, elle accepta de la main de Notre Seigneur les tourments d'une nouvelle obsession et possession afin d'obtenir la conversion du célèbre général Ducrot. La conversion obtenue, elle fut délivrée à Lourdes le 3 septembre, 1875, par les prières des 15,000 pèlerins qui s'y trouvaient réunis. *Obsession et possession renouvelées* avaient duré cinq ans.

Plus jamais, pendant les quarante ans qu'elle avait encore à vivre, elle ne fut possédée ; mais elle continua à être obsédée tantôt plus, tantôt moins. Les souffrances de toutes sortes, qu'elle endura alors, eurent pour but d'obtenir le salut et le triomphe du clergé.

Quant aux raisons et au but des premières persécutions diaboliques qu'elle subit pendant dix-neuf ans et dont elle fut délivrée par les exorcismes officiels, ils sont restés inconnus. *Une Possédée Contemporaine* (1834–1914), pp. 171–2.

[86] A fragment of the soutane of this most holy Pontiff was taken to Hélène and during one of her fits placed upon her forehead. At the contact she cried out : "Le Pape est un saint, oui un grand saint." (The Pope is a Saint, truly a great Saint !)

[87] Pour y être admis, il faut apporter une ou plusiers hosties consacrées, les remettre au démon qui, sous forme corporelle ou visible, préside l'assemblée. Il faut les profaner d'une manière horrible, adorer le démon lui-même et commettre avec lui et les autres sociétaires les actes d'impudicité les plus révoltants. Trois villes : Paris, Rome, et Tours sont les sièges de cette société infernale.

[88] La seconde possession fut plus terrible que la première. 1e : Par la durée ; la première fut de treize mois, la seconde de cinq ans. 2e : La première fut adoucie par de nombreuses consolations surnaturelles ; la seconde très peu. 3e : Les dévices abondèrent dans la première ; dans la seconde les avanies morales l'emportèrent de beaucoup sur les avanies physiques. *Une Possédée Contemporaine* (1834–1914), p. 405.

[89] *Spirit Possession,* Henry M. Hugunin, published in Sycamore, Ill., U.S.A.

[90] One should note the implication that science and faith are opposed. Dr. Wilfred T. Grenfell pointedly comments : "This question seems inept. To me the terms are not in antithesis, i.e. logical *v.* spiritual.

[91] Edited by Huntly Carter. Fisher Unwin, 1920.

[92] Whose contribution, *From Non-Religion to Religion,* opens with the following inepitude : "I think that the renewal of Spiritualism is mainly due to a real increase in our knowledge of psychical facts." This phrase could only have been written by one wholly ignorant of mystical theology, and, it would seem, of historical Christianity.

[93] *Spiritualism, Its Present-Day Meaning,* p. 258.

[94] *Idem,* p. 269.

[95] *Idem,* pp. 270-1.

[96] *Idem,* p. 245.

[97] *Idem,* p. 206.

[98] *Idem,* pp. 206–7.

[99] *Idem,* p. 205. The words are those of Father Bernard Vaughan.

[100] "Seventeen Elementary Facts concerning Spiritualism." *Light,* 21 February, 1925. Here we also have the frank avowal : "Modern Spiritualism is only a revival of phenomena and experiences that were well known in ancient times." It should be remarked that similar phenomena, believed to be a genuine case of haunting, occurred at the house of Mr. Samuel Wesley, at Epworth, Lincolnshire, in 1716, and attracted universal attention. It is

said that the knockings at the house of Parsons, Cock Lane, West Smithfield, in 1760, were proved to be fraud, but I do not know that the case has ever been candidly studied.

[101] She took part in a séance on 25 October, 1860, but this seems to have been exceptional.

[102] *Washington Daily Star*, 7 March, 1893, quoted in *The Medium and the Daybreak*, 7 April, 1893.

[103] In the "educational" primers prepared by certain spiritists for use by children the story of the Fox Sisters is told in glowing colours to a point, but the history of their downfall is suppressed.

[104] He died at Bedford, 5 September, 1892. His control was the spirit Imperator, who claimed to be the prophet Malachias. For a very full biography see Arthur Lillie's *Modern Mystics and Modern Magic*. London. 1894.

[105] For Mrs. Bassett see *The Medium*, 11 April and 18 April, 1873, pp. 174 and 182; for Miss Showers, *The Medium*, 8 May and 22 May, pp. 294 and 326.

[106] *Medium and Daybreak*, 15 November, 1878, p. 730.

[107] *L'Eclair*, 6 April, 1909.

[108] Dr. Grasset, *L'Occultisme*, pp. 56, *sqq.*; p. 424.

[109] *Procès des Spirites*, 8vo. Paris. 1875.

[110] *La Revue Spirite* and *L'Echo du Mentalisme*, Nov., 1908.

[111] Who apparently believes that Spiritism is authorized by the Scriptures, and that many of the prophets, nay, even Our Divine Lord Himself, were but mediums.

[112] *Light*. Saturday, 21 February, 1925, p. 89.

[113] Organized in 1882 for the scientific examination of "debatable phenomena."

[114] See the Report presented 11 May, 1922, and published by The Magic Circle, Anderton's Hotel, Fleet Street.

[115] *The Goligher Circle, May to August*, 1921. Experiences of E. E. Fournier d'Albe, D.SC. London, Watkins, 1922.

[116] *The Classification of Psychic Phenomena*, by W. Loftus Hare. *The Occult Review*, July, 1924, p. 38.

[117] Her real name appears to be Marthe Béraud. Professor Richet is satisfied that in his experiments with this medium at the Villa Carmen (Algiers) in 1905 genuine materialization was effected.

[118] Who, as noted above, specializes in the Ouija-Board and Automatic Writing.

[119] He has written such works as *The New Revelation*, and compiled *The Spiritualists' Reader*, "A Collection of Spirit Messages from many sources, specially prepared for Short Readings."

[120] In all of whose documents the distinction is clearly drawn between legitimate scientific investigation and superstitious abuses.

CHAPTER VII

THE WITCH IN DRAMATIC LITERATURE

THE English theatre, in common with every other form of the world's drama, had a religious, or even more exactly a liturgical, origin. At the Norman Conquest as the English monasteries began to be filled with cultured French scholars there is evidence that Latin dialogues, the legends of saints and martyrs, something after the fashion of Hrotsvitha's comedies, which we do not imagine to have been a unique phenomenon, found their way here also, and from recitation to the representation of these was an easy and indeed inevitable step. For it is almost impossible to declaim without appropriate action. From the very heart of the liturgy itself arose the Mystery Play.

The method of performing these early English guild plays has been frequently and exactly described, and I would only draw attention to one feature of the movable scaffold which passed from station to station, that is the dark cavern at the side of the last of the three sedes, Hell-mouth. No pains were spared to make this as horrible and realistic as might be. Demons with hideous heads issued from it, whilst ever and anon lurid flames burst forth and dismal cries were heard. Thus the Digby S. Mary Magdalen play has the stage-direction: "a stage, and Helle ondyrneth that stage." At Coventry the Cappers had a "hell-mouth" for the Harrowing of Hell, and the Weavers another for Doomsday. This was provided with fire, a windlass, and a barrel for the earth-quake. In the stage-directions to Jordan's Cornish Creation of the World Lucifer descends to hell "apareled fowle wth fyre about hem" and the place is filled with "every degre of devylls of lether and spirytis on cordis." Among the "establies" required for the Rouen play of 1474 was "Enfer fait en maniere d'une grande gueulle se cloant et ouvrant quant besoing en est." The last stage-direction of the

Sponsus, a liturgical play from Limoges,—assigned by M. M. W. Cloetta and G. Paris to the earlier half of the twelfth century—which deals with the Wise and Foolish Virgins runs as follows: "*Modo accipiant eas [fatuas uirgines] dæmones et præcipitentur in infernum.*"

The Devil himself is one of the most prominent characters in the Mystery, the villain of the piece. So the York cycle commences with *The Creation and the Fall of Lucifer.* Whilst the Angels are singing "Holy, Holy, Holy" before the throne of God, Satan appears exulting in his pride to be cast down speedily into hell whence he howls his complaint beginning "Owte, owte! harrowe!" There is a curious incident in the episode of the Dream of Pilate's wife. Whilst she sleeps Satan whispers in her ear the vision which moves her to try to stay the condemnation of Jesus whereby mankind is to be redeemed. The last play of the York cycle is the *Day of Judgement.*

In like manner the Towneley cycle opens with *The Creation*, and presently we have the stage-direction *hic deus recedit à suo solio & lucifer sedebit in eodem solio.* The scene soon shifts to hell when we hear the demons reproaching Lucifer for his pride. After the creation of Adam and Eve follows Lucifer's lament. In the long episode of *Doomsday* a number of demons appear and are kept inordinately busy.

The Devil was represented as black, with goat's horns, ass's ears, cloven hoofs, and an immense phallus. He is, in fact, the Satyr of the old Dionysiac processions, a nature-spirit, the essence of joyous freedom and unrestrained delight, shameless if you will, for the old Greek knew not shame. He is the figure who danced light-heartedly across the Aristophanaic stage, stark nude in broad midday,[1] animally physical, exuberant, ecstatic, crying aloud the primitive refrain, Φαλῆς, ἑταῖρε Βακχίου, ξύγκωμε, νυκτεροπλάνητε, μοιχέ, παιδεραστά, (Phales, boon mate of Bacchus, joyous comrade in the dance, wanton wanderer o' nights, fornicating Phales), in a word he was Paganism incarnate, and Paganism was the Christian's deadliest foe; so they took him, the Bacchic reveller, they smutted him from horn to hoof, and he remained the Christian's deadliest foe, the Devil.[2]

It was long before the phallic demon was banished the stage, for strange as it may seem, positive evidence exists that he was known there as late as Shakespeare's day. In 1620 was published in London by Edward Wright *A Courtly Masque: The Deuice called, The World tost at Tennis.* "As it hath beene diuers times Presented to the Contentment of many Noble and Worthy Spectators: By the Prince his Seruants." It was "Inuented and set downe by Tho: Middleton, Gent. and William Rowley, Gent." The title-page presents a rough engraving of the various characters in this masque, doubtless from a sketch made at the actual performance. Outside the main group stands a hideous black figure "The Diuele," who made his appearance towards the end to take part in the last dance, furnished with horns, hoofs, talons, tail, and a monstrous phallus. It may be remarked that these horns are prominent on the goat-like head (a clear satyr) of the Devil in *Doctor Faustus* as depicted on the title-page of the Marlovian quarto. A phallus, to which reference is made in the text, was also worn by the character dressed up as the monkey (*Bavian*) in the May-dance scene in Shakespeare & Fletcher's *The Two Noble Kinsman*, Act III, 5, 1613. It is worth remembering that troops of phallic demons formed a standing characteristic of the old German carnival comedy. Moreover, several of the grotesque types of the Commedia dell' arte in the second decade of the seventeenth century were traditionally equipped in like manner.[3] That the Devil was so represented in the English theatre is important. It gives us the popular idea of the Prince of Evil, and incidentally throws a side-light upon much of the grotesque and obscene evidence in the contemporary witch-trials.

In Skelton's lost *Nigramansir* one of the stage directions is stated to have been "Enter Balsebub with a beard," no doubt the black vizard with an immense goatish beard familiar to the old religious drama. Presumably the chief use of the Necromancer, who gives his name to this play, was indeed but to speak the Prologue which summons the Devil who buffets and kicks him for his pains. However, we only know the play from Warton, who describes it as having been shown him by William Collins, the poet, at Chichester, about 1759. He says: "It is the Nigramansir, a morall *Enterlude* and a pithie, written by Maister Skelton laureate, and plaid before the King and other estatys at Woodstoke on Palme Sunday. It was printed by Wynkyn de Worde in a thin quarto, in the year 1504. It must have been presented before Henry VII, at the royal manor or palace at Woodstock in Oxfordshire, now destroyed. The characters are a Necromancer or conjurer, the devil, a notary public, Simony, and Philargyria or Avarice. It is partly a satire on some abuses in the Church. . . . The story, or plot, is the trial of Simony and Avarice." Beyond what Warton tells us nothing further is known of the play. Ritson, *Bibliographia Poetica*, 106, declared : " it is utterly incredible that the *Nigramansir* . . . ever existed." It has been shown, too, that Warton as a literary historian is not infrequently suspect, and E. G. Duff, *Hand Lists of English Printers*, can trace no extant copy of this " morall *Enterlude*."

In the English moralities the Devil plays an important part, and, as in their French originals or analogues, he is consistently hampering and opposing the moral purpose or lesson which the action of these compositions is designed to enforce. In the later English plays also which evolved with added regularity from these interludes the Devil is always a popular character. He is generally attended by the Vice, who although in some sort a serving-man or jester in the fiend's employ, devotes his time to twitting, teazing, tormenting, and thwarting his master for the edification, not unmixed with fun, of the audience. In *The Castell of Perseverance* Lucifer appears shouting in good old fashion " Out herowe I rore," just as he was wont to announce himself in the Mysteries, and he is wearing his " devil's array " over the habit of a " prowde galaunt." Wever's *Lusty Juventus* has unmistakable traces of the slime of the evil days of Edward VI, in whose reign it was written, and when the Devil calls Hipocrisy to his aid we are prepared for a flood of empty but bitter abuse which embodies the sour Puritan hatred against the Catholic Church, and towards the end, under the misnomer God's Merciful Promises, we are not surprised to meet a tiresome old gentleman who cantingly expounds the doctrine of Justification by Faith.

In the interlude to which Collier has assigned the name *Mankind* Mischief summons to her aid the fiend Titivillus, who had appeared in the *Judicium* of the Towneley Mysteries. Once the Devil's registrar and tollsman, he is best known as

"Master Lollard." According to a silly old superstition Titivillus was an imp whose business it was to pick up the words any priest might drop and omit whilst saying Mass.

When we pass to the beginnings of the regular drama we find an extremely interesting play that introduces, if not magic, at least fortune-telling, John Lyly's "Pleasant Conceited Comedie" *Mother Bombie*, acted by the children of Paul's and first printed in 1594. Although the plot is of the utmost complexity and artificiality it does not seem to be derived, as are most of Lyly's stories, from any classical or pseudo-classical source, whilst the cunning old woman of Rochester, who supplies the title, has in fact little to say or do, except that her intervention helps to bring about the unravelling of a perfect maze and criss-cross of incidents. When Selena addresses the beldame with "They say, you are a witch," Mother Bombie quickly retorts "They lie, I am a cunning woman," a passage not without significance.

Upon a very different level from Lyly's play stands Marlowe's magnificent drama *The Tragical History of Dr. Faustus*. The legend of a man who sells his soul to the Devil for infinite knowledge and absolute power seems to have crystallized about the sixth century, when the story of *Theophilus* was supposed to have been related in Greek by his pupil Eutychianus. Of course, every warlock had bartered his soul to Satan, and throughout the whole of the Middle Ages judicial records, the courts of the Inquisition, to say nothing of popular knowledge, could have told of a thousand such. But this particular legend seems to have captured the imagination of both Western and Eastern Christendom; it is met with in a variety of forms; it was introduced into the collections of Jacopo à Voragine; it found its way into the minstrel repertory through Rutebeuf, a French *trouvère* of the thirteenth century; it reappeared in early English narrative and in Low-German drama. Icelandic variants of the story have been traced. It was made the subject of a poem by William Forrest, priest and poet, in 1572; and it also formed the material for two seventeenth-century Jesuit "comedies."

That the original Faust was a real personage,[4] a wandering conjurer and medical quack, who was well known in the south-west of the German Empire, as well as in Thuringia,

Saxony, and the adjoining countries somewhere between the years 1510–1540, does not now admit of any serious doubt. Philip Begardi, a physician of Worms, author of an *Index Sanitatis* (1539), mentions this charlatan, many of whose dupes he personally knew. He says that Faust was at one time frequently seen, although of later years nothing had been heard of him. It has indeed been suggested the whole legend originated in the strange history of Pope S. Clement I and his father Faustus, or Faustinianus, as related in the *Recognitions*, which were immensely popular throughout the Middle Ages. But Melanchthon knew a Johannes Faustus born at Knütlingen, in Wurtemberg, not far from his own home, who studied magic at Cracow, and afterwards "roamed about and talked of secret things." There was a doctor Faustus in the early part of the sixteenth century, a friend of Paracelsus and Cornelius Agrippa, a scholar who won an infamous reputation for the practice of necromancy. In 1513 Conrad Mutt, the Humanist, came across a vagabond magician at Erfurt named Georgius Faustus Hermitheus of Heidelberg. Trithemius in 1506, met a Faustus junior whose boast it was that if all the works of Plato and Aristotle were burned he could restore them from memory. It seems probable that it was to the Dr. Faustus, the companion of Paracelsus and Cornelius[5] Agrippa, that the legend became finally and definitely attached. The first literary version of the story was the *Volksbuch*, which was published by Johann Spies in 1587, at Frankfort-on-the-Main, who tells us that he obtained the manuscript "from a good friend at Spier," and it soon afterwards appeared in England as *The History of the Damnable Life and Deserved Death of Dr. John Faustus*, a chap-book to which Marlowe mainly adhered for the incidents in his play. The tragedy was carried across to Germany by the English actors who visited that country in the last years of the sixteenth and the earlier part of the seventeenth century, and thus, while it was itself derived from a German source, it greatly influenced, if it did not actually give rise to, the treatment of the same theme by the German popular drama and puppet-play. These were seldom printed, and usually for the most part extemporized, keeping all the while more or less closely to the theme. Scheible in his *Kloster* (1847), Volume V, gives the excellent Ulm piece, and there are marionette versions edited by W. Hamm (1850; English translation by T. C. H. Hedderwick, 1887), O. Schade (1856), K. Engel (1874), Bielschowsky (1882), and Kralik and Winter (1885).

Lessing projected two presentations of the story, and Klinger worked the subject into a romance, *Fausts Leben, Thaten, und Höllenfahrt* (1791; translated into English by George Barrow in 1826). A bombast tragedy was published by Klingemann in 1815, whilst Lenau issued his epico-dramatic *Faust* in 1836. Heine's ballet *Der Doctor Faust, ein Tanzpoem* appeared in 1851. The libretto for Spohr's opera (1814) was written by Bernard.

Goethe's masterpiece, planned as early as 1774, was given to the world in 1808, but the second part was delayed until 1831.

General evidence points to 1588 as the date of the first production of Marlowe's *Doctor Faustus*, for it seems certain that the ballad of the *Life and Death of Doctor Faustus the great Conjurer*, entered in the Stationers' Register, February, 1589, did not precede but was suggested by the drama. The first extant quarto is 1604, but already it had been subjected to more than one revision. Upon the stage *Doctor Faustus* long remained popular, and in England, at least, however fragmentary Marlowe's tragedy may be it has never been supplemented by any other literary handling of its theme. Old Prynne in his *Histriomastix* (1633) retails an absurd story to the effect that the Devil *in propria persona* "appeared on the stage at the *Belsavage* Playhouse in Queen *Elizabeth's* days" whilst the tragedy was being performed, "the truth of which I have heard from many now alive who well remember it." It was revived after the Restoration, and on Monday, 26 May, 1662, Pepys and his wife witnessed the production at the Red Bull, "but so wretchedly and poorly done that we were sick of it." It was being performed at the Theatre Royal in the autumn of 1675, but no details are recorded. In 1685–6 at Dorset Garden appeared William Mountfort's *The Life and Death of Doctor Faustus, Made into a Farce, with the Humours of Harlequin and Scaramouch*, a queer mixture of Marlowe's scenes with the Italian *commedia dell' arte*. Harlequin was acted by nimble Thomas Jevon, the first English harlequin, and Scaramouch by Antony Leigh, the most whimsical of comedians. At the end of the third act after Faustus has been carried away by Lucifer and Mephistopheles, his body is discovered torn in pieces. Then "Faustus *Limbs come together. A Dance and Song.*" This farce was continually revived with great applause, and during the whole of the eighteenth century Faust was the central figure of pantomime after pantomime. Nearly forty dramatic versions of the Faust legend might be enumerated. Many are wildly romantic and were especially beloved of the minor theatres: such are *Faustus* by G. Soane and D. Terry, produced at Drury Lane 16 May, 1825, with "O" Smith as Mephistopheles; H. P. Grattan's *Faust, or The Demon of the Drachenfels* performed at Sadlers Wells, 5 September, 1842, with Henry Marston, Mephistopheles, T. Lyon, Faust, "the Magician of Wittenberg," Caroline Rankley, Marguerite; T. W. Robertson's *Faust and Marguerite*, played at the Princess's Theatre in April, 1854: some are operatic; the ever-popular *Faust* of Gounod, with libretto by Barbier and Carré, first seen at the Théâtre Lyrique, Paris, in 1859; and Hector Berlioz' *The Damnation of Faust*, which, adapted to the English stage by T. H. Friend, was performed at the Court, Liverpool, 3 February, 1894; many more are burlesques, descendants of the eighteenth-century farces, amongst which may be remembered F. C. Burnard's *Faust and Marguerite*, S. James, 9 July, 1864; C. H. Hazlewood's *Faust: or Marguerite's Mangle*, Britannia Theatre, 25 March, 1867; Byron's *Little Doctor Faust* (1877); *Faust in Three Flashes* (1884); *Faust in Forty Minutes* (1885); and the most famous of all the travesties *Faust Up to Date*, produced at the Gaiety, 30 October, 1888, with E. J. Lonnen as Mephistopheles and Florence St. John as Marguerite. In France the *Faust*—après Goethe—of Theaulou and Gondelier first seen at the Nouveautés, 27 October, 1827, had a great success, and in the following year no less than three pens, Antony Béraud, Charles Nodier, and Merle, combined to produce a *Faust* in three acts, the music of which is by Louis Alexandre Piccini, the grandson of Gluck's famous rival. In 1858 Adolphe Dennery gave the Parisian stage *Faust*, a "drame fantastique" in five acts and sixteen tableaux, a drama of the Grattan school, effective enough in a lurid Sadlers Wells way, which is, at any rate, a vein greater dramatists have exploited with profit and applause.

Of more recent English dramas which have the Faust legend as their theme the most striking is undoubtedly the adaptation by W. G. Wills from the first part of Goethe's tragedy, which was produced at the Lyceum 19 December, 1885, with H. H. Conway as Faust; George Alexander, Valentine; Mrs. Stirling, Martha; Miss Ellen Terry, Margaret; and Henry Irving, Mephistopheles. Not merely in view of the masterpieces of Marlowe and Goethe, but even by the side of theatrical versions of the legend from far lesser men the play itself was naught, a superb pantomime, a thing helped out by a witches' kitchen, by a bacchanalia of demons, by chromo-lithographic effects, by the mechanist and the brushes of Telbin and Hawes Craven, but it was informed throughout and raised to heights of greatness, nay, even to awe and terror, by the genius of Irving as the red-plumed Mephistopheles, that sardonic, weary, restless figure, horribly unreal yet mockingly alert and alive, who dominated the whole.

To attempt a comparison between Marlowe and Goethe were not a little absurd, and it is superfluous to expatiate upon the supreme merits of either masterpiece. In Goethe's mighty and complex work the story is in truth refined away beneath a wealth of immortal philosophy. Marlowe adheres quite simply to the chap-book incidents, and yet in all profane literature I scarcely know words of more shuddering dread and complete agony than Faust's last great speech:

> Ah, Faustus,
> Now hast thou but one bare hour to live.
> And then thou must be damned perpetually!

The scene becomes intolerable. It is almost too painful to be read, too overcharged with hopeless darkness and despair.

As it is in some sense at least akin to the Faust story it may not be impertinent briefly to mention here an early Dutch secular drama, which has been called "one of the gems of Dutch mediæval literature," *A Marvellous History of Mary of Nimmegen, who for more than seven years lived and had ado with the Devil,*[6] printed by William Vorsterman of Antwerp about 1520. It is only necessary to call attention to a few features of the legend. Mary, the niece of the old priest Sir Gysbucht, one night meets the Devil in the shape of *Moonen with the single eye.* He undertakes to teach her all the secrets of necromancy if she will but refrain from crossing herself and change her name to Lena of Gretchen. But Mary, who has had a devotion to our Lady, insists upon retaining at least the M in her new nomenclature, and so becomes Emmekin. "Thus Emma and Moonen lived at Antwerp at the sign of the Golden Tree in the market, where daily of his contrivings were many murders and slayings together with every sort of wickedness." Emma then resolves to visit her uncle, and insists upon Moonen accompanying her to Nimmegen. It is a high holiday and she sees by chance the mystery of *Maskeroon* on a pageant-waggon in a public square. Our Lady is pleading before the throne of God for mankind, and Emma is filled with strange remorse to hear such blessed words. Moonen carries her off, but she falls and is found in a swoon by the old priest, her uncle. No priest of Nimmegen dared shrive her, not even the Bishop of Cologne, and so she journeyed to Rome, where the Holy Father heard her confession and bade her wear in penitence three strong bands of iron fastened upon neck and arms. Thus she returned to Maestricht to the cloister of the Converted Sinners, and there her sorrow was so prevailing and her humility so unfeigned that an Angel in token of Divine forgiveness removed the irons as she slept.

> And go ye to Maestricht, an ye be able
> And in the Converted Sinners shall ye see
> The grave of Emma, and there all three
> The rings be hung above her grave.[7]

Magic and fairy-land loom large in the plays of Robert Greene, whose place in English literature rests at least as much upon his prose-tracts as on his dramas. It seems to me fairly obvious that *The Honourable History of Friar Bacon and Friar Bungay*, which almost certainly dates from 1589, although the first quarto is 1594, was composed owing to the success of Marlowe's *Doctor Faustus.* Greene was not the man to lose an opportunity of exploiting fashion, and with his solid British bent I have no doubt he considered an old English tale of an Oxford magician would be just as effective as imported legends from Frankfort and Wittenberg. To say that the later play is on an entirely different level is not to deny it interest and considerable charm. But in spite of Bacon's avowal

> Thou know'st that I have divèd into hell
> And sought the darkest palaces of fiends;
> That with my magic spells great Belcephon,
> Hath left his lodge and kneeled at my cell,

his sorceries are in lighter vein than those of Faustus; moreover neither his arts nor the magic of Friar Bungay form the essential theme of the play, which also sketches the love of Edward, Prince of Wales (afterwards Edward I) for Margaret, "the fair Maid of Fressingfield." It is true Bacon conjures up spirits enough, and we are shown his study at Brasenose with the episode of the Brazen Head. It may be noted that Miles, Bacon's servant, is exactly the Vice of the Moralities, and at the end he rides off farcically enough on the Devil's back, whilst Bacon announces his intention of spending the remainder of his years in becoming penitence for his necromancy and magic.

In Greene's *Orlando Furioso*, 4to, 1594, which is based on Ariosto, canto XXIII, we meet Melissa, an enchantress: and in *Alphonsus, King of Arragon*, 4to, 1599, which is directly imitative of *Tamburlaine*, a sibyl with the classical name Medea, conjures up Calehas "in a white surplice and cardinal's mitre," and here we also have a Brazen Head through which Mahomet speaks. A far more interesting play is *A Looking Glasse for London and England*, 4to, 1594, an elaborated Mystery upon the history of the prophet Jonah and the repentance of Nineveh. Among the characters are a Good Angel, an Evil Angel, and "one clad in Devil's attire," who is soundly drubbed by Adam the buffoon. In 1598 was published, "As it hath bene sundrie times publikely plaide," *The Scottish Historie of Iames the fourth, slaine at Flodden. Entermixed with a pleasant Comedie, presented by Oboram, King of Fayeries.* But the fairies only appear in a species of prose prologue, and in brief interludes between the acts.

George Peele's charming piece of folk-lore *The Old Wives' Tale* introduces among its quaint commixture of episodes the warlock Sacripant, son of a famous witch Meroe,[8] who has stolen away and keeps under a spell the princess Delia. His power depends upon a light placed in a magic glass which can only be broken under certain conditions. Eventually Sacripant is overcome by the aid of a friendly ghost, Jack, the glass broken, the light extinguished, and the lady restored to her lover and friends.

Other magicians who appear in various dramas of the days of Elizabeth and her immediate successors are Brian Sansfoy in the primitive *Sir Clyomon and Sir Clamydes*, 4to, 1599; the Magician in *The Wars of Cyrus;* Friar Bacon, Friar Bungay, and Jaques Vandermast in Greene's *Friar Bacon and Friar Bungay*, Merlin and Proximus in the pseudo-Shakespearean *The Birth of Merlin*, where the Devil also figures; Ormandini and Argalio in *The Seven Champions of Christendom*, where we likewise have Calib, a witch, her incubus Tarpax, and Suckabus their clownish son; Comus in Milton's masque; Mago the conjurer with his three familiars Eo, Meo, and Areo in Cokain's *Trappolin Creduto Principe, Trappolin suppos'd a Prince*, 4to, 1656, excellent light fare, which Nahum Tate turned into *A Duke and No Duke* and produced at Drury Lane in November, 1684, and which in one form or another, sometimes "a comic melodramatic burletta," sometimes a ballad opera, sometimes a farce, was popular until the early decades of the nineteenth century.

Seeing that actors are "the abstracts and brief chronicles of the time," it is not surprising to find that Witchcraft has a very important part in the theatre of Shakespeare. Setting aside such a purely fairy fantasy as *A Midsummer-Night's Dream*, such figures as the "threadbare juggler" Pinch in *The Comedy of Errors*, such scenes as the hobgoblin mask beneath Herne's haunted oak, such references as that to Mother Prat, the old woman of Brainford, who worked "by charms, by spells, by the figure," or the vile abuse by Richard, Duke of Gloucester, of "Edward's wife, that monstrous witch, Consorted with that harlot strumpet Shore," we have one historical drama *King Henry VI*, Part II, in which an incantation scene plays no small part; we have one romantic comedy *The Tempest*, one tragedy *Macbeth*, the very motives and development of which are due to magic and supernatural charms. It must perhaps be remarked that *King Henry VI*, Part I, is defiled by the obscene caricature of S. Joan of Arc, surely the most foul and abominable irreverence that shames English literature. It is too loathsome for words, and I would only point out the enumeration in one scene where various familiars are introduced of the most revolting details of contemporary witch-trials, but to think of such horrors in connexion with S. Joan revolts and sickens the imagination.

In *King Henry VI* (Part II) the Duchess of Gloucester employs John Hume and John Southwell, two priests; Bolingbroke, a conjurer; and Margery Jourdemain, a witch, to raise a spirit who shall reveal the several destinies of the King, and the Dukes of Suffolk and Somerset. The scene is written with extraordinary power and has not a little of awe and terror. Just as the demon is dismissed 'mid thunder and lightning the Duke of York with his guards rush in and arrest the sorcerers. Later the two priests and Bolingbroke are condemned to the gallows, the witch in Smithfield is "burn'd to ashes," whilst the Duchess of Gloucester after three days' public penance is banished for life to the Isle of Man.

The incidents as employed by Shakespeare are fairly correct. It is certain that the Duchess of Gloucester, an ambitious and licentious woman, called to her counsels Margery Jourdemain, commonly known as the Witch of Eye, Roger Bolingbroke an astrologer, Thomas Southwell, Canon of S. Stephen's, a priest named Sir John Hume or Hun, and a certain William Wodham. These persons frequently met in secret, and it was discovered that they had fashioned according to the usual mode a wax image of the King which they melted before a slow fire. Bolingbroke confessed, and Hume also turned informer; and in 1441 Bolingbroke was placed on a high scaffold before Paul's Cross together with a chair curiously carved and painted, found at his lodging, which was supposed to be an instrument of necromancy, and in the presence of Cardinal Beaufort of Winchester, Henry Chicheley, Archbishop of Canterbury, and an imposing array of bishops, he was compelled to make abjuration of his wicked arts. The Duchess of Gloucester, being refused sanctuary at Westminster, was arrested and confined in Leeds Castle, near Maidstone. She was brought to trial with her accomplices in October, when sentence was passed upon her as has been related above. Margery Jourdemain perished at the stake as a witch and relapsed heretic; Thomas Southwell died in prison; and Bolingbroke was hanged at Tyburn, 18 November.

In *The Tempest* Prospero is a philosopher rather than a wizard, and Ariel is a fairy not a familiar. The magic of Prospero is of the intellect, and throughout, Shakespeare is careful to insist upon a certain detachment from human passions and ambitions. His love for Miranda, indeed, is exquisitely portrayed, and once—at the base ingratitude of Caliban—his anger flashes forth, but none the less, albeit superintending the fortunes of those over whom he watches tenderly, and utterly abhorring the thought of revenge, he seems to stand apart like Providence divinely guiding the events to the desired issue of reconciliation and forgiveness. Even so, the situation was delicate to place before an Elizabethan audience, and how nobly and with what art does Shakespeare touch upon Prospero's "rough magic"! In Sycorax we recognize the typical witch, wholly evil, vile, malignant, terrible for mischief, the consort and mistress of devils.

There are few scenes which have so caught the world's fancy as the wild overture to *Macbeth*. In storm and wilderness we are suddenly brought face to face with three mysterious phantasms that ride on the wind and mingle with the mist in thunder, lightning, and in rain. They are not agents of evil, they are evil; nameless, spectral, wholly horrible. And then, after the briefest of intervals, they reappear to relate such exploits as killing swine and begging chestnuts from a sailor's wife, to brag of having secured such talismans as the thumb of a drowned pilot, businesses proper to Mother Demdike or Anne Bishop of Wincanton, Somerset. Can this change have been intentional? I think not, and its very violence and quickness are jarring to a degree. The meeting with Hecate, who is angry, and scolds them "beldames as you are, Saucy and overbold" does not mend matters, and in spite of the horror when the apparitions are evoked, the ingredients of the cauldron, however noisome and hideous, are too material for "A deed without a name." There is a weakness here, and it says much for the genius of the tragedy that this weakness is not obtrusively felt.

Nevertheless it was upon this that the actors seized when for theatrical effect the incantation scenes had to be "written up" by the interpolation of fresh matter. Davenant also in his frankly operatic version of *Macbeth*, produced at Dorset Garden in February, 1672–3 elaborated the witch scenes to an incredible extent, although by ample conveyance from Middleton's *The Witch* together with songs and dances he was merely following theatrical tradition.[9]

There seems no reasonable doubt that *The Witch* is a later play than *Macbeth*, but it is only fair to say that the date of *The Witch* is unknown—it was first printed in 1778 from a manuscript now in the Bodleian—and the date of *Macbeth* (earlier than 1610, probably 1606) is not demonstrably certain. *The Witch* is a good but not a distinguished play. Owing to the incantation scenes and its connexion with *Macbeth* it has acquired an accidental interest, and an enduring reputation. The witches themselves, Hecate and her crew, stand midway between the mystic Norns of the first scene in *Macbeth*, and the miserable hag of Dekker in *The Witch of Edmonton;* they are just a little below the Witches in *Macbeth* as they appear after the opening lines. There is a ghastly fantasy in their revels which is not lessened by the material grossness of Firestone the clown, Hecate's son. They raise "jars, jealousies, strifes, and heart-burning disagreements, like a thick scurf o'er life," and although their figures are often grotesque their power for evil is not to be despised. Much of their jargon, their charms and gaucheries complete, are taken word for word from Reginald Scott's *Discoverie of Witchcraft*, London, 1584.

The village witch, as she appeared to her contemporaries, a filthy old doting crone, hunch-backed, ignorant, malevolent, hateful to God and man, is shown with photographic detail in *The Witch of Edmonton; A known True Story* by Rowley, Dekker, and Ford, produced at the Cockpit in Drury Lane during the autumn or winter of 1621. It seems to have been very popular at the time, and not only was it applauded in the public theatre, but it was presented before King James at Court. It did not, however, find its way into print until as late as 1658.

The trial and execution (19 April, 1621) of Elizabeth Sawyer attracted a considerable amount of attention.

Remarkable numbers of ballads and doggerel songs were made upon the event, detailing her enchantments, how she had blighted standing corn, how a ferret and an owl constantly attended her, and of many demons and familiars who companied with her in the prison. Not only were these ditties trolled out the day of the execution but many were published as broadsides, and sold widely. Accordingly the Newgate Ordinary hastened to pen *The Wonderfull Discoverie of Elizabeth Sawyer, a Witch, Late of Edmonton, Her Conviction, and Condemnation, and Death, Together with the Relation of the Divels Accesse to Her, and Their Conference Together*, " Written by Henry Goodcole, Minister of the Word of God, and her Continual Visiter in the Gaole of Newgate," Published by Authority, 4to, 1621. This tractate is in the form of a dialogue, question and answer, between Goodcole and the prisoner, who makes ample confession of her crimes.

In some ways *The Witch of Edmonton* is the most interesting and valuable of the witch dramas, because here we have the hag stripped of the least vestige of glamour and romance presented to us in the starkest realism. We see her dwelling apart in a wretched hovel, " shunned and hated like a sickness," miserably poor, buckl'd and bent together, dragging her palsied limbs wearily through the fields, as she clutches her dirty rags round her withered frame. And if she but dare to gather a few dried sticks in a corner she is driven from the spot with hard words and blows. What wonder her mouth is full of cursing and revenge ?

'Tis all one
To be a witch as to be counted one.

Then appears the Black Dog and seals a contract with her blood. She blights the corn and sends a murrain on the cattle of her persecutors ; here a horse has the glanders, there a sow casts her farrow ; the maid churns butter nine hours and it will not come ; above all a farmer's wife, whom she hates, goes mad and dies in frantic agony ; mischief and evil run riot through the town. But presently her familiar deserts her, she falls into the hands of human justice, and after due trial is dragged to Tyburn shrieking and crying out in hideous despair. It is a sordid and a terrible, but one cannot doubt, a true picture.

It is obvious that in this drama[10] Frank Thorney, a most

subtle and minute study of weakness and degeneracy, is wholly Ford's. Frank Thorney may be closely paralleled with Giovanni in *'Tis Pity She's a Whore.* Winnifride, too, has all the sentimental charm of Ford's heroines, Annabella and Penthea.

Carter is unmistakably the creation of Dekker. Simon Eyre and Orlando Friscobaldo are the same hearty, bluff, hospitable, essentially honest old fellows. To Dekker also I would assign Mother Sawyer herself.

Rowley's hand is especially discernible in the scenes where Cuddy Banks and the clowns make their appearance.

It may be mentioned that Elizabeth Sawyer figures in Caulfield's *Portraits, Memoirs, and Characters of Remarkable Persons*, 1794; and she is also referred to in Robinson's *History and Antiquities of the Parish of Edmonton* with a woodcut " from a rare print in the collection of W. Beckford, esq."

A second drama which was also actually founded upon a contemporary trial is Heywood and Brome's *The Late Lancashire Witches*, " A Well Received Comedy " produced at the Globe in 1634.[11] In the previous year, 1633, a number of trials for Witchcraft had drawn the attention of all England to Pendle Forest. A boy, by name Edmund Robinson, eleven years of age, who dwelt here with his father, a poor wood-cutter, told a long and detailed story which led to numerous arrests throughout the district. Upon All Saints' Day when gathering " bulloes " in a field he saw two greyhounds, one black, the other brown, each wearing a collar of gold. They fawned upon him, and immediately a hare rose quite near at hand. But the dogs refused to course, whereupon he beat them with a little switch, and the black greyhound started up in the shape of an old woman whom he recognized as Mother Dickenson, a notorious witch, and the other as a little boy whom he did not know. The beldame offered him money, either to buy his silence or as the price of his soul, but he refused. Whereupon taking something like a Bridle " that gingled " from her pocket she threw it over the little boy's head and he became a white horse. Seizing young Robinson in her arms they mounted and were conveyed with the utmost speed to a large house where had assembled some sixty other persons. A bright fire was burning on the hearth with roast meat before it. He was invited to partake of "Flesh and Bread upon a Trencher and Drink in a Glass," which he tasted, but at once rejected. He was next led into an adjoining barn where seven old women were pulling at seven halters that hung from the roof. As they tugged large pieces of meat, butter in lumps, loaves of bread, black puddings, milk, and all manner of rustic dainties fell down into large basins which were placed under the ropes. When the seven hags were tired their places were taken by seven others. But as they were engaged at their extraordinary task their faces seemed so fiendish and their glances were so evil that Robinson took to his heels. He was instantly pursued, and he saw that the foremost of his enemies was a certain Mother Lloynd. But luckily for himself two horsemen, travellers, came up, whereupon the witches vanished. A little later when he was sent in the evening to fetch home two kine, a boy met him in the dusk and fought him, bruising him badly. Looking down he saw that his opponent had a cloven foot, whereupon he ran away, only to meet Mother Lloynd with a lantern in her hand. She drove him back and he was again mauled by the cloven-footed boy.[12]

Such was the story told to the justices and corroborated by Robinson's father. A reign of terror ensued. Mother Dickenson and Mother Lloynd were at once thrown into jail, and in the next few days more than eighteen persons were arrested. The informer and his father netted a good sum by going round from church to church to point out in the congregations persons whom he recognized as having been in the house and barn to which he was led. A little quiet blackmail of the wealthier county families, threats to disclose the presence of various individuals at the witches' feast, brought in several hundreds of pounds.

The trial took place at Lancaster Assizes and seventeen of the accused were incontinently found guilty. But the judge, completely dissatisfied with so fantastic a story, obtained a reprieve. Four of the prisoners were sent up to London, where they were examined by the Court physicians. King Charles himself also questioned one of these poor wretches and, discerning that the whole history was a fraud, forthwith pardoned all who had been involved. Meantime

Dr. John Bridgeman, the Bishop of Chester, had also been holding a special inquiry into the case. Young Robinson was lodged separately, being allowed to hold no communication with his relatives, and when closely interrogated he gave way and confessed that the scare from beginning to end had been manœuvred by his father, who carefully coached him in his lies. In spite of this fiasco the talk did not die down immediately, and there were many who continued to maintain that Mother Dickenson was indeed a witch, however false the evidence on this occasion might be. It must be remembered, moreover, that twenty-two years before, in the very same district, a coven of thirteen witches, of whom the chief was Elizabeth Demdike, had been brought to justice, " at the Assizes and Generall Gaole-Delivery, holden at Lancaster, before Sir Edward Bromley and Sir James Eltham." Old Demdike herself—she was blind and over eighty years of age—died in prison, but ten of the accused were executed, and the trial, which lasted two days, occasioned a tremendous stir.

It seems not at all improbable that Heywood had written a topical play in 1612 dealing with this first sensational prosecution, and that when practically the same events repeated themselves in the same place less than a quarter of a century after he and the ever-ready Brome fashioned anew the old scenes. In the character of the honourable country-gentleman Master Generous, whose wife is discovered to be guilty of Witchcraft, there is something truly noble, and his tender forgiveness of her crime when she repents is touched with the loving pathos that informs *A Woman Kilde with Kindnesse*, whilst his agony at her subsequent relapse is very real, although Heywood has wisely refrained from any attempt to show a broken heart save by a few quite simple but poignant words. The play as a whole is a faithful picture of country life, homely enough, yet not without a certain winsome beauty. The comic episodes are sufficiently broad in their humour ; we have a household turned topsy-turvy by enchantment, a wedding-breakfast bewitched : the kitchen invaded by snakes, bats, frogs, beetles, and hornets, whilst to cap all the unfortunate bridegroom is rendered impotent. In Act II we have the incident of a Boy with a switch (young Edmund Robinson) and the two greyhounds.

Gammer Dickison carries him off against his will "to a brave feast," where we see the witches pulling ropes for food:

> Pul for the poultry, foule and fish,
> For emptie shall not be a dish.

In Act V the Boy tells Doughty the story of his encounter with the Devil: "He came to thee like a boy, thou sayest, about thine owne bisnesse?" they ask him, and the whole scene meticulously follows the detailed evidence given before the judge at Lancaster. Of the witches, Goody Dickison, Mal Spencer, Mother Hargrave, Granny Johnson, Meg, Mawd, are actual individuals who were accused by Robinson; Mrs. Generous alone is the poet's fiction. When Robin, the blunt serving-man, refuses to saddle the grey gelding she shakes a bridle over his head and using him as a horse makes him carry her to the satanical assembly. There is a mill, which is haunted by spirits in the shape of cats, and here a soldier undertakes to watch. For two nights he is undisturbed, but on the third "*Enter* Mrs. Generous, Mal, *all the* Witches and *their Spirits* (*at severall dores*)." "*The* Spirits *come about him with a dreadfull noise*," but he beats them thence with his sword, lopping off a tabby's paw in the hurly-burly. In the morning a hand is found, white and shapely, with jewels on the fingers. These Generous recognizes as being his wife's rings, and Mrs. Generous, who is in bed ill, is found to have one hand cut off at the wrist. This seals her fate. All the witches are dragged in and in spite of their charms and bug-words are identified by several witnesses including the boy who "saw them all in the barne together, and many more, at their feast and witchery."

The play was evidently produced just after the Lancaster Assizes, whilst four of the accused were in the Fleet prison, London, for further examination, and the King's pardon had not as yet been pronounced. This is evident from the Epilogue, which commences:

> Now while the witches must expect their due,
> By lawfull justice, we appeale to you
> For favourable censure; what their crime
> May bring upon 'em ripens yet of time
> Has not reveal'd. Perhaps great mercy may,
> After just condemnation, give them day
> Of longer life.

It will be convenient to consider in this connexion a drama largely founded upon Heywood and Brome, and produced nearly half a century later at the Duke's House, Dorset Garden, Shadwell's *The Lancashire Witches and Teague o Divelly, the Irish Priest,* which was first seen in the autumn of 1681 (probably in September). The idea of using magic in a play was obviously suggested to Shadwell by his idolized Ben Jonson's *Masque of Queens,* performed at Whitehall, 2 February, 1609. In close imitation of his model Shadwell has further appended copious notes to Acts one, two, three, and five, giving his references for the details of his enchantments. In the Preface (4to, 1682) he naïvely confesses: "For the magical part I had no hopes of equalling *Shakespear* in fancy, who created his witchcraft for the most part out of his own imagination (in which faculty no man ever excell'd him), and therefore I resolved to take mine from authority. And to that end there is not one action in the Play, nay, scarce a word concerning it, but is borrowed from some antient, or modern witchmonger. Which you will find in the notes, wherein I have presented you a great part of the doctrine of witchcraft, believe it who will." And he has indeed copious citations from Vergil, Horace, Ovid, Propertius, Juvenal, Tibullus, Seneca, Tacitus, Lucan, Petronius, Pliny, Apuleius, Aristotle, Theocritus, Lucian, Theophrastus; S. Augustine, S. Thomas Aquinas; Baptista Porta; Ben Jonson (*The Sad Shepherd*); from the *Malleus Maleficarum* of James Sprenger, O.P., and Henry Institor (Heinrich Kramer), written *circa* 1485–89, from Jean Bodin's (1520–96) *La Demonomanie des Sorciers,* 1580; the *Dæmonolatria,* 1595, of Nicolas Remy; *Disquisitionum Magicarum libri six* of Martin Delrio, S.J. (1551–1608); *Historia Rerum Scoticarum,* Paris, 1527, of Hector Boece (1465–1536); *Formicarius,* 5 vols., Douai, 1602, of John Nider, O.P. (1380–1438); *De Præstigiis Dæmonum,* 1563, by the celebrated John Weyer, physician to the Duke of Cleves; *De Gentibus Septentrionalibus,*[13] Rome, 1555, by Olaus Magnus, the famous Archbishop of Upsala; *Discoverie of Witchcraft,* 1584, by Reginald Scot; *Dæmonomagia,* by Philip Ludwig Elich, 1607; *De Strigimagis,* by Sylvester Mazzolini, O.P. (1460–1523), Master of the Sacred Palace and champion of the Holy See against the heresiarch Luther; *Compendium Maleficarum* (Milan,

1608), by Francesco Maria Guazzo of the Congregation of S. Ambrose; *Disputatio de Magis* (Frankfort, 1584), by Johan Georg Godelmann; *Tractatus de Strigiis et Lamiis* of Bartolommeo Spina, O.P.; the *Decretum* (about 1020) of Burchard, Bishop of Worms; the *De Sortilegiis* (Lyons, 1533) of Paolo Grilland; the *De Occulta Philosophia* (Antwerp, 1531) of Cornelius Agrippa; the *Apologie pour tous les Grands Hommes qui ont este faussement supconnez de Magie* (1625) of Gabriel Naudé, librarian to Cardinal Mazarin; *De Subtilitate* (libri XXI, Nuremberg, 1550) of Girolamo Cardano, the famous physician and astrologer; *De magna et occulta Philosophia* of Paracelsus; *IIII Livres des Spectres* (Angers, 1586) by Pierre le Loyer, Sieur de Brosse, of which Shadwell used the English version (1605) *A treatise of Specters* . . . translated by Z. Jones.

It will be seen that no less than forty-one authors, authorities on magic, are quoted by Shadwell in these notes, whilst not infrequently the same author is cited again and again, and extracts of some length, not merely general references, are given.

But for all this parade of learning, perchance because of all this parade of learning, Shadwell's witch scenes are intolerably clumsy, they are gross without being terrible. Shadwell was a clever dramatist, he was able to draw a character, especially a crank, with quite remarkable vigour, and his scenes are a triumph of photographic realism. True, he could not discriminate and select; he threw his world *en masse* higgledy piggledy on to the stage, and as even in the reign of the Merry Monarch there were a few tedious folk about, so now and again—but not very often—one chances upon heavy passages in Shadwell's robust comedies. On the other hand *The Sullen Lovers*, *Epsom Wells*, *The Virtuoso*, *Bury Fair*, *The Squire of Alsatia*, *The Volunteers*, in fact all his native plays, are full of bustle and fun, albeit a trifle riotous and rude as the custom was. Dryden, who very well knew what he was about, for purposes of his own cleverly dubbed Shadwell dull. And dull he has been dubbed ever since by those who have not read him. But Shadwell had not a spark of poetry in his whole fat composition. And so his witches become farcical, yet farcical in a grimy unpleasant way, for we are spared none of the loathsome details of the

Sabbat, and should anyone object, why, there is the authority of Remy or Guazzo, the precise passage from Prierias or Burchard to support the author. Indeed we feel that these witches are very real in spite of their materialism. They present a clear picture of one side of the diabolic cult, however crude and crass.

Even so, these incantation scenes are not, I venture to think, the worst thing in the play. The obscene caricature of the Catholic priest, Teague o Divelly, is frankly disgusting beyond words. He is represented as ignorant, idle, lecherous, a liar, a coward, a buffoon, too simiously cunning to be a fool, too basely mean to be a villain. It is a filthy piece of work, malignant and harmful prepense.[14]

But Shadwell showed scant respect for the Protestants too, since Smerk, Sir Edward Hartfort's chaplain, is described as "foolish, knavish, popish, arrogant, insolent; yet for his interest, slavish."

It is hardly a matter for surprise that after the play had been in the actors' hands about a fortnight complaints from such high quarters were lodged with Charles Killigrew, the Master of the Revels, that he promptly sent for the script, which at first he seems to have passed carelessly enough, and would only allow the rehearsals to proceed on condition that a quantity of scurrilous matter was expunged. Even so the dialogue is sufficiently offensive and profane. There was something like a riot in the theatre at the first performance, and the play was as heartily hissed as it deserved. Yet it managed to make a stand: those were the days of the Third Exclusion Bill and rank disloyalty, but the tide was on the turn, a rebel Parliament had been dissolved on the 28th March, on the 31st of August Stephen College, a perjured fanatic doubly dyed in treason and every conceivable rascality, had met his just reward on the gallows, whilst the atrocious Shaftesbury himself was to be smartly laid by the heels in the November following. That part of the dialogue which was not allowed to be spoken on the stage Shadwell has printed in italic letter,[15] and so we plainly see that the censor was amply justified in his demands. The political satire is of the muddiest; the railing against the Church is lewd and rancorous.

Such success as *The Lancashire Witches* had in the theatre—

and it was not infrequently revived—was wholly due to the mechanist and the scenic effects, the "flyings" of the witches, and the music, this last so prominent a feature that Downes does not hesitate to call it "a kind of Opera."

In Shadwell's Sabbat scenes the Devil himself appears, once in the form of a Buck Goat and once in human shape, whilst his satellites adore him with disgusting ceremonies. The witches are Mother Demdike, Mother Dickenson, Mother Hargrave, Mal Spencer, Madge, and others unnamed.

Elizabeth Demdike and Jennet Hargreaves belonged to the first Lancashire witch-trials, the prosecutions of 1612; Frances Dickenson and Mal Spencer were involved in the Robinson disclosures of 1633; so it is obvious that Shadwell has intermingled the two incidents. In his play we have a coursing scene where the hare suddenly changes to Mother Demdike; the witches raise a storm and carouse in Sir Edward's cellar something after the fashion of Madge Gray, Goody Price, and Goody Jones in *The Ingoldsby Legends;* Mal Spencer bridles Clod, a country yokel, and rides him to a witches' festival, where Madge is admitted to the infernal sisterhood; the witches in the guise of cats beset a number of persons with horrible scratchings and miauling, Tom Shacklehead strikes off a grimalkin's paw and Mother Hargreave's hand is found to be missing: "the cutting off the hand is an old story," says Shadwell in his notes. It will be seen that the later dramatist took many of his incidents from Heywood and Brome, although it is only fair to add that he has also largely drawn from original sources.

Shortly after the Restoration was published a play dealing with one of the most famous of English sibyls, *The Life of Mother Shipton.* "A New Comedy. As it was Acted Nineteen dayes together with great Applause. . . . Written by T[homas] T[homson]." Among the Dramatis Personæ appear Pluto, the King of Hell, with Proserpina, his Queen; Radamon, A chief Spirit; Four other Devils. The scene is "The City of York, or Naseborough Grove in Yorkshire." It is a rough piece of work, largely patched together from Middleton's *A Chaste Maid in Cheapside* and Massinger's *The City Madam,* whilst the episodes in which Mother Shipton is concerned would seem to be founded on one of the many old chap-books that relate her marvellous adventures and prophetic skill. Agatha Shipton (her name is usually given as Ursula) is complaining of her hard lot when she encounters Radamon, a demon who holds high rank in the court of Dis. He arranges to meet her later, and returns to his own place to boast of his success. He reappears to her dressed as a wealthy nobleman; he marries her; and for a while she is seen in great affluence and state. At the commencement of Act III she finds herself in her poor cottage again. As she laments Radamon enters, he informs her who he really is, and bestows upon her magical powers. Her fame spreads far and wide, and as popular story tells, the abbot of Beverley in disguise visits her to make trial of her art. She at once recognizes him, and foretells to his great chagrin the suppression of the monasteries with other events. In the end Mother Shipton outwits and discomforts the devils who attempt to seize her, she is vouchsafed a heavenly vision, and turns to penitence and prayer. The whole thing is a crude enough commixture, of more curiosity than value.

There are some well-written episodes in Nevil Payne's powerful tragedy *The Fatal Jealousie*,[16] produced at Dorset Garden early in August, 1672. Among the characters we have Witch, Aunt of Jasper, the villain of the piece. Jasper, who is servant to Antonio, applies to his aunt to help him in his malignant schemes. At first he believes she is a genuine sorceress, but she disabuses him and frankly acknowledges:

> I can raise no Devils,
> Yet I Confederate with Rogues and Taylors,
> Things that can shape themselves like Elves,
> And Goblins——

Her imps *Ranter* and *Swash*, *Dive*, *Fop*, *Snap*, *Gilt*, and *Picklock*, are slim lads in masquing habits, trained to trickery. None the less they manage an incantation scene to deceive Antonio and persuade him that his wife, Caelia, is false. An "Antick Dance of Devils" which follows is interrupted by the forcible entry of the Watch. The Aunt shows Jasper a secret hiding-place, whereupon he murders her and conceals the body in the hole. He pretends that she was in truth a witch and has vanished by magic. The Captain of the Watch, however, had detected her charlatanry long before, and presently a demon's vizor and a domino are found on the premises.

Later a little boy, who is caught in his devil's attire, confesses the impostures, and trembling adds that in one of their secret chambers they have discovered their mistress's corpse stabbed to death. Finally Jasper is unmasked, and only escapes condign punishment by his dagger. The character of the Witch is not unlike that of Heywood's *Wise Woman of Hogsdon,* although in *The Fatal Jealousie* the events take a tragic and bloody turn. Smith acted Antonio; Mrs. Shadwell, Caelia; Mrs. Norris, the Witch; and Sandford was famous in the rôle of Jasper.

There are incantation scenes in Dryden's tragedies, but these hardly come within our survey, as the magicians are treated romantically, one might even say decoratively, and certainly here no touch of realism is sought or intended. We have the famous episode in *The Indian-Queen* (produced at the Theatre Royal in January, 1663–4), when Zempoalla seeks Ismeron the prophet who raises the God of Dreams to prophesy her destiny;[17] in the fourth act of *Tyrannick Love* (Theatre Royal, June, 1669), the scene is an Indian cave, where at the instigation of Placidius the magician Nigrinus raises a vision of the sleeping S. Catharine, various astral spirits appear only to fly before the descent of Amariel, the Saint's Guardian-Angel; in *Œdipus,* by Dryden and Lee (Dorset Garden, December, 1678), Teresias plays a considerable part, and Act III is mainly concerned with a necromantic spell that raises the ghost of Laius in the depths of a hallowed grove. In *The Duke of Guise,* moreover (Theatre Royal, December, 1682), there is something of real horror in the figures of Malicorne and his familiar Melanax, and the scene[18] when the miserable wizard, whose bond is forfeit, is carried shrieking to endless bale, cannot be read without a shudder even after the last moments of Marlowe's *Faustus.* Act IV of Lee's *Sophonisba* (Theatre Royal, April, 1675) commences with the temple of Bellona, whose priestesses are shown at their dread rites. Cumana is inspired by the divinity, she raves in fury of obsession, there is a dance of spirits, and various visions are evoked.

In Otway's curious rehandling of *Romeo and Juliet* which he Latinized as *The History and Fall of Caius Marius* produced at Dorset Garden in the autumn of 1679, the Syrian witch Martha only appears for a moment to prophesy good fortune to Marius and to introduce a dance of spirits by the waving of her wand.

Charles Davenant's operatic *Circe* (Dorset Garden, March, 1676–7) is an amazing distortion of mythological story. There are songs without number, a dance of magicians, storms, dreams, an apparition of Pluto in a Chariot drawn by Black Horses, but all these are very much of the stage, stagey, born of candle-light and violins, hardly to be endured in cold print. Ragusa, the Sorceress in Tate's *Brutus of Alba: or the Enchanted Lovers* (Dorset Garden, May, 1678) is a far more formidable figure. Tate has managed his magic not without skill, and the conclusion of Act III, an incantation, was deservedly praised by Lamb. Curiously enough the plot of *Brutus of Alba* is the story of Dido and Aeneas, Vergil's names being altered "rather than be guilty of a breach of Modesty," Tate says. But Tate supplied Henry Purcell with the libretto for his opera *Dido and Aeneas*, wherein also witches appear. It must not be forgotten that *Macbeth* was immensely popular throughout the whole of the Restoration period, when, as has been noted above, the witch scenes were elaborated and presented with every resource of scenery, mechanism, dance, song, and meretricious ornament. Revival followed revival, each more decorative than the last, and the theatre was unceasingly thronged. Duffett undertook to burlesque this fashion, which he did in an extraordinary Epilogue to his skit *The Empress of Morocco*, produced at the Theatre Royal in the spring of 1674, but for all his japeries *Macbeth* never waned in public favour.

Spirits in abundance appear in the Earl of Orrery's unpublished tragedy *Zoroastres*,[19] the principal character being described as "King of Persia, the first Magician." He is attended by "several spirits in black with ghastly vizards," and at the end furies and demons arise shaking dark torches at the monarch whom they pull down to hell, the sky raining fire upon them. It was almost certainly never acted, and is the wildest type of transpontine melodrama.

Edward Ravenscroft's "recantation play" *Dame Dobson, or, The Cunning Woman* (produced at Dorset Garden in the early autumn of 1683) is an English version of *La Devineresse; ou les faux Enchantements* (sometimes known as *Madame Jobin*), a capital comedy by Thomas Corneille and Jean

Donneau de Vise. This French original had been produced in 1679, and both the stage-craft and the adroit way in which the various tricks and conjurations are managed must be allowed to be consummately clever. An English comedy on a similar theme is *The Wise Woman of Hogsdon*, the intricacies of which are a triumph of technique. *La Devineresse* was published in 1680 with a frontispiece picturing a grimalkin, a hand of glory, noxious weeds, two blazing torches and other objects beloved of necromancy. There are, moreover, eight folding plates which embellish the little book, and these have no small interest as they depict scenes in the comedy. But *Dame Dobson* cannot be accounted a play of witchcraft; it is no more than an amusing study of dextrous charlatanry. The protagonist herself[20] is of that immortal sisterhood graced by Heywood's sibyl, of whom it is said "She is a cunning woman, neither hath she her name for nothing, who out of her ignorance can fool so many that think themselves wise."

Mrs. Behn, in her amusing comedy *The Luckey Chance; or, An Alderman's Bargain*, produced at Drury Lane in the late winter of 1686, 4to, 1687, has made some play with pretended magic in the capital scenes where Gayman (Betterton) is secretly brought by the prentice Bredwel (Bowman), disguised as a devil, to the house of Lady Fulbank (Mrs. Barry). Here he is received by Pert, the maid, who is dressed as an old witch, and conducted to his inamorata's embraces. But the whole episode is somewhat farcically treated, and it is, of course, an elaborate masquerade for the sake of an intrigue.[21]

Shadwell in 1681 took Witchcraft seriously, and notwithstanding the half-hearted disclaimer in his address "To the Reader" that prefaces *The Lancashire Witches* I think he was sensible enough to recognize the truth which lies at the core of the matter in spite of the grotesqueness of the formulæ and spells doting hags and warlocks are wont to employ. Witchcraft was still a capital offence when some fifteen years later Congreve lightly laughed it out of court. Foresight (*Love for Love*), "an illiterate old Fellow, peevish and positive, superstitious, and pretending to understand Astrology, Palmistry, Phisiognomy, Omens, Dreams, etc.," is in close confabulation with his young daughter's Nurse, when

Angelica his niece trips in to ask the loan of his coach, her own being out of order. He says no, and presses her to remain at home, muttering to himself some old doggerel which bodes no good to the house if all the womenfolk are gadding abroad. The lady fleers him, twits him with jealousy of his young wife: "Uncle, I'm afraid you are not Lord of the Ascendant, ha! ha! ha!" He is obstinate in his refusal; and she retorts: "I can make Oath of your unlawful Midnight Practices; you and the Old Nurse there. . . . I saw you together, through the Key-hole of the Closet, one Night, like *Saul* and the Witch of *Endor*, turning the Sieve and Sheers, and pricking your Thumbs to write poor innocent Servants' Names in Blood about a little Nutmeg-Grater, which she had forgot in the Caudle-Cup." "Hussy, Cockatrice," storms the old fellow beside himself with rage. Angelica mocks him even more bitterly, accuses him and the Nurse of nourishing a familiar, "a young Devil in the shape of a Tabby-Cat," and with a few last thrusts she departs, trilling with merriment, in a sedan-chair.

To return for a brief space to an earlier generation when it would have hardly been possible, or at least highly inadvisable, to treat Witchcraft in this blithesome mood, of two plays that would almost certainly have been of great interest in this connexion we have only the names, *The Witch of Islington*, acted in 1597, and *The Witch Traveller*, licensed in 1623.

In addition to *The Masque of Queens*, which as has already been noted, served to some extent for a model to Shadwell when inditing his encyclopædic notes on magic, Ben Jonson in that sweet pastoral *The Sad Shepherd* introduces a Scotch witch, Maudlin. The character is drawn with vigorous strokes; realism mingles with romance.

During the quarrel scene which opens *The Alchemist* Face threatens Subtle:

I'll bring thee, rogue, within
The statute of sorcerie, *tricesimo tertio*
Of Harry the Eight.

Dapper the gull asks Subtle for a familiar, as Face explains (I, 2):

Why, he do's aske one but for cups, and horses,
A rifling flye: none o' your great familiars.

And later in order to trick him thoroughly Dol Common appears as the "Queene of Faerie." The Queen of Elphin or Elfhame, who is particularly mentioned in the Scotch witch-trials, seems to be identical with the French Reine du Sabbat. In 1670 Jean Weir confessed: "That when she keeped a school at Dalkeith, and teached childering, ane tall woman came to the declarant's hous when the childering were there; and that she had, as appeared to her, ane chyld upon her back, and one or two at her foot; and that the said woman disyred that the declarant should imploy her to spick for her to the Queen of Farie, and strik and battle in her behalf with the said Queen, (which was her own words)."[22]

Beaumont and Fletcher afford us but few instances of witchcraft in the many dramas that conveniently go under their names. We have, it is true, a she-devil, Lucifera, in *The Prophetess*, but the incident is little better than clowning. Delphia herself is a severely classical pythoness far removed from the Sawyers, Demdikes, and Dickensons Sulpitia, in *The Custom of the County* dons a conjurer's robe and at Hippolita's bidding blasts Zenocia almost to death by her spells, but yet she is more bawd than witch. Peter Vecchio in *The Chances*, "a reputed wizard," is as sharp and cozening a practitioner as Forobosco, the mountebank, a petty pilferer, who is exposed and sent to the galleys at the end of *The Fair Maid of the Inn;* or Shirley's Doctor Sharkino[23] whom silly serving-men consult about the loss of silver spoons and napkins; or Tomkis's Albumazar; nay, Jonson's Subtle himself.[24]

In Marston's *Sophonisba* (4to, 1606) appears Erictho, borrowed from Lucan. The Friar in Chapman's *Bassy d'Ambois* (4to, 1607) puts on a magician's habit, and after a sonorous Latin invocation raises the spirits Behemoth and Cartophylax in the presence of Bussy and Tamyra.

A far more interesting drama than these is Shirley's *S. Patrick for Ireland*, acted in Dublin, 1639–40, which has as its theme the conversion of Ireland by S. Patrick and the opposition of the Druids under their leader Archimagus. The character of S. Patrick moves throughout with a quiet spiritual dignity that has true beauty, and the magicians in their baffled potency for evil are only less effective. This drama is a work of stirling merit, to which I would unhesitatingly assign a very high place in Shirley's theatre. We are shown the various attempts upon S. Patrick's life: poison is administered in a cup of wine, the Saint drinks and remains unharmed; Milcho, a great officer, whose servant S. Patrick once was, locks him and his friends in a house and fires it. The Christians pass out unscathed through the flames which devour the incendiary. In the last scene whilst S. Patrick sleeps Archimagus summons a vast number of hideous serpents to devour him, but the Apostle of Ireland wakes, and expels for ever all venomous reptiles from his isle, whereon the earth gapes and swallows the warlock alive. Particularly impressive is the arrival of S. Patrick, when as the King and his two sons, his druids and nobles, are gathered in anxious consultation at the gates of their temple, they see passing in solemn procession through the woods a fair company with gleaming crosses, silken banners, bright tapers and incense, what time the sweet music of a hymn strikes upon the ear:

Post maris sæui fremitus Iernæ
(Nauitas cœlo tremulas beante)
Uidimus gratum iubar enatantes
Littus inaurans.

(Now that we have crossed the fierce waves of ocean to Ireland's coast, and Heaven has blessed its poor fearful wanderers, wending our way along with joy do we see a sunbeam of light gilding these shores.)

As Marlowe's *Dr. Faustus* has already been treated in this connexion it may not be altogether impertinent very briefly to consider some three or four other Elizabethan plays in which the Devil appears among the Dramatis Personæ, even if he act no very prominent part. These for the most part fluctuate between the semi-serious and merest buffoonery. Thus the prologue of *The Merry Devil of Edmonton* (4to, 1608), in which the enchanter Peter Fabell tricks the demon who has come to demand the fulfilment of his contract, is at the opening managed with due decorum, but it soon adopts a lighter, and even trivial, vein. William Rowley's *The Birth of Merlin, or The Childe hath found his Father* (not printed until 1662) is a curious medley of farce and romance, informed with a certain awkward vigour and not wholly destitute of poetry. Dekker's *If it be not good, the Divel is in it* (4to, 1612), which may be traced to the old prose *History of Friar Rush*, depicts the exploits of three lesser fiends who are dispatched to spread their master's kingdom in Naples. It is an unequal play, the satire of which falls very flat, since it is obvious that the poet was not sincere in his extravagant theme.[25]

Ben Jonson's *The Devil is an Ass*, acted in 1616, is wholly comic. Pug, "the less devil," who visits the earth, and engages himself as servant to a Norfolk squire, Fabian Fitzdottrel, is hopelessly outwitted on every occasion by the cunning of mere mortals. Eventually he finds himself lodged in Newgate, and in imminent danger of the gallows were he not rescued by the Vice, Iniquity, by whom he is carried off rejoicing to the nether regions. His fate may be compared with that of Roderigo in Wilson's excellent comedy *Belphegor: or, The Marriage of the Devil* (produced at Dorset Garden in the summer of 1690), who with his two attendant devils flies back to his native hell to escape the woes of earth.

In *The Devil's Charter*, however, by Barnaby Barnes (1607), we have what is undoubtedly a perfectly serious tragedy, which if not exactly modelled upon, at least owes many hints to Marlowe's *Faustus*. It is flamboyant melodrama and wildly unhistorical throughout, a very tophet of infernal horror. The chief character is a loathsome caricature of Pope Alexander VI,[26] and, as we might expect, all the lies and libels of Renaissance satirists and Protestant pamphleteers are heaped together to portray an impossible monster of lust and crime. The filthiest scandals of Burchard, Sanudo, Giustiniani, Filippo Nerli, Guicciardini, Paolo Giovio, Sannazzaro and the Neapolitans, have been employed with one might almost say a scrupulous conscientiousness. The black art, in particular, occupies a very prominent place in these lurid scenes. Alexander has signed a bond with a demon Astaroth, and it is to this contract that all his success is ascribed. In Act IV there is a long incantation when the Pope puts on his magical robes, takes his rod and pentacle, and standing within the circle he has traced conjures in strange terms, commencing a Latin exorcism which tails off into mere gibberish. Various devils appear, and he is shown a vision of Gandia's murder by Cæsar,[27] with other atrocities. At the climax of the piece we have the banquet with Cardinal

Adrian of Corneto, and whilst the guests talk "The Devill commeth and changeth the Popes bottles." The Borgias are poisoned, and in a far too protracted "Scena Ultima" Alexander discourses and disputes frantically with the demons who appear to mock and torment him. There is the old device of an ambiguous contract; presently a "Devil like a Poast" enters winding a horn to summon the unhappy wretch, who raves and shrieks out meaningless ejaculations as he is dragged away amid thunder and lightning. This sort of thing pandered to the most brutalized appetites of the groundlings, and *The Devil's Charter* may be summed up as a disgusting burlesque not without its quota of vile stuff that is so repulsive as to be physically sickening.

Upon a careful consideration of those seventeenth-century plays which have Witchcraft as their main theme, and leaving on one side, for our purpose, the essentially romantic treatment of the subject, however realistic some details of the picture may be, it is, I think, beyond dispute that *The Witch of Edmonton* in the figure of Mother Sawyer offers us the best contemporary illustration of the Elizabethan witch. The drama itself is one of no ordinary merit and power, whilst the understanding and restraint which set the play apart from its fellows also raises it to the level of genuine tragedy. It should be noticed that we see a witch, so to speak, in the process of making. Mother Sawyer is in truth the victim of the prejudices of the village hinds and ignorant yokels. When she first appears it is merely as a poor old crone driven to desperation by her brutal neighbours; the farmers declare she is a witch, and at length persecution makes her one. She is malignant and evil enough once the compact with the demon has been confirmed; she longs from the first to be revenged upon her enemies and mutters to herself "by what art May the thing called Familiar be purchased?" But, in one sense, she is urged and hounded to her destiny, and the authors, although never doubting her compact with the powers of darkness, her vile and poisonous life, show a detached but very real sympathy for her. It is this touch of humanity, the pathos and pity of the poor old hag, repulsive, wicked, and baleful as she may be, which must place *The Witch of Edmonton* in my opinion among the greatest and most moving of all Elizabethan plays.

It is no pleasant task to turn now to the theatre of the eighteenth century in this connexion. The witch became degraded; she was comic, burlesqued, buffooned; a mere property for a Christmas pantomime: *Harlequin Mother Bunch, Mother Goose, Harlequin Dame Trot*, Charles Dibdin's *The Lancashire Witches, or The Distresses of Harlequin*[28] whose tinsel, music, and mummery drew all the macaronis and cyprians in London to the Circus during the winter of 1782–3.

Some subtle premonition of the great success of Harrison Ainsworth's powerful story *The Lancashire Witches*—for this and the macabre *Rookwood* are probably the best of the work of a talented writer now unduly depreciated and decried—seems to have suggested to the prolific Edward Fitzball his "Legendary Drama in Three Acts," *The Lancashire Witches, A Romance of Pendle Forest*, produced at the Adelphi Theatre, 3 January, 1848. It was quick work, for it was only a month before, 3 December, 1847, that Ainsworth, writing to his friend Crossley of Manchester, states that he has accepted the liberal offer of the *Sunday Times*—£1000 and the copyright to revert to the author on the completion of the work—that his new romance *The Lancashire Witches* should make its appearance as a serial in the paper. He had already sketched out the plan, and he must have given Fitzball an idea of this, or at least have allowed the dramatist the use of some few rough notes, for although the play and the novel have little, one might say nothing essential, in common, the chief character in the theatre, Bess of the Woods, "140 years old, formerly Abbess of S. Magdalen's, doomed for her crimes to an unearthly age," is none other than the anchoress Isolde de Heton.[29] The fourth scene of the second act presents the ruins of Whalley Abbey by moonlight. During an incantation the picture gradually changes; the broken arches form themselves into perfect masonry; the ivy disappears from the windows to show the ruby and gold of coloured glass; the decaying altar glitters with piled plate and the gleam of myriad tapers. A choir of nuns rises from the grave to dance with spectral gallants. Among the votaries are Nutter, Demdike, and Chattox "Three Weird Sisters, doomed for their frailties to become Witches." But they utter no word, and have no part save this in the action.

This scene must have proved extraordinarily effective upon the stage. It owes much to the haunted convent in Meyerbeer's *Robert le Diable*, produced at the Académie Royale in November, 1831, and given in a piratical form both at Drury Lane and Covent Garden within a few weeks. Nor is it comparable to its original. In Fitzball's melodrama O. Smith appeared as Gipsy Dallan, a new character; and Miss Faucit (Mrs. Bland) as Bess of the Woods. The play, for what it is, a luridly theatrical and Surrey-side sensation, has merit; but to speak of it in the same breath as Middleton or even as Barnes would be absurd.

Shelley's genius has with wondrous beauty translated for us scenes from Calderon's *El Magico Prodigioso*, one of the loveliest songs of the Spanish nightingale. On another plane, admittedly, but yet, I think, far from lacking a simple comeliness of its own and surely not without most poignant pathos, is Longfellow's New England Tragedy *Giles Corey of the Salem Farms.*[30] The honest sincerity of Cotton Mather, the bluff irascible heartiness of Corey himself, the inopportune scepticism of his wife—which to many would seem sound common sense—the hysteria of Mary Walcot, the villainy of John Gloyd, all these are sketched with extraordinary power, a few quiet telling touches which make each character, individual, alert, alive.

In the French theatre we have an early fourteenth-century *Miracle de Nostre Dame de Robert le Dyable*, and in 1505 was acted *Le mystère du Chevalier qui donna sa femme au Diable*, à dix personnages. As one might well expect during the long classical period of the drama Witchcraft could have found no place in the scenes of the French dramatists. It would have been altogether too wild, too monstrous a fantasy. And so it is not until the 24 floréal, An XIII (11 June, 1805) that a play which interweaves sorcery as its theme is seen at the Théâtre français, when *Les Templiers* of Raynouard was given there. A few years later *Le Vampire*, a thrilling melodrama by Charles Nodier and Carmouche, produced on 13 August, 1820, was to draw all idle Paris to the Porte-Saint-Martin. In 1821 two facile writers quick to gauge the public appetite, Frédéric Dupetit-Mèré and Victor Ducagne, found some favour with *La Sorcière, ou l'Orphelin écossais.* Alexandre Dumas, and one of his many ghosts Auguste

Maquet, collaborated (if one may use the term) in a grandiose five-act drama *Urbain Grandier*, 1850. *La Sorcière Canidie*, a one-act play by Aurélien Vivie, produced at Bordeaux in 1888 is of little account. *La Reine de l'Esprit* (1891) of Maurice Pottecher is founded to some extent on the *Comte de Gabalis*, whilst the same author's three-act *Chacun cherche son Trésor*, "histoire des sorciers" (1899) was not a little helped by the music of Lucien Michelet. There are many excuses for passing over with a mere mention *Les Noces de Sathan* (1892), a "drama ésoterique," by Jules Bois, and *Les Basques ou la Sorcière d'Espelette*, a lyric drama in three acts by Loquin and Mégret de Belligny, produced at Bordeaux in 1892, has an interest which is almost purely local. Alphonse Tavan's *Les Mases* (sorciers), a legendary drama of five acts of alternating prose and verse seen in 1897 was helped out by every theatrical resource, a ballet, chorus, mechanical effects, and confident advertisement. Serge Basset's *Vers le Sabbat* "évocation de sorcellerie en un acte" which appeared in the same year need not be seriously considered. Nor does an elaborate episode "Le Sabbat et la Herse Infernale," wherein Mons. Benglia appeared as Satan, that was seen in the Folies Bergère revue, *Un Soir de Folie*, 1925–6, call for more than the briefest passing mention.

In more recent days Victor Sardou's *La Sorcière* is a violent, but effective, melodrama. Produced at the Théâtre Sarah-Bernhardt, 15 December, 1903, with De Max as Cardinal Ximenes and Sarah Bernhardt as the moresque Zoraya, it obtained a not undeserved success. The locale of the tragedy is Toledo, anno domini 1506; Act IV, the Inquisition scene; and Act V, the square before the Cathedral with the grim pyre ready for the torch, were—owing to the genius of a great actress—truly harrowing. Of course it is very flamboyant, very unbalanced, very unhistorical, but in its gaudy theatrical way—all the old tricks are there—*La Sorcière* had an exciting thrill for those who were content to be unsophisticated awhile.

John Masefield's adaptation from the Norwegian of Wiers-Jennsen, *The Witch*,[31] a drama in four acts, is a very different thing. Here we have psychology comparable to that of Dekker and Ford. Nor will the performances of Miss Janet

Achurch as Merete Beyer and Miss Lillah McCarthy as Anne Pedersdotter easily be forgotten. As a picture of the horror of Witchcraft in cold Scandinavia, the gloom and depression of formidable fanaticism engendered by Lutheran dogma and discipline with the shadow of destiny lowering implacably over all, this is probably the finest piece of work dealing in domestic fashion with the warlock and the sorceress that has been seen on the English stage since the reign of wise King James three hundred years ago.

NOTES TO CHAPTER VII

[1] The *Floralia*, the most wanton of Roman festivals, commenced on the fourth day before the Kalends of May, and during these celebrations the spectators insisted that the *mimæ* should play naked, "agebantur [*Floralia*] a meretricibus ueste exutis omni cum uerborum licentia, motuumque obscænitate," says the old commentator on Martial I, 1. "Lasciui Floralia laeta theatri" Ausonius names them, *De Feriis Romanis*, 25. Lactantius, *De Institutionibus Diuinis*, I, 20, writes: "Celebrantur ergo illi ludi cum omni lasciuia, conuenientes memoriæ meretricis. Nam praeter uerborum licentiam, quibus obscænitas omnis effunditur; exuuntur etiam uestibus populo flagitante meretrices; quæ tunc mimorum funguntur officio; et in conspectu populi usque ad satietatem impudicorum luminum cum pudendis motibus detinentur." Both S. Augustine and Arnobius reprehend the lewdness of these naked dances. At Sens during the Feast of Fools, when every licence prevailed, men were led in procession *nudi*. Warton (*History of English Poetry*, by T. Warton, edited by W. C. Hazlitt, 4 vols., 1871), II, 223, states that in the Mystery Plays "Adam and Eve are both exhibited on the stage naked, and conversing about their nakedness; this very pertinently introduces the next scene, in which they have coverings of fig-leaves." In a stage-direction of the Chester Plays we find: "Statim nudi sunt. . . . Tunc Adam et Eua cooperiant genitalia sua cum foliis." Chambers, *The Mediæval Stage*, II, 143, doubts whether the players were actually nude, and suggests a suit of white leather. Warton, however, is probably right.

[2] Phales was an early deity, very similar to Priapus, and closely associated with the Bacchic mysteries. For the refrain see *The Acharnians*, 263–265.

[3] See Callot's series of character-etchings, *I Balli di Sfessanio*.

[4] Not to be confused with the printer Fust, as was at one time frequently supposed.

[5] In Marlowe's play Faust welcomes "German Valdes and Cornelius." Who Valdes is has not been satisfactorily explained. The suggestion of Dr. Havelock Ellis that Paracelsus seems intended is no doubt correct.

[6] Translated from the Middle Dutch by Harry Morgan Ayres, with an Introduction by Adriaan J. Barnouw. *The Dutch Library*, The Hague: Martinus Nijhoff. 1924.

[7] The International Theatre Society gave a private subscription performance of *Mary of Nimmegen* at Maskelyne's Theatre on Sunday, 22 February, 1925. But such a play, presenting crowded scenes of burgher life, the streets, the market-place, to be effective demands a large stage and costly production.

[8] Meroe is the hag "saga et diuina" in Apuleius, *Metamorphoseon*, I.

[9] *Macbeth* was tinkered at almost from the first. Upon the revival of the play immediately after the Restoration the witch scenes were given great theatrical prominence. 7 January, 1667, Pepys declared himself highly delighted with the "divertissement, though it be a deep tragedy."

[10] *The Witch of Edmonton* was revived under my direction for two performances at the Lyric Theatre, Hammersmith, 24 and 26 April, 1921.

Sybil Thorndike played the Witch, Russell Thorndike, the Familiar; Ion Swinley, Frank Thorney; Edith Evans, Ann Ratcliffe; and Frank Cochrane, Cuddy Banks.

11 4to 1634: *Stationers' Register*, 28 October.

12 In a famous Scotch trial for witchcraft, 1661, Jonet Watson of Dalkeith confessed "that the Deivill apeired vnto her in the liknes of ane prettie boy, in grein clothes."

13 Liber III. *De Magis et Maleficis Finnorum.*

14 Tegue o' Divelly was acted by Antony Leigh, the most famous comedian of his day, and an intimate friend of Shadwell.

15 Curiously enough Halliwell in *The Poetry of Witchcraft*, a private reprint of Heywood and Shadwell's plays, 80 copies only, 1853, has not reproduced the italic letter but gives all the dialogue in roman to the great detriment of this edition.

16 Licensed for printing 2 November, 1672, and published quarto with date 1673.

17 At a later revival Ismeron's recitative "Ye twice ten hundred Deities" was set by Purcell.

18 Dryden's. He wrote the first scene of the first act, the whole of the fourth act, rather more than one-half of act five, and Lee is responsible for the rest of the tragedy.

19 For a full analysis and critical examination of *Zoroastres* see my article in the *Modern Language Review*, XII, Jan., 1917.

20 The title-rôle Dame Dobson was played by Mrs. Corey, a mistress of broad comedy, who was much admired for her humour by Samuel Pepys.

21 Mrs. Behn owes a hint to Shirley's *The Lady of Pleasure*, licensed by Sir Henry Herbert, 15 October, 1635; 4to. 1637. It must be confessed that she has managed her scenes with more wit and spirit than the older dramatist, whose charming verse is perhaps too seriously poetical for the actual situation.

22 George Sinclar, *Satan's Invisible World Discovered*, 1685. Reprint, Edinburgh, 1871. Supplement, I, p. xii.

23 *The Maid's Revenge*, acted 1626, printed 1639.

24 Compare Mopus in Wilson's *The Cheats* (acted in 1662); Stargaze in *The City Madam*; Rusee, Norbrett, and their accomplices in *Rollo*; Iacchelino in Ariosto's *Il Negromante*; and a score beside.

25 Sir Adolphus Ward, *English Dramatic Literature*, 1899, II, 465, says that Langbaine wrongly supposed the source of this play to be "Machiavelli's celebrated *Novella* on the marriage of Belphegor." But this is hardly correct. Langbaine wrote: "The beginning of his Play seems to be writ in imitation of *Matchiavel's* Novel of *Belphegor*: where *Pluto* summons the Devils to Councel."

26 For a fitting account of Alexander VI see *Le Pape Alexandre VI et les Borgia*, Paris, 1870, by Père Ollivier, O.P.; also Leonetti *Papa Alessandro VI secondo documenti e carteggi del tempo*, 3 vols., Bologna, 1880. *Chronicles of the House of Borgia*, by Frederick, Baron Corvo, 1901, may be studied with profit. Monsignor de Roo's *Material for a History of Pope Alexander VI*, 5 vols., Bruges, 1924, is of the greatest value, and completely authoritative.

27 The murderer of the Duke of Gandia is unknown to history, if not to historians.

28 The songs only are printed, 8vo, 1783.

29 Fosbrooke, *British Monachism*, says that in the reign of Henry VI one Isolde de Heton petitioned the King to let her be admitted as an anchoress in the Abbey of Whalley. But afterwards she left the enclosure and broke her vows, whereupon the King dissolved the hermitage.

30 The incidents are historically correct. See Cotton Mather's *Wonders of the Invisible World*. Corey refusing to plead was pressed to death.

31 Originally produced 10 October, 1910, at the Royalty, Glasgow: in London, 31 January, 1911, at the Court. Revived at the Court, 29 October, 1913, when it ran for a month, and was afterwards included in the subsequent three weeks' repertory season.

BIBLIOGRAPHY

THIS Bibliography does not aim at anything beyond presenting a brief and convenient hand-list of some of the more important books upon Witchcraft. It does not even purport to give all those monographs to which reference is made in the body of this study. A large number of books I have thought it superfluous to include. Thus I have omitted general works of reference such as the *Encyclopædia Britannica*, Du Cange's *Glossarium ad scriptores mediæ et infimæ latinitatis*, Dugdale's *Monasticon;* daily companions such as the Missal, the Breviary, the Bible; Homer, Vergil, Horace, Ovid, Petronius, Lucan; Shakespeare, Marlowe, Ford, Dryden, Burton's *Anatomy of Melancholy*, and English classics; those histories which are on every library shelf, Gibbon, Lingard, Ranke; and such histories as the *Cambridge Modern History.*

On the other hand, I have of purpose included various books which may not seem at first sight to have much connexion with Witchcraft, although they are, as a matter of fact, by no means impertinent. In order to appreciate this vast subject in all its bearings, even the desultory or amateur investigator should at least be fairly grounded in theology, philosophy, and psychology. The student must be a capable theologian.

I have devoted some particular attention to the works of the demonologists, now almost universally neglected, but a close study of which is essential to the understanding of occultism and the appreciation of the grave dangers that may lurk there.

I am only too conscious of the plentiful lacunæ in this Bibliography. However, to attempt anything like a complete catalogue—if, indeed, it were possible to essay so illimitable a task—would involve the listing of very many thousands of books, and would itself require no inconsiderable a tale of volumes.

I need hardly point out that side by side with works of the highest importance it has been found necessary to include a few of no great value, which yet have their use to illustrate some one point or special phase.

GENERAL

CAILLET, ALBERT L. *Manuel bibliographique des sciences psychiques ou occultes, science des Mages, hermétique, astrologie, Kabbale, Franc-maçonnerie, médecine ancienne, mesmérisme, sorcellerie, singularités, etc.* 3 vols. Paris, 1913.

GRÆSSE, JOHAN GEORG THEODOR. *Bibliotheca magica et pneumatica.* Leipzig, 1843. (In spite of obvious defects a very valuable bibliography.)

YVE-PLESSIS, R. *Bibliographie française de la sorcellerie.* Paris, 1900. (An immense and exhaustive work on French books.)

AARON THE GREEK [Simon Blocquel]. *La Magie rouge.* Paris, 1821.

ABNER, THEODORE. *Les apparitions du Diable.* Brussels, 1879.

ACONTIUS. *Stratagemata Satanæ.* Libri VIII. Basle, 1565.

Acta Sanctorum. Par les Bollandistes. Antwerp, Tongerloo, Brussels, 1644 *sqq.* Reprinted, Paris, 1863 *sqq.*

ADHÉMAR DE CHABANNES. *Chronicle :* in *Monumenta Germaniæ historica.* Ed. G. A. Pertz, etc. Vol. IV.

AGOBARD, S. *Opera omnia.* Migne, *Patrologia latina.* Vol. CIV.

AGRIPPA, HEINRICH CORNELIUS *La philosophie occulte de Henr. Corn. Agrippa . . . traduite du latin* [par A. Levasseur]. 2 vols. Hague, 1727.

Œuvres magiques . . . mises en français par Pierre d'Aban. Rome, 1744. (Of the last rarity. There are other editions, Liège, 1788 ; Rome, 1800 ; Rome, 1744 (*circa* 1830) ; but all these are extremely scarce.)

ALANUS (Alain de Lille). *Aduersus hæreticos et Waldenses.* Ed. J. Masson. Paris, 1612.

ALANUS, HENRICUS. *Ciceronis de Divinatione et de Fato.* 1839.

ALBERT, LE PETIT. *Alberti Parui Lucii libellus de mirabilibus Naturæ arcanis.* (This treatise which tells how to confect philtres, make talismans, use the hand of glory, discover treasures, etc., has been very frequently translated into French, generally under the running title *Les secrets merveilleux de la magie naturelle et cabalistique. . . .*)

BL. ALBERTUS MAGNUS, O.P. *Opera omnia.* Ed. Father Peter Jammy, O.P. 21 vols. Lyons, 1651, etc.

De alchimia. (This treatise is said to be doubtful.)

De secretis mulierum. (This work is certainly not from the pen of the great Dominican doctor, to whom, however, it was universally ascribed. There are a vast number of editions, and translations, especially into French. *Les secretz des femmes et homes . . . stampato in Torino par Pietro Ranot,* N.D. *circa* 1540. *Les secrets admirables du grand Albert.* Paris, 1895.)

Commentaria. Lib. IV, dist. 34. *An maleficii impedimento aliquis potest impediri a potentia cocundi.* (*Nœud de l'aiguillette.*)

ALEXANDER III, POPE. *Epistolæ* apud *Regesta R. R. Pontificum.* Nos. 10, 584–14, 424. Ed. Jaffé. And Löwenfeld's *Epistolæ Pontif. Rom. ineditæ.* Leipzig, 1885.

ALEXIS. *Secreti del reverendo Donno Alessio Piemontese.* Venice, 1555. (Attributed by Girolamo Muzio to the alchemist Girolamo Ruscelli.)

ALLARD, PAUL. *Histoire des persécutions.* 5 vols. Paris, 1892.

Julien l'Apostat. 3 vols. Paris, 1900.

ALPHONSUS LIGUORI, S. *Theologia Moralis.* 9 vols. Malines, 1828. Also ed. P. Gaudé, C. SS. R. Rome, 1905.

ALVARO, PELAYO. *De Planctu Ecclesiæ.* Venice, 1560.
AMBROISE DA VIGNATE (c. 1408). *Tractatus de Hæreticis.* Rome, 1581.
AMBROSE, S. *Opera omnia.* Ed. Paolo Angelo Ballerini. 6 vols. Folio. Milan, 1875.
ANANIA, GIOVANNI LORENZO. *De Natura Dæmonum.* Apud Vol. II. *Malleus Maleficarum.* 1669.
Anonymi Gesta Francorum et Aliorum Hierosolymitanorum. Oxford.
ANTONELLI, G. PROF. *Lo spiritismo. Fede e Scienza,* II. 11, 12. Rome.
ANTONINUS, O. P. S. *Confessionale.* Florence, 1496.
ANTONIO A SPIRITU SANCTO, O.D.C. *Directorium Mysticum.* Paris, 1904.
AREMI (LE SAGE). *Secrets de vieux Druide.* Lille, 1840.
ARETINI, ANGELO. *Tractatus de maleficiis.* 1521.
ARIES, MARTIN. *De superstitionibus maleficorum.* Romé, 1559.
ARIMINENSIS, AUGUSTINUS. *Additiones in Angeli Aretini Tractatum de maleficiis.* Milan, 1514.
ARNAULD DE VILLENEUVE. *De Maleficiis.* Lyons, 1509.
ARNOULD, ARTHUR. *Histoire de l'Inquisition.* Paris, 1869.
AROUX. *Mystères de la Chevalerie et de l'amour platonique.* 1857–8.
ARPE (PETR. FRID.). *De Prodigiosis Naturæ et Artis Operibus Talismanes et Amuleta.* Hamburg, 1717.
ATHANASIUS, S. *Opera omnia.* Migne, *Pat. Graeci.* Vols. XXIII–XXVIII.
ATWOOD, M. A. *A Suggestive Inquiry into the Hermetic Mystery.*
AUGUSTINE, S. *Opera omnia.* Migne. *Pat. Lat.* Vols. XXXIX–XLVII.
De Ciuitate Dei. Ed. J. E. C. Welldon, D.D., Dean of Durham. 2 vols. 1924. (The introduction and appendices must be used with caution.)
Confessiones. Ed. P. Knöll. *Corpus Scriptorum Eccl. Latinorum* (Vienna.) XXXIII.
D'AUTUN, JACQUES. *L'Incredulité savante.* Lyons, 1674.
D'AVALLON, ANDRÉ, ET CONDIS. *Dictionnaire de droit canonique.*
AZPILCEUTA, MARTIN. *Opera omnia.* 3 vols. Lyons, 1589.
BACO, R. *De secretis operibus magiæ.* Paris, 1542.
BACON, ROGER. *Epistola de secretis operibus.* Hamburg, 1608; 1618. (The same work as *De mirabili potestate artis et naturæ et de nullitate magiæ.* Paris, 1542; Oxford, 1604; London, 1859.
BAISSAC, JULES. *Les grands jours de la sorcellerie.* Paris, 1890.
BALLERINI, ANTONIO, S.J. *Opus theologicum morale.* 7 vols. Prati, 1892.
BANG. *Norske Hexeformularer.* Christiania, 1902.
BARONIUS, CESARE VEN. *Annales ecclesiastici.* 38 vols. Lucca, 1738–59.
BARRETT. *Magus or Celestial Intelligencer; Being a complete system of Occult Philosophy, etc.* 1801.
BASIL, S. *Opera omnia.* Paris, 1839.
BASIN, BERNARDUS. *De artibus magicis.* 1482; and Paris, 1506.
BECANUS, MARTIN, S.J. *Opuscula Theologica sive Controversiæ Fidei inter Catholicos et Hæreticos hujus temporis.* Duaci, 1634.
BEER, M. *Social Struggles in the Middle Ages.* London, 1924.
BEKKER, BALTHASAR. *De Betoverde Wereld.* 4 vols. Amsterdam, 1691–93.
BENEDICT XIII. *Vita del Sommo Pontefice Benedetto XIII.* Venezia, 1737.
BENEDICT XIV, POPE. *De Beatificatione et Canonizatione.* 9 vols. Rome, 1787.
BENOIST, J., O.P. *Histoire des Albigeoises et des Vaudois.* Paris, 1691.
BERNARD, S. *Opera omnia.* Migne, *Pat. Lat.* CLXXXII–CLXXXV.
BERNARD OF COMO, O.P. *Lucerna inquisitorum hæreticæ prauitatis . . . et eiusdem Tractatus de Strigibus. . . .* Milan, 1566; Rome, 1584.
BERNARD OF LUXEMBURG, O.P. *Catalogus hæreticorum omnium.* Erfurt, 1522.
BERTAGNA, J. B. *De casuum reseruatione in Sacramento Pœnitentiæ.* Turin, 1868.
BERTHIER, O.P. *L'Étude de la Somme Théologique de S. Thomas d'Aquin.* Paris, 1905. (Appendix III. *Spiritisme et hypnotisme d'après S. Thomas.*)
BESTERMAN, THEODORE. *Crystal-Gazing.*

BIEL, GABRIEL. *Supplementum in 28 distinctiones ultimas 4ti magistri sententiarum.* (1486.) Basle, 1520.
BINSFELD, PETER. *De Confessionibus Maleficorum.* Treves, 1589.
BODIN, JEAN. *De la démonomanie des sorciers.* Paris, 1580.
Le fleav des demons et sorciers. Nyort, 1616.
BOGUET, HENRY. *Discours des Sorciers.* 3rd ed. Lyons, 1590.
BOISSARDUS, JAN. JAC. *De Diuinatione et Magicis Prasetigiis.* Oppenheimii, 1615.
BONAVENTURA, S. *Opera omnia.* 10 vols. Quaracchi, 1882–1902.
BRAND, J. *Observations on Popular Antiquities.* 2 vols. 1813.
BRETT, G. S. *A History of Psychology.* Vol. I, Ancient and Patristic; Vol. II, Mediæval and Early Modern; Vol. III, Modern Psychology.
BROGNOLI, O.F.M. *Alexicacon, hoc est de maleficiis.* Venice, 1714.
BRUNUS, CONRADUS. *De hæreticis et schismaticis.* Rome, 1584.
BUDGE, SIR E. A. WALLIS. *Tutankhamen: Amenism, Atenism, and Egyptian Monotheism, with Hieroglyphic Texts of Hymns to Amen and Aten.*
Egyptian Magic. Third Impression. London, N.D. [1923].
Bullarium Papæ Benedicti XIV. Rome, 1746.
BURCHARD, WORMACIENSIS. *Decretum.* Migne, *Pat. Lat.* Vol. CLX.
BURKITT, F. G. *The Religion of the Manichees.* Cambridge, 1925.
BUTLER, ALBAN. *Lives of the Saints.* 1756–9; 2 vols. Dublin, 1833.
BZOVIUS, A. *Historiæ Ecclesiasticæ.* Apud Zilettum, *q.u.*
CÆSALPINUS, ANDREAS. *Dæmonum inuestigatio.* Florence, 1580.
CAIETANUS, THOMAS. *De Maleficiis.* 1500.
CALMET, AUGUSTIN DOM, O.S.B. *Traité sur les Apparitions des Esprits, et sur les Vampires.* 2 vols. Paris, 1751.
CAPPELLO, S.J., FELIX M. *De Censuris.* Rome, 1919.
CARENA. *Tractatus de officio Sanctæ Inquisitionis.* Lyons, 1669.
CASSINIS, SAMUEL DE. *Question de la strie.* 1505.
CAUZ, C. F. DE. *De Cultibus Magicis.* 1771.
CHARLEY, T. *News from the Invisible World.* Wakefield, n.s. (*circa* 1850).
CHRYSOSTOM, S. JOHN. *Opera omnia Græce.* Edidit H. Savile. 8 vols. Etonæ, 1612.
CHURCHWARD, ALBERT. *The Arcana of Freemasonry.*
CIRVELIUS, PETRUS. *De magica superstitione.* 1521.
Clementis Alexandrini Opera. 2 vols. Venice, 1757.
Collectanea Chemica. (Select Treatises on Alchemy and Hermetic Medicine.) 1893.
COLLIN DE PLANCY, J. A. S. *Dictionnaire Infernal.* Editio princeps. 2 vols. Paris, 1818. (I have used the sixth, and last, edition, one vol. Paris, H. Plon. 4to, 1863. The six editions differ widely from one another. This famous work is valuable, but often uncritical and even erroneous.)
COLLIUS, FRANCIS. *De Animabus Paganorum.* Milan, 1622.
CONCONIER. *L'âme humaine.* Paris, 1890.
L'hypnotisme franc. Paris, 1898.
CONDROCHIUS, BAPTISTA. *De morbis ueneficis ac ueneficiis.* Libri IV. Venice, 1595.
COUNCELL, R. W. *Apologia Alchymiæ.*
CRESPET, PÈRE CELESTINE. *La haine de Sathan contre l'homme.* Paris, 1590.
CROWE, CATHERINE. *The Night Side of Nature.* 2 vols. 1848. (A standard work; very frequently reprinted.)
CUTHBERT, O.S.F.C., FATHER. *God and the Supernatural.* London, 1920.
DANEAU, LAMBERT. *Les Sorciers.* 1574. There is an English tr. *A Dialogue of Witches,* 1575. [London ?]
DAYNES, GILVBERT W. *The Untrodden Paths of Masonic Research.*
DE LANCRE, PIERRE. *Tableau de l'inconstance des mauvais anges et démons.* Paris, 1612.
L'incredvlité et mescréance dv sortilège. Paris, 1622.
Du Sortilège. 1627. (This is the rarest of De Lancre's books, and very little known.)
DELASSUS, JULES. *Les Incubes et les Succubes.* Paris, 1897.

DELEHAYE, H., S.J. *Légendes Hagiographiques.* Brussels, 1906. Trans. by Mrs. V. M. Crawford as *The Legends of the Saints.* (*The Westminster Library.*)
DELRIO, MARTIN ANTON, S.J. *Disquisitionum Magicarum Libri Sex.* Louvain, 1599.
Devil, History of the, Ancient and Modern, with a Description of the Devil's Dwellings. Durham, 1822.
DIANA, R. P. D. ANTONINUS. *Resolutiones morales.* Lyons, 1633.
DIDRON, M. *Iconographie chrétienne. Histoire de Dieu.* Paris, 1843. Eng. tr. 2 vols. by E. J. Millington. London, 1851. Bohn's Library.
DOBBINS, F. S. *False Gods, or the Idol Worship of the World.* Boston, *circa* 1870.
DORAT, S.J., JOSEPH. *Psychologia.* Vol. VI of *Summa Philosophiæ Christianæ.* 8 vols. Rome.
DRAGO, LUIGI VINCENZO. *Il materialismo e il dogma. Fede e Scienza.* IV, 40 Rome.
DULAURE, J. A. *Des Cultes qui ont précédé et amené l'idolâtrie.* 1805.
Des Divinités Génératrices. Paris, 1805.
DU PREL, CARL. Tr. C. C. Massey. *The Philosophy of Mysticism.* 2 vols. London, 1889.
ELICH, PHILIP LUDWIG. *Dæmonomagia, siue de dæmonis cacurgia.* Frankfort, 1607.
ENNEMOSER, JOSEPH. *The History of Magic.* 2 vols. London, 1854.
ERASTUS, THOMAS. *De lamiis seu strigibus.* Basle, 1577.
Errores Gazariorum seu illorum qui scobam uel baculum equitare probantur. 1450.
EVENIUS, SIGISMUND. *Dissertatio physica de magia.* 1512.
EWICK, JOHN. *De sagorum quos uulgo ueneficos appellant natura.* Bremen, 1584.
EYMERIC, O.P., NICHOLAS. *Directorium Inquisitorum.* Rome, 1585 ; Venice, 1607.
FERRERES, S.J., I. B. *Theologia Moralis.* 11th ed. Rome, 1921.
FRANZELIN, S.J., CARDINAL I.B. *De Deo Uno.* Rome.
FRAZER, SIR JAMES. *Folk-Lore in the Old Testament.* London, 1923.
FREDERICQ, DR. PAUL. *Corpus documentorum Inquisitionis hæreticæ prauitatis neerlandicæ.* 5 vols. Ghent, 1889 *sqq.*
Geschiednes der Inquisitie de Neerlanden tot aen hare herinrichting onder Keizer Karel V (1025–1520). Ghent, 1892 *sqq.*
FREUD, SIGISMUND. *Totem and Taboo. Resemblances between the Psychic Lives of Savages and Neurotics.* London, 1919.
GAFFARELLUS, JAC. *Curiositates Inauditæ.* Hamburg, 1706.
GAMS, PIUS BONIFACIUS, O.S.B. *Die Kirchengeschichte von Spanien.* 5 vols. Regensburg, 1862.
GARRIGON-LEGRANGE, O.P., REGINALD. *De Reuelatione.* 2nd ed. 1921.
GAYA, LOUIS DE. *Cérémonies nuptiales de toutes les nations.* Paris, 1680.
GEBHART, EMILE. *L'Italie mystique.* Paris, 1893.
GEILER, JOHANN. *Die Emeis. Dies ist das Buch von der Omeissen.* 1516.
GEMELLI, O.F.M., AGOSTINO. *Psicologia e Biologia.* Rome, 1920.
Non Moechaberis. Milan, 1923.
GERBERT. *Epistolæ.* Migne. *Pat. Lat.* Vol. CXXXIX.
GERUASIUS OF TILBURY. *Otia imperialia.* Written *circa* 1214.
GIESSLER, J. C. L. *Ecclesiastical History.* Eng. tr. 1853.
GILLY, WILLIAM STEPHEN. *Narrative of Researches among the Vaudois.* London, 1824.
GIUSTINIANUS, BERNARDUS. *Historia Generale della Monarchia Spagnuola Antica, e Moderna.* Venezia, 1674.
GODELMANN, JOHAN GEORG. *Disputatio de Magis.* Frankfort, 1584.
Tractatus de Magis. 1591.
GODWIN, WILLIAM. *Lives of the Necromancers.* London, 1834.
GÖRRES, JOHANN JOSEPH. *Die christliche Mystik.* 4 vols. 1836–42. French translation : *La Mystique Divine, Naturelle, et Diabolique. . . .* 5 vols. Paris, 1861.

GOUGENOT DES MOUSSEAU, HENRI ROGER.
Dieu et les Dieux. Paris, 1854.
Mœurs et pratiques des Démons. Paris, 1854.
La magie au dix-neuvième siècle. Paris, 1860.
Les médiateurs et les moyens de la magie. Paris, 1863.
Les hauts phénomènes de la magie. Paris, 1864.
(Vampires ; the Incubus and the Succubus.)

GOUJET, ABBÉ. *Histoire des inquisitions.* 2 vols. Cologne, 1759.

GREGOROVIUS, FERDINAND. *Geschichte der Stadt Rom im Mittlealter.* 7 vols. 5th ed. Stuttgard and Berlin, 1903 *sqq.*

GREGORY VII, POPE S. *Epistolarum libri* apud Mansi *Sacrorum conciliorum nona . . . collectio.* Florence, 1759. Also *S. Gregorii VII epistolæ et diplomata.* Ed. Horoy. Paris, 1877.

GREGORY XV, POPE. *Gesta Pontificum Romanorum.* Venice, 1688. IV, 522–36.

GREGORY THE GREAT, POPE S. *Opera omnia.* Ed. J. B. Gallicoli. 17 vols. Venice, 1765–76. Reprinted by Migne. *Pat. Lat.* LXXV–LXXIX.

GREGORY OF NAZIANZUS, S. *Opera omnia.* Paris, 1609–11. Migne. *Pat. Gr.* 4 vols. XXXV–XXXVIII.

GREGORY OF TOURS, S. *Scriptores Rerum Merovinginarum* apud *monumenta Germaniæ historica.* I, Pt. I, pp. 1–30. 1884–5.

GRILLANDUS, PAULUS. *De sortilegiis.* Lyons, 1533.

GUAITA, STANISLAS DE. *Essais de sciences maudites.* Paris and Brussels, 1886.

GUAZZO, FRANCESCO MARIA, AMBROSIAN. *Compendium Maleficarum.* Milan, 1608. (One of the most valuable of the earlier writers.)

GUI, BERNARD. *Practica Inquisitionis hæreticæ prauitatis.* Ed. Mgr. C. Douais. Paris, 1886.

GURY, S.J., I. P. *Theologia moralis.* 15th ed. Rome, 1907. Cum supplemento, Acta et Decreta nouissima. 2 vols. Rome, 1915.

HALES, ALEXANDER OF. *Summa uniuersæ theologiæ.* Cologne, 1622.

HANSEN, J. *Quellen und Untersuchungen zur Geschichte des Hexenwahns.* Bonn, 1901.

HARTMANN, FRANZ. *The Life of Phillippus Theophrastus Bombast, of Hohenheim, known by the name of Paracelsus, and the Substance of his Teachings.*
Magic, White and Black.

HASKINS, CHARLES HOMER. *Studies in the History of Mediæval Science.* London, 1924.

HAUBER, E. D. *Bibliotheca magica et scripta magica.* 1738–45.

HAURÉAU, B. *Histoire de la Philosophie Scolastique.* Paris, 1880.

HECKETHORN, CHARLES WILLIAM. *Secret Societies of All Ages and Countries.* 2 vols. London, 1897.

HEDELIN, FRANÇOIS. *Des Satyres, Brutes, Monstres et Demons.* Paris, 1627. Reprinted, Liseux, 1888.

HEINER, FREDERICH. *De Processu Criminali Ecclesiastico.* Rome, 1920.

HEISTERBACH, CÆSARIUS. *Dialogus Miraculorum.* *Circa* 1225. Reprints, 1861, 1901.

HERRMANN. *Institutiones Theologiæ Dogmaticæ.* 2 vols. Rome, 1914.

HETZENAUER, O.M.C., MICHAEL. *Commentarius in librum Genesis.* Rome, 1910.

HILDEBERT, S. *Opera omnia.* Paris, 1708.

HINCMAR. *Opera omnia.* Migne, *Pat. Lat.* Vols. CXXV, CXXVI.

HOCHSTRATEN, JACOB VON. *Quam grauiter peccent quærentes auxilium a maleficiis.* 1510.

HOFFMANN, FRIDOLIN. *Geschichte des Inquisition.* 2 vols. Bonn, 1878.

HOLMES, EDMOND. *The Albigensian or Catharist Heresy.* London, 1925. (A truly amazing defence of the Albigensians. The author has completely misunderstood their heresies.)

HOWEY, M. OLDFIELD. *The Horse in Magic and Myth.* London, 1923.

HUEBER. *Menologium S. Francisci.* Munich, 1608.

HUGON, R. P. *De Deo Uno et Trino.* 2 vols. Rome.

Inquisition. Orden que Comunmente se Guarda en el Santo Oficio de la Inquisition. Valencia, 1736. (Contains all the forms and procedure of the Holy Office.)

IVES, GEORGE. *A History of Penal Methods.* 1914. Chapter II: "The Witch Trials." (The whole volume is valuable.)
JACOLLIOT, LOUIS. *Occult Science in India and among the Ancients.*
JACQUERIUS, NICOLAS. *Flagellum Dæmonum Fascinariorum.* 1458.
JADEROSA, FEDERICO. *Theologia Moralis.* Rome, 1922.
JAUER, NICOLAUS VON. *Tractatus de superstitionibus.* 1405.
JENNINGS, HARGRAVE. *The Rosicrucians: their Rites and Mysteries.*
JORDANUS DE BERGAMO. *Quæstio de strigis.* 1476. MS. 3446. Bibliothèque nationale, Paris.
KELLY, EDWARD *The Alchemical Writings of Edward Kelly.* Trans. from the Hamburg Edition of 1676. 1893.
KHUNRATH, H. *Amphitheatrum Sapientiæ Æternæ Solius Veræ, Christiano-Kabalisticum, Diuino-Magicum, nec non Physico-Chymicum, Tertriunum, Catholicon.* Hanover, 1609.
KRAKEWITZ VON, ALBERT JOACHIM. *De theologia dæmonum.* Wittenberg, 1715.
KRONE. *Fra Dolcino und die Patarerer.* Leipzig, 1844.
LAURENT-NAGOUR. *Occultismus und Liebe,* 1903.
LAVATER, LOYS. *De spectris, lemuribus, etc.* Geneva, 1570.
LEA, HENRY CHARLES. *History of the Inquisition of the Middle Ages.* New York, 1887; London, 1888; and 3 vols., 1906.
Superstition and Force. Philadelphia, 1866. 3rd ed., 1878; 4th ed., 1892.
Studies in Church History. Philadelphia, 1869.
History of the Inquisition in Spain. 4 vols. London, 1906–7.
The Inquisition in the Spanish Dependencies. New York, 1908.
(The works of Henry Charles Lea, lengthy and laborious as they are, must be used with the utmost caution and need continually to be corrected. They are insecure, and bitterly biased, since even when facts are not widely distorted a wrong interpretation is inevitably placed upon them. Their value and merit can but be regarded as fundamentally shaken. The following criticism will be found useful: Paul Maria Baumgarten: *Die Werke von Henry Charles Lea und verwandte Bücher,* 1908. Eng. tr.: *H. C. Lea's Historical Writings: A critical inquiry into their method and merit.* 1909.)
LEE, FREDERICK GEORGE, D.D. *The Other World.* 2 vols. London, 1875.
More Glimpses of the World Unseen. 1878.
Glimpses in the Twilight. 1885.
Sights and Shadows. 1894.
(Scholarly and valuable works.)
LEHMANN. *Aberglaube.* 2nd ed. 1908.
LEHMKUHL, S.J., AUG. *Casus conscientiæ.* 2 vols. Rome, 1913.
LE LOYER, PIERRE. *Discours et histoires des spectres.* Paris, 1605.
LÉVI, ELIPHAS (ALPHONSE LOUIS CONSTANT). *The History of Magic.* Trans. by Arthur Edward Waite. 1922.
The Paradoxes of the Highest Science. (Footnotes by a Master of the Wisdom.)
Transcendental Magic. (Translated, annotated, and introduced by Arthur Edward Waite.)
LEYSER, AUGUST. *De crimine magiæ.* Wittenberg, 1737.
LICOSTHENES, CONRAD. *De prodigiis et ostentis.* 1557.
LOCATI, UMBERTO. *Opus iudiciale inquisitorum.* Rome, 1572.
LOMBARD, PETER. *Quatuor Libri Sententiarium.* Printed 1472. Paris, 1892. (Best edition is that found in the Commentary of S. Bonaventura. *Opera S. Bonauenturæ.* Quaracchi, 1885, I–IV.
LOMEIER, J. *Epimenides sive De Ueterum Gentilium Lustrationibus Syntagma.* Zutphen, 1700
LOTTINI, O.P., GIOVANNI. *Compendium Philosophiæ Scholasticæ.* 3 vols. Rome, 1912.
LUANCO, J. RAMÓN DE. *Ramón Lull considerado come Alquimista.* Barcelona, 1870.
LULL, BL. RAMÓN. *Opera omnia.* 10 vols. Mainz, 1721–42.

MACKAY, CHARLES. *Memoirs of Extraordinary Popular Delusions.* 2 vols. London, 1852. (Must be used with caution, very frequently reprinted.)
MADDEN, R. R. *Phantasmata.* 2 vols. 1857.
MAIER, M. *Themis Aurea* (on the Rosicrucians). Frankfurt, 1618.
MAMOR, PIETRO. *Flagellum maleficorum.* *Circa* 1462.
MANGETUS. *Bibliotheca Chemico Curiosa.* 1702.
MARÉCHAUX, O.S.B., BERNARD-MARIE. *La Réalité des Apparitions Angéliques.* Paris, 1901.
MARCHESE. *Diario Domenicano.* Naples, 1668–81.
MARTINDALE, C. C., S.J. *Antichrist.* C.T.S. (Do. 83).
Theosophy.
MAURITIUS, E. *De denunciatione sagarum.* Tubingen, 1664.
MAYER, J. B. *Ancient Philosophy.* Cambridge, 1895.
MAYO, HERBERT. *On the Truths contained in Popular Superstitions.* Edinburgh, 1851.
MAZZARA. *Leggendario francescano.* Venice, 1721.
MAZZELLA, HOR. *Prælectiones Scholastico-Dogmaticæ.* 4 vols. Rome.
MAZZOLINI (MOZOLINI, PRIERIAS), O.P., SYLVESTER. *De strigimagorum libri III.* Rome, 1521.
MECHLINIA, JOHANNES DE. *Utrum perfecta dei opera possint impediri dæmonis malicia.* *Circa* 1450.
MEMMINGIUS, NICOLAS. *Admonitio de superstitionibus magicis uitandis.* *s.l.* 1575.
MENANT, JOACHIM. *Les Yezidiz. Episodes de l'histoire des adorateurs du Diable.* Paris, 1892.
MENGO, GIROLAMO, CAPUCHIN. *Flagellum Dæmonum.* Bologna, 1578.
Euersio dæmonum e corporibus oppressis. Bologna, 1588.
Fustis dæmonum. Bologna, 1589.
Menologium Cisterciense.
MERCER, REV. J. E. *Alchemy : its Science and Romance.*
MERIC, MGR. *L'Autre vie.* 13 ed. Paris, 1919.
L'Imagination et les Prodigues. Paris, 1918.
Revue de Monde Invisible. Edited by Mgr. Meric. 1909—in continuation.
MICHELET, JULES. *La sorcière.* Paris, 1862. (This original edition is of the last rarity. Reprinted 1862.)
MIRANDOLA, G. P. P. DELLA. *Strix siue de ludificatione dæmonum.* 1523.
MOLITOR, ULRICH. *De lamiis et phitonicis mulieribus, teutonice unholden uel hexen.* 1489.
MOREAU, PAUL. *Des Aberrations du Sens Génésique.* 4th ed. 1887.
MOSHEIM, J. J. VON. *Institutes of Ecclesiasticæ History.* Eng. tr. 2nd ed. 1850.
MURNER, O.M., THOMAS. *De phitonico contractu.* 1499.
MURRAY, MARGARET ALICE. *The Witch-Cult in Western Europe.* Oxford, 1921.
NAUDÉ, GABRIEL. *Apologie povr tovs les grands hommes qui ont esté faussement soupconnez de magie.* Paris, 1625.
NEALE, REV. JOHN MASON. *The Unseen World.* 1847.
NEVIUS, REV. JOHN L. *Demon Possession and Allied Themes.* New York, 1893.
NIDER, JOHAN, O.P. *Formicarius.* 5 vols. Douai, 1602.
Occult Review, The. (In continuation.)
PAPUS (pseud. of Gérard Encausse). *Absolute Key to Occult Science : The Tarot of the Bohemians.* Trans. by A. P. Morton. 1896.
PARACELSUS (Aureolus Philippus, i.e. Theophrastus Bombast von Hohenheim). *Philosophy Reformed and Improved.* Made English by H. Pinnell. 2 vols. 1657.
PARAMO, LUDOVICO À. *De origine et progressu officii Sanctæ Inquisitionis.* Madrid, 1598.
PASCH, G. *De operationibus Dæmonum duo problemata curiosa utrum possint generare et utrum homines in bestias transformari.* 1684.
—— PATRICIUS, FR. *Magia Philosophica.* Hamburg, 1593.

PEEBLES, J. M. *The Demonism of the Ages.* Battle Creek, Mich., 1904.
PEÑA, FRANCESCO. *Inquirendorum hæreticorum lucerna.* Rome, 1572.
PERRY, W. J. *The Origin of Magic and Religion.*
PEUCER, CASPAR. *Commentarius De Præcipuis Generibus Diuinationum.* Witenberga, 1560.
PIGNATARO, F. S. J. *De Disciplina Pœnitentiali.*
PONS, VINCENT. *De potentia Dæmonum.* Aquis Sextiis, 1613.
PONZINIBIO, FRANCESCO. *De lamiis.* Apud *Thesaurus iurisconsultorum.* Venice, 1584.
PRUMMER, O.P., DOMINIC. *Manuale Theologiæ Moralis secundum principia S. Thomæ Aquinatis.* 3 vols. Rome, 1915.
PRYCE, F. N. *The Fame and Confession of the Fraternity of R. C., commonly of the Rosie Cross.* London, 1652.
QUÉTIF-ECHARD. *Scriptores Ordinis Prædicatorum.* 2 vols. Paris, 1719.
RAMUS, S.J., LE PÈRE MARIE. *La Dévotion à Sainte Anne.* Lyons, 1888.
REDGROVE, H. STANLEY. *Alchemy, Ancient and Modern.*
REGINO, ABBOT OF PRÜM. *Libri duo de synodalibus causis.* Migne. *Pat. Lat*; Vol. CXXXII.
REMY, NICOLAS (Remigius). *Dæmonolatriæ libri tres.* Lyons, 1595.
Repertorium penitile de prauitate hæreticorum. 1494.
RÉVILLE, A. *The Devil.* London, 1871.
RIBADENEIRA, S.J., PEDRO. *Uita Ignatii.* Naples, 1572.
RIBET, M. J. *La Mystique Divine.* 4 vols. Paris, 1895.
RICARDUS, ANGENTNUS. *De præstigiis et incantationibus dæmonum.* Basle, 1568.
RICHALMUS, B. (Reichhelm). *Liber de Insidiis Dæmonum. Circa* 1270.
RÖMER, WILHELM. *Die Hexenbulle des Papster Innocenz VIII.* Schaffhausen, 1889.
ROSKOFF, GUSTAV. *Geschichte des Teufels.* 2 vols. Leipzig, 1859.
ROYAS, À J. *De Hæreticis.* Apud Zilettum, *q.u.*
SABETTI, ALOYSIUS, S.J. *Compendium Theologiæ Moralis.* Ed. Uicesima Quinta. Recog. a Timotheo Barrett, S.J. 1916. (Tractatus VI. 2. *De Uitiis Religioni Oppositis.* 3. *De Diuinatione.* 4. *De Magia et maleficio.*)
SAINT-HEBIN, ALEXANDRE. *Du culte de Satan.* Paris, 1867.
SBARALEA. *Bullarium Franciscanum* 5 vols. Rome, 1759 *sqq.*
SCHELTEMA, JACOBUS. *Geschiedenis der Heksenprocessen, eene bijdrage tot den roem des vaderlands.* Haarlem, 1828.
SCHERARTZ, SIGISMUND. *Libellus de spectris.* Wittenberg, 1620.
SCHMIDT. *Histoire et Doctrine de la secte des Cathares ou Albigeois.* Paris, 1849.
SCHRAM, DOMINIC, O.S.B. *Institutiones Theologiæ Mysticæ.* 2 vols. Ausburg, 1774. (A most valuable work.)
SCHWAB, J. B. *Jean Gerson.* Würzburg, 1858.
SCOTUS, DUNS. *Opera omnia.* 12 vols. Ed. Wadding. Lyons, 1639. Reprint, 26 vols. (Vives) Paris, 1891–95.
SIMANCAS. *De Catholicis Institutionibus.* Apud Zilettum, *q.u.*
SINISTRARI, O.M., LUDOVICO MARIA. *Opera omnia.* Rome. 3 vols. 1753–4. *De Dæmonialitate.* First published by Liseux. Paris, 1875. Eng. tr. *Demonality, or Incubi and Succubi.* Paris, 1879.
SOCINUS, MARIANUS. *De sortilegiis. Circa* 1465.
SOLE, JACOBUS. *De Delictis et Pœnis.* Rome, 1920.
SPEE, S.J., FREDERICH. *Cautio criminalis.* 1631. Cologne, 1632.
SPENCE, LEWIS. *An Encyclopedia of Occultism : a Compendium of Information on the Occult Sciences, Occult Personalities, Psychic Sciences, Magic, Demonology, Spiritism, and Mysticism.* London, 1920.
Spicilegium dæmonolatriæ. Circa 1330.
SPINA, BARTOLOMEO, O.P. *Tractatus de Strigibus et Lamiis.* Venice, 1523.
SPRENGER, O.P., JAMES and KRAMER (Institor), HEINRICH. (*Editio princeps*) *Malleus Maleficarum.* Nuremburg, 1494 and 1496. Cologne, 1489 and 1494. Frankfort, 1582. Cologne, 1511 and 1520. Lyons, 1595 and (a fuller edition) 1620. (There are several other issues.) Of this authoritative work I have used the Lyons edition.

Sumptibus Claudii Bovrgeat. 4 vols. 1669, which contains the following valuable collections :—
Vol. I.
NIDER, O.P., JOHN. *Formicarius de maleficiis.*
SPRENGER and KRAMER. *Malleus Maleficarum.*
Vol. II.
ANANIA, GIOVANNI LORENZO. *De Natura Dœmonum.*
BASIN, BERNARD. *De Artibus magicis.*
BERNARD OF COMO, O.P. *De Strigibus.* (With the annotations of Francesco Peña.)
CASTRO, O.M., ALFONSO À. *De impia Sortilegarum hæresi.*
DE VIGNATE, AMBROSE. *Quœstio de Lamiis.* (With a commentary by Peña.)
GERSON, JOHN. *De Probatione Spirituum. De erroribus circa artem magicam reprobatis.*
GRILLAND, PAUL. *De Sortilegiis.*
LEONE, GIOVANNI FRANCESCO. *De Sortilegiis.*
MOLITOR, ULRICH. *De Pythonicis mulieribus.*
MURNER, O.M., THOMAS. *De Pythonico Contractu.*
SIMANCAS, IAGO. *De Lamiis.*
SPINA, O.P., BARTOLOMEO. *De Strigibus.*
In Ponzinibium de Lamiis Apolegia.
Vol. III
GORICHEN, HEINRICH DE. *De superstitioris quibusdam casibus.*
MAMOR, PIETRO. *Flagellum maleficorum.*
MENGO, GIROLAMO, CAPUCHIN. *Flagellum Dœmonum.*
Fustis Dœmonum.
STAMPA, PIETRO ANTONIO. *Fuga Satanœ.*
Vol. IV.
Ars exorcistica tribus partibus.
(It is hardly possible to overestimate the value of this collection.)

STEAD, W. T. *Real Ghost Stories* Reprinted from " The Review of Reviews," 1891–2. London, 1897.

STEINER, RUDOLF. *Les Mystères antiques et le Mystère chrétien.* Paris, 1920.

STENGESIUS, G. *De Monstris et Monstrosis.* 1647 (?).

STRIDTHECKH, CHRISTIAN. *De Sagis, siue Fœminis, commercium cum Malo Spiritu habentibus.* Leipzig, 1691.

SUTTER, PAUL ABBÉ. *Lucifer.* Tr. by the Rev. Theophilus Borer. London, 1922.

TAGEREAU, VINCENT. *Discours sur l'impuissance de l'homme et de la femme.* Paris, 1612.

TAILLEPIED, FRÈRE NOEL. *Psichologie, ou traité de l'apparition des Esprits.* Paris, 1588 ; and many other eds.

TARREGA, RAIMUNDUS. *De inuocatione dœmonum. Circa* 1370.

TARTAROTTI, GIROLAMO. *Del Congresso Notturno delle Lammie.* Rovereto, 1749.

TAXIL, JEAN. *Traicté de l'Epilepsie.* Lyons, 1602. C. XVII (pp. 150–162) treats of demoniacs, sorcerers, and possession.

THEATINUS, JOHANN BAPISTA. *Aduersus artem magicam et striges. Circa* 1510.

Theatrum Diabolorum. 1587.

S. THOMAS AQUINAS. *Opera omnia iussu edita Leonis XIII., P.M.* The Leonine edition.

THUMMIUS, THEODORE. *De Sagarum impictate.* Tubingen, 2nd ed., 1666.

TINCTOR, JOHANNES. *Sermo de secta Uaudensium.* 1460.

TOMASETTI. Ed. *Bullarium . . . Romanorum Pontificum.* 22 vols. Turin, 1857, etc. ; and Naples, 1867–85.

TRIEZ, ROBERT DU. *Les ruses, finesses, et impostures des Esprits malins.* Cambrai, 1563.

TRITHEMIUS, JOHANNES. *Liber Octo quœstionum.* 1508.
Antipalus Maleficiorum. 1508.

TUBERVILLE, A. S. *Mediœval Heresy and the Inquisition.* London, 1920.

UGOLINI, ZANCHINO. *De Hœreticis.* Apud Zilettum, *q.u.*

Ulrichs, K. H. *Incubus, Urningsliebe, und Blutgier.* Leipzig, 1869.
Ulysse, Robert. *Les signes d'infamie au Moyen Age.* Paris, 1891.
Urstisius. *Germanicæ historiæ scriptores.* Frankfort, 1585.
Vair, Leonard. *Trois livres des charmes, sorceleges, ou enchantments. . . . Faits en latin par Leonard Vair et mis en Francois par Iulian Bavdon, Angeuin.* Paris, 1583.
De Valle de Moura. *De incantationibus.* 1620.
Valois, N. *La France et le Grand Schisme d'Orient.* Paris, 1896–1902
Vaughan, Thomas (Eugenius Philalethes). *Magical Writings of Thomas Vaughan.* Edited by Arthur Edward Waite. 1888.
Veritable Dragon Rouge ou il est traite de l'Art de commander les esprits infernaux aeriens et terrestres, faire apparaitre les morts . . . plus La Poule Noire. Sur l'Edition de 1521 [*circa* 1900].
Verpoorten, G. P. *De Dæmonum existentia.* 1779.
Vicecomes, Girolamo. *Lamiarum siue striarum opusculum.* 1460, printed 1490.
Villalpando, Francisco Torreblanca. *Dæmonologia sive de Magia Naturali, Dæmoniaca, licitia, et illicita.* Mainz, 1603.
Vincentius, Joannes. *Liber aduersus magicas artes et eos qui dicunt eisdem nullam inesse efficaciam. Circa* 1475.
Vinetus, Joannes. *Tractatus contra dæmonum inuocatores. Circa* 1450. Printed 1480.
Vivet, O.P., John. *Tractatus contra dæmonum inuocatores.* (*Sine l. et d.*) Black letter.
Waite, Arthur Edward. *Book of Black Magic, and of Pacts, including the Rites and Mysteries of Goëtic Theurgy, Sorcery, and Infernal Necromancy.* 1898.
Mysteries of Magic. A Digest of the Writings of Eliphas Lévi. 1886.
The Occult Sciences. 1891.
The Real History of the Rosicrucians. 1887
Studies in Mysticism. 1906.
Wake, C. S. *Serpent Worship.* 1888.
Ward, J. S. M. *Freemasonry and the Ancient Gods.*
Weyer, Johan (Wierus). *De præstigiis dæmonum et incantationibus et uenificiis.* Basle, 1563. *De Lamiis* and *Pseudo-monarchia Dæmonum* are appended to the ed. of 1577.
Wright, Dudley. *Druidism.* London, 1924.
The Eleusinian Mysteries and Rites.
Masonic Legend and Tradition.
Vampires and Vampirism. 2nd ed. London, 1925.
Wright, Thomas. *Narratives of Sorcery and Magic.* 2 vols. 1851.
Wulf, M. de. *History of Mediæval Philosophy.* Eng. tr. 1909.
Wünschelburg, Johannes. *Tractatus de superstitionibus. Circa* 1440.
Zancherius, Ugolini. *Tractatus de hæreticis.* Mantua, 1567. Rome, 1579.
Zilettus. *Tractatus Uniuersi iuris.* Venice, 1633.

SCRIPTURAL AND ORIENTAL

Baudissen, Grafen Wolf Wilhelm. *Studien zur semitischen Religionsgeschichte.* 2 vols. Leipzig, 1876 and 1878.
Bochartus, Sam. *Hierozoicon.* Ed. Tert. Lugd. et Traj., 1682.
Bousset, W. *The Antichrist Legend.* Trans. by A. H. Keane. London, 1896.
Brecher. *Das transcendentale Magie und magische Heilarten im Talmud.* Wien, 1850.
Brinton, D. G. *Religions of Primitive Peoples.* London and New York, 1897.
Charles, R. H. *The Book of Enoch.* Oxford, 1893.
Constans. *Relation sur une epidemie d'hystero-demonopathie.* Paris, 1863.
Cornill, Carl Heinrich. *The Culture of Ancient Israel.*
Crook, W. *Folklore of Northern India.* 2 vols. 2nd ed. London, 1896.
Davies, T. Witton. *Magic, Divination and Demonology.* London, 1898. (This work should be used with reserve.)

DENNYS, B. N. *The Folklore of China.* London, 1876.
EDERSHEIM, ALFRED. *Life and Times of the Messiah.* London, 1888.
GINSBERG. *The Kabbalah.* London, 1865. Reprinted, 1925.
GRANGER, F. *The Worship of the Romans.* London, 1895.
GRANT, JAMES. *The Mysteries of all Nations.* Leith, 1880.
HILLEBRANDT. *Ritualliteratur. Vedische Opfer und Zauber.* Strasburg, 1897.
HUGHES, T. P. *Dictionary of Islam.* London, 1885.
HUMMELAUR DE, S. J. *Commentarius in libros Samuel.* (*I et II Regum.*) Rome.
KING, J. *Babylonian Magic and Sorcery.* London, 1896.
KOHUT, A. *Jüdische Angel. und Dämonologie.* Leipzig, 1866.
LENORMANT, F. *Chaldean Magic.* London, 1877.
Divination, et la science des presages. Paris, 1875.
LESÊTRE. *Dictionnaire de la Bible.* (Sub uoce *Demoniaques.*)
MARTIGNY. *Dictionnaire des antiquités chrétiennes* (p. 312). Paris, 1877.
MASPERO. *Histoire ancienne des peuples de l'Orient.*
MEINERS, PROF. *Geschichte aller Religionen.* 2 vols. 1806.
MICHAELIS, J. D. *Commentaries on the Laws of Moses.* From the German. 4 vols. London, 1814.
PAUVERT. *La vie de N. S. Jésus-Christ.*
PERRONE, S.J., GIOVANNI. *De Deo creatore.* Pt. I, c. v, prop. 1, 11.
PICK, BERNHARD. *The Cabala.*
SCHENKEL, D. *Bibel-Lexicon.*
SCHRADER. *Die Keilinschriften u. d. alte Testament.* 2nd ed. Geissen, 1883.
SMIT, J. *De Demoniacis in Historia Evangelica Dissertatio Exegetico Apologetica.* Romæ, 1913.
SPENCER. *De Legibus Hebrœorum ritualibus earumque rationibus.* Ed. C. M. Pfaff. 2 vols. Tubingae, 1732.
STEHELIN, J. P. *Traditions of the Jews.* 2 vols. London, 1743.
STRAENE, A. W. *A Translation of the Treatise Chagigah, from the Babylonian Talmud.* Cambridge, 1891.
TERTULLIAN. *Apologia.* Migne, *Pat. Lat. I.*
TIELE, C. P. *Geschichte der Religion im Alterthum.* Vol. I. Gotha, 1896.
VIGOUROUX. *Les livres saints et la critique rationaliste.* Paris, 1891.
TORREBLANCA. *De Magia.* Ed. novissima. Lugduni, 1678.
WAFFELAERT. *Dictionnaire apologétique de la foi catholique.* Paris, 1889. (Sub uoce Possession diabolique.)
WEBER, TERD. VON. *Judische Theologie.* 2te verbesserte Auflage. Leipzig, 1897.
WIEDEMANN, ALFRED. *Religion of the Ancient Egyptians.* London, 1897.
ZIMMERN. *Die Beschwörungstafeln Surpu.* Leipzig, 1896.

ENGLAND, SCOTLAND, AND IRELAND

Abbotsford Club Miscellany. Vol. I. Edinburgh, 1837.
ADY, THOMAS. *A Candle in the Dark.* London, 1656.
ARNOT, HUGO. *Criminal Trials.* Edinburgh, 1785.
ASHTON, JOHN. *The Devil in Britain and America.* London, 1896.
BAXTER, RICHARD. *Certainty of the World of Spirits.* London, 1691.
BEAUMONT, JOHN. *Historical Treatise of Spirits.* London, 1705.
BEDE, VEN. *Ecclesiastical History* (ed. Giles). London, 1843.
BERNARD, RICHARD. *Guide to Grand-Iury men.* London, 1627.
BLACK, G. F. *Scottish Antiquary,* Vol. IX. Edinburgh, 1895.
Blackwood's Magazine, Vol. I. Edinburgh, 1817.
BOULTON, R. *Compleat History of Magick, Sorcery and Witchcraft.* 2 vols. London, 1715.
BOVETT, R. *Pandœmonium.* London, 1658.
BRAND, JOHN. *History and Antiquities of . . . Newcastle.* London, 1789.
BROMHALL, THOMAS. *Treatise of Spectres.* London, 1658.
BURNS, BEGG. *Proceedings of Soc. of Antiquaries of Scotland.* New Series. Vol. X. Edinburgh.
BURTON, JOHN HILL. *Criminal Trials.* London, 1852.

BUTLER, SAMUEL. *Hudibras.* (Ed. Zachary Grey.) 2 vols. Cambridge, 1744.
Calendar of State Papers. Domestic. 1584. London, 1865.
Camden Society. Lady Alice Kyteler. London, 1843.
COOPER, THOMAS. *Mystery of Witchcraft.* London, 1617.
Pleasant Treatise of Witches. London, 1673.
COTTA, JOHN. *Infallible, true and assured Witch.* London, 1625.
Trial of Witchcraft. London, 1616.
County Folklore, III. London, 1901.
DALYELL, JOHN GRAHAME. *Darker Superstitions of Scotland.* Edinburgh, 1834.
DAVENPORT, JOHN. *Witches of Huntingdon.* London, 1646.
DAVIES, J. CEREDIG. *Welsh Folklore.* Aberystwith, 1911.
Denham Tracts. London, 1895.
DRAGE, W. *A Physical Nosonomy . . . with Daimonomagia.* 1665.
FAIRFAX, EDWARD. *Demonologia* (ed. W. Grainge). Harrogate, 1882,
FORBES, WILLIAM. *Institutes of the Law of Scotland.* Edinburgh, 1722–30.
FOSTER. *Tryall of Ann Foster.* Northampton, 1881.
FOUNTAINHALL, LORD. *Decisions.* Edinburgh, 1759.
FULLER, THOMAS. *Church History of Britain.* London, 1655. And edition of J. S. Brewer. Oxford, 1845.
GARDINER, RALPH. *England's Grievance Discovered.* London, 1655.
GAULE, JOHN. *Select cases of Conscience.* London, 1646.
GERISH, WILLIAM BLYTH. *Relation of Mary Hall of Gadsden.* 1912.
The Divel's Delusions. Bishops Stortford, 1914.
The Severall Practices of Johane Harrison. 1909.
GIBBONS, A. *Ely Episcopal Records.* Lincoln, 1891.
GIFFARD, GEORGE. *Discourse of the subtill Practices of Devilles.* London, 1587
Dialogue concerning Witches, Percy Society, VIII. London, 1843.
GILBERT, WILLIAM. *Witchcraft in Essex.* London, 1909.
GLANVILL, JOSEPH. *Sadducismus Triumphatus.* London, 1681.
GOLDSMID, E. *Confessions of Witches under Torture.* Edinburgh, 1886.
HALE, JOHN. *A Modest Enquiry* (ed. Burr). New York, 1914.
HALE, SIR MATTHEW. *Collection of Modern Relations.* London, 1693.
HECTOR, WILLIAM. *Judicial Records of Renfrewshire.* Paisley, 1876.
HELE, N. F. *Notes of Jottings about Aldeburgh.* Ipswich, 1890.
HIBBERT, SAMUEL. *Description of the Shetland Isles.* Edinburgh, 1822.
Highland Papers. Vol. III. Witchcraft in Bute. Edinburgh, 1920.
HOLLAND, HENRY. *A treatise against Witchcraft.* Cambridge, 1590.
HOLLINGSWORTH, A. G. *History of Stowmarket.* Ipswich, 1844.
HORNECK, ANTHONY. *Appendix to Glanvill's Sadducismus Triumphatus.* London, 1681.
HORNES, N. *Dæmonologie and Theologie.* London, 1650.
HOWELL, JAMES. *Familiar Letters.* (Ed. Joseph Jacobs.) London, 1890–2
HOWELL, THOMAS BAYLY. *State Trials.* London, 1816.
HUNT, WILLIAM. *History of the English Church.* London, 1901.
HUTCHINSON, BISHOP FRANCIS. *Historical Essay.* London, 1718.
INCH. *Trial of Isabel Inch.* Ardrossan, *circa* 1855.
JAMES, I. *Demonologie.* Edinburgh, 1597.
Journal of Anatomy. Vols. XIII and XXV. London, 1879, 1891.
Justiciary Court of Edinburgh, Records of Proceedings. Edinburgh, 1905.
KINLOCH, GEORGE RITCHIE. *Reliquiæ Antiquæ Scoticæ.* Edinburgh, 1848.
KNAPP AND BALDWIN. *Newgate Calendar.* London, 1825.
LAMONT, JOHN. *Diary, Maitland Club.* Edinburgh, 1830.
LAW, ROBERT. *Memorialls.* (Ed. Sharpe.) Edinburgh, 1818.
Lawes against Witches and Conivration. Published by Authority. London, 1745.
LYNN LINTON, MRS. *Witch Stories.* London, 1861 and 1883. (A diligent but uncritical work.)
MACKENZIE, SIR G. *Laws and Customs of Scotland.* Edinburgh, 1699.
MAITLAND, S. R. *Puritan Thaumaturgy.*
Maitland Club Miscellany. Vol. II. Glasgow, 1840.
MASON, J. *Anatomie of Sorcery.* 1612.

MELVILLE, SIR CHARLES. *Memoirs. Bannatyne Club.* Edinburgh.
Moore Rental. Chetham Society. Vol. XII. Manchester, 1847.
MORE, HENRY. *Antidote against Atheism.* London, 1655.
Narrative of the Sufferings of a young Girle. Edinburgh, 1698.
NICHOLLS, JOHN. *History and Antiquities of the County of Leicester.* London, 1795–1815.
NICOLL, JOHN. *Diary. Bannatyne Club.* Edinburgh, 1836.
NOTESTEIN, WALLACE. *History of Witchcraft in England.* Washington, 1911.
OSBORNE, FRANCIS. *Traditional Memoirs of the Reigns of Q. Elizabeth and King James I.* London, 1658.
Miscellany of Sundry Essays. London, 1659.
OWEN, H. and BLAKEWAY, J. B. *History of Shrewsbury.* London, 1825.
Percy Society, Giffard's Dialogues of Witches. London, 1843.
PERKINS, WILLIAM. *Discourse of the damned Art of Witchcraft.* Cambridge, 1608.
PETERSON. *Tryall of Mrs. Joan Peterson. Thomason Tracts.* London, 1652.
PETTO, SAMUEL. *A faithful Narrative.* London, 1693.
Philobiblion Society. Examination of certain Witches. London, 1863–4.
PIKE, L. O. *History of Crime in England.* London, 1873.
PITCAIRN, ROBERT. *Criminal Trials.* Edinburgh, 1833.
Pittenweem, A true and full Relation of the Witches of. Edinburgh, 1704.
POLLOCK and MAITLAND. *History of English Law.* 2nd ed. Cambridge, 1898.
Prodigious and Tragicall History. London, 1652.
QUIBELL, JAMES EDWARD. *Hierakonpolis.* II. London, 1902.
Register of the Privy Council of Scotland. Edinburgh, 1881.
Registrum Magni Sigilli Regum Scotorum. Edinburgh, 1886.
ROBERTS, ALEXANDER. *Treatise of Witchcraft.* London, 1616.
Sadducismus Debellatus. London, 1698.
SANDYS, GEORGE. *Relation of a Journey.* London, 1632.
SAUNDERS, W. H. B. *Legends and Traditions of Huntingdonshire.* 1888.
SCOT, REGINALD. *Discoverie of Witchcraft.* London, 1584.
SCOTT, SIR WALTER. *Demonology and Witchcraft.*
Scottish History Society. Vol. XXV. Edinburgh, 1896.
SEYMOUR, S. JOHN D. *Irish Witchcraft and Demonology.* Dublin, 1913.
SHARPE, CHARLES K. *Historical Account of Witchcraft in Scotland.* London, 1884.
SHAW. *Elinor Shaw and Mary Phillips.* Northampton, 1866.
SINCLAR, GEORGE. *The Hydrostaticks.* Edinburgh, 1672.
Satan's Invisible World Discovered. Edinburgh, 1871.
SMITH, CHARLOTTE FELL. *John Dee* (1527–1608). London, 1909.
Spalding Club Miscellany. Aberdeen, 1841.
SPOTTISWODE, JOHN. *History of the Church of Scotland.* Edinburgh, 1847–50.
STEPHEN, SIR J. F. *History of the Criminal Law in England.* London, 1883.
STEVENSON, J. *Chronicon de Lanercost. Maitland Club.* Glasgow, 1839.
STEWART, WILLIAM GRANT. *Popular Superstitions of the Highlands.* Edinburgh, 1823.
STRYPE, JOHN. *Annals of the Reformation.* London, 1709–31. Oxford, 1824.
Surtees Society. Vol. XL. Durham, 1861.
TAYLOR, JOHN. *Tracts relating to Northamptonshire.* Northampton, 1866.
THORPE, BENJAMIN. *Monumenta Ecclesiastica.* London, 1840.
VETTER, THEODOR. *Relations between England and Zurich during the Reformation.* London, 1904.
VICKARS, K. H. *Humphrey, Duke of Gloucester.* London, 1907.
WAGSTAFFE, JOHN. *Displaying of Supposed Witchcraft.* London, 1671.
WALSH. *Examination of John Walsh.* London, 1566.
WHITAKER, T. D. *History of Whalley.* London, 1818.
WILKINS, DAVID. *Concilia Magnæ Britanniæ.* London, 1737.
WILSON, ARTHUR. *Life and Reign of James I.* London, 1653.
Witchcraft, Collection of rare and curious tracts on. Edinburgh, 1891.
Witchcraft, Collections of rare and curious Tracts relating to. London, 1838.
Witchcraft Detected. 1826.
ZIMMERMAN, G. *De Mutata Saxonum veterum religione.* 1839.

ENGLAND: THE PAMPHLET LITERATURE

(Arranged in chronological order)

The Examination and confession of certaine Wytches at Chensforde in the Countie of Essex before the Quenes maiesties Judges, the XXVI daye of July Anno 1566.

A Rehearsall both straung and true of hainous and horrible actes committed by Elizabeth Stile, alias Rockingham, Mother Dutten, Mother Devell, Mother Margaret. Fower notorious Witches apprehended at Winsore in the Countie of Barks, and at Abington arraigned, condemned and executed on the 28 *daye of Februarie last anno* 1579.

A Detection of damnable driftes, practised by three Witches arraigned at Chelmsforde in Essex . . . whiche were executed in Aprill 1579. 1579.

The apprehension and confession of three notorious Witches arraigned and by Justice condemnede in the Countye of Essex the 5 *day of Julye last past.* 1589.

A True and just Recorde of the Information, Examination and Confessions of all the Witches taken at St. Oses in the countie of Essex: wherefore some were executed, and other some entreated accordingly to the determination of Lawe. . . . Written orderly, as the cases were tryed by evidence, by W. W. 1582.

The most strange and admirable discoverie of the three Witches of Warboys, arraigned, convicted and executed at the last assizes at Huntingdon. London, 1593.

(This was one of the most famous cases of English Witchcraft. A whole literature grew up in connexion therewith. In *Notes and Queries*, Twelfth Series, I, 1916, p. 283 and p. 304, will be found: "The Witches of Warboys: Bibliographical Note," where twenty-eight entries are made.)

The most wonderfull and true storie of a certaine Witch named Alse Gooderidge of Stapenhill, who was arraigned and convicted at Darbie. . . . As also a true Report of the strange Torments of Thomas Darling, a boy of thirteen years of age, that was possessed by the Devill, with his horrible Fittes and terrible apparitions by him uttered at Burton upon Trent, in the county of Stafford, and of his marvellous deliverance. London, 1597. [By John Denison.]

The Arraignment and Execution of 3 *detestable Witches, John Newell, Joane his wife, and Hellen Calles; two executed at Barnett, and one at Braynford,* 1 *Dec.* 1595.

The severall Facts of Witchcrafte approved on Margaret Haskett of Stanmore, 1585. Black letter.

An Account of Margaret Hacket, a notorious Witch, who consumed a young Man to Death, rotted his Bowells and back bone asunder, who was executed at Tiborn, 19 *Feb.* 1585. London, 1585.

The Examination and Confession of a notorious Witch named Mother Arnold, alias Whitecote, alias Glastonbury, at the Assise of Burntwood in July, 1574*: who was hanged for Witchcraft at Barking.* 1575.

(The four preceding pamphlets although referred to by Lowndes and other bibliographers apparently have not been traced.)

A true report of three Straunge Witches, lately found at Newnham Regis.

(Not traced. Hazlitt, *Handbook*, p. 231.

A short treatise declaringe the detestable wickednesse of magicall sciences, as Necromancie, Coniuration of Spirites, Curiouse Astrologie and such lyke. . . . Made by Francis Coxe. [London, 1561.] Black letter.

The Examination of John Walsh, before Master Thomas Williams, Commissary to the Reverend father in God, William, bishop of Excester, upon certayne Interrogatories touchyng Wytch-crafte and Sorcerye, in the presence of divers gentlemen and others, the XX of August, 1566. 1566. Black letter.

The disclosying of a late counterfeyted possession by the devyl in two maydens within the Citie of London. [1574.] Black letter.

The Wonderfull Worke of God shewed upon a Chylde, whose name is William Withers, being in the Towne of Walsam . . . Suffolk, who, being Eleven Yeeres of age, laye in a Traunce the Space of tenne Days . . . and hath continued the Space of Three Weeks. London, 1581.

A Most Wicked worke of a Wretched Witch (the like whereof none can record these manie yeares in England) wrought on the Person of one Richard Burt, servant to Maister Edling of Woodhall in the Parrish of Pinner in the Countie of Myddlesex, a myle beyond Harrow. Latelie committed in March last, An. 1592 *and newly recognized acording to the truth. By* G. B. *maister of Artes.* [London, 1593.]

A defensative against the poyson of supposed prophecies, not hitherto confuted by the penne of any man; which being eyther uppon the warrant and authority of old paynted bookes, expositions of dreames, oracles, revelations, invocations of damned spirits . . . have been causes of great disorder in the commonwealth and chiefly among the simple and unlearned people. Circa 1581–3.

The scratchinge of the wytches. 1579.

A warnynge to wytches. 1585.

A lamentable songe of Three Wytches of Warbos, and executed at Huntingdon. 1593.

(The three preceding are ballads. See Hazlitt, *Bibliographical Collections and Notes,* 2nd Series. London, 1882.)

A poosye in forme of a visyon, agaynste wytche Crafte, and Sosyrye.

A Breife Narration of the possession, dispossession, and repossession of William Sommers . . . Together with certaine depositions taken at Nottingham. 1598.

An Apologie, or defence of the possession of William Sommers, a yong man of the towne of Nottingham. . . . By John Darrell, Minister of Christ Jesus. [1599 ?] Black letter.

The Triall of Maist. Dorrel, or A Collection of Defences against Allegations. . . 1599.

(Apparently written by Darrel himself; but the Huth catalogue (V. 1643) ascribes it to James Bamford.)

A brief Apologie proving the possession of William Sommers. Written by John Dorrel, a faithful Minister of the Gospell, but published without his knowledge. . . . 1599.

A Discovery of the Fraudulent Practises of John Darrel, Bacheler of Artes. . . . London, 1599. (By Samuel Harsnett.)

A True Narration of the strange and grevous Vexation by the Devil of seven persons in Lancashire. . . . 1600. Written by Darrel.

(Reprinted in 1641, and again in the *Somers Tracts,* III.)

A True Discourse concerning the certaine possession and dispossession of 7 *persons in one familie in Lancashire, which also may serve as part of an Answere to a fayned and false Discoverie. . . . By George More, Minister and Preacher of the Worde of God. . . .* 1600.

A Detection of that sinnful, shamful, lying, and ridiculous discours of Samuel Harshnet. 1600. (By Darrel in answer to Harsnett.)

A Summarie Answere to al the Material Points in any of Master Darel his bookes, More especiallie to that one Booke of his, intituled, the Doctrine of the Possession and Dispossession of Demoniaks out of the word of God. By John Deacon [*and*] *John Walker, Preachers.* London, 1601.

A Survey of Certaine Dialogical Discourses, written by John Deacon and John Walker. . . . By John Darrell, minister of the gospel. . . . 1602.

The Replie of John Darrell, to the Answer of John Deacon, and John Walker concerning the doctrine of the Possession and Dispossession of Demoniakes. . . . 1602.

A True and Breife Report of Mary Glover's Vexation, and of her deliverance by the meanes of fastinge and prayer. . . . By John Swan, student in Divinitie. . . . 1603.

Elizabeth Jackson was indicted on the charge of having bewitched Mary Glover, but Dr. Edward Jorden, who examined the girl declared her an hysterical impostor in his pamphlet

A briefe discourse of a disease called the Suffocation of the Mother, Written uppon occasion which hath beene of late taken thereby, to suspect possession of an evill spirit. . . . London, 1603.

A history of the case of Catherine Wright.

The strange Newes out of Sommersetshire, Anno 1584, *tearmed, a dreadfull discourse of the dispossessing of one Maggaret Cooper at Ditchet, from a devill in the likenes of a headlesse beare. Discovery of the Fraudulent Practices of John Darrel.* 1584.

The Most Cruell and Bloody Murther committed by an Inn-keepers Wife called Annis Dell, and her Sonne George Dell, Foure Years since. . . . With the severall Witch-crafts and most damnable practices of one Iohane Harrison and her Daughter, upon several persons men and women at Royston, who were all executed at Hartford the 4 of August last past 1606. London, 1606.

The Witches of Northamptonshire.

Agnes Browne { *Arthur Bill* } *Witches*
Joane Vaughan { *Hellen Jenkenson* }
Mary Barber

Who were all executed at Northampton the 22 *of July last.* 1612. 1612.

The severall notorious and lewd Cosenages of Iohn West and Alice West, falsely called the King and Queene of Fayries . . . convicted. . . . 1613. London, 1613.

The Wonderfull Discoverie of Witches in the countie of Lancaster. With the Arraignment and Triall of Nineteene notorious Witches, at the Assizes and Gaole deliverie, holden at the Castle of Lancaster, upon Munday, the seventeenth of August last, 1612. *Before Sir James Altham, and Sir Edward Bromley.* London, 1613.

(Reprinted by the Chetham Society, edited James Crossley. 1845. One of the most famous of the witch-trials.)

Witches Apprehended, Examined and Executed, for notable villanies by them committed both by Land and Water. With a strange and most true trial how to know whether a woman be a Witch or not. London, 1613.

A Booke of the Wytches Lately condemned and executed at Bedford, 1612–1613.

A Treatise of Witchcraft. . . . With a true Narration of the Witchcrafts which Mary Smith, wife of Henry Smith, Glover, did practise . . . and lastly, of her death and execution. . . . By Alexander Roberts, B.D. and Preacher of Gods Word at Kings-Linne in Norffolke. London, 1616.

The Wonderful Discoverie of the Witchcrafts of Margaret and Phillip Flower, daughters of Joan Flower neere Bever Castle: executed at Lincolne, March 11, 1618. *Who were specially arraigned and condemned . . . for confessing themselves actors in the destruction of Henry, Lord Rosse, with their damnable practises against others the Children of the Right Honourable Francis Earle of Rutland. Together with the severall Examinations and Confessions of Anne Baker, Joan Willimot, and Ellen Greene, Witches of Leicestershire.* London, 1619.

Strange and wonderfull Witchcrafts, discovering the damnable Practises of seven Witches against the Lives of certain noble Personages and others of this Kingdom; with an approved Triall how to find out either Witch or any Apprentise to Witchcraft. 1621. Another edition in 1635.

The Wonderfull discoverie of Elizabeth Sawyer . . . late of Edmonton, her conviction, condemnation and Death. . . . Written by Henry Goodcole, Minister of the word of God, and her continuall Visiter in the Gaole of Newgate. . . . 1621.

(Reprinted in Vol. I (lxxxi–cvii) of Bullen's recension of the Dyce-Gifford *Ford*. 3 vols. London, 1895.)

The Boy of Bilson: or A True Discovery of the Late Notorious Impostures of Certaine Romish Priests in their pretended Exorcisme, or expulsion of the Divell out of a young Boy, named William Perry. . . . London, 1622.

A Discourse of Witchcraft As it was acted in the Family of Mr. Edward Fairfax of Fuystone in the County of York, in the year 1621. Edited by R. Monckton Milnes (Lord Houghton) for Vol. V of *Miscellanies of the Philobiblon Soc.* London, 1858–1859. (The editor says the original MS. is still in existence.)

A Most certain, strange and true Discovery of a Witch, Being overtaken by some of the Parliament Forces, as she was standing on a small Planck-board and sayling on it over the River of Newbury, Together with the strange and true manner of her death. 1643.

A Confirmation and Discovery of Witch-craft . . . together with the Confessions of many of those executed since May, 1645. . . . By John Stearne.

The Examination, Confession, Triall, and Execution of Joane Williford, Joan Cariden and Jane Hott: who were executed at Faversham, in Kent . . . all attested under the hand of Robert Greenstreet, Maior of Faversham.

A true and exact Relation of the severall Informations, Examinations, and Confessions of the late Witches arraigned . . . and condemned at the late Sessions, holden at Chelmsford before the Right Honorable Robert, Earle of Warwicke, and severall of his Majesties Justices of Peace, the 29 of July, 1645.

A True Relation of the Arraignment of eighteene Witches at St. Edmundsbury, 27th August, 1645. . . . As Also a List of the names of those that were executed.

Strange and fearfull newes from Plaisto in the parish of Westham neere Bow foure miles from London. London, 1645.

The Lawes against Witches and Conjuration, and Some brief Notes and Observations for the Discovery of Witches. Being very Usefull for these Times wherein the Devil reignes and prevailes. . . . Also The Confession of Mother Lakeland, who was arraigned and condemned for a Witch at Ipswich in Suffolke. . . . By Authority. London, 1645.

Signes and Wonders from Heaven. . . . Likewise a new discovery of Witches in Stepney Parish. And how 20. Witches more were executed in Suffolk this last Assize. Also how the Divell came to Sofforn to a Farmer's house in the habit of a Gentlewoman on horse backe. London [1645].

Relation of a boy who was entertained by the Devil to be Servant to him . . . about Credition in the West, and how the Devil carried him up in the aire, and showed him the torments of Hell, and some of the Cavaliers there, etc., with a coppie of a Letter from Maior Generall Massie, concerning these strange and Wonderfull things, with a certaine box of Reliques and Crucifixes found in Tiverton Church. 1645.

(A ridiculous, but not uninteresting, publication.)

The Witches of Huntingdon, their Examinations and Confessions. . . . London, 1646.

(The Dedication is signed by John Davenport.)

The Discovery of Witches: in answer to severall Queries, lately Delivered to the Judges of Assize for the County of Norfolk. And now published by Matthew Hopkins, Witchfinder. For the Benefit of the Whole Kingdome. . . London, 1647.

(The most famous of the "Hopkins series.")

A strange and true Relation of a Young Woman possest with the Devill. By name Joyce Dovey dwelling at Bewdley neer Worcester. . . . Also a Letter from Cambridge, wherein is related the late conference between the Devil (in the shape of a Mr. of Arts) and one Ashbourner, a Scholler of S. Johns Colledge . . . who was afterwards carried away by him and never heard of since onely his Gown found in the River. London, 1647.

The Full Tryals, Examination and Condemnation of Four Notorious Witches, At the Assizes held in Worcester on Tuseday the 4th of March. . . . As also Their Confessions and last Dying Speeches at the place of Execution, with other Amazing Particulars. . . . London, no date.

The Divels Delusions or A faithfull relation of John Palmer and Elizabeth Knot two notorious Witches lately condemned at the Sessions of Oyer and Terminer in St. Albans. 1649.

Wonderfull News from the North, Or a True Relation of the Sad and Grievous Torments Inflicted upon the Bodies of three Children of Mr. George Muschamp, late of the County of Northumberland, by Witchcraft. . . . As also the prosecution of the sayd Witches, as by Oaths, and their own Confessions will appear and by the Indictment found by the Jury against one of them, at the Sessions of the Peace held at Alnwick, the 24 day of April, 1650. London, 1650.

The strange Witch at Greenwich haunting a Wench, 1650.

A Strange Witch at Greenwich, 1650.

The Witch of Wapping, or an Exact and Perfect Relation of the Life and Devilish Practises of Joan Peterson, who dwelt in Spruce Island, near Wapping; Who was condemned for practising Witchcraft, and sentenced to be Hanged at Tyburn, on Munday the 11*th of April*, 1652. London, 1652.

A Declaration in Answer to several lying Pamphlets concerning the Witch of Wapping, . . . shewing the Bloudy Plot and wicked Conspiracy of one Abraham Vandenhemde, Thomas Crompton, Thomas Collet, and others. London, 1652.

The Tryall and Examinations of Mrs. Joan Peterson before the Honourable Bench at the Sessions house in the Old Bayley yesterday. [1652.]

Doctor Lamb's Darling, or Strange and terrible News from Salisbury; Being A true, exact, and perfect Relation of the great and wonderful Contract and Engagement made between the Devil, and Mistris Anne Bodenham; with the manner how she could transform herself into the shape of a Mastive Dog, a black Lyon, a white Bear, a Woolf, a Bull, and a Cat. . . . The Tryal, Examinations, and Confession . . . before the Lord Chief Baron Wild. . . . By James [Edmond ?] Bower, Cleric. London, 1653.

Doctor Lamb Revived, or, Witchcraft condemn'd in Anne Bodenham . . . who was Arraigned and Executed the Lent Assizes last at Salisbury, before the Right Honourable the Lord Chief Baron Wild, Judge of the Assize. . . . By Edmund Bower, an eye and ear Witness of her Examination and Confession. London, 1653. (Bower's second and more detailed account.)

A Prodigious and Tragicall History of the Arraignment, Tryall, Confession, and Condemnation of six Witches at Maidstone, in Kent, at the Assizes there held in July, Fryday 30, *this present year*, 1652. *Before the Right Honorable, Peter Warburton. . . . Collected from the Observations of E. G. Gent, a learned person, present at their Convictions and Condemnation* London, 1652.

The most true and wonderfull Narration of two women bewitched in Yorkshire: Who comming to the Assizes at York to give Evidence against the Witch after a most horrible noise to the terror and amazement of all the beholders, did vomit forth before the Judges, Pins, wool. . . . Also a most true Relation of a young Maid . . . who . . . did . . . vomit forth wadds of straw, with pins a crosse in them, iron Nails, Needles, . . . as it is attested under the hand of that most famous Phisition Doctor Henry Heers. . . . 1658.

A more Exact Relation of the most lamentable and horrid Contract with Lydia Rogers, living in Pump-Alley in Wapping, made with the Divel. . . Together with the great pains and prayers of many eminent Divines. . . 1658.

The Snare of the Devill Discovered: Or, A True and perfect Relation of the sad and deplorable Condition of Lydia the Wife of John Rogers House Carpenter, living in Greenbank in Pumpe alley in Wappin. . . . Also her Examination by Mr. Johnson the Minister of Wappin, and her Confession. As also in what a sad Condition she continues. . . . London, 1658.

Strange and Terrible Newes from Cambridge, being A true Relation of the Quakers bewitching of Mary Philips . . . into the shape of a Bay Mare, riding her from Dinton towards the University. With the manner how she became visible again . . . in her own Likeness and Shape, with her sides all rent and torn, as if they had been spur-galled, . . . and the Names of the Quakers brought to tryal on Friday last at the Assizes held at Cambridge. . . . London, 1659.

The Power of Witchcraft, Being a most strange but true Relation of the most miraculous and wonderful deliverance of one Mr. William Harrison of Cambden in the County of Gloucester, Steward to the Lady Nowel. . . . London, 1662.

A True and Perfect Account of the Examination, Confession, Tryal, Condemnation and Execution of Joan Perry and her two Sons . . . for the supposed murder of William Harrison, Gent. . . . London, 1676.

A Tryal of Witches at the assizes held at Bury St. Edmonds for the County of Suffolk; on the tenth day of March, 1664. London, 1682; and 1716.

The Lord's Arm Stratched Out in an Answer of Prayer or a True Relation of the Wonderful Deliverance of James Barrow, the Son of John Barrow of Olaves Southwark, London, 1664. (A Baptist tract.)

The wonder of Suffolke, being a true relation of one that reports he made a league with the Devil for three years, to do mischief, and now breaks open houses, robs people daily . . . and can neither be shot nor taken, but leaps over walls fifteen feet high, runs five or six miles in a quarter of an hour, and sometimes vanishes in the midst of multitudes that go to take him. Faithfully written in a letter from a solemn person, dated not long since, to a friend in Ship-Yard near Temple-bar, and ready to be attested by hundreds. . . . London, 1677.

Daimonomageia : a small Treatise of Sicknesses and Diseases from Witchcraft and Supernatural Causes. . . . Being useful to others besides Physicians, in that it confutes Atheistical, Sadducistical, and Sceptical Principles and Imaginations. . . . London, 1665.

Hartford-shire Wonder. Or, Strange News from Ware, Being an Exact and true Relation of one Jane Stretton . . . who hath been visited in a strange kind of manner by extraordinary and unusual fits. . . . London, 1669.

A Magicall Vision, Or a Perfect Discovery of the Fallacies of Witchcraft, As it was lately represented in a pleasant sweet Dream to a Holysweet Sister, a faithful and pretious Assertor of the Family of the Stand-Hups, for preservation of the Saints from being tainted with the heresies of the Congregation of the Doe-Littles. London, 1673. (Hazlitt, *Bibliographical Collections,* fourth series, *s. u.* Witchcraft.)

A Full and True Relation of The Tryal, Condemnation, and Execution of Ann Foster . . . at the place of Execution at Northampton. With the Manner how she by her Malice and Witchcraft set all the Barns and Corn on Fire . . . and bewitched a whole Flock of Sheep. . . . London, 1674.

Strange News from Arpington near Bexby in Kent : Being a True Narrative of a yong Maid who was Possest with several Devils. . . . London, 1679.

Strange and Wonderful News from Yowell in Surry ; Giving a True and Just Account of One Elizabeth Burgess, Who was most strangely Bewitched and Tortured at a sad rate. London, 1681.

An Account of the Tryal and Examination of Joan Buts, for being a Common Witch and Inchantress, before the Right Honourable Sir Francis Pemberton, Lord Chief Justice, at the Assizes. . . . 1682. Single leaf.

The Tryal, Condemnation, and Execution of Three Witches, viz., Temperance Floyd, Mary Floyd, and Susanna Edwards. Who were Arraigned at Exeter on the 18th of August, 1682. London, 1682.

A True and Impartial Relation of the Informations against Three Witches, viz., Temperance Lloyd, Mary Trembles, and Susanna Edwards, who were . . . Convicted at the Assizes holden . . . at . . . Exon, Aug. 14, 1682. *With their several Confessions . . . as also Their . . . Behaviour, at the . . . Execution on the Twenty fifth of the said Month.* London, 1682.

Witchraft discovered and punished Or the Tryals and Condemnation of three Notorious Witches, who were Tryed the last Assizes, holden at the Castle of Exeter . . . where they received sentence of Death, for bewitching severall Persons, destroying Ships at Sea, and Cattel by Land. To the Tune of Doctor Faustus ; or Fortune my Foe.
(A ballad. Roxburghe Collection. Broadside.)

The Life and Conversation of Temperance Floyd, Mary Lloyd and Susanna Edwards . . .; Lately Condemned at Exeter Assizes ; together with a full Account of their first Agreement with the Devil : With the manner how they prosecuted their devilish Sorceries. . . . London, 1687.

A Full and True Account of the Proceedings at the Sessions of Oyer and Terminer . . . which began at the Sessions House in the Old Bayley on Thursday, June 1st, and Ended on Fryday, June 2nd, 1682. *Wherein is Contained the Tryall of Jane Kent for Witchcraft.*

Strange and Dreadful News from the Town of Deptford in the County of Kent, Being a Full, True, and Sad Relation of one Anne Arthur. 1684–5. One leaf, folio.

Strange newes from Shadwell, being a . . . relation of the death of Alice Fowler, who had for many years been accounted a witch. London, 1685.

A True Account of a Strange and Wonderful Relation of one John Tonken, of Pensans in Cornwall, said to be Bewitched by some Women : two of which on Suspition are committed to Prison. London, 1686.

News from Panier Alley ; or a True Relation of Some Pranks the Devil hath lately play'd with a Plaster Pot there. London, 1687.

A faithful narrative of the . . . fits which . . . Thomas Spatchet . . . was under by witchcraft. . . . 1693.

The Second Part of the Boy of Bilson, Or a True and Particular Relation of the Imposter Susanna Fowles, wife of John Fowles of Hammersmith in the Co. of Midd., who pretended herself to be possessed. London, 1698.

A Full and True Account Both of the Life : And also the Manner and Method of carrying on the Delusions, Blasphemies, and Notorious Cheats of Susan Fowls, as the same was Contrived, Plotted, Invented, and Managed by wicked Popish Priests and other Papists.

The trial of Susannah Fowles, of Hammersmith, for blaspheming Jesus Christ, and cursing the Lord's Prayer. . . . London, 1698.

The Case of Witchcraft at Coggeshall, Essex, in the year 1699. Being the Narrative of the Rev. J. Boys, Minister of the Parish. Printed from his manuscript in the possession of the publisher (A. Russell Smith). London, 1901.

A True and Impartial Account of the Dark and Hellish Power of Witchcraft, Lately Exercised on the Body of the Reverend Mr. Wood, Minister of Bodmyn. In a Letter from a Gentleman there, to his Friend in Exon, in Confirmation thereof. Exeter, 1700.

A Full and True Account of the Apprehending and Taking of Mrs. Sarah Moordike, Who is accused for a Witch, Being taken near Pauls' Wharf . . . for having Bewitched one Richard Hetheway. . . . With her Examination before the Right Worshipful Sir Thomas Lane, Sir Oven Buckingham, and Dr. Hambleton in Bowe-lane. 1701.

A short Account of the Trial held at Surry Assizes, in the Borough of Southwark ; on an Information against Richard Hathway . . . for Riot and Assault. London, 1702.

The Tryall of Richard Hathaway, upon an Information For being a Cheat and Imposter. For endeavouring to take away the Life of Sarah Morduck, For being a Witch at Surry Assizes. . . . London, 1702.

A Full and True Account of the Discovery, Apprehending, and taking of a Notorious Witch, who was carried before Justice Bateman in Well-Close on Sunday, July the 23. Together with her Examination and Commitment to Bridewel, Clerkenwell. London, 1704.

An Account of the Tryals, Examination, and Condemnation of Elinor Shaw and Mary Phillips. . . . 1705.

The Northamptonshire Witches. . . . 1705.

The Devil Turned Casuist, or the Cheats of Rome Laid open in the Exorcism of a Despairing Devil at the House of Thomas Bennington in Oriel. . . . By Zachary Taylor, M.A., Chaplain to the Right reverend Father in God, Nicholas, Lord Bishop of Chester, and Rector of Wigan. London, 1696.

The Surey Demoniack, Or an Account of Satan's Strange and Dreadful Actings, In and about the Body of Richard Dugdale of Surey, near Whalley in Lancashire. And How he was Dispossest by Gods blessing on the Fastings and Prayers of divers Ministers and People. London, 1697.

The Surey Imposter, being an answer to a late Fanatical Pamphlet, entituled The Surey Demoniack. By Zachary Taylor. London, 1697.

A Vindication of the Surey Demoniack as no Imposter : Or, A Reply to a certain Pamphlet publish'd by Mr. Zach. Taylor, called The Surey Imposter. . . . By T. J., London, 1698.

Popery, Supersitition, Ignorance and Knavery very unjustly by a letter in the general pretended ; but as far as was charg'd very fully proved upon the Dissenters that were concerned in the Surey Imposture. 1698. Written by Zachary Taylor.

The Lancashire Levite Rebuked, or a Vindication of the Dissenters from Popery, Superstition, Ignorance, and Knavery, unjustly Charged on them by Mr. Zachary Taylor. . . . London, 1698.

The Lancashire Levite Rebuked, or a Farther Vindication. 1698.

Popery, Superstition, Ignorance, and Knavery, Confess'd and fully Proved on the Surey Dissenters, from a Second Letter of an Apostate Friend, to Zach. Taylor. To which is added a Refutation of T. Jollie's Vindication. . . . London, 1699. Written by Zachary Taylor.

A Refutation of Mr. T. Jolly's Vindication of the Devil in Dugdale; Or, The Surey Demoniack. London, 1699.

The Portsmouth Ghost, or A Full and true Account of a Strange, wonderful, and dreadful Appearing of the Ghost of Madam Johnson, a beautiful young Lady of Portsmouth, Shewing, 1. *Her falling in Love with Mr. John Hunt, a Captain in one of the Regiments sent to Spain.* 2. *Of his promising her Marriage, and leaving her big With Child.* 3. *Of her selling herself to the Devil to be revenged on the Captain.* 4. *Of her ripping open her own Belly, and the Devil's flying away with her Body, and leaving the Child in the room.* . . . 7. *Of her Carrying* [*the Captain*] *away in the night in a flame of fire.* Printed and sold by Cluer Dicey and Co. in Aldermary Church Yard, Bow Lane. *Circa* 1704.

A Looking Glass for Swearers, Drunkards, Blasphemers, Sabbath Breakers, Rash Wishers, and Murderers. Being a True Relation of one Elizabeth Hale, in Scotch Yard in White Cross Street; who having sold herself to the Devil to be reveng'd on her Neighbours, did on Sunday last, in a wicked manner, put a quantity of Poyson into a Pot where a Piece of Beef was a boyling for several Poor Women and Children, Two of which dropt down dead, and Twelve more are dangerously Ill; the Truth of which will be Attested by several in the Neighbourhood. Her Examination upon the Crowners Inquest and her Commitment to Newgate. Printed by W. Wise and M. Holt in Fleet Street, 1708.

The Witch of the Woodlands; Or, The Cobler's New Translation. Printed and Sold in Aldermary Church Yard, Bow Lane, London. No date, but about 1710. This pamphlet merely relates an old legend, but is interesting as reproducing with appropriate woodcuts intimate details of the mediæval Sabbat.

An Account of the Tryal, Examination, and Condemnation of Jane Wenham, on an Indictment of Witchcraft, for Bewitching of Matthew Gilston and Anne Thorne of Walcorne, in the County of Hertford. . . .

A Full and Impartial Account of the Discovery of Sorcery and Witchcraft, Practis'd by Jane Wenham of Walkerne in Hertfordshire, upon the bodies of Anne Thorn, Anne Street, &c. . . . till she . . . receiv'd Sentence of Death for the same, March 4, 1711–12. London, 1712.

Witchcraft Farther Display'd. Containing (I) An Account of the Witchcraft practis'd by Jane Wenham of Walkerne, in Hertfordshire, since her Condemnation, upon the bodies of Anne Thorne and Anne Street. . . . (II) An Answer to the most general Objections against the Being and Power of Witches: With some Remarks upon the Case of Jane Wenham in particular, and on Mr. Justice Powel's procedure therein. . . . London, 1712.

A Full Confutation of Witchcraft: More particularly of the Depositions against Jane Wenham, Lately Condemned for a Witch; at Hertford. In which the Modern Notions of Witches are overthrown, and the Ill Consequences of such Doctrines are exposed by Arguments; proving that, Witchcraft is Priestcraft. . . . In a Letter from a Physician in Hertfordshire, to his Friend in London. London, 1712.

The Impossibility of Witchcraft, Plainly Proving, From Scripture and Reason, That there never was a Witch; and that it is both Irrational and Impious to believe there ever was. In which the Depositions against Jane Wenham, Lately Try'd and Condemned for a Witch, at Hertford, are Confuted and Expos'd. London, 1712.

The Belief of Witchcraft Vindicated; proving from Scripture, there have been Witches; and from Reason, that there may be Such still. In answer to a late Pamphlet, Intituled, The Impossibility of Witchcraft. . . By G. R., A.M. London, 1712.

The Case of the Hertfordshire Witchcraft Consider'd. Being an Examination of a book entitl'd, A Full and Impartial Account. . . . London, 1712.

A Defense of the Proceedings against Jane Wenham, wherein the Possibility and Reality of Witchcraft are Demonstrated from Scripture. . . . In Answer to Two Pamphlets Entituled : (I) The Impossibility of Witchcraft, etc. (II) A Full Confutation of Witchcraft. By Francis Bragge, A.B., London, 1712.

The Impossibility of Witchcraft Further Demonstrated, Both from Scripture and Reason . . . with some Cursory Remarks on two trifling Pamphlets in Defense of the existence of Witches. 1712.

An Account of The Tryals, Examination and Condemnation of Elinor Shaw and Mary Phillips (Two notorious Witches) on Wednesday the 7th of March, 1705, *for Bewitching a Woman, and two children. . . . With an Account of their strange Confessions.* This is signed at the end, "Ralph Davis, March 8, 1705." It was followed very shortly by a completer account, written after the execution, and entitled :

The Northamptonshire Witches, Being a true and faithful account of the Births, Educations, Lives, and Conversations of Elinor Shaw and Mary Phillips (The two notorious Witches) That were Executed at Northampton on Saturday, March the 17th, 1705 *. . . with their full Confession to the Minister, and last Dying Speeches at the place of Execution, the like never before heard of. . . . Communicated in a Letter last Post, from Mr. Ralph Davis of Northampton, to Mr. William Simons, Merchantt in London.* London, 1705.

The Whole Trial and Examination of Mrs. Mary Hicks and her Daughter Elizabeth, But of Nine Years of Age, who were Condemn'd the last Assizes held at Huntingdon for Witchcraft, and there Executed on Saturday, the 28*th of July,* 1716 *. . . the like never heard before ; their Behaviour with several Divines who came to converse with 'em whilst under their sentence of Death ; and last Dying Speeches and Confession at the place of execution.* London, 1716. There is a copy in the Bodleian Library.

(These last three pamphlets are almost certainly spurious.)

A Terrible and seasonable Warning to young Men. Being a very particular and True Relation of one Abraham Joiner a young Man about 17 *or* 18 *Years of Age, living in Shakesby's Walks in Shadwell, being a Ballast Man by Profession, who on Saturday Night last pick'd up a leud Woman, and spent what Money he had about him in Treating her, saying afterwards if she wou'd have any more he must go to the Devil for it, and slipping out of her Company, he went to the Cock and Lyon in King Street, the Devil appear'd to him, and gave him a Pistole, . . . appointing to meet him the next Night at the World's End at Stepney ; Also how his Brother perswaded him to throw the Money away, which he did ; but was suddenly Taken in a very strange manner ; so that they were fain to send for the Reverend Mr. Constable and other Ministers to pray with him, he appearing now to be very Penitent. . . .* Printed for J. Dulton, near Fleet Street. *Circa* 1718.

A Timely Warning to Rash and Disobedient Children Being a strange and wonderful Relation of a young Gentleman in the Parish of Stepheny in the Suburbs of London, that sold himself to the Devil for 12 *years to have the Power of being revenged on his Father and Mother, and how his Time being expired, he lay in a sad and deplorable Condition to the Amazement af all Spectators.* Edinburgh : Printed Anno 1721.

The Kentish Miracle, Or, a Seasonable Warning to all Sinners Shewn in The Wonderful Relation of one Mary Moore, whose Husband died some time ago, and left her with two Children, who was reduced to great Want. . . . How the Devil appeared to her, and the many great Offers he made to her to deny Christ, and enter into his Service ; and how she confounded Satan by powerful Arguments . . . with an Account how an Angel appeared to her and relieved her. . . . Edinburgh : Printed in the Year 1741.

(This is probably a reprint. The style of the pamphlet seems some thirty or forty years earlier.)

Trial of Thomas Colley, to which is annexed some Further Particulars of the Affair from the Mouth of John Osborne. 1751. (The trial took place at Hertford Assizes, 30 July, 1751.)

Remarkable Confession and Last Dying Words of Thomas Colley. 1751.

FRANCE

BARTHÉTY, H. *La sorcellerie en Béarn et dans le pays basque.* Pau, 1879.

BERNOU, J. *La chasse aux sorcières dans le Labourd* (1609). Agen, 1897.

BEUGNOT, A. *Histoire de la destruction du Paganisme en occident.* 2 vols. Paris, 1835.

BOIS, JULES. *Le Satanisme et la magie. Les Petites Religions de Paris.*

BONNEMÈRE, EUGÈNE. *Histoire des Camisardes des Cévennes.* Paris, 1869.

BOUCHARD, H. E. *Annette Taudet, ou les sorciers du Poitou au XIXme siècle* Paris, 1867.

BOURIGNON, ANTOINETTE. *La Parole de Dieu.* Amsterdam, 1683.

La vie extérieure. Amsterdam, 1683.

BOURNON, JACQUES. *Chroniques de la Lorraine.* Nancy, 1838.

BRÉVANNES, ROLAND. *L'Orgie Satanique.* Paris, 1904.

BRICAUD, JOANNY. *J. K. Huysmans et le Satanisme.* Paris, 1912.

Huysmans, occultiste et magicien. Paris, 1913.

Un disciple de Cl. de Saint-Martin. Paris, 1911.

Eléments d'Astrologie. Paris, 1911.

Premiers Elements d'Occultisme. Paris, 1912.

CANNAERT, J. B. *Olim : procès des sorcières en Belgique soûs Philippe II* Ghent, 1847.

CAUFEYNON ET JAF, DRS. *Les Messes Noires.* Paris, 1905. (A valuable work.)

CAUZONS, THEODORE DE. *La Magie et la Sorcellerie en France.* 4 vols. Paris, 1900, etc. (A very important study.)

CHABLOZ, FRITZ. *Les sorcières neuchatéloises.* Neuchatel, 1868.

CHRISTIAN, PAUL (Paul Pitois). *Histoire de la Magie.* Paris, 1870.

CLOSMADEUC, DR. G. DE. *Les sorciers de Lorient.* Vannes, 1885.

DEBAY, DR. A. *Histoire des sciences occultes.* Paris, 1860.

DE LA MARTINIÈRE. *Voyage des Pais Septentrionaux.* Paris, 1682.

Discours sur la mort et condamnation de Charles de Franchillon Baron de Chenevieres, exécuté . . . pour Crime de Sortilège et de Magie. Paris, 1626.

DRAZOR, H. R. *Histoire tragique de trois magiciens qvi ont accvsé à la mort Mazarin en Italie.* Paris, 1649.

ELVEN, HENRY VON. *La Tradition.* Vol. V. Paris, 1891.

FIGUIER, LOUIS. *Histoire du merveilleux dans les temps modernes.* 4 vols. Paris, 1860–1.

FONTENELLE, BERNARD LE BOVIER DE. *Histoire des oracles.* Paris, 1687. (Often reprinted.)

FOURNIER, ALBAN. *Epidémie de Sorcellerie en Lorraine.* Nancy, 1891.

GARINET, JULES. *Histoire de la magie en France.* Paris, 1818.

GARSAULT, F. ALEXANDRE. *Faits des causes célèbres et intéressantes.* Amsterdam and Paris, 1757.

HARON, ALFRED. *La Tradition.* Vol. VI. Paris, 1892.

Histoire prodigieuse et espouvantable de plus de deux cens 50 sorciers et sorcières emmenez pour leur estre fait et parfait leur procès au parlement de Tholoze. Paris, 1649.

Histoire véritable des crimes horribles commis à Boulogne par deux moynes, deux gentils-hommes, et deux damoiselles, sur le S. Sacrement de l'Autel, qu'ils ont fait consumer à une Cheure et à un Oye, et sur trois enfants, qu'ils ont fait distiler sur la lambique. Paris, 1651.

Histoire véritable de l'exécrable Docteur Vanini, autrement nommé Luciolo. Paris, 1619.

JAF, LE DR. *Physonomie du vice.* Paris, *circa* 1903.

L'Amour secret. Paris, *circa* 1904.

Journal d'un bourgeois de Paris. Panthéon Litteraire. Paris, 1838.

LADAME, DR. *Procès criminel de la derni re sorcière brulée à Genève, le 6 avril, 1652.* Paris, 1888.
LAVANCHY, L'ABBÉ J. M. *Sabbats ou synagogues sur les bords du lac d'Annecy.* Annecy, 1885.
LECANU, L'ABBE. *Histoire de Satan.* 1861.
LECOCQ, AD. *Les sorciers de la Beauce.* Chartres, 1861.
LEMOINE, JULES. *La Tradition.* Vol. VI. Paris, 1892.
Les Enfers Lubriques. Paris, *circa* 1900.
LES GOUVELLES, LE VICOMTE HIPPOLYTE. *Apparitions d'une âme du Purgatoire en Bretagne.* 4th ed. Paris, 1919. (An apparition which visited Jeanne Audouis [Sœur Marie des Sept Douleurs]).
Les sorceleries de Henry de Valois, et les oblations qu'il faisoit au Diable dans le bois de Vincennes. 15 pp. Paris, 1589.
(This attack on Henry III has been reprinted several times; as by Cimber and Darignon *Archives curieuses de l'Histoire de France.* Vol. XII, and L'Estoile, *Journal de Henri III.*
LILLIE, ARTHUR. *The Worship of Satan in Modern France.* 1896.
LOUÏSE, TH. *De la sorcellerie et de la justice criminelle à Valenciennes.* Valenciennes, 1861.
Magie. 2 vols. Paris, *circa* 1904.
MATTER, JACQUES. *Histoire critique du gnosticisme.* 3 vols. Paris, 1828.
MAURY, ALFRED. *Histoire des religions de la Grèce antique.* 3 vols. Paris, 1857–9.
La Magie et l'Astrologie. Paris, 1860. (Often reprinted.)
MONNOYER, JULES. *La sorcellerie en Hainault . . . avec analyse de procès pour sortilèges* (1568–1683). Mons, 1886.
MONSEUR, EUGÈNE. *Le folklore Wallon.* Brussels, 1892.
ROUÉ, PAUL. *Causes sales.* Paris, 1902.
SALVERTE, A. J. E. B. DE. *Essai sur la Magie.* Brussels, 1817.
SCHURÉ, EDOUARD. *Les grandes légendes de France.* 19th ed. Paris, 1922.
SIMONET, L'ABBE. *Realité de la Magie.* Paris, 1819.
THUIS, L'ABBÉ JEAN-BAPTISTE. *Traite des superstitions qui regardent les Sacraments.* 3 vols. Paris, 1703. Reprinted 4 vols., 1741; and 4 vols., 1777.
Tradition, La. Vol. V contains Van Elvan's *Les Procès de sorcellerie au moyen âge.* Paris, 1891. Vol. VI contains Harou's *Sorciers et sorcières.* Par Paris, 1892, also Lemoine's *Sorcellerie contemporaine.* Paris, 1892.
UN BADAUD (Paul Marrin). *Coup d'œil sur la Magie as XIXme siècle.* Paris, 1891.
Coup d'œil sur les thaumaturges et les médiums du XIXme siècle. Paris, 1891.
WAITE, ARTHUR EDWARD. *Devil-Worship in France.* London, 1896.

FRANCE: SPECIAL CASES

Madeleine Bavent

YVELIN, DR. *Examen de la possession des religieuses de Louviers.* Paris, 1643.
Responce à l'Examen de la possession des religieuses de Louviers, n.d.
Récit véritable de ce qui s'est fait et passé à Louviers, touchant les religieuses possédées, n.d.
LE GAUFFRE. *Exorcismes de plusieurs religieuses de la ville de Louuiers en présence de Monsieur le Penitencier d'Evreux et de Monsieur Le Gauffre.*
LE BRETON, JEAN. *La défense de la vérité touchant la possession des religieuses de Lovviers.* Evreux, 1643.
DELANGLE. *Procès-verbal de Monsieur le Penitencier d'Evreux.* Paris, 1643.
Trois questions touchant l'accident arrivé aux religieuses de Louviers, n.d.
DESMARETS, PÈRE. *Histoire de Magdelaine Bavent, religieuse du monastère de Saint-Louis de Louviers avec sa confession générale et testamentaire, ou elle déclare les abominations, impietez et sacrilèges qu'elle a pratiqué et veu pratiquer, tant dans ledit monastère qu'au Sabbat.* Paris, 1652.
HUMIER. *Discours théologique sur l'histoire de Magdelaine Bavent.* Nyort, 1659.

MORIN, LOUIS RENÉ. *Histoire de Louviers.* Rouen, 1822.
DIBON. *Essai historique sur Louviers.* Rouen, 1836.
DU BOIS, L. *Recherches archéologiques . . . sur la Normandie.* Paris, 1843.
PIERART, Z. *La magnétisme, le somnambulisme et le spiritualisme dans l'histoire. Affaire curieuse des possédées de Louviers.* Paris, 1858.

Marie Benoist, La Bucaille

Arrest donné par la chambre ordonée par le Roy au temps des vacations contre Marie Benoist. Rouen, 1699.
Le tableau prétendu de la pénitence ou le caractère de la dévotion de sœur Marie Bucaille, accusé d'être sorcière. Rouen, 1699.
Almanach historique, ecclésiastique et politique du Diocèse de Coutances pour l'année 1774.

La Cadière and Père Girard

Justification de demoiselle Catherine Cadière. 1731.
Factum pour Marie Catherine Cadière contre le Père J-B. Girard, jésuite, où ce religieux est accusé de l'avoir portée par un abominable Quietisme aux plus criminels excès de l'impudicité. Hague, 1731.
LOUIS, BISHOP OF TOULON. *Mémoires des faits qui se sont passés sous les yeux de M. l'Evêque de Toulon, lors de l'origine de l'affaire du P. Girard, jésuite, et de la Cadière.* Toulon, 1731.
CHAUDON. *Réponse a l'écrit qui a pour titre " Memoires des faits, etc."* Aix, 1731.
Les veritables sentiments de Mademoiselle Cadière . . . écrits de sa propre main. Aix, 1731.
BOYER D'AIGUILLES. *Conclusions de M. le procureur général du roi . . . au sujet de procès d'entre le P. Girard. . . .* n.d.
Sentence de monsieur l'official de l'évêché de Toulon, qui renvoie le P. Girard absous des accusations . . . n.d.

Leonora Galigai

La Juste pvnition de Lycaon, Florentin, Marquis d'Ancre. Paris, 1617.
Arrest de la Cour de Parlement contre le marechal d'Ancre et sa femmé, prononce et exécuté à Paris le 8 *juillet,* 1617.
Harangve de la marquise d'Ancre, estant sur l'echaffaut. 1617.
Bref récit de ce qui s'est passé pour l'exécution . . . de la marquise d'Anchre. Paris, 1617.
Discours sur le mort de Eléonor Galligay, femme de Conchine, marquis d'Ancre. Paris, 1617.
La Médée de la France, dépeinte en personne de la Marguerite d'Ancre. Paris, 1617.

Louis Gaufridi and Madeleine de la Palud

Arrest de la Covr de Parlement de Provence, portant condamnation contre Messire Louis Gaufridi . . . convaincu de Magie et autres crimes abominables. . . . Aix, 1611.
Confession faicte par Messire Lovys Gaufridi, prestre en l'église Accoules de Marseille, prince de magiciens depuis Constantinople jusques à Paris. . . . Aix, 1611.
FONTAINE, JACQUES. *Discovrs des marqves des sorciers . . . sur le subiect di procez de . . . Louys Gauffridy.* Paris, 1611.
MICHAËLIS, PÈRE. *Histoire admirable de la possession et conversion d'une pénitente séduite par un magicien. . . .* Paris, 1612.
DOOMS. *Actes des exorcismes faits à la Sainte-Baume . . . sur Louis Copeau, Magdeleine de la Palud et Louis Gauffridy.* Douai, 1613.
ROSSET, FRANÇOIS DE. *Les histoires tragiqves de nostre temps.* Paris, 1614.
LENORMANT DE CHIREMONT, J. *Histoire veritable, mémorable de ce qvi c'est passé sovs l'exorcisme de trois filles possédées ès païs de Flandre . . . ou il est avssi traité de la police du Sabbat.* Paris, 1623.
GINESTE, RAOUL. *Louis Gaufridi et Magdeleine de la Palud.* Paris, 1904. (A modern study which must be used with reserve.)

Urbain Grandier

Interrogatoire de maistre Urbain Grandier, prêtre, curé de Saint Pierre-du-Marché de Loudun, avec les confrontations des religieuses possédées contre ledict Grandier. Paris, 1634.

Arrest et condamnation de mort contre Maistre Vrbain Grandier . . . atteint et convaincu du crime de magie. Paris, 1634.

Relation veritable de ce qui s'est passé à la mort du curé de Loudun, bruslé tout vif le vendredi 18 *aoust* 1634.

TRANQUILLE, PÈRE. *Véritable relation des justes procédures observées au faict de la possession des Ursulines de Loudun.* Paris, 1634.

La démonomanie de Lodun, qui montre la véritable possession des religieuses urselines et autres séculières. La Flèche, 1634.

DUNCAN, MARC. *Discours de la possession des religieuses Ursulines de Loudun.* 1634.

Récit véritable de ce qui s'est passé à Loudun contre Maistre Urbain Grandier. Paris, 1634.

LA FOUCAULDIÈRE, M. DE. *Les effets miraculeux de l'église romain sur les estranges et affroyables action des démons.* Paris, 1635.

Relation de la sortie du démon Balam du corps de la mère prieure des ursulines de Loudun. Paris, 1635.

SURIN, PÈRE. *Lettre écrite à Monseigneur l'Evêque de Poictiers par un des Pères Jésuites qui exorcisèrent à Loudun.* Paris, 1635.

La gloire de St. Joseph, victorieux des principaux démons de la possession des Ursulines de Loudun. Le Mans, 1636.

LUCHÉ, PÈRE MATHIEU DE. *Les interrogatoires et exorcismes nouvellement faites à un démon sur le sujet de la possession des filles urcellines de Loudun.* Paris, 1637.

SAINTE-CATHERINE. *Le grand pécheur converty, représenté dans les deux estats de la vie de M. de Queriolet.* Lyons, 1690.

AUBIN. *Histoire des diables de Loudun.* Amsterdam, 1693.

LA MÉNARDAYE, M. DE. *Examen et discussion critique de l'histoire des diables de Loudun.* Paris, 1747.

Histoire abrégée de la possession des Ursulines de Loudun. Paris, 1828.

DUMAS, ALEXANDRE. *Crimes célèbres.* 6 vols Paris, 1839–41. (A highly romantic treatment. This survey must be used with caution.)

SAUZÉ, CHARLES. *Etude médico-historique sur les possédées de Loudun.* Paris, 1840.

LERICHE, L'ABBÉ. *Etudes sur les possessions en général et sur celle de Loudun en particulier.* Paris, 1859.

LEGUÉ, DR. G. *Documents pour servir à l'histoire médicale des possédées de Loudun.* Paris, 1874.

Urbain Grandier et les possédées de Loudun. Paris, 1880.

JEAN DE POITIERS. *Les diables de Loudun.* Paris, 1878.

S. Joan of Arc

LENGLET-DUFRESNOY, L'ABBÉ N. *Histoire de Jeanne d'Arc.* Paris, 1753–4.

GUILBERT. *Eloge historique de Jeanne d'Arc.* Rouen, 1803.

BUCHON, J. A. *Chronique et procès de la Pucelle d'Orleans.* Paris, 1817.

LE BRUN DES CHARMETTES. *Histoire de Jeanne d'Arc.* Paris, 1817.

QUATREMÈRE-ROISSY, J. A. *Quelques pièces curieuses sur le mariage prétendu de Jeanne d'Arc.* Paris, 1830.

QUICHERAT, JULES. *Aperçus nouveaux sur l'histoire de Jeanne d'Arc.* Paris, 1841.

Relation inédite sur Jeanne d'Arc. Orleans, 1879.

BEAUREGARD, B. DE. *Histoire de Jeanne d'Arc.* Paris, 1847.

MICHELET, JULES. *Jeanne d'Arc.* Paris, 1853.

BRIERE DE BOISMONT, DR. A. *De l'hallucination historique, ou étude . . . sur les voix et les révélations de Jeanne d'Arc.* Paris, 1861.

VALLET DE VIRIVILLE. *Procès de condamnation de Jeanne d'Arc.* Paris, 1867.

O'REILLY, E. *Les Deux Procès de condamnation . . . de Jeanne d'Arc.* Paris, 1869.

ROBILLARD DE BEAUREPAIRE. *Recherches sur le procès de condamnation de Jeanne d'Arc.* Rouen, 1869.
CHEVALIER, A. *Jeanne d'Arc. Bio-Bibliographie.* Montbeliard, 1878.
LUCE, SIMÉON. *Jeanne d'Arc à Domremy.* Paris, 1886.
LÉO TAXIL, G. J. P. and FESCH, PAUL. *Le Martyr de Jeanne d'Arc.* Paris, 1890.
BEAUREPAIRE, CHARLES DE. *Notes sur les juges et les assesseurs du procès de condamnation de Jeanne d'Arc.* Rouen, 1890.

La Voisin and her Confederates

DUFEY DE L'YONNE. *La Bastille, mémoires pour servir à l'histoire secrète. . . .* Paris, 1833.
CLÈMENT, PIERRE. *La police de Paris sous Louis XIV.* Paris, 1866.
RAVAISSON, FRANÇOIS. *Archives de la Bastille.* 17 vols. Paris, 1866–74.
MONTIFAUD, M. DE. *Racine et la Voisin.* Paris, 1878.
LOISELEUR, JULES. *La Saint-Barthélemy, l'affaire des poisons et Mme de Montespan.* Paris, 1882.
JOURDY, G. *La Citadelle de Besançon . . . ou épilogue de l'Affaire des poisons.* 1888.
LEGUÉ, DR. G. *Medécins et empoisonneurs au XVIIme siècle.* Paris, 1890.
NASS, DR. L. *Les empoisonnements sous Louis XIV.* Paris, 1898.
FUNCK-BRENTANO, F. *Le drame des poisons.* Paris, 1899.

Palladism

BATAILLE (Dr. Hacks). *Le diable au XIXme siècle ou les mystères du Spiritisme.* Paris, 1893.
MARGIOTTA, D. *Le Palladisme. Culte de Satan.* Grenoble, 1895.
VAUGHAN, MISS DIANA. (i.e. LÉO TAXIL.) *Le Palladium régénéré et libre. Lien des groupes lucifériens independants.* Paris, 1895.
Mémoires d'une ex-palladiste. Paris, 1896.
La Restauration du Paganisme. Transition décrétée par le Sanctum Regnum, pour préparer l'etablissement du culte public de Lucifer. Paris, 1896.
SURLABRÈCHE, E. *La confusion de Satan.* Paris, 1896.
PAPUS. *Catholicisme, satanisme et occultisme.* Paris, 1897.

Gilles de Rais

MEURET, F. C. *Annales de Nantes.* Nantes, *circa* 1840.
Petite histoire nantaise . . . du Barbe-Bleue nantais, ou du Maréchal de Retz. Nantes, 1841.
STENDHAL, H. BEYLE. *Mémoires d'un touriste.* Paris, 1854.
GUERAUD, ARMAND. *Notice sur Gilles de Rais.* Rennes, 1855.
MARCHEGAY. *Récit authentique de l'exécution de Gilles de Rays.* Nantes, s.d.
LACROIX, PAUL. *Crimes étranges. Le maréchal de Rays.* Brussels, 1855.
BOSSARD, L'ABBÉ E. *Gilles de Rais . . . dit Barbe-Bleue.* Paris, 1885.
HUYSMANS, J. K. *La Magie en Poitou. Gilles de Rais.* 1899.

The Templars

MESSIE, PIERRE (Pedro Mexia). *Les diverses leçons de Pierre Messie.* Paris, 1556.
DUPUY, PIERRE. *Traité concernant l'histoire de France.* Paris, 1654.
Histoire de l'abolition de l'ordre des Templiers. Paris, 1779.
NICOLAÏ, FREDERIC. *Essai sur les accusations intentées aux Templiers et sur le secret de cet ordre.* Amsterdam, 1783.
GROUVELLE, P. *Mémoires historiques sur les Templiers.* Paris, 1805.
RAYNOUARD, F. J. M. *Monumens historiques relatifs à la condamnation des Chevaliers du Temple.* Paris, 1813.
REY, E. *Etude sur les Templiers.* Arcis-sur-Aube, 1891.
HAMNER, JOSEPH DE. *Mémoires sur deux coffrets gnostiques du Moyen-Age du cabinet de M. le duc de Blacas.* Paris, 1832.
BARGINET, F. A. *Discours sur l'histoire civile et religieuse de l'ordre du Temple.* Paris, 1833.

MAILLARD DE CHAMBURE, C. H. *Règles et statuts secrets des Templiers.* Paris, 1841.
HAVEMANN. *Geschichte des Ausgangs des Tempelherernordens.* Stuttgart, 1846.
MIGNARD, T. J. A. P. *Monographie du coffret de M. le duc de Blacas.* Paris, 1852.
DAUNANT, DE. *Le procès des Templiers.* Nimes, 1863.
LOISELEUR, JULES. *La doctrine secrète des Templiers.* Paris, 1872.
GAIDOZ, H. *Note sur un statuette en bronze représentant un homme assis les jambes croisées.*
PRUTZ, HANS DR. *Geheimlehre und Geheimstatuten des Tempelherren-Ordens.* Berlin, 1879.
Entwicklung und Untergang des Tempelherrenordens. Berlin, 1888.
JACQUOT, F. *Défense des Templiers.* Paris, 1882.
CURZON, HENRI DE. *La Règle du Temple.* Paris, 1886.
SCHOTTMULLER. *Der Untergang des Tempelordens.* 2 vols. Berlin, 1887.
LAVOCAT. *Procès des frères et de l'ordre du Temple.* Paris, 1888.
NAEF, F. *Recherches sur les opinions religieuses des Templiers.* Nimes, 1890.
GMELIN. *Schuld oder Unschuld des Templerordens.* Stuttgart, 1893.

ITALY

Archivio storico italiano. 4 serie. Florence, 1842–85.
BOFFITO. *Gli eretici in Piemonte.* 1897.
BONNI, F. *L' Inquisizione e i Calabro-Valdesi.* Milan, 1864.
BORELLI. *Editti antichi e nuovi.* Turin, 1681.
BORGIA, STEFANO. *Memorie istoriche della pontificia cittá di Benevento.* Rome, 1769.
CANTÙ, CESARE. *Gli Eretici d' Italia.* 3 vols. Turin, 1865–7.
Storia della Diocesi di Como. 2 vols. Como, 1829–31.
CAPPELLETTI. *Le Chiese d' Italia.* Venice, 1844.
CARUTTI. *Storia della citta di Pinerolo.* Pinerolo, 1893.
CASTRO, G. DE. *Il Mondo Segreto.* 9 vols. Milan, 1864.
Arnaldo da Brescia. Leghorn, 1875.
CATTANI, FRA. *Discorso sopra la Superstizione dell' Arte Magica.* Florence, 1567.
CIGOGNA, STROZZI. *Pelagii de gli incanti.* Vicenza, 1605.
CORIO, B. *L' Istoria di Milano.* Padua, 1646.
DANDALO, C. T. *La Signora di Monza.* Milan, 1855.
DE BLASIO, PROF. ABELE. *La Mala Vita a Napoli.* Naples, 1905.
DEJOB. *De l'influence du concile de Trente.* Paris, 1884.
FOLENGO, GIROLAMO. *Opus Macaronicum.* 2 vols. Mantua, 1771.
GALVANI. *Osservazioni sulla Poesia de' Trovatori.* Modena, 1839.
GIANNONE, P. *Istoria civile del Regno di Napoli.* 7 vols. Naples, 1770.
GORI. *Storia di Chiusi.*
GRIMALDO, CONSTANTINI. *Dissertatione in cui si investiga quali sian le operazioni che dependono della magia.* Rome, 1751.
GUICCIARDINI, FRANCESCO. *Delle istorie d' Italia.* 8 vols. Florence, 1818. Also ed. Resini. 5 vols. Turin, 1874.
LAMI. *Lezioni d' antichitá toscane.* 2 vols. Florence, 1766.
LELAND, C. G. *Etruscan Remains.* London, 1892.
Lettera dal Inquisitore da Barzalone allo Inquisitore de Novara, n.d.
MASTRIANI, F. *I Vermi.* 2 vols. Naples, 1877.
Misteri dell' Inquisizione. Paris, 1847. (A catchpenny.)
MONNIER, M. *La Camorra.* Paris, 1863.
MURATORI, L. A. *Rerum italicarum scriptores.* 28 vols. Milan, 1723 *et seq.*
Continuatio opera Jo. Mar. Tartini. 2 vols. Florence, 1748–80.
Antiquitates italicæ medii aevi. 6 vols. Milan, 1738.
Annali d' Italia. 5 vols. Milan, 1838.
MUTINELLI. *Storia Arcana d' Italia.* 4 vols. Venice, 1858.
MUZI. *Memorie ecclesiastiche e civili di Cittá di Castello.* Rome, 1842–7.

NICEFORO, A. E SIGHELE. *La Mala Vita a Roma.* Rome, 1899.
L' Italia barbara. Rome, 1898.
NOVELLIS. *Biografia Savigliancse.* Turin, 1840.
OGNIBEN, ANDREA. *I Guglielmiti del secolo XIII.* Perugia, 1847.
PECCI, GIOVANNI ANTONIO. *Storia del vescovado della cittá di Siena.* Lucca, 1748.
PELLET, M. *Naples contemporaine.* Paris, 1894.
PERINI, O. *Storia delle Societá Segrete.* 2 vols. Milan, 1863.
ROSSETTI, GABRIELE. *Disquisitions on the Antipapal Spirit . . . its Secret Influence. . . .* 2 vols. 1834. (Translated by Miss C. Ward.)
SEGNI, GIOVANNI BATTISTA. *Del vero cristiano contra l' arte planetaria.* Ferrara, 1592.
SILVAGNI, D. *La Corte e la Societá Romana nei XVIII e XIX secoli.* 2nd ed. 3 vols. Florence, 1882–5.
Successo di Giustitia fatta nella cittá di Munich di sei scelerati strigoni. Genoa, 1641.
TOCCO. *L' Eresia nel medio Evo.* Florence, 1884.
TORRICELLO. *Dialogo di Otto Lupano, nel qual si ragiona delle statute e miracoli de demoni e spiriti.* Milan, 1540.
TURLETTI. *Storia di Savigliano.*
UGHELLI. *Italia sacra.* 10 vols. Venice, 1721.
VAYRA, P. *Le Streghe nel Canarese* (*Curiositá di Storia Subalpina*). 1874.
VIZZINI, A. *La Mafia.* Rome, 1880.

NORTH AMERICA

A True though Sad Relation of Six Sea-men (Belonging to the Margaret *of* Boston) *Who Sold Themselves to the* Devil *And were Invisibly Carry'd away.* A pamphlet of 8 pages. N.D. *Circa* 1698.
BANCROFT. *History of the United States.*
BURR, GEORGE LINCOLN. *Narratives of the Witchcraft Cases.* New York, 1914.
The Witchcraft Persecutions. Univ. of Pennsylvania Translations and Reprints. Vol. III. No. 4. Philadelphia, 1903.
CALEF, ROBERT. *The Wonders of the Invisible World.* Boston, 1700.
DRAKE, SAMUEL G. *Annals of Witchcraft.* 1869.
GREEN, SAMUEL ABBOTT. *Groton in the Witchcraft Times.* Cambridge, Mass., 1883.
HUTCHINSON, JOHN. *History of the Province of Massachuset's Bay.*
KITTREDGE, G. L. *Notes on Witchcraft.* American Antiquarian Soc. Proceedings. N.S. xviii. 1906–7.
MATHER, COTTON. *The Wonders of the Invisible World.* Boston, 1693.
MATHER, INCREASE. *Remarkable Providences.* Boston, 1683–4.
NEAL, D. *History of New England.* London, 1747.
NEVINS, W. S. *Witchcraft in Salem Village.* Boston, 1892.
POOLE, W. F. *Salem Witchcraft.* Boston, 1869.
TAYLOR, John. *The Witchcraft Delusion in Colonial Connecticut.* New York, n.d.
UPHAM, CLEMENT WENTWORTH. *History of Salem Witchcraft.* 2 vols.
UPHAM, CAROLINE E. *Salem Witchcraft in Outline.* Illustrated. 3rd ed. Salem, Mass., 1891.
(This is mainly a compendium of C. W. Upham's larger work.)
WINSOR, J. *The Literature of Witchcraft in New England.* 1896. (Reprinted from Proc. Am. Antiq. Soc., 1895.)

GERMANY

BUCHINGER. *Julius Echter von Melpresbrunn.*
DIECKHOFF. *Die Waldenser im Mittelalter.* Gottingen, 1851.
DIEFFENBACH, JOHANN. *Der Hexenwahn vor und nach der Glaubensspaltung in Deutschland.* Mainz, 1886.

DUHR. *Stellung des Jesuiten in der deutschen Hexenprozessen.* Freiburg, 1900.
DURINGSFELD. *Das festliche Jahr.* Leipzig.
FLÜGEL, G. *Mani, seine Lehre und seine Schriften.* Leipzig, 1862.
GAAR, G. S. J. *Christliche Anred nächst dem Scheiterhaufen, worauff der Leichnam Mariæ Renatæ, einer durchs Schwert hingerichtetin Zauberin, den 21ten Jun. An.* 1749, *ausser der Stadt Würzburg, verbrennet worden, an ein Zahlreich versammeltes Volk gethan.* . . . (Contemporary and important.)
GLAUBRECHT, OTTO. *Die Schreckensjahre von Lindheim.* Stuttgart, 1886.
Handbuch der deutschen Mythologie.
HANSEN, JOSEPH. *Quellen und Untersuchungen zur Geschichte des Hexenwahns und der Hexenverfolgung im Mittelalter.* Bonn, 1901. (A valuable and important study.)
HELBING. *Die Tortur, Geschichte der Folter, etc.* 2 vols. Berlin, 1902.
Historia tragica adolescentis prænobilis Ernesti ab Ernberg. (Written by his confessor, a Jesuit father. Collect. Gropp. Vol. II, pp. 287, *sqq.*)
HORST, GEORG CONRAD. *Dæmonomagie, oder Geschichte des Glaubens an Zauberci und dæmonische Wunder.* Frankfort. 2 vols. 1818.
HORST, VICTOR. *Zauberbibliothek.* 6 vols.
KESSLER. *Mâni Forschungen über die manichäissche Religion.* 2 vols. Berlin, 1889, *sqq.*
Kleiner Beitrag zur Geschichte des Hexenwesens im 16 *Jahrhundert.* Trier, 1830.
KOPP. *Die Hexenprozesse und ihre Gegner in Tyrol.* Innsbruck, 1874.
KRONE. *Fra Dolcino und die Patarerer.* Leipzig, 1844.
LEHMANN. *Aberglaube und Zauberei.* Stuttgart, 1908.
LEITSCHUH, FRIEDRICH DR. *Beitræge zur Geschichte des Hexenwesens in Franken.* Bamberg, 1883.
Der letzte Hexenprocess in Deutschland. Pirna, 1849.
LOSCHART, OSWALD, C.R.P. *Die wahrhafte und umständliche Nachricht von dem Zufalle, so das jungfräuliche Kloster Unterzell Nächst Würzburg betroffen, verfasset im Jahr* 1749. 1749.
MEYER, LUDWIG. *Die Periode der Hexenprocesse.*
MÜLLER, KARL. *Die Waldenser und ihre einzelnen Gruppen bis zum Anfang des* 14 *Iahrhunderts.* Gotha, 1886.
OCHSENBEIN. *Aus dem Schweizer Volksleben des XV Iahrhunderts.* 1881.
PAULUS. *Hexenwahn und Hexenprozess in* 16 *Jahrh.* Freiburg, 1910.
RAPP, LUDWIG. *Die Hexenprozesse und ihre Gegner aus Tyrol.*
REINSBURG, O. F. VON. *Bavaria Landes und Volkskunde des Königreichs Bayern.* Munich, 1860–66.
RIETZLER. *Hexenprozesse in Bayern.* Stuttgart, 1896.
SCHERR, J. *Hammerschläge und Historien.* Vol. II. sub *Die letzte Reichshexe.*
SCHINDLER. *Der Aberglaube des Mittelalters.* Breslau, 1858.
SCHREIBER. *Die Hexenprozesse im Breisgau.*
SCHUMACHER, H. A. *Die Stedinger, Beitrag zur Geschichte der Wesenmarschen.* Bremen, 1865.
SILBERSTEIN, AUGUST. *Denksäulen im Gebeite der Cultur und Literatur.* Vienna, 1879.
SOLDAN-HEPPE. *Geschichte der Hexenprozesse.* 2 vols. Stuttgart, 1880. (Soldan's famous work " neu gearbitet von Dr. Heinrich Heppe.")
STECK, RUDOLFF. *Die Akten des Jetzerprozesses nebst dem Defensorium.* Basel, 1904.
STEINER. *Geschichte der Stads Dieburg.* Darmstadt, 1829.
TRUMMER, C. *Vorträge über Tortur, Hexenverfolgungen, Vehmgerichte,* etc., in *Der Hamburgischen Rechtsgeschichte.* Vol. I.
VOLK, FR. *Hexen in der Landvogtei Ortenau und Reichstadt Offenburg.*
WITZSCHEL, AUGUST. *Sitten, Sagen, und Gevräuche aus Thuringen.* Vienna, 1878.
Wunderbarliche Geheimnussen der Zauberey. 4to. 1630.
ZINGERLE, IGNAZ, DR. *Barbara Pachlerin, die Sarnthaler Hexe.* Innsbruck, 1858.

SPIRITISM

"ADEPTE, UN." *Katie King, Histoire de ses Apparitions.* Paris, 1879.
BALLOU, ADIN. *Spirit Manifestations.* Boston, 1852; Liverpool, 1853.
BENSON, VERY REV. MGR. HUGH. *Spiritualism.* C.T.S. No. 36.
BLACKMORE, S.J., SIMON AUGUSTINE. *Spiritism, Facts and Frauds.* London, 1925. (The best concise study of the subject. The work is fairly and authoritatively written, and the conclusions are eminently sane.)
BROWSON. *The Spirit-Rapper.* Boston, 1854. In Vol. IX of Works. Detroit, 1884.
BUTT, G. BASEDEN. *Modern Psychism.* London, 1925.
CAPRON, E. W. *Modern Spiritualism.* New York, 1855.
CARRINGTON, HEREWARD. *Physical Phenomena.* 1920.
The Physical Phenomena of Spiritualism. Boston, 1902.
CARTER, HUNTLY. *Spiritualism, Its Present-Day Meaning. A Symposium.* London, 1920.
COATES, JAMES. *Seeing the Invisible: practical studies in Psychometry,* etc.
CRAWFORD, W. J. *Experiments in Psychical Science.*
The Reality of Psychic Phenomena.
Some practical Hints for those investigating . . . Spiritualism.
DELANNE, G. and G. BOURNIQUET. *Ecoutons les Morts.* Paris, 1923.
DUNRAVEN, EARL OF. *Experiences in Spiritualism with D. D. Home.*
DURVILLE. *Le Fântome des Vivants.* Paris, 1909.
FOURNIER D'ALBE, E. E. *The Goligher Circle, May to August,* 1921. London, 1922.
GASPARIN, COUNT AGENOR DE. *Des tables tournantes.* Paris, 1854.
GURNEY, MYERS, and PODMORE. *Phantasms of the Living.* 2 vols. London, 1886.
GUTHERLET. *Der Kampf und die Seele.* 2nd ed. Mainz, 1903.
JUNG, J. H. *Theorie der Geisterkunde.*
LANSLOTO, O.S.B., D. I. *Spiritism Unveiled.* St. Louis, 1913. (An excellent and most valuable work.)
LEPICIER, O.S.M., ALEXIS. *The Unseen World.* London, 1906.
LILLIE, ARTHUR. *Modern Mystics and Modern Magic.* London, 1894.
LODGE, SIR OLIVER. *Raymond, or Life after Death.* London, 1916
PAILLOUX, C. S. *Le Magnetisme, le Spiritisme, et la possession.*
RAUPERT, J. GODFREY. *Spiritistic Phenomena; their interpretation.*
New Black Magic. 1924.
Modern Spiritism. London, 1907.
SARGENT, EPES. *Planchette or the Despair of Science.* Boston, 1869.
SCHRENCK-NOTZING, BARON VON. *Phenomena of Materialization.* Trans. by E. E. Fournier d'Albe. London, 1923.
SEMENOFF, MARC. *Introduction à la vie secrète.* Paris, 1925.
SPICER, HENRY. *Sights and Sounds; the Mystery of the Day.* London, 1853.
SURBLED. *Spiritualism et spiritisme.* Paris, 1898.
Spirites et mediums. Paris, 1901.
THURSTON, S.J., HERBERT F. *The Problems of Materialization. The Month,* Oct., 1922. (And a number of valuable articles which have been published of recent years in *The Month.*)
TRETHEWY, A. W. *The Controls of Stainton Moses.* London, 1925.
WALLACE, A. R. *Miracles and Modern Spiritualism.* London, 1897.

INDEX